THE ISRAEL-ARAB READER

This is the story of a continuing crisis — the struggle of two diametrically opposed peoples for one territory. Here are their points of view presented in the words of their own heads of state, in official documents, unofficial letters, and the articles of experts in the field.

In this extraordinary collection of Zionist and Arab declarations and various commission reports are the deep-rooted grievances of both sides — the reasons for their beginnings, their aggravations through eighty years of hostility, and the possibilities of their continuance in the future.

The Israel-Arab Reader

A DOCUMENTARY HISTORY OF THE MIDDLE EAST CONFLICT

Edited by Walter Laqueur

Director of the Institute of Contemporary History and Wiener
Library (London); Professor of History, University of Reading;
Professor in the History of Ideas, Brandeis University

THE CITADEL PRESS • NEW YORK

Published by The Citadel Press
222 Park Avenue South, New York, N. Y. 10003
(by arrangement with B. L. Mazel, Inc.)

Library of Congress Catalog Number 68-25146

PRINTED IN THE UNITED STATES OF AMERICA

Contents

115523

PART III: *ISRAEL AND THE ARAB WORLD 1948-1967*

PART IV: *VIEWS AND COMMENTS: THE ARAB-ISRAELI CONFLICT TODAY AND TOMORROW*

Introduction

This collection of documents and comment aims to provide a better understanding of the background of the Arab-Jewish conflict, which has led to three wars within two decades. There is no certainty that war will not break out again, nor can it be taken for granted that it will always be possible to localize it.

Zionism and the Arab national movement appeared on the political scene at about the same time. When Britain received the Mandate for Palestine on behalf of the League of Nations, the total population of the country was less than a million. It was widely believed at the time that the aspirations of Jews and Arabs could be combined. By 1937, a British Commission of Enquiry found that an "irrepressible conflict" had arisen between two national communities within the narrow boundaries of one small country. Jewish immigration grew by leaps and bounds following the rise of Nazism in Europe; the Arabs, supported by public opinion in the neighboring countries, demanded that no more Jews should be permitted to enter Palestine.

In this collection, the story of the unfolding crisis is traced on the basis of Zionist and Arab declarations, and of the findings and recommendations of the various commissions of enquiry during the nineteen thirties and forties. The partition of Palestine, decided by the United Nations in 1947, was rejected by the Arabs; it led to the establishment of the State of Israel and the first Arab–Israeli war

in 1948. As a result of the war, new problems were created—such as the refugee question—which made a reconciliation between the two peoples even more difficult. Arab
guerrillas carried the war into Israel even after the armistice agreements had been signed and Israel retaliated by
raids beyond its borders. The neighboring Arab states refused to recognize the existence of the Jewish state which,
in their view, was illegitimate; they boycotted Israeli
goods, blocked the Suez Canal and the Gulf of Aqabah.
The war of 1956 ensued, and after a decade of uneasy
truce, there was a new escalation culminating in the Six
Days' War in 1967.

The selection of documents has been made with an eye
to the interests of the general reader, not the expert in
international law. The armistice agreements of 1949, whatever their intrinsic importance, are mainly of a technical
character and therefore of no great relevance in the present context. In many cases, substantial cuts in the documents were necessary; such deletions are indicated in the
text. The historian always dislikes such procedure, for it
opens him to charges of suppression of evidence, however
careful and impartial his selection. But there was no other
choice, for it is the aim of the present collection to present
pertinent documents, viewpoints and opinions; it is not a
legal source book. No useful purpose would have been
served, for example, by reprinting the whole of Herzl's
The Jewish State or the unabridged text of Nasser's
speeches.

The editor has refrained (not without a struggle) from
commenting in detail on the documents. A reader of this
kind includes by necessity not only views with which he
disagrees, but also statements which are factually untrue.
But this is well nigh inevitable in polemics on a subject
which is so highly charged with emotion; those claiming to
speak with detachment and objectivity are not necessarily
nearer to truth and justice than the self-avowed partisans.
The discussions of the merits and demerits of the Jewish
and the Arab case will continue for a long time and there
will be no lack of involvement on the part of the partici-

pants. The task of a reader is more modest: to present a survey of representative views, past and present, on the Arab–Israeli conflict, but not to pass judgment on their intrinsic value.

I would like to record my gratitude to the Middle Eastern Document Section at the Institute of Contemporary History (The Wiener Library) in London and in particular to Mrs. Christa Wichmann and Mr. Ze'ev Ben Shlomo in assisting me to collect the documents, as well as to my publisher, B. L. Mazel, for his help during this entire project.

Walter Laqueur

PART I

From the Bilu to the
British Mandate

Part I of the Reader covers the period from the first stirrings of the Jewish and Arab national movements to 1917, the date of the Balfour Declaration. The tie between the Jewish communities in what was still commonly defined as the diaspora had been submerged but never entirely severed; it survived, for instance, in the traditional prayer ("Next year in Jerusalem") and found its political expression in the emergence of the Zionist movement in the last decade of the nineteenth century. There was no specific Arab Palestinian national consciousness, but among the leaders of the Arab population of the Ottoman Empire the demand for national self-determination gained ground. After the defeat of the Turks in 1918, this movement quickly gathered momentum.

Document 1

The Manifesto of the Bilu

Bilu are the first letters of a passage in Isaiah, Chapter 2, Verse 5: "House of Jacob, come let us go." The Biluim, about five hundred young people mainly from the Kharkov region, were part of the wider movement of the "Lovers of Zion" (*Hovevei Zion*) which had developed in Russia in the early eighteen-eighties mainly under the impact of the pogroms of 1881. This manifesto was issued by a Bilu group in Constantinople in 1882.

To our brothers and sisters in Exile!
'If I help not myself, who will help me?'
Nearly two thousand years have elapsed since, in an evil hour, after a heroic struggle, the glory of our Temple vanished in fire and our kings and chieftains changed their crowns and diadems for the chains of exile. We lost our country where dwelt our beloved sires. Into the Exile we took with us, of all our glories, only a spark of the fire by which our Temple, the abode of our Great One, was engirdled, and this little spark kept us alive while the towers of our enemies crumbled into dust, and this spark leapt into celestial flame and shed light on the heroes of our race and inspired them to endure the horrors of the dance of death and the tortures of the *autos-da-fé*. And this spark is again kindling and will shine for us, a true pillar of fire going before us on the road to Zion, while behind us is a pillar of cloud, the pillar of oppression threatening to destroy us. Sleepest thou, O our nation? What hast thou been doing until 1882? Sleeping, and dreaming the false dream of Assimilation. Now, thank God, thou art awak-

ened from thy slothful slumber. The Pogroms have awakened thee from thy charmed sleep. Thine eyes are open to recognise the cloudy delusive hopes. Canst thou listen silently to the taunts and mockeries of thine enemies? . . . Where is thy ancient pride, thine olden spirit? Remember that thou wast a nation possessing a wise religion, a law, a constitution, a celestial Temple whose wall* is still a silent witness to the glories of the past; that thy sons dwelt in palaces and towers, and thy cities flourished in the splendour of civilisation, while these enemies of thine dwelt like beasts in the muddy marshes of their dark woods. While thy children were clad in purple and fine linen, they wore the rough skins of the wolf and the bear. Art thou not ashamed?

Hopeless is your state in the West; the star of your future is gleaming in the East. Deeply conscious of all this, and inspired by the true teaching of our great master, Hillel, 'If I help not myself, who will help me?' we propose to form the following society for national ends.

1. The Society will be named 'BILU', according to the motto 'House of Jacob, come, let us go'. It will be divided into local branches according to the numbers of its members.

2. The seat of the Committee shall be Jerusalem.

3. Donations and contributions shall be unfixed and unlimited.

WE WANT:

1. A home in our country. It was given us by the mercy of God; it is ours as registered in the archives of history.

2. To beg it of the Sultan himself, and if it be impossible to obtain this, to beg that we may at least possess it as a state within a larger state; the internal administration to be ours, to have our civil and political rights, and to act with the Turkish Empire only in foreign affairs, so as to help our brother Ishmael in the time of his need.

We hope that the interests of our glorious nation will rouse the national spirit in rich and powerful men, and that everyone, rich or poor, will give his best labours to the holy cause.

Greetings, dear brothers and sisters!

HEAR, O ISRAEL! The Lord our God, the Lord is one, and our land Zion is our one hope.

GOD be with us! THE PIONEERS OF BILU.

---

* The Wailing Wall.

Document 2

Negib Azouri: Program of the League of the Arab Fatherland*

N. Azouri, a Christian Arab, edited the journal *L'Indépendance Arabe* in Paris before the first world war. His *"Réveil de la Nation Arabe dans l'Asie Turque . . ."* (1905) from which this excerpt is drawn was the "first open demand for the secession of the Arab lands from the Ottoman Empire." (Sylvia G. Haim: *Arab Nationalism*)

. . . There is nothing more liberal than the league's program. The league wants, before anything else, to separate the civil and the religious power, in the interest of Islam and the Arab nation, and to form an Arab empire stretching from the Tigris and the Euphrates to the Suez Isthmus, and from the Mediterranean to the Arabian Sea.

The mode of government will be a constitutional sultanate based on the freedom of all the religions and the equality of all the citizens before the law. It will respect the interests of Europe, all the concessions and all the privileges which had been granted to her up to now by the Turks. It will also respect the autonomy of the Lebanon, and the independence of the principalities of Yemen, Nejd, and Iraq.

The league offers the throne of the Arab Empire to that prince of the Khedivial family of Egypt who will openly declare himself in its favor and who will devote his energy and his resources to this end.

It rejects the idea of unifying Egypt and the Arab Empire under the same monarchy, because the Egyptians do not belong to the Arab race; they are of the African Berber family and the language which they spoke before Islam bears no similarity to Arabic. There exists, moreover, between Egypt and the Arab Empire a natural frontier which must be respected in order to avoid the introduction, in the new state, of the germs of discord and destruction. Never, as a matter of fact, have the ancient Arab caliphs succeeded for any length of time in controlling the two countries at the same time. . . .

* Translated by Sylvia G. Haim.

Document 3

Theodor Herzl: The Jewish State

Theodor Herzl (1860-1904) was the founder of modern political Zionism. In the preface to *Der Judenstaat* (published in 1896) he says: "The Idea which I have developed in this pamphlet is a very old one: it is the restoration of the Jewish State."

. . . The Jewish question still exists. It would be foolish to deny it. It is a remnant of the Middle Ages, which civilized nations do not even yet seem able to shake off, try as they will. They certainly showed a generous desire to do so when they emancipated us. The Jewish question exists wherever Jews live in perceptible numbers. Where it does not exist, it is carried by Jews in the course of their migrations. We naturally move to those places where we are not persecuted, and there our presence produces persecution. This is the case in every country, and will remain so, even in those highly civilized—for instance, France—until the Jewish question finds a solution on a political basis. The unfortunate Jews are now carrying the seeds of Anti-Semitism into England; they have already introduced it into America.

I believe that I understand Anti-Semitism, which is really a highly complex movement. I consider it from a Jewish standpoint, yet without fear or hatred. I believe that I can see what elements there are in it of vulgar sport, of common trade jealousy, of inherited prejudice, of religious intolerance, and also of pretended self-defence. I think the Jewish question is no more a social than a religious one, notwithstanding that it sometimes takes these and other forms. It is a national question, which can only be solved by making it a political world-question to be discussed and settled by the civilized nations of the world in council.

We are a people—one people.

We have honestly endeavored everywhere to merge ourselves in the social life of surrounding communities and to preserve the faith of our fathers. We are not permitted to do so. In vain are we loyal patriots, our loyalty in some places running to extremes; in vain do we make the same sacrifices of life and property as our fellow-citizens; in vain do we strive to increase the fame of our native land in science and art, or her wealth by trade and commerce. In countries where we have lived for centuries we are still cried down as strangers, and often by those whose ancestors were not yet domiciled in the land where Jews had already had experience of suffering. The majority many decide which are the strangers; for this, as indeed every point which arises in the relations between nations, is a question of might. I do not here surrender any portion of our prescriptive right, when I make this statement merely in my own name as an individual. In the world as it now is and for an indefinite period will probably remain, might precedes right. It is useless, therefore, for us to be loyal patriots, as were the Huguenots who were forced to emigrate. If we could only be left in peace. . . .

But I think we shall not be left in peace.

Oppression and persecution cannot exterminate us. No nation on earth has survived such struggles and sufferings as we have gone through. Jew-baiting has merely stripped off our weaklings; the strong among us were invariably true to their race when persecution broke out against them. This attitude was most clearly apparent in the period immediately following the emancipation of the Jews. Those Jews who were advanced intellectually and materially entirely lost the feeling of belonging to their race. Wherever our political well-being has lasted for any length of time, we have assimilated with our surroundings. I think this is not discreditable. Hence, the statesman who would wish to see a Jewish strain in his nation would have to provide for the duration of our political well-being; and even a Bismarck could not do that.

For old prejudices against us still lie deep in the hearts of the people. He who would have proofs of this need only listen to the people where they speak with frankness and simplicity: proverb and fairy-tale are both Anti-Semitic. A nation is everywhere a great child, which can certainly be educated; but its education would, even in most favorable circumstances, occupy such a vast amount of time that we could, as already mentioned, remove our own difficulties by other means long before the process was accomplished.

Assimilation, by which I understood not only external conformity in dress, habits, customs, and language, but also identity of feeling and manner—assimilation of Jews could be effected only by intermarriage. But the need for mixed marriages would have to be felt by the majority; their mere recognition by law would certainly not suffice. . . .

No one can deny the gravity of the situation of the Jews. Wherever they live in perceptible numbers, they are more or less persecuted. Their equality before the law, granted by statute, has become practically a dead letter. They are debarred from filling even moderately high positions, either in the army, or in any public or private capacity. And attempts are made to thrust them out of business also: "Don't buy from Jews!"

Attacks in Parliaments, in assemblies, in the press, in the pulpit, in the street, on journeys—for example, their exclusion from certain hotels—even in places of recreation, become daily more numerous. The forms of persecutions varying according to the countries and social circles in which they occur. In Russia, imposts are levied on Jewish villages; in Rumania, a few persons are put to death; in Germany, they get a good beating occasionally; in Austria, Anti-Semites exercise terrorism over all public life; in Algeria, there are travelling agitators; in Paris, the Jews are shut out of the so-called best social circles and excluded from clubs. Shades of anti-Jewish feeling are innumerable. But this is not to be an attempt to make out a doleful category of Jewish hardships.

I do not intend to arouse sympathetic emotions on our behalf. That would be foolish, futile, and undignified proceeding. I shall content myself with putting the following questions to the Jews: Is it not true that, in countries where we live in perceptible numbers, the position of Jewish lawyers, doctors, technicians, teachers, and employees of all descriptions becomes daily more intolerable? Is it not true, that the Jewish middle classes are seriously threatened? Is it not true, that the passions of the mob are incited against our wealthy people? Is it not true, that our poor endure greater sufferings than any other proletariat? I think that this external pressure makes itself felt everywhere. In our economically upper classes it causes discomfort, in our middle classes continual and grave anxieties, in our lower classes absolute despair.

Everything tends, in fact, to one and the same conclusion, which is clearly enunciated in that classic Berlin phrase: *"Juden Raus!"* (Out with the Jews!)

I shall now put the Question in the briefest possible form: Are we to "get out" now and where to?

Or, may we yet remain? And, how long?

Let us first settle the point of staying where we are. Can we hope for better days, can we possess our souls in patience, can we wait in pious resignation till the princes and peoples of this earth are more mercifully disposed towards us? I say that we cannot hope for a change in the current of feeling. And why not? Even if we were as near to the hearts of princes as are their other subjects, they could not protect us. They would only feel popular hatred by showing us too much favor. By "too much," I really mean less than is claimed as a right by every ordinary citizen, or by every race. The nations in whose midst Jews live are all either covertly or openly Anti-Semitic.

The common people have not, and indeed cannot have, any historic comprehension. They do not know that the sins of the Middle Ages are now being visited on the nations of Europe. We are what the Ghetto made us. We have attained pre-eminence in finance, because mediaeval conditions drove us to it. The same process is now being repeated. We are again being forced into finance, now it is the stock exchange, by being kept out of other branches of economic activity. Being on the stock exchange, we are consequently exposed afresh to contempt. At the same time we continue to produce an abundance of mediocre intellects who find no outlet, and this endangers our social position as much as does our increasing wealth. Educated Jews without means are now rapidly becoming Socialists. Hence we are certain to suffer very severely in the struggle between classes, because we stand in the most exposed position in the camps of both Socialists and capitalists. . . .

The Plan

The whole plan is in its essence perfectly simple, as it must necessarily be if it is to come within the comprehension of all.

Let the sovereignty be granted us over a portion of the globe large enough to satisfy the rightful requirements of a nation; the rest we shall manage for ourselves.

The creation of a new State is neither ridiculous nor impossible. We have in our day witnessed the process in connection with nations which were not largely members of the middle class, but poorer, less educated, and consequently weaker than ourselves. The Governments of all countries scourged by Anti-Semitism will be keenly interested in assisting us to obtain the sovereignty we want.

The plan, simple in design, but complicated in execution, will be carried out by two agencies: The Society of Jews and the Jewish Company.

The Society of Jews will do the preparatory work in the

domains of science and politics, which the Jewish Company will afterwards apply practically.

The Jewish Company will be the liquidating agent of the business interests of departing Jews, and will organize commerce and trade in the new country.

We must not imagine the departure of the Jews to be a sudden one. It will be gradual, continuous, and will cover many decades. The poorest will go first to cultivate the soil. In accordance with a preconceived plan, they will construct roads, bridges, railways and telegraph installations; regulate rivers; and build their own dwellings; their labor will create trade, trade will create markets and markets will attract new settlers, for every man will go voluntarily, at his own expense and his own risk. The labor expended on the land will enhance its value, and the Jews will soon perceive that a new and permanent sphere of operation is opening here for that spirit of enterprise which has heretofore met only with hatred and obloquy.

If we wish to found a State today, we shall not do it in the way which would have been the only possible one a thousand years ago. It is foolish to revert to old stages of civilization, as many Zionists would like to do. Supposing, for example, we were obliged to clear a country of wild beasts, we should not set about the task in the fashion of Europeans of the fifth century. We should not take spear and lance and go out singly in pursuit of bears; we would organize a large and active hunting party, drive the animals together, and throw a melinite bomb into their midst.

If we wish to conduct building operations, we shall not plant a mass of stakes and piles on the shore of a lake, but we shall build as men build now. Indeed, we shall build in a bolder and more stately style than was ever adopted before, for we now possess means which men never yet possessed.

The emigrants standing lowest in the economic scale will be slowly followed by those of a higher grade. Those who at this moment are living in despair will go first. They will be led by the mediocre intellects which we produce so superabundantly and which are persecuted everywhere.

This pamphlet will open a general discussion on the Jewish Question, but that does not mean that there will be any voting on it. Such a result would ruin the cause from the outset, and dissidents must remember that allegiance or opposition is entirely voluntary. He who will not come with us should remain behind.

Let all who are willing to join us, fall in behind our banner and fight for our cause with voice and pen and deed.

Those Jews who agree with our idea of a State will attach themselves to the Society, which will thereby be authorized to confer and treat with Governments in the name of our people. The Society will thus be acknowledged in its relations with Governments as a State-creating power. This acknowledgment will practically create the State.

Should the Powers declare themselves willing to admit our sovereignty over a neutral piece of land, then the Society will enter into negotiations for the possession of this land. Here two territories come under consideration, Palestine and Argentine. In both countries important experiments in colonization have been made, though on the mistaken principle of a gradual infiltration of Jews. An infiltration is bound to end badly. It continues till the inevitable moment when the native population feels itself threatened, and forces the Government to stop a further influx of Jews. Immigration is consequently futile unless we have the sovereign right to continue such immigration.

The Society of Jews will treat with the present masters of the land, putting itself under the protectorate of the European Powers, if they prove friendly to the plan. We could offer the present possessors of the land enormous advantages, assume part of the public debt, build new roads for traffic, which our presence in the country would render necessary, and do many other things. The creation of our State would be beneficial to adjacent countries, because the cultivation of a strip of land increases the value of its surrounding districts in innumerable ways.

Document 4

The Basle Declaration

This official statement of Zionist purpose was adopted by the first Zionist Congress in Basle in August 1897.

The aim of Zionism is to create for the Jewish people a home in Palestine secured by public law.

The Congress contemplates the following means to the attainment of this end:

1. The promotion, on suitable lines, of the colonization of Palestine by Jewish agricultural and industrial workers.

2. The organization and binding together of the whole of Jewry by means of appropriate institutions, local and international, in accordance with the laws of each country.

3. The strengthening and fostering of Jewish national sentiment and consciousness.

4. Preparatory steps towards obtaining government consent, where necessary, to the attainment of the aim of Zionism.

Document 5

The Sykes–Picot Agreement

Sir Mark Sykes (1873-1919), a distinguished British orientalist, and Charles Georges-Picot, formerly French Consul in Beirut, prepared a draft agreement in 1915–16 about the post-war division of the Middle East, which was also approved in principle by Russia.

1. *Sir Edward Grey to Paul Cambon, 15 May 1916*

I shall have the honour to reply fully in a further note to your Excellency's note of the 9th instant, relative to the creation of an Arab State, but I should meanwhile be grateful if your Excellency could assure me that in those regions which, under the conditions recorded in that communication, become entirely French, or in which French interests are recognised as predominant, any existing British concessions, rights of navigation or development, and the rights and privileges of any British religious, scholastic, or medical institutions will be maintained.

His Majesty's Government are, of course, ready to give a reciprocal assurance in regard to the British area.

2. *Grey to Cambon, 16 May 1916*

I have the honour to acknowledge the receipt of your Excellency's note of the 9th instant, stating that the French Government accept the limits of a future Arab State, or Confederation of States, and of those parts of Syria where French interests predominate, together with certain conditions attached thereto, such as they result from recent discussions in London and Petrograd on the subject.

I have the honour to inform your Excellency in reply that the acceptance of the whole project, as it now stands, will involve the abdication of considerable British interests, but, since His Majesty's Government recognise the advantage to the general cause of the Allies entailed in producing a more favourable internal political situation in Turkey, they are ready to accept the arrangement now arrived at, provided that the co-operation of the Arabs is secured, and that the Arabs fulfil the conditions and obtain the towns of Homs, Hama, Damascus, and Aleppo.

It is accordingly understood between the French and British Governments—

1. That France and Great Britain are prepared to recognize and protect an independent Arab State or a Confederation of Arab States in the areas (A) and (B) marked on the annexed map (*map not reproduced: Ed.*), under the suzerainty of an Arab chief. That in area (A) France, and in area (B) Great Britain, shall have priority of right of enterprise and local loans. That in area (A) France, and in area (B) Great Britain, shall alone supply advisers or foreign functionaries at the request of the Arab State or Confederation of Arab States.

2. That in the blue area France, and in the red area Great Britain, shall be allowed to establish such direct or indirect administration or control as they desire and as they may think fit to arrange with the Arab State or Confederation of Arab States.

3. That in the brown area there shall be established an international administration, the form of which is to be decided upon after consultation with Russia, and subsequently in consultation with the other Allies, and the representatives of the Shereef of Mecca.

4. That Great Britain be accorded (1) the ports of Haifa and Acre, (2) guarantee of a given supply of water from the Tigris and Euphrates in area (A) for area (B). His Majesty's Government, on their part, undertake that they will at no time enter into negotiations for the cession of Cyprus to any third Power without the previous consent of the French Government.

5. That Alexandretta shall be a free port as regards the trade of the British Empire, and that there shall be no discrimination in port charges or facilities as regards British shipping and British goods; that there shall be freedom of transit for British goods through Alexandretta and by railway through the blue area, whether those goods are intended for or originate in the red area, or (B) area, or area (A); and there shall be no discrimination, direct or indirect against British

goods on any railway or against British goods or ships at any port serving the areas mentioned.

That Haifa shall be a free port as regards the trade of France, her dominions and protectorates, and there shall be no discrimination in port charges or facilities as regards French shipping and French goods. There shall be freedom of transit for French goods through Haifa and by the British railway through the brown area, whether those goods are intended for or originate in the blue area, area (A), or area (B), and there shall be no discrimination, direct or indirect, against French goods on any railway, or against French goods or ships at any port serving the areas mentioned.

6. That in area (A) the Bagdad Railway shall not be extended southwards beyond Mosul, and in area (B) northwards beyond Samarra, until a railway connecting Baghdad with Aleppo via the Euphrates Valley has been completed, and then only with the concurrence of the two Governments.

7. That Great Britain has the right to build, administer, and be sole owner of a railway connecting Haifa with area (B), and shall have a perpetual right to transport troops along such a line at all times.

It is to be understood by both Governments that this railway is to facilitate the connexion of Baghdad with Haifa by rail, and it is further understood that, if the engineering difficulties and expense entailed by keeping this connecting line in the brown area only make the project unfeasible, that the French Government shall be prepared to consider that the line in question may also traverse the polygon Banias-Keis Marib-Salkhab Tell Otsda-Mesmie before reaching area (B).

8. For a period of twenty years the existing Turkish customs tariff shall remain in force throughout the whole of the blue and red areas, as well as in areas (A) and (B), and no increase in the rates of duty or conversion from *ad valorem* to specific rates shall be made except by agreement between the two Powers.

There shall be no interior customs barriers between any of the above-mentioned areas. The customs duties leviable on goods destined for the interior shall be collected at the port of entry and handed over to the administration of the area of destination.

9. It shall be agreed that the French Government will at no time enter into any negotiations for the cession of their rights and will not cede such rights in the blue area to any third Power, except the Arab State or Confederation of Arab States

without the previous agreement of His Majesty's Government, who, on their part, will give a similar undertaking to the French Government regarding the red area.

10. The British and French Governments, as the protectors of the Arab State, shall agree that they will not themselves acquire and will not consent to a third Power acquiring territorial possessions in the Arabian peninsula, nor consent to a third Power installing a naval base either on the east coast, or on the islands, of the Red Sea. This, however, shall not prevent such adjustment of the Aden frontier as may be necessary in consequence of recent Turkish aggression.

11. The negotiations with the Arabs as to the boundaries of the Arab State or Confederation of Arab States shall be continued through the same channel as heretofore on behalf of the two Powers.

12. It is agreed that measures to control the importation of arms into the Arab territories will be considered by the two Governments.

I have further the honour to state that, in order to make the agreement complete, His Majesty's Government are proposing to the Russian Government to exchange notes analogous to those exchanged by the latter and your Excellency's Government on the 26th April last. Copies of these notes will be communicated to your Excellency as soon as exchanged.

I would also venture to remind your Excellency that the conclusion of the present agreement raises, for practical consideration, the question of the claims of Italy to a share in any partition or rearrangement of Turkey in Asia, as formulated in article 9 of the agreement of the 26th April, 1915, between Italy and the Allies.

His Majesty's Government further consider that the Japanese Government should be informed of the arrangement now concluded.

Document 6

The McMahon Letter

Sir Henry McMahon (1862–1949), British High Commissioner in Cairo, negotiated in 1915–16 with Husain Ibn Ali, the Sherif of Mecca. The British government promised to support his bid for the restoration of the Caliphate (and leadership in the Arab world) if Husain supported the British war effort against Turkey. Palestine was not mentioned by name in this exchange: the Arabs subsequently claimed that it had been included in the promise of an independent Arab state. The British denied this—as evidenced by McMahon's letter published in the London *Times* in 1937.

October 24, 1915.

I have received your letter of the 29th Shawal, 1333, with much pleasure and your expression of friendliness and sincerity have given me the greatest satisfaction.

I regret that you should have received from my last letter the impression that I regarded the question of limits and boundaries with coldness and hesitation; such was not the case, but it appeared to me that the time had not yet come when that question could be discussed in a conclusive manner.

I have realised, however, from your last letter that you regard this question as one of vital and urgent importance. I have, therefore, lost no time in informing the Government of Great Britain of the contents of your letter, and it is with great pleasure that I communicate to you on their behalf the following statement, which I am confident you will receive with satisfaction.

The two districts of Mersina and Alexandretta and portions of Syria lying to the west of the districts of Damascus, Homs, Hama and Aleppo cannot be said to be purely Arab, and should be excluded from the limits demanded.

With the above modification, and without prejudice to our existing treaties with Arab chiefs, we accept those limits.

As for those regions lying within those frontiers wherein Great Britain is free to act without detriment to the interests of her ally, France, I am empowered in the name of the Government of Great Britain to give the following assurances and make the following reply to your letter:

(1) Subject to the above modifications, Great Britain is prepared to recognise and support the independence of the Arabs in all the regions within the limits demanded by the Sherif of Mecca.

(2) Great Britain will guarantee the Holy Places against all external aggression and will recognise their inviolability.

(3) When the situation admits, Great Britain will give to the Arabs her advice and will assist them to establish what may appear to be the most suitable forms of government in those various territories.

(4) On the other hand, it is understood that the Arabs have decided to seek the advice and guidance of Great Britain only, and that such European advisers and officials as may be required for the formation of a sound form of administration will be British.

(5) With regard to the *vilayets* of Bagdad and Basra, the Arabs will recognise that the established position and interests of Great Britain necessitate special administrative arrangements in order to secure these territories from foreign aggression to promote the welfare of the local populations and to safeguard our mutual economic interests.

I am convinced that this declaration will assure you beyond all possible doubt of the sympathy of Great Britain towards the aspirations of her friends the Arabs and will result in a firm and lasting alliance, the immediate results of which will be the expulsion of the Turks from the Arab countries and the freeing of the Arab peoples from the Turkish yoke, which for so many years has pressed heavily upon them.

I have confined myself in this letter to the more vital and important questions, and if there are any other matters dealt with in your letters which I have omitted to mention, we may discuss them at some convenient date in the future.

It was with very great relief and satisfaction that I heard of the safe arrival of the Holy Carpet and the accompanying offerings which, thanks to the clearness of your directions and the excellence of your arrangements, were landed without trouble or mishap in spite of the dangers and difficulties occasioned by the present sad war. May God soon bring a lasting peace and freedom of all peoples.

I am sending this letter by the hand of your trusted and excellent messenger, Sheikh Mohammed ibn Arif ibn Uraifan, and he will inform you of the various matters of interest, but of less vital importance, which I have not mentioned in this letter.

(Compliments).

(Signed): A. HENRY McMAHON.

Document 7

The Balfour Declaration

British policy during the war years became gradually committed to the idea of the establishment of a Jewish home in Palestine. After discussions on cabinet level and con-

sultation with Jewish leaders, the decision was made
known in the form of a letter by Arthur James Lord
Balfour (1848-1930) to Lord Rothschild.

                                        Foreign Office
                                   November 2nd, 1917.
Dear Lord Rothschild,
   I have much pleasure in conveying to you, on behalf of His
Majesty's Government, the following declaration of sympathy
with Jewish Zionist aspirations which has been submitted to,
and approved by, the Cabinet.

   "His Majesty's Government view with favour the establishment in Palestine of a national home for the Jewish people,
and will use their best endeavours to facilitate the achievement of this object, it being clearly understood that nothing
shall be done which may prejudice the civil and religious
rights of existing non-Jewish communities in Palestine, or the
rights and political status enjoyed by Jews in any other country."

   I should be grateful if you would bring this declaration to
the knowledge of the Zionist Federation.
                                   Yours sincerely,
                                   ARTHUR JAMES BALFOUR.

Document 8

The Feisal–Weizmann agreement and
Feisal–Frankfurter letters

During the peace conference Emir Feisal (1855-1933),
the son of Husain, the Sherif of Mecca, met various Jewish
leaders and signed an agreement with Dr. Chaim Weizmann (1877-1952), leader of the Zionist movement.
Feisal, who in 1921 became King of Iraq, had it announced ten years later that "His Majesty does not remember having written anything of that kind with his
knowledge."

Agreement Between Emir Feisal and
Dr. Weizmann January 3, 1919

   His Royal Highness the Emir Feisal, representing and acting on behalf of the Arab Kingdom of Hedjaz, and Dr. Chaim

Weizmann, representing and acting on behalf of the Zionist Organisation, mindful of the racial kinship and ancient bonds existing between the Arabs and the Jewish people, and realising that the surest means of working out the consummation of their national aspirations is through the closest possible collaboration in the development of the Arab State and Palestine, and being desirous further of confirming the good understanding which exists between them, have agreed upon the following Articles:

ARTICLE I

The Arab State and Palestine in all their relations and undertakings shall be controlled by the most cordial goodwill and understanding, and to this end Arab and Jewish duly accredited agents shall be established and maintained in the respective territories.

ARTICLE II

Immediately following the completion of the deliberations of the Peace Conference, the definite boundaries between the Arab State and Palestine shall be determined by a Commission to be agreed upon by the parties hereto.

ARTICLE III

In the establishment of the Constitution and Administration of Palestine all such measures shall be adopted as will afford the fullest guarantees for carrying into effect the British Government's Declaration of the 2d of November, 1917.

ARTICLE IV

All necessary measures shall be taken to encourage and stimulate immigration of Jews into Palestine on a large scale, and as quickly as possible to settle Jewish immigrants upon the land through closer settlement and intensive cultivation of the soil. In taking such measures the Arab peasant and tenant farmers shall be protected in their rights, and shall be assisted in forwarding their economic development.

ARTICLE V

No regulation nor law shall be made prohibiting or interfering in any way with the free exercise of religion; and further the free exercise and enjoyment of religious profession and worship without discrimination or reference shall forever be allowed. No religious test shall ever be required for the exercise of civil or political rights.

ARTICLE VI

The Mohammedan Holy Places shall be under Mohammedan control.

ARTICLE VII

The Zionist Organisation proposes to send to Palestine a Commission of experts to make a survey of the economic possibilities of the country, and to report upon the best means for its development. The Zionist Organisation will place the aforementioned Commission at the disposal of the Arab State for the purpose of a survey of the economic possibilities of the Arab State and to report upon the best means for its development. The Zionist Organisation will use its best efforts to assist the Arab State in providing the means for developing the natural resources and economic possibilities thereof.

ARTICLE VIII

The parties hereto agree to act in complete accord and harmony on all matters embraced herein before the Peace Congress.

ARTICLE IX

Any matters of dispute which may arise between the contracting parties shall be referred to the British Government for arbitration.

Given under our hand at London, England, the third day of January, one thousand nine hundred and nineteen.

CHAIM WEIZMANN.
FEISAL IBN-HUSSEIN.

RESERVATION BY THE EMIR FEISAL

If the Arabs are established as I have asked in my manifesto of January 4th addressed to the British Secretary of State for Foreign Affairs, I will carry out what is written in this agreement. If changes are made, I cannot be answerable for failing to carry out this agreement.

FEISAL IBN-HUSSEIN.

Feisal-Frankfurter Correspondence

DELEGATION HEDJAZIENNE, *Paris, March 3, 1919.*

DEAR MR. FRANKFURTER: I want to take this opportunity of my first contact with American Zionists to tell you what I have often been able to say to Dr. Weizmann in Arabia and Europe.

We feel that the Arabs and Jews are cousins in race, having suffered similar oppressions at the hands of powers stronger than themselves, and by a happy coincidence have been able to take the first step towards the attainment of their national ideals together.

We Arabs, especially the educated among us, look with the deepest sympathy on the Zionist movement. Our deputation here in Paris is fully acquainted with the proposals submitted yesterday by the Zionist Organization to the Peace Conference, and we regard them as moderate and proper. We will do our best, in so far as we are concerned, to help them through: we will wish the Jews a most hearty welcome home.

With the chiefs of your movement, especially with Dr. Weizmann, we have had and continue to have the closest relations. He has been a great helper of our cause, and I hope the Arabs may soon be in a position to make the Jews some return for their kindness. We are working together for a reformed and revived Near East, and our two movements complete one another. The Jewish movement is national and not imperialist. Our movement is national and not imperialist, and there is room in Syria for us both. Indeed I think that neither can be a real success without the other.

People less informed and less responsible than our leaders and yours, ignoring the need for cooperation of the Arabs and Zionists have been trying to exploit the local difficulties that must necessarily arise in Palestine in the early stages of our movements. Some of them have, I am afraid, misrepresented your aims to the Arab peasantry, and our aims to the Jewish peasantry, with the result that interested parties have been able to make capital out of what they call our differences.

I wish to give you my firm conviction that these differences are not on questions of principle, but on matters of detail such as must inevitably occur in every contact of neighbouring peoples, and as are easily adjusted by mutual goodwill. Indeed nearly all of them will disappear with fuller knowledge.

I look forward, and my people with me look forward, to a future in which we will help you and you will help us, so that the countries in which we are mutually interested may once again take their places in the community of civilised peoples of the world.

Believe me,
    Yours sincerely,

(*Sgd.*) FEISAL.
5TH MARCH, 1919.

ROYAL HIGHNESS:

Allow me, on behalf of the Zionist Organisation, to acknowledge your recent letter with deep appreciation.

Those of us who come from the United States have already been gratified by the friendly relations and the active cooperation maintained between you and the Zionist leaders, particularly Dr. Weizmann. We knew it could not be otherwise; we knew that the aspirations of the Arab and the Jewish peoples were parallel, that each aspired to reestablish its nationality in its own homeland, each making its own distinctive contribution to civilisation, each seeking its own peaceful mode of life.

The Zionist leaders and the Jewish people for whom they speak have watched with satisfaction the spiritual vigour of the Arab movement. Themselves seeking justice, they are anxious that the just national aims of the Arab people be confirmed and safeguarded by the Peace Conference.

We knew from your acts and your past utterances that the Zionist movement—in other words the national aims of the Jewish people—had your support and the support of the Arab people for whom you speak. These aims are now before the Peace Conference as definite proposals by the Zionist Organisation. We are happy indeed that you consider these proposals "moderate and proper," and that we have in you a staunch supporter for their realisation. For both the Arab and the Jewish peoples there are difficulties ahead—difficulties that challenge the united statesmanship of Arab and Jewish leaders. For it is no easy task to rebuild two great civilisations that have been suffering oppression and misrule for centuries. We each have our difficulties we shall work out as friends, friends who are animated by similar purposes, seeking a free and full development for the two neighbouring peoples. The Arabs and Jews are neighbours in territory; we cannot but live side by side as friends.

Very respectfully,

(Sgd.) FELIX FRANKFURTER.

Document 9

Recommendations of the King–Crane Commission

The King–Crane Commission was appointed by President Wilson, following a suggestion by Dr. Howard Bliss, President of the American University in Beirut and a sympathizer with the Arab cause. Its main function was to determine which of the Western nations should act as the mandatory power for Palestine.

August 28, 1919

The Commissioners make to the Peace Conference the following recommendations for the treatment of Syria:

1. We recommend, as most important of all, and in strict harmony with our instructions, that whatever foreign administration (whether of one or more powers) is brought into Syria, should come in, not at all as a colonization Power in the old sense of that term, but as a Mandatory under the League of Nations, with the clear consciousness that "the well-being and development" of the Syrian people form for it a "sacred trust".

(1) To this end the mandate should have a limited term, the time of expiration to be determined by the League of Nations, in the light of all the facts as brought out from year to year, in the annual reports of the Mandatory to the League or in other ways.

(2) The Mandatory Administration should have, however, a period and power sufficient to ensure the success of the new State; and especially to make possible carrying through important educational and economic undertakings, essential to secure founding of the State.

(3) The Mandatory Administration should be characterized from the beginning by a strong and vital educational emphasis in clear recognition of the imperative necessity of education for the citizens of a democratic state, and the development of a sound national spirit. This systematic cultivation of national spirit is particularly required in a country like Syria, which has only recently come to self-consciousness.

(4) The Mandatory should definitely seek, from the beginning of its trusteeship, to train the Syrian people to independent self-government as rapidly as conditions allow, by

setting up all the institutions of a democratic state, and by sharing with them increasingly the work of administration and so forming gradually an intelligent citizenship, interested unselfishly in the progress of the country, and forming at the same time a large group of disciplined civil servants.

(5) The period of "tutelage" should not be unduly prolonged, but independent self-government should be granted as soon as it can safely be done; remembering that the primary business of government is not the accomplishment of certain things, but the development of citizens.

(6) It is peculiarly the duty of the Mandatory in a country like Syria, and in this modern age, to see that complete religious liberty is ensured, both in the constitution and in the practice of the state, and that a jealous care is exercised for the rights of all minorities. Nothing is more vital than this for the enduring success of the new Arab State.

(7) In the economic development of Syria, a dangerous amount of indebtedness on the part of the new State should be avoided, as well as any entanglements financially with the affairs of the Mandatory Power. On the other hand the legitimate established privileges of foreigners such as rights to maintain schools, commercial concessions, etc., should be preserved, but subject to review and modification under the authority of the League of Nations in the interest of Syria. The Mandatory Power should not take advantage of its position to force a monopolistic control at any point to the detriment either of Syria or of other nations; but it should seek to bring the new State as rapidly as possible to economic independence as well as to political independence. Whatever is done concerning the further recommendations of the Commission, the fulfillment of at least the conditions now named should be assured, if the Peace Conference and the League of Nations are true to the policy of mandatories already embodied in "The Covenant of the League of Nations". This should effectively guard the most essential interests of Syria, however the machinery of administration is finally organized. The Damascus Congress betrayed in many ways their intense fear that their country would become, though under some other name, simply a colonial possession of some other Power. That fear must be completely allayed.

2. We recommend, in the second place that the unity of Syria be preserved, in accordance with the earnest petition of the great majority of the people of Syria.

(1) The territory concerned is too limited, the population

too small, and the economic, geographic, racial and language unity too manifest to make the setting up of independent states within its boundaries desirable, if such division can possibly be avoided. The country is very largely Arab in language, culture, traditions, and customs.

(2) This recommendation is in line with important "general considerations" already urged, and with the principles of the League of Nations, as well as in answer to the desires of the majority of the population concerned.

(3) The precise boundaries of Syria should be determined by a special commission on boundaries, after the Syrian territory has been in general allotted. The Commissioners believe, however, that the claim of the Damascus Conference to include Cilicia in Syria is not justified, either historically or by commercial or language relations. The line between the Arabic-speaking and the Turkish-speaking populations would quite certainly class Cilicia with Asia Minor rather than with Syria. Syria, too, has no such need of further sea coast as the large interior sections of Asia Minor.

(4) In standing thus for the recognition of the unity of Syria, the natural desires of regions like the Lebanon, which have already had a measure of independence, should not be forgotten. It will make for real unity, undoubtedly, to give a large measure of local autonomy, and especially in the case of strongly unified groups. Even the "Damascus Program" which presses so earnestly the unity of Syria, itself urges a government "on broad decentralization principles".

Lebanon has achieved a considerable degree of prosperity and autonomy within the Turkish Empire. She certainly should not find her legitimate aspirations less possible within a Syrian national State. On the contrary, it may be confidently expected that both her economic and political relations with the rest of Syria would be better if she were a constituent member of the State, rather than entirely independent of it.

As a predominantly Christian country, too, Lebanon naturally fears Moslem domination in a unified Syria. But against such domination she would have a four-fold safeguard: her own large autonomy; the presence of a strong Mandatory for the considerable period in which the constitution and practice of the new State would be forming; the oversight of the League of Nations, with its insistence upon religious liberty and the rights of minorities; and the certainty that the Arab Government would feel the necessity of such a state, if it were to commend itself to the League of Nations. Moreover, there would be less danger of reactionary Moslem attitude, if Christians were present in the state in considerable numbers, rather than largely segregated outside the state, as experience of the relations of different religious faiths in India suggests.

As a predominantly Christian country, it is also to be noted that Lebanon would be in a position to exert a stronger and more helpful influence if she were within the Syrian State, feeling its problems and needs, and sharing all its life, instead of outside it, absorbed simply in her own narrow concerns. For the sake of the larger interests, both of Lebanon and of Syria, then, the unity of Syria is to be urged. It is certain that many of the more thoughtful Lebanese themselves hold this view. A similar statement might be made for Palestine; though, as "the Holy Land" for Jews and Christians and Moslems alike, its situation is unique, and might more readily justify unique treatment, if such treatment were justified anywhere. This will be discussed more particularly in connection with the recommendation concerning Zionism.

3. We recommend, in the third place, that Syria be placed under an (e) Mandatory Power, as the natural way to secure real and efficient unity.

(1) To divide the administration of the provinces of Syria among several mandatories, even if existing national unity were recognized; or to attempt a joint mandatory of the whole on the commission plan:—neither of these courses would be naturally suggested as the best way to secure and promote the unity of the new State, or even the general unity of the whole people. It is conceivable that circumstances might drive the Peace Conference to some such form of divided mandate; but it is not a solution to be voluntarily chosen, from the point of view of the larger interests of the people, as considerations already urged indicate.

(2) It is not to be forgotten, either, that, however they are handled politically, the people of Syria are there, forced to get on together in some fashion. They are obliged to live with one another—the Arabs of the East and the people of the Coast, the Moslems and the Christians. Will they be helped or hindered, in establishing tolerable and finally cordial relations, by a single mandatory? No doubt the quick mechanical solution of the problem of different relations is to split the people up into little independent fragments. And sometimes, undoubtedly, as in the case of the Turks and Armenians, the relations are so intolerable as to make some division impera-

tive and inevitable. But in general, to attempt complete separation only accentuates the differences and increases the antagonism. The whole lesson of the modern social consciousness points to the necessity of understanding "the other half", as it can be understood only by close and living relations. Granting reasonable local autonomy to reduce friction among groups, a single mandatory ought to form a constant and increasingly effective help to unity of feeling throughout the state, and ought to steadily improve group relations.

The people of Syria, in our hearings, have themselves often insisted that, so far as unpleasant relations have hitherto prevailed among various groups, it has been very largely due to the direct instigation of the Turkish Government. When justice is done impartially to all; when it becomes plain that the aim of the common government is the service of all classes alike, not their exploitation, decent human relations are pretty certain to prevail, and a permanent foundation for such relations to be secured—a foundation which could not be obtained by dividing men off from one another in antagonistic groups.

The Commissioners urge, therefore, for the largest future good of all groups and regions alike, the placing of the whole of Syria under a single mandate.

4. We recommend, in the fourth place, that Emir Feisal be made the head of the new united Syrian State.

(1) This is expressly and unanimously asked for by the representative Damascus Congress in the name of the Syrian people, and there seems to be no reason to doubt that the great majority of the population of Syria sincerely desire to have Emir Feisal as ruler.

(2) A constitutional monarchy along democratic lines, seems naturally adapted to the Arabs, with their long training under tribal conditions, and with their traditional respect for their chiefs. They seem to need, more than most people, a King as the personal symbol of the power of the State.

(3) Emir Feisal has come, too, naturally into his present place of power, and there is no one else who could well replace him. He had the great advantage of being the son of the Sherif of Mecca, and as such honored throughout the Moslem world. He was one of the prominent Arab leaders who assumed responsibility for the Arab uprising against the Turks, and so shared in the complete deliverance of the Arab-speaking portions of the Turkish Empire. He was consequently hailed by the "Damascus Congress" as having "merited their full confidence and entire reliance". He was taken up and

supported by the British as the most promising candidate for the headship of the new Arab State—as Arab of the Arabs, but with a position of wide appeal through his Sherifian connection, and through his broad sympathies with the best in the Occident. His relations with the Arabs to the east of Syria are friendly, and his kingdom would not be threatened from that side. He undoubtedly does not make so strong an appeal to the Christians of the West Coast, as to the Arabs of the East; but no man can be named who would have a stronger general appeal. He is tolerant and wise, skilful in dealing with men, winning in manner, a man of sincerity, insight, and power. Whether he has the full strength needed for his difficult task it is too early to say; but certainly no other Arab leader combines so many elements of power as he, and he will have invaluable help throughout the mandatory period.

The Peace Conference may take genuine satisfaction in the fact that an Arab of such qualities is available for the headship of this new state in the Near East.

5. We recommend, in the fifth place, serious modification of the extreme Zionist program for Palestine of unlimited immigration of Jews, looking finally to making Palestine distinctly a Jewish State.

(1) The Commissioners began their study of Zionism with minds predisposed in its favor, but the actual facts in Palestine, coupled with the force of the general principles proclaimed by the Allies and accepted by the Syrians have driven them to the recommendation here made.

(2) The Commission was abundantly supplied with literature on the Zionist program by the Zionist Commission to Palestine; heard in conferences much concerning the Zionist colonies and their claims and personally saw something of what had been accomplished. They found much to approve in the aspirations and plans of the Zionists, and had warm appreciation for the devotion of many of the colonists, and for their success, by modern methods, in overcoming great natural obstacles.

(3) The Commission recognized also that definite encouragement had been given to the Zionists by the Allies in Mr. Balfour's often quoted statement, in its approval by other representatives of the Allies. If, however, the strict terms of the Balfour Statement are adhered to—favoring "the establishment in Palestine of a national home for the Jewish people," "it being clearly understood that nothing shall be done which may prejudice the civil and religious rights of existing non-

Jewish communities in Palestine"—it can hardly be doubted that the extreme Zionist Program must be greatly modified. For "a national home for the Jewish people" is not equivalent to making Palestine into a Jewish State; nor can the erection of such a Jewish State be accomplished without the gravest trespass upon the "civil and religious rights of existing non-Jewish communities in Palestine". The fact came out repeatedly in the Commission's conference with Jewish representatives, that the Zionists looked forward to a practically complete dispossession of the present non-Jewish inhabitants of Palestine, by various forms of purchase.

In his address of July 4, 1918, President Wilson laid down the following principle as one of the four great "ends for which the associated peoples of the world were fighting": "The settlement of every question, whether of territory, of sovereignty, of economic arrangement, or of political relationship upon the basis of the free acceptance of that settlement by the people immediately concerned, and not upon the basis of the material interest or advantage of any other nation or people which may desire a different settlement for the sake of its own exterior influence or mastery". If that principle is to rule, and so the wishes of Palestine's population are to be decisive as to what is to be done with Palestine, then it is to be remembered that the non-Jewish population of Palestine—nearly nine-tenths of the whole—are emphatically against the entire Zionist program. The tables show that there was no one thing upon which the population of Palestine were more agreed than upon this. To subject a people so minded to unlimited Jewish immigration, and to steady financial and social pressure to surrender the land, would be a gross violation of the principle just quoted, and of the peoples' rights, though it kept within the forms of law.

It is to be noted also that the feeling against the Zionist program is not confined to Palestine, but shared very generally by the people throughout Syria, as our conferences clearly showed. More than 72 per cent—1350 in all—of all the petitions in the whole of Syria were directed against the Zionist program. Only two requests—those for a united Syria and for independence—had a larger support. This general feeling was only voiced by the "General Syrian Congress," in the seventh, eighth and tenth resolutions of their statement.

The Peace Conference should not shut its eyes to the fact that the anti-Zionist feeling in Palestine and Syria is intense and not lightly to be flouted. No British officer, consulted by the Commissioners, believed that the Zionist program could be carried out except by force of arms. The officers generally thought that a force of not less than fifty thousand soldiers would be required even to initiate the program. That of itself is evidence of a strong sense of the injustice of the Zionist program, on the part of the non-Jewish populations of Palestine and Syria. Decisions, requiring armies to carry them out, are sometimes necessary, but they are surely not gratuitously to be taken in the interests of a serious injustice. For the initial claim, often submitted by Zionist representatives, that they have a "right" to Palestine, based on an occupation of two thousand years ago, can hardly be seriously considered.

There is a further consideration that cannot justly be ignored, if the world is to look forward to Palestine becoming a definitely Jewish state, however gradually that may take place. That consideration grows out of the fact that Palestine is "the Holy Land" for Jews, Christians, and Moslems alike. Millions of Christians and Moslems all over the world are quite as much concerned as the Jews with conditions in Palestine, especially with those conditions which touch upon religious feelings and rights. The relations in these matters in Palestine are most delicate and difficult. With the best possible intentions, it may be doubted whether the Jews could possibly seem to either Christians or Moslems proper guardians of the holy places, or custodians of the Holy Land as a whole. The reason is this: the places which are most sacred to Christians—those having to do with Jesus—and which are also sacred to Moslems, are not only not sacred to Jews, but abhorrent to them. It is simply impossible, under those circumstances, for Moslems and Christians to feel satisfied to have these places in Jewish hands, or under the custody of Jews. There are still other places about which Moslems must have the same feeling. In fact, from this point of view, the Moslems, just because the sacred places of all three religions are sacred to them, have made very naturally much more satisfactory custodians of the holy places than the Jews could be. It must be believed that the precise meaning, in this respect, of the complete Jewish occupation of Palestine has not been fully sensed by those who urge the extreme Zionist program. For it would intensify, with a certainty like fate, the anti-Jewish feeling both in Palestine and in all other portions of the world which look to Palestine as "the Holy Land".

In view of all these considerations, and with a deep sense of sympathy for the Jewish cause, the Commissioners feel bound to recommend that only a greatly reduced Zionist program be attempted by the Peace Conference and even that, only very gradually initiated. This would have to mean that Jewish immigration should be definitely limited, and that the project for making Palestine distinctly a Jewish commonwealth should be given up.

There would then be no reason why Palestine could not be included in a united Syrian State, just as other portions of the country, the holy places being cared for by an International and Inter-religious Commission, somewhat as at present, under the oversight and approval of the Mandatory and of the League of Nations. The Jews, of course, would have representation upon this Commission.

[The remaining part of this document recommended that the United States be asked to undertake the single Mandate for all Syria. Ed.]

Document 10

Memorandum Presented to the King–Crane Commission by the General Syrian Congress

This is one of the first Arab statements on record opposing Jewish migration to Palestine.

July 2, 1919

We the undersigned members of the General Syrian Congress, meeting in Damascus on Wednesday, July 2nd, 1919, made up of representatives from the three Zones, viz., the Southern, Eastern, and Western, provided with credentials and authorizations by the inhabitants of our various districts, Moslems, Christians, and Jews, have agreed upon the following statement of the desires of the people of the country who have elected us to present them to the American Section of the International Commission; the fifth article was passed by a very large majority; all the other articles were accepted unanimously.

1. We ask absolutely complete political independence for Syria within these boundaries: the Taurus System on the North; Rafah and a line running from Al Jauf to the south of the Syrian and the Hejazian line to Akaba on the south; the Euphrates and Khabur Rivers and a line extending east of Abu Kamal to the east of Al Jauf on the east; and the Mediterranean on the west.

2.   We ask that the Government of this Syrian country should be a democratic civil constitutional Monarchy on broad decentralization principles, safeguarding the rights of minorities, and that the King be the Emir Feisal, who carried on a glorious struggle in the cause of our liberation and merited our full confidence and entire reliance.

3.   Considering the fact that the Arabs inhabiting the Syrian area are not naturally less gifted than other more advanced races and that they are by no means less developed than the Bulgarians, Serbians, Greeks, and Roumanians at the beginning of their independence, we protest against Article 22 of the Covenant of the League of Nations, placing us among the nations in their middle stage of development which stand in need of a mandatory power.

4.   In the event of the rejection by the Peace Conference of this just protest for certain considerations that we may not understand, we, relying on the declarations of President Wilson that his object in waging war was to put an end to the ambition of conquest and colonization, can only regard the mandate mentioned in the Covenant of the League of Nations as equivalent to the rendering of economical and technical assistance that does not prejudice our complete independence. And desiring that our country should not fall a prey to colonization is farthest from any thought of colonization and has no political ambition in our country, we will seek the technical and economical assistance from the United States of America, provided that such assistance does not exceed 20 years.

5.   In the event of America not finding herself in a position to accept our desire for assistance, we will seek this assistance from Great Britain, also provided that such assistance does not infringe the complete independence and unity of our country and that the duration of such assistance does not exceed that mentioned in the previous article.

6.   We do not acknowledge any right claimed by the French Government in any part whatever of our Syrian country and refuse that she should assist us or have a hand in our country under any circumstances and in any place.

7.   We oppose the pretensions of the Zionists to create a Jewish commonwealth in the southern part of Syria,

known as Palestine, and oppose Zionist migration to any part of our country; for we do not acknowledge their title but consider them a grave peril to our people from the national, economical, and political points of view. Our Jewish compatriots shall enjoy our common rights and assume the common responsibilities.

8.   We ask that there should be no separation of the southern part of Syria, known as Palestine, nor of the littoral western zone, which includes Lebanon, from the Syrian country. We desire that the unity of the country should be guaranteed against partition under whatever circumstances.

9.   We ask complete independence for emancipated Mesopotamia and that there should be no economical barriers between the two countries.

10. The fundamental principles laid down by President Wilson in condemnation of secret treaties impel us to protest most emphatically against any treaty that stipulates the partition of our Syrian country and against any private engagement aiming at the establishment of Zionism in the southern part of Syria; therefore we ask the complete annulment of these conventions and agreements.

The noble principles enunciated by President Wilson strengthen our confidence that our desires emanating from the depths of our hearts, shall be the decisive factor in determining our future; and that President Wilson and the free American people will be our supporters for the realization of our hopes thereby proving their sincerity and noble sympathy with the aspiration of the weaker nations in general and our Arab people in particular.

We also have the fullest confidence that the Peace Conference will realize that we would not have risen against the Turks, with whom we had participated in all civil, political, and representative privileges, but for their violation of our national rights, and so will grant us our desires in full in order that our political rights may not be less after the war than they were before, since we have shed so much blood in the cause of our liberty and independence.

We request to be allowed to send a delegation to represent us at the Peace Conference to defend our rights and secure the realization of our aspirations.

Document 11

The British Mandate

The San Remo Conference decided on April 24, 1920 to assign the Mandate under the League of Nations to Britain. The terms of the Mandate were also discussed with the United States which was not a member of the League. An agreed text was confirmed by the Council of the League of Nations on July 24, 1922, and it came into operation in September 1923.

"The Council of the League of Nations:

Whereas the Principal Allied Powers have agreed, for the purpose of giving effect to the provisions of Article 22 of the Covenant of the League of Nations, to entrust to a Mandatory selected by the said Powers the administration of the territory of Palestine, which formerly belonged to the Turkish Empire, within such boundaries as may be fixed by them; and

Whereas the Principal Allied Powers have also agreed that the Mandatory should be responsible for putting into effect the declaration originally made on November 2nd, 1917, by the Government of His Britannic Majesty, and adopted by the said Powers, in favour of the establishment in Palestine of a national home for the Jewish people, it being clearly understood that nothing should be done which might prejudice the civil and religious rights of existing non-Jewish communities in Palestine, or the rights and political status enjoyed by Jews in any other country; and

Whereas recognition has thereby been given to the historical connexion of the Jewish people with Palestine and to the grounds for reconstituting their national home in that country; and

Whereas the Principal Allied Powers have selected His Britannic Majesty as the Mandatory for Palestine; and

Whereas the mandate in respect of Palestine has been formulated in the following terms and submitted to the Council of the League for approval; and

Whereas His Britannic Majesty has accepted the mandate in respect of Palestine and undertaken to exercise it on behalf of the League of Nations in conformity with the following provisions; and

Whereas by the aforementioned Article 22 (paragraph 8), it is provided that the degree of authority, control or administration to be exercised by the Mandatory, not having been previously agreed upon by the Members of the League, shall be explicitly defined by the Council of the League of Nations;

Confirming the said Mandate, defines its terms as follows:

ARTICLE 1.

The Mandatory shall have full powers of legislation and of administration, save as they may be limited by the terms of this mandate.

ARTICLE 2.

The Mandatory shall be responsible for placing the country under such political, administrative and economic conditions as will secure the establishment of the Jewish national home, as laid down in the preamble, and the development of self-governing institutions, and also for safeguarding the civil and religious rights of all the inhabitants of Palestine, irrespective of race and religion.

ARTICLE 3.

The Mandatory shall, so far as circumstances permit, encourage local autonomy.

ARTICLE 4.

An appropriate Jewish agency shall be recognized as a public body for the purpose of advising and cooperating with the Administration of Palestine in such economic, social and other matters as may affect the establishment of the Jewish national home and the interests of the Jewish population in Palestine, and, subject always to the control of the Administration, to assist and take part in the development of the country.

The Zionist Organization, so long as its organization and constitution are in the opinion of the Mandatory appropriate, shall be recognized as such agency. It shall take steps in consultation with His Britannic Majesty's Government to secure the cooperation of all Jews who are willing to assist in the establishment of the Jewish national home.

ARTICLE 5.

The Mandatory shall be responsible for seeing that no Palestine territory shall be ceded or leased to, or in any way placed under the control of, the Government of any foreign Power.

ARTICLE 6.

The Administration of Palestine, while ensuring that the rights and position of other sections of the population are not prejudiced, shall facilitate Jewish immigration under suitable conditions and shall encourage, in co-operation with the Jewish agency referred to in Article 4, close settlement by Jews on the land, including State lands and waste lands not required for public purposes.

ARTICLE 7.

The Administration of Palestine shall be responsible for enacting a nationality law. There shall be included in this law provisions framed so as to facilitate the acquisition of Palestinian citizenship by Jews who take up their permanent residence in Palestine.

ARTICLE 8.

The privileges and immunities of foreigners, including the benefits of consular jurisdiction and protection as formerly enjoyed by Capitulation or usage in the Ottoman Empire, shall not be applicable in Palestine.

Unless the Powers whose nationals enjoyed the aforementioned privileges and immunities on August 1st, 1914, shall have previously renounced the right to their re-establishment, or shall have agreed to their non-application for a specified period, these privileges and immunities shall, at the expiration of the mandate, be immediately re-established in their entirety or with such modifications as may have been agreed upon between the Powers concerned.

ARTICLE 9.

The Mandatory shall be responsible for seeing that the judicial system established in Palestine shall assure to foreigners, as well as to natives, a complete guarantee of their rights.

Respect for the personal status of the various peoples and communities and for their religious interests shall be fully guaranteed. In particular, the control and administration of Waqfs shall be exercised in accordance with religious law and the dispositions of the founders.

ARTICLE 10.

Pending the making of special extradition agreements relating to Palestine, the extradition treaties in force between the Mandatory and other foreign Powers shall apply to Palestine.

ARTICLE 11.

The Administration of Palestine shall take all necessary measures to safeguard the interests of the community in connection with the development of the country, and, subject to any international obligations accepted by the Mandatory, shall have full power to provide for public ownership or control of any of the natural resources of the country or of the public works, services and utilities established or to be established therein. It shall introduce a land system appropriate to the needs of the country having regard, among other things, to the desirability of promoting the close settlement and intensive cultivation of the land.

The Administration may arrange with the Jewish agency mentioned in Article 4 to construct or operate, upon fair and equitable terms, any public works, services and utilities, and to develop any of the natural resources of the country, in so far as these matters are not directly undertaken by the Administration. Any such arrangements shall provide that no profits distributed by such agency, directly or indirectly, shall exceed a reasonable rate of interest on the capital, and any further profits shall be utilized by it for the benefit of the country in a manner approved by the Administration.

ARTICLE 12.

The Mandatory shall be entrusted with the control of the foreign relations of Palestine, and the right to issue exequaturs to consuls appointed by foreign Powers. He shall also be entitled to afford diplomatic and consular protection to citizens of Palestine when outside its territorial limits.

ARTICLE 13.

All responsibility in connexion with the Holy Places and religious buildings or sites in Palestine, including that of preserving existing rights and of securing free access to the Holy Places, religious buildings and sites and the free exercise of worship, while ensuring the requirements of public order and decorum, is assumed by the Mandatory, who shall be responsible solely to the League of Nations in all matters connected herewith, provided that nothing in this article shall prevent the Mandatory from entering into such arrangements as he may deem reasonable with the Administration for the purpose of carrying the provisions of this article into effect; and provided also that nothing in this Mandate shall be construed as conferring upon the Mandatory authority to interfere with the fabric or the management of purely Moslem sacred shrines, the immunities of which are guaranteed.

ARTICLE 14.

A special Commission shall be appointed by the Mandatory to study, define and determine the rights and claims in connection with the Holy Places and the rights and claims relating to the different religious communities in Palestine. The method of nomination, the composition and the functions of this Commission shall be submitted to the Council of the League for its approval, and the Commission shall not be appointed or enter upon its functions without the approval of the Council.

ARTICLE 15.

The Mandatory shall see that complete freedom of conscience and the free exercise of all forms of worship, subject only to the maintenance of public order and morals, are ensured to all. No discrimination of any kind shall be made between the inhabitants of Palestine on the ground of race, religion or language. No person shall be excluded from Palestine on the sole ground of his religious belief.

The right of each community to maintain its own schools for the education of its own members in its own language, while conforming to such educational requirements of a general nature as the Administration may impose, shall not be denied or impaired.

ARTICLE 16.

The Mandatory shall be responsible for exercising such supervision over religious or eleemosynary bodies of all faiths in Palestine as may be required for the maintenance of public order and good government. Subject to such supervision, no measures shall be taken in Palestine to obstruct or interfere with the enterprise of such bodies or to discriminate against any representative or member of them on the ground of his religion or nationality.

ARTICLE 17.

The Administration of Palestine may organize on a voluntary basis the forces necessary for the preservation of peace and order, and also for the defence of the country, subject, however, to the supervision of the Mandatory, but shall not use them for purposes other than those above specified save with the consent of the Mandatory. Except for such purposes, no military, naval or air forces shall be raised or maintained by the Administration of Palestine.

Nothing in this article shall preclude the Administration of Palestine from contributing to the cost of the maintenance of the forces of the Mandatory in Palestine.

The Mandatory shall be entitled at all times to use the roads, railways and ports of Palestine for the movement of armed forces and the carriage of fuel and supplies.

ARTICLE 18.

The Mandatory shall see that there is no discrimination in Palestine against the nationals of any State Member of the League of Nations (including companies incorporated under its laws) as compared with those of the Mandatory or of any foreign State in matters concerning taxation, commerce or navigation, the exercise of industries or professions, or in the treatment of merchant vessels or civil aircraft. Similarly, there shall be no discrimination in Palestine against goods originating in or destined for any of the said States, and there shall be freedom of transit under equitable conditions across the mandated area.

Subject as aforesaid and to the other provisions of this mandate, the Administration of Palestine may, on the advice of the Mandatory, impose such taxes and customs duties as it may consider necessary, and take such steps as it may think best to promote the development of the natural resources of the country and to safeguard the interests of the population. It may also, on the advice of the Mandatory, conclude a special customs agreement with any State the territory of which in 1914 was wholly included in Asiatic Turkey or Arabia.

ARTICLE 19.

The Mandatory shall adhere on behalf of the Administration of Palestine to any general international conventions already existing, or which may be concluded hereafter with the approval of the League of Nations, respecting the slave traffic, the traffic in arms and ammunition, or the traffic in drugs, or relating to commercial equality, freedom of transit and navigation, aerial navigation and postal, telegraphic and wireless communication or literary, artistic or industrial property.

ARTICLE 20.

The Mandatory shall co-operate on behalf of the Administration of Palestine, so far as religious, social and other conditions may permit, in the execution of any common policy adopted by the League of Nations for preventing and combating disease, including diseases of plants and animals.

ARTICLE 21.

The Mandatory shall secure the enactment within twelve months from this date, and shall ensure the execution of a Law of Antiquities based on the following rules. This law shall ensure equality of treatment in the matter of excavations and archaeological research to the nationals of all States Members of the League of Nations. . . .

ARTICLE 22.

English, Arabic and Hebrew shall be the official languages of Palestine. Any statement or inscription in Arabic on stamps or money in Palestine shall be repeated in Hebrew and any statement or inscription in Hebrew shall be repeated in Arabic.

ARTICLE 23.

The Administration of Palestine shall recognize the holy days of the respective communities in Palestine as legal days of rest for the members of such communities.

ARTICLE 24.

The Mandatory shall make to the Council of the League of Nations an annual report to the satisfaction of the Council as to the measures taken during the year to carry out the provisions of the mandate. Copies of all laws and regulations promulgated or issued during the year shall be communicated with the report.

ARTICLE 25.

In the territories lying between the Jordan and the eastern boundary of Palestine as ultimately determined, the Mandatory shall be entitled, with the consent of the Council of the League of Nations, to postpone or withhold application of such provisions of this mandate as he may consider inapplicable to the existing local conditions, and to make such provision for the administration of the territories as he may consider suitable to those conditions, provided that no action shall be taken which is inconsistent with the provisions of Articles 15, 16 and 18.

ARTICLE 26.

The Mandatory agrees that if any dispute whatever should arise between the Mandatory and another Member of the League of Nations relating to the interpretation or the application of the provisions of the mandate, such dispute, if it cannot be settled by negotiation, shall be submitted to the Permanent Court of International Justice provided for by Article 14 of the Covenant of the League of Nations.

ARTICLE 27.

The consent of the Council of the League of Nations is required for any modification of the terms of this mandate.

ARTICLE 28.

In the event of the termination of the mandate hereby conferred upon the Mandatory, the Council of the League of Nations shall make such arrangements as may be deemed necessary for safeguarding in perpetuity, under guarantee of the League, the rights secured by Articles 13 and 14, and shall use its influence for securing, under the guarantee of the League, that the Government of Palestine will fully honour the financial obligations legitimately incurred by the Administration of Palestine during the period of the mandate, including the rights of public servants to pensions or gratuities.

The present instrument shall be deposited in original in the archives of the League of Nations and certified copies shall be forwarded by the Secretary General of the League of Nations to all Members of the League.

DONE AT LONDON the twenty-fourth day of July, one thousand nine hundred and twenty-two."

PART II

Palestine 1920-1947

Part II of the Reader deals with the unhappy history of the British Mandate, from the Balfour Declaration promising the establishment of a Jewish Home in Palestine to the British decision to return the Mandate to the United Nations, and the U.N. resolution about partition and the establishment of an Arab and a Jewish state in Palestine. During this period Arab opposition grew against Jewish colonization and immigration; there was frequent unrest (in 1920–21, 1928, 1933, 1936–39) and the various suggestions for a solution to the conflict were rejected as impractical.

Document 12

The Churchill White Paper—1922

In view of growing opposition to Zionism, a new statement of policy was drafted in 1922 by the then British Colonial Secretary, which, while not explicitly opposing the idea of a Jewish state, "redeemed the Balfour promise in depreciated currency" to quote a contemporary British source.

STATEMENT OF BRITISH POLICY IN PALESTINE ISSUED BY MR. CHURCHILL IN JUNE, 1922.

The Secretary of State for the Colonies has given renewed consideration to the existing political situation in Palestine, with a very earnest desire to arrive at a settlement of the outstanding questions which have given rise to uncertainty and unrest among certain sections of the population. After consultation with the High Commissioner for Palestine the following statement has been drawn up. It summarizes the essential parts of the correspondence that has already taken place between the Secretary of State and a Delegation from the Moslem Christian Society of Palestine, which has been for some time in England, and it states the further conclusions which have since been reached.

The tension which has prevailed from time to time in Palestine is mainly due to apprehensions, which are entertained both by sections of the Arab and by sections of the Jewish population. These apprehensions, so far as the Arabs are concerned, are partly based upon exaggerated interpretations of the meaning of the Declaration favouring the establishment of a Jewish National Home in Palestine, made on behalf of His Majesty's Government on 2nd November, 1917. Unauthorized statements have been made to the effect that the purpose in view is to create a wholly Jewish Palestine. Phrases have been used such as that Palestine is to become "as Jewish as England is English." His Majesty's Government regard any such expectation as impracticable and have no such aim in view. Nor have they at any time contemplated, as appears to be feared by the Arab Delegation, the disappearance or the subordination of the Arabic population, language, or culture in Palestine. They would draw attention to the fact that the terms of the Declaration referred to do not contemplate that Palestine as a whole should be converted into a Jewish National Home, but that such a Home should be founded *in Palestine*. In this connection it has been observed with satisfaction that at the meeting of the Zionist Congress, the supreme governing body of the Zionist Organization, held at Carlsbad in September, 1921, a resolution was passed expressing as the official statement of Zionist aims "the determination of the Jewish people to live with the Arab people on terms of unity and mutual respect, and together with them to make the common home into a flourishing community, the upbuilding of which may assure to each of its peoples an undisturbed national development."

It is also necessary to point out that the Zionist Commission in Palestine, now termed the Palestine Zionist Executive, has not desired to possess, and does not possess, any share in the general administration of the country. Nor does the special position assigned to the Zionist Organization in Article IV of the Draft Mandate for Palestine imply any such functions. That special position relates to the measures to be taken in Palestine affecting the Jewish population, and contemplates that the Organization may assist in the general development of the country, but does not entitle it to share in any degree in its Government.

Further, it is contemplated that the status of all citizens of Palestine in the eyes of the law shall be Palestinian, and it has never been intended that they, or any section of them, should possess any other juridical status.

So far as the Jewish population of Palestine are concerned it appears that some among them are apprehensive that His Majesty's Government may depart from the policy embodied in the Declaration of 1917. It is necessary, therefore, once more to affirm that these fears are unfounded, and that that

Declaration, re-affirmed by the Conference of the Principal Allied Powers at San Remo and again in the Treaty of Sèvres, is not susceptible of change.

During the last two or three generations the Jews have recreated in Palestine a community, now numbering 80,000, of whom about one-fourth are farmers or workers upon the land. This community has its own political organs; an elected assembly for the direction of its domestic concerns; elected councils in the towns; and an organization for the control of its schools. It has its elected Chief Rabbinate and Rabbinical Council for the direction of its religious affairs. Its business is conducted in Hebrew as a vernacular language, and a Hebrew Press serves its needs. It has its distinctive intellectual life and displays considerable economic activity. This community, then, with its town and country population, its political, religious, and social organizations, its own language, its own customs, its own life, has in fact "national" characteristics. When it is asked what is meant by the development of the Jewish National Home in Palestine, it may be answered that it is not the imposition of a Jewish nationality upon the inhabitants of Palestine as a whole, but the further development of the existing Jewish community, with the assistance of Jews in other parts of the world, in order that it may become a centre in which the Jewish people as a whole may take, on grounds of religion and race, an interest and a pride. But in order that this community should have the best prospect of free development and provide a full opportunity for the Jewish people to display its capacities, it is essential that it should know that it is in Palestine as of right and not on sufferance. That is the reason why it is necessary that the existence of a Jewish National Home in Palestine should be internationally guaranteed, and that it should be formally recognized to rest upon ancient historic connection.

This, then, is the interpretation which His Majesty's Government place upon the Declaration of 1917, and, so understood, the Secretary of State is of opinion that it does not contain or imply anything which need cause either alarm to the Arab population of Palestine or disappointment to the Jews.

For the fulfilment of this policy it is necessary that the Jewish community in Palestine should be able to increase its numbers by immigration. This immigration cannot be so great in volume as to exceed whatever may be the economic capacity of the country at the time to absorb new arrivals. It is essential to ensure that the immigrants should not be a burden upon the people of Palestine as a whole, and that they should not deprive any section of the present population of their employment. Hitherto the immigration has fulfilled these conditions. The number of immigrants since the British occupation has been about 25,000.

It is necessary also to ensure that persons who are politically undesirable are excluded from Palestine, and every precaution has been and will be taken by the Administration to that end.

It is intended that a special committee should be established in Palestine, consisting entirely of members of the new Legislative Council elected by the people, to confer with the administration upon matters relating to the regulation of immigration. Should any difference of opinion arise between this committee and the Administration the matter will be referred to His Majesty's Government, who will give it special consideration. In addition, under Article 81 of the draft Palestine Order in Council, any religious community or considerable section of the population of Palestine will have a general right to appeal, through the High Commissioner and the Secretary of State, to the League of Nations on any matter on which they may consider that the terms of the Mandate are not being fulfilled by the Government of Palestine.

With reference to the Constitution which it is now intended to establish in Palestine, the draft of which has already been published, it is desirable to make certain points clear. In the first place, it is not the case, as has been represented by the Arab Delegation, that during the war His Majesty's Government gave an undertaking that an independent national government should be at once established in Palestine. This representation mainly rests upon a letter dated the 24th October, 1915, from Sir Henry McMahon, then His Majesty's High Commissioner in Egypt, to the Sherif of Mecca, now King Hussein of the Kingdom of the Hejaz. That letter is quoted as conveying the promise to the Sherif of Mecca to recognise and support the independence of the Arabs within the territories proposed by him. But this promise was given subject to a reservation made in the same letter, which excluded from its scope, among other territories, the portions of Syria lying to the west of the district of Damascus. This reservation has always been regarded by His Majesty's Government as covering the vilayet of Beirut and the independent Sanjak of Jerusalem. The whole of Palestine west of the Jordan was thus excluded from Sir H. McMahon's pledge.

Nevertheless, it is the intention of His Majesty's Government to foster the establishment of a full measure of self-government in Palestine. But they are of opinion that, in the special circumstances of that country, this should be accomplished by gradual stages and not suddenly. The first step was taken when, on the institution of a Civil Administration, the nominated Advisory Council, which now exists, was established. It was stated at the time by the High Commissioner that this was the first step in the development of self-governing institutions, and it is now proposed to take a second step by the establishment of a Legislative Council containing a large proportion of members elected on a wide franchise. It was proposed in the published draft that three of the members of this Council should be non-official persons nominated by the High Commissioner, but representations having been made in opposition to this provision, based on cogent considerations, the Secretary of State is prepared to omit it. The Legislative Council would then consist of the High Commissioner as President and twelve elected and ten official members. The Secretary of State is of opinion that before a further measure of self-government is extended to Palestine and the Assembly placed in control over the Executive, it would be wise to allow some time to elapse. During this period the institutions of the country will have become well established; its financial credit will be based on firm foundations, and the Palestinian officials will have been enabled to gain experience of sound methods of government. After a few years the situation will be again reviewed, and if the experience of the working of the constitution now to be established so warranted, a larger share of authority would then be extended to the elected representatives of the people.

The Secretary of State would point out that already the present Administration has transferred to a Supreme Council elected by the Moslem community of Palestine the entire control of Moslem religious endowments (Wakfs), and of the Moslem religious Courts. To this Council the Administration has also voluntarily restored considerable revenues derived from ancient endowments which had been sequestrated by the Turkish Government. The Education Department is also advised by a committee representative of all sections of the population, and the Department of Commerce and Industry has the benefit of the co-operation of the Chambers of Commerce which have been established in the principal centres.

It is the intention of the Administration to associate in an increased degree similar representative committees with the various Departments of the Government.

The Secretary of State believes that a policy upon these lines, coupled with the maintenance of the fullest religious liberty in Palestine and with scrupulous regard for the rights of each community with reference to its Holy Places, cannot but commend itself to the various sections of the population, and that upon this basis may be built up that spirit of co-operation upon which the future progress and prosperity of the Holy Land must largely depend.

Document 13

The MacDonald Letter

Following the Arab riots of 1929, the British Labor government published a new statement of policy (the Passfield White Paper), which urged the restriction of immigration and of land sales to Jews. It was bitterly denounced by Zionist leaders as a violation of the letter and the spirit of the Mandate. The MacDonald letter, while not openly repudiating the Passfield report, gave assurances that the terms of the Mandate would be fulfilled. It was rejected by the Arabs as the "Black Letter". James Ramsay Mac-Donald (1866-1937) was Prime Minister in 1931; Lord Passfield (Sidney Webb, 1859-1947) was Colonial Secretary in the Labor cabinet.

Premier MacDonald's Letter
Addressed to Dr. Chaim Weizmann
February 13, 1931

DEAR DR. WEIZMANN:

In order to remove certain misconceptions and misunderstandings which have arisen as to the policy of his Majesty's Government with regard to Palestine, as set forth in the White Paper of October, 1930, and which were the subject of a debate in the House of Commons on Nov. 17, and also to meet certain criticisms put forward by the Jewish Agency, I have pleasure in forwarding you the following statement of our position, which will fall to be read as the authoritative interpretation of the White Paper on the matters with which this letter deals.

It has been said that the policy of his Majesty's Government involves a serious departure from the obligations of the mandate as hitherto understood; that it misconceives the mandatory obligations, and that it foreshadows a policy which is inconsistent with the obligations of the mandatory to the Jewish people.

His Majesty's Government did not regard it as necessary to quote in extenso the declarations of policy which have been previously made, but attention is drawn to the fact that, not only does the White Paper of 1930 refer to and endorse the White Paper of 1922, which has been accepted by the Jewish Agency, but it recognizes that the undertaking of the mandate is an undertaking to the Jewish people and not only to the Jewish population of Palestine. The White Paper places in the foreground of its statement my speech in the House of Commons on the 3d of April, 1930, in which I announced, in words that could not have been made more plain, that it was the intention of his Majesty's Government to continue to administer Palestine in accordance with the terms of the mandate as approved by the Council of the League of Nations. That position has been reaffirmed and again made plain by my speech in the House of Commons on the 17th of November. In my speech on the 3d of April I used the following language:

> His Majesty's Government will continue to administer Palestine in accordance with the terms of the mandate as approved by the Council of the League of Nations. This is an international obligation from which there can be no question of receding.
>
> Under the terms of the mandate his Majesty's Government are responsible for promoting the establishment of a national home for the Jewish people, it being clearly understood that nothing shall be done which might prejudice the civil and religious rights of existing non-Jewish communities in Palestine or the rights and political status enjoyed by Jews in any other country.
>
> A double undertaking is involved, to the Jewish people on the one hand and to the non-Jewish population of Palestine on the other; and it is the firm resolve of his Majesty's Government to give effect, in equal measure, to both parts of the declaration and to do equal justice to all sections of the population of Palestine. That is a duty from which they will not shrink and to discharge of which they will apply all the resources at their command.

That declaration is in conformity not only with the articles but also with the preamble of the mandate, which is hereby explicitly reaffirmed.

In carrying out the policy of the mandate the mandatory cannot ignore the existence of the differing interests and viewpoints. These, indeed, are not in themselves irreconcilable, but they can only be reconciled if there is a proper realization that the full solution of the problem depends upon an understanding between the Jews and the Arabs. Until that is reached, considerations of balance must inevitably enter into the definition of policy.

A good deal of criticism has been directed to the White Paper upon the assertion that it contains injurious allegations against the Jewish people and Jewish labor organizations. Any such intention on the part of his Majesty's Government is expressly disavowed. It is recognized that the Jewish Agency have all along given willing cooperation in carrying out the policy of the mandate and that the constructive work done by the Jewish people in Palestine has had beneficial effects on the development and well-being of the country as a whole. His Majesty's Government also recognizes the value of the services of labor and trades union organizations in Palestine, to which they desire to give every encouragement.

A question has arisen as to the meaning to be attached to the words 'safeguarding the civil and religious rights of all inhabitants of Palestine irrespective of race and religion' occurring in Article II, and the words 'insuring that the rights and position of other sections of the population are not prejudiced' occurring in Article VI of the mandate. The words 'safeguarding the civil and religious rights' occurring in Article II cannot be read as meaning that the civil and religious rights of individual citizens are unalterable. In the case of Suleiman Murra, to which reference has been made, the Privy Council, in construing these words of Article II said 'It does not mean . . . that all the civil rights of every inhabitant of Palestine which existed at the date of the mandate are to remain unaltered throughout its duration; for if that were to be a condition of the mandatory jurisdiction, no effective legislation would be possible.' The words, accordingly, must be read in another sense, and the key to the true purpose and meaning of the sentence is to be found in the concluding words of the article, 'irrespective of race and religion.' These words indicate that in respect of civil and religious rights the mandatory is not to discriminate between persons on the ground of religion or race, and this protective provision applies equally to Jews, Arabs and all sections of the population.

The words 'rights and position of other sections of the population,' occurring in Article VI, plainly refer to the non-Jewish community. These rights and position are not TO BE prejudiced; that is, are not to be impaired or made worse. The effect of the policy of immigration and settlement on the economic position of the non-Jewish community cannot be excluded from consideration. But the words are not to be read as implying that existing economic conditions in Palestine should be crystallized. On the contrary, the obligation to facilitate Jewish immigration and to encourage close settlement by Jews on the land remains a positive obligation of the mandate and it can be fulfilled without prejudice to the rights and position of other sections of the population of Palestine.

We may proceed to the contention that the mandate has been interpreted in a manner highly prejudicial to Jewish interests in the vital matters of land settlement and immigration. It has been said that the policy of the White Paper would place an embargo on immigration and would suspend, if not indeed terminate, the close settlement of the Jews on the land, which is a primary purpose of the mandate. In support of this contention particular stress has been laid upon the passage referring to State lands in the White Paper, which says that 'it would not be possible to make available for Jewish settlement in view of their actual occupation by Arab cultivators and of the importance of making available suitable land on which to place the Arab cultivators who are now landless.'

The language of this passage needs to be read in the light of the policy as a whole. It is desirable to make it clear that the landless Arabs, to whom it was intended to refer in the passage quoted, were such Arabs as can be shown to have been displaced from the lands which they occupied in consequence of the land passing into Jewish hands, and who have not obtained other holdings on which they can establish themselves, or other equally satisfactory occupation. The number of such displaced Arabs must be a matter for careful inquiry. It is to landless Arabs within this category that his Majesty's Government feels itself under an obligation to facilitate their settlement upon the land. The recognition of this obligation in no way detracts from the larger purposes of development which his Majesty's Government regards as the most effectual means of furthering the establishment of a national home for the Jews. . . .

Further, the statement of policy of his Majesty's Government did not imply a prohibition of acquisition of additional land by Jews. It contains no such prohibition, nor is any such intended. What it does contemplate is such temporary control of land disposition and transfers as may be necessary not to impair the harmony and effectiveness of the scheme of land settlement to be undertaken. His Majesty's Government feels bound to point out that it alone of the governments which have been responsible for the administration of Palestine since the acceptance of the mandate has declared its definite intention to initiate an active policy of development, which it is believed will result in a substantial and lasting benefit to both Jews and Arabs.

Cognate to this question is the control of immigration. It must first of all be pointed out that such control is not in any sense a departure from previous policy. From 1920 onward, when the original immigration ordinance came into force, regulations for the control of immigration have been issued from time to time, directed to prevent illicit entry and to define and facilitate authorized entry. This right of regulation has at no time been challenged.

But the intention of his Majesty's Government appears to have been represented as being that 'no further immigration of Jews is to be permitted so long as it might prevent any Arab from obtaining employment.' His Majesty's Government never proposed to pursue such a policy. They were concerned to state that, in the regulation of Jewish immigration, the following principles should apply: viz., that 'it is essential to insure that the immigrants should not be a burden on the people of Palestine as a whole, and that they should not deprive any section of the present population as a whole, and that they should not deprive any section of the present population of their employment.' (White Paper 1922.)

In one aspect, his Majesty's Government have to be mindful of their obligations to facilitate Jewish immigration under suitable conditions, and to encourage close settlement by Jews on the land; in the other aspect, they have to be equally mindful of their duty to insure that no prejudice results to the rights and position of the non-Jewish community. It is because of this apparent conflict of obligations that his Majesty's Government have felt bound to emphasize the necessity of the proper application of the absorptive principle.

That principle is vital to any scheme of development, the primary purpose of which must be the settlement both of Jews and of displaced Arabs on the land. It is for that reason that his Majesty's Government have insisted, and are compelled to insist, that government immigration regulations must be properly applied. The considerations relevant to the limits of absorptive capacity are purely economic considerations.

His Majesty's Government did not prescribe and do not contemplate any stoppage or prohibition of Jewish immigration in any of its categories. The practice of sanctioning a labor schedule of wage-earning immigrants will continue. In each case consideration will be given to anticipated labor requirements for works which, being dependent upon Jewish or mainly Jewish capital, would not be or would not have been undertaken unless Jewish labor was available. With regard to public and municipal works failing to be financed out of public funds, the claim of Jewish labor to a due share of the employment available, taking into account Jewish contributions to public revenue, shall be taken into consideration. As regards other kinds of employment, it will be necessary in each case to take into account the factors bearing upon the demand for labor, including the factor of unemployment among both the Jews and the Arabs.

Immigrants with prospects of employment other than employment of a purely ephemeral character will not be excluded on the sole ground that the employment cannot be guaranteed to be of unlimited duration.

In determining the extent to which immigration at any time may be permitted it is necessary also to have regard to the declared policy of the Jewish Agency to the effect that 'in all the works or undertakings carried out or furthered by the Agency it shall be deemed to be a matter of principle that Jewish labor shall be employed.' His Majesty's Government do not in any way challenge the right of the Agency to formulate or approve and endorse this policy. The principle of preferential, and indeed exclusive, employment of Jewish labor by Jewish organizations is a principle which the Jewish Agency are entitled to affirm. But it must be pointed out that if in consequence of this policy Arab labor is displaced or existing unemployment becomes aggravated, that is a factor in the situation to which the mandatory is bound to have regard.

His Majesty's Government desire to say, finally, as they have repeatedly and unequivocally affirmed, that the obligations imposed upon the mandatory by its acceptance of the mandate are solemn international obligations from which there is not now, nor has there been at any time, any intention to depart. To the tasks imposed by the mandate, his Majesty's Government have set their hand, and they will not withdraw it. But if their efforts are to be successful, there is need for coöperation, confidence, readiness on all sides to appreciate the difficulties and complexities of the problem, and, above all, there must be a full and unqualified recognition that no solution can be satisfactory or permanent which is not based upon justice, both to the Jewish people and to the non-Jewish communities of Palestine.

RAMSAY MACDONALD

Document 14

From the Report of the Palestine Royal Commission (Peel Commission)—1937

A Royal Commission headed by Lord Peel was appointed in 1936, following the outbreak of fresh Arab riots earlier that year. Its report, published in July 1937, stated that the desire of the Arabs for national independence and their hatred and fear of the establishment of the Jewish National Home were the underlying causes of the disturbances. It found that Arab and Jewish interests could not be reconciled under the Mandate and it suggested, therefore, the partition of Palestine. The Jewish state was to comprise Galilee, the Yezreel Valley and the Coastal Plain to a point midway between Gaza and Jaffe, altogether about twenty per cent of the area of the country. The rest, Arab Palestine, was to be united with Transjordan. Jerusalem, Bethlehem, a corridor linking them to the Sea, and, possibly, Nazareth and the Sea of Genezareth would remain a British mandatory zone. The Arab leadership rejected the plan, the Zionist Congress accepted it with qualifications—against the wish of a substantial minority. The British government which had initially favored partition eventually rejected it in November 1938. (Document 16)

. . . To foster Jewish immigration in the hope that it might ultimately lead to the creation of a Jewish majority and the establishment of a Jewish State with the consent or at least the acquiescence of the Arabs was one thing. It was quite another to contemplate, however remotely, the forcible conversion of Palestine into a Jewish State against the will of the Arabs. For that would clearly violate the spirit and intention of the Mandate System. It would mean that national self-determination had been withheld when the Arabs were a majority in Palestine and only conceded when the Jews were a majority. It would mean that the Arabs had been denied the opportunity of standing by themselves: that they had, in fact, after an interval of conflict, been bartered about from Turkish sovereignty to Jewish sovereignty. It is true that in the light of history Jewish rule over Palestine could not be regarded as foreign rule in the same sense as Turkish; but the international recognition of the right of the Jews to return to their old homeland did not involve the recognition of the right of the Jews to govern the Arabs in it against their will. The case stated by Lord Milner against an Arab control of Palestine applies equally to a Jewish control. . . .

An irrepressible conflict has arisen between two national communities within the narrow bounds of one small country. About 1,000,000 Arabs are in strife, open or latent, with some 400,000 Jews. There is no common ground between them. The Arab community is predominantly Asiatic in character, the Jewish community predominantly European. They differ in religion and in language. Their cultural and social life, their ways of thought and conduct, are as incompatible as their national aspirations. These last are the greatest bar to peace. Arabs and Jews might possibly learn to live and work together in Palestine if they would make a genuine effort to reconcile and combine their national ideals and so build up in time a joint or dual nationality. But this they cannot do. The War and its sequel have inspired all Arabs with the hope of reviving in a free and united Arab world the traditions of the Arab golden age. The Jews similarly are inspired by their historic past. They mean to show what the Jewish nation can achieve when restored to the land of its birth. National assimilation between Arabs and Jews is thus ruled out. In the Arab picture the Jews could only occupy the place they occupied in Arab Egypt or Arab Spain. The Arabs would be as much outside the Jewish picture as the Canaanites in the old land of Israel. The National Home, as we have said before, cannot be half-national. In these circumstances to maintain that Palestinian citizenship has any moral meaning is a mischievous pretense. Neither Arab nor Jew has any sense of service to a single State. . . .

Document 15

V. Jabotinsky: A Jewish State Now: Evidence Submitted to the Palestine Royal Commission*

Vladimir Ze'ev Jabotinsky (1880-1940) was the leader of the Zionist–Revisionists advocating the establishment of a Jewish state in its historic borders.

The conception of Zionism which I have the honour to represent here is based on what I should call the humanitarian aspect. By that I do not mean to say that we do not respect the other, the purely spiritual aspects of Jewish nationalism, such as the desire for self-expression, the rebuilding of a Hebrew culture, or creating some "model community of which the Jewish people could be proud." All that, of course, is most important; but as compared with our actual needs and our real position in the world to-day, all that has rather the character of luxury. The Commission have already heard a description of the situation of World Jewry especially in Eastern Europe, and I am not going to repeat any details, but you will allow me to quote a recent reference in *The New York Times* describing the position of Jewry in Eastern Europe as "a disaster of historic magnitude." I only wish to add that it would be very naïve, and although many Jews make this mistake I disapprove of it—it would be very naïve to ascribe that state of disaster, permanent disaster, only to the guilt of men, whether it be crowds and multitudes, or whether it be Governments. The thing goes much deeper than that. I am very much afraid that what I am going to say will not be popular with many among my co-religionists, and I regret that, but the truth is the truth. We are facing an elemental calamity, a kind of social earthquake. Three generations of Jewish thinkers and Zionists among whom there were many great minds—I am not going to fatigue you by quoting them

* V. Jabotinsky, House of Lords, London: February 11, 1937.

—three generations have given much thought to analysing
the Jewish position and have come to the conclusion that
the cause of our suffering is the very fact of the "Diaspora," the
bedrock fact that we are everywhere a minority. It is not the
anti-Semitism of men; it is, above all, the anti-Semitism of
things, the inherent xenophobia of the body social or the body
economic under which we suffer. Of course, there are ups and
downs; but there are moments, there are whole periods in
history when this "xenophobia of Life itself" takes dimensions
which no people can stand, and that is what we are facing
now. I do not mean to suggest that I would recognise that all
the Governments concerned have done all they ought to have
done; I would be the last man to concede that. I think many
Governments, East and West, ought to do much more to protect the Jews than they do; but the best of Governments could
perhaps only soften the calamity to quite an insignificant extent, but the core of the calamity is an earthquake which
stands and remains. I want to mention here that, since one of
those Governments (the Polish Government) has recently
tried what amounts to bringing to the notice of the League of
Nations and the whole of humanity that it is humanity's duty
to provide the Jews with an area where they could build up
their own body social undisturbed by anyone, I think the sincerity of the Polish Government, and of any other Governments who, I hope, will follow, should not be suspected, but
on the contrary it should be recognised and acknowledged
with due gratitude.—Perhaps the greatest gap in all I am
going to say and in all the Commission have heard up to now
is the impossibility of really going to the root of the problem,
really bringing before you a picture of what that Jewish hell
looks like, and I feel I cannot do it. I do hope that the day
may come when some Jewish representative may be allowed
to appear at the Bar of one of these two Houses just to tell
them what it really is, and to ask the English people: "What
are you going to advise us? Where is the way out? Or, standing up and facing God, say that there is no way out and that
we Jews have just to go under." But unfortunately I cannot
do it, so I will simply assume that the Royal Commission are
sufficiently informed of all this situation, and then I want you
to realise this: the phenomenon called Zionism may include
all kinds of dreams—a "model community", Hebrew culture,
perhaps even a second edition of the Bible—but all this longing for wonderful toys of velvet and silver is nothing in comparison with that tangible momentum of irresistible distress

and need by which we are propelled and borne. We are not free agents. We cannot "concede" anything. Whenever I hear the Zionist, most often my own Party, accused of asking for too much—Gentlemen, I really cannot understand it. Yes, we do want a State; every nation on earth, every normal nation, beginning with the smallest and the humblest who do not claim any merit, any role in humanity's development, they all have States of their own. That is the normal condition for a people. Yet, when we, the most abnormal of peoples and therefore the most unfortunate, ask only for the same condition as the Albanians enjoy, to say nothing of the French and the English, then it is called too much. I should understand it if the answer were, "It is impossible," but when the answer is, "It is too much" I cannot understand it. I would remind you (excuse me for quoting an example known to every one of you) of the commotion which was produced in that famous institution when Oliver Twist came and asked for "more." He said "more" because he did not know how to express it; what Oliver Twist really meant was this: "Will you just give me that normal portion which is necessary for a boy of my age to be able to live." I assure you that you face here to-day, in the Jewish people with its demands, an Oliver Twist who has, unfortunately, no concessions to make. What can be the concessions? We have got to save millions, many *millions*. I do not know whether it is a question of re-housing one-third of the Jewish race, half of the Jewish race, or a quarter of the Jewish race; I do not know; but it is a question of millions. Certainly the way out is to evacuate those portions of the Diaspora which have become no good, which hold no promise of any possibility of a livelihood, and to concentrate all those refugees in some place which should *not* be Diaspora, not a repetition of the position where the Jews are an unabsorbed minority within a foreign social, or economic, or political organism. Naturally, if that process of evacuation is allowed to develop, as it ought to be allowed to develop, there will very soon be reached a moment when the Jews will become a majority in Palestine. I am going to make a "terrible" confession. Our demand for a Jewish majority is not our maximum—it is our minimum: it is just an inevitable stage if only we are allowed to go on salvaging our people. The point when the Jews will reach a majority in that country will not be the point of saturation yet—because with 1,000,000 more Jews in Palestine to-day you could already have a Jewish majority, but there are certainly 3,000,000 or 4,000,000 in the East who are virtually knocking at the door asking for admission, i.e., for salvation.

I have the profoundest feeling for the Arab case, in so far as that Arab case is not exaggerated. This Commission have already been able to make up their minds as to whether there is any individual hardship to the Arabs of Palestine as men, deriving from the Jewish colonisation. We maintain unanimously that the economic position of the Palestinian Arabs, under the Jewish colonisation and owing to the Jewish colonisation, has become the object of envy in all the surrounding Arab countries, so that the Arabs from those countries show a clear tendency to immigrate into Palestine. I have also shown to you already that, in our submission, there is no question of ousting the Arabs. On the contrary, the idea is that Palestine on both sides of the Jordan should hold the Arabs, their progeny, *and* many millions of Jews. What I do not deny is that in that process the Arabs of Palestine will necessarily become a minority in the country of Palestine. What I do deny is that *that* is a hardship. It is not a hardship on any race, any nation, possessing so many National States now and so many more National States in the future. One fraction, one branch of that race, and not a big one, will have to live in someone else's State: well, that is the case with all the mightiest nations of the world. I could hardly mention one of the big nations, having their States, mighty and powerful, who had not one branch living in someone else's State. That is only normal and there is no "hardship" attached to that. So when we hear the Arab claim confronted with the Jewish claim; I fully understand that any minority would prefer to be a majority, it is quite understandable that the Arabs of Palestine would also prefer Palestine to be the Arab State No. 4, No. 5, or No. 6—that I quite understand; but when the Arab claim is confronted with our Jewish demand to be saved, it is like the claims of appetite versus the claims of starvation. No tribunal has ever had the luck of trying a case where all the justice was on the side of one Party and the other Party had no case whatsoever. Usually in human affairs any tribunal, including this tribunal, in trying two cases, has to concede that both sides have a case on their side and, in order to do justice, they must take into consideration what should constitute the basic justification of all human demands, individual or mass demands—the decisive terrible balance of Need. I think it is clear.

Document 16

Against Partition: British Statement of Policy November, 1938

. . . 3. His Majesty's Government have now received the report of the Palestine Partition Commission who have carried out their investigations with great thoroughness and efficiency, and have collected material which will be very valuable in the further consideration of policy. Their report is now published, together with a summary of their conclusions. It will be noted that the four members of the Commission advise unanimously against the adoption of the scheme of partition outlined by the Royal Commission. In addition to the Royal Commission's scheme, two other schemes described as plans B and C are examined in the report. One member prefers plan B. Two other members, including the Chairman, consider that plan C is the best scheme of partition which, under the terms of reference, can be devised. A fourth member, while agreeing that plan C is the best that can be devised under the terms of reference, regards both plans as impracticable. The report points out that under either plan, while the budget of the Jewish State is likely to show a substantial surplus, the budgets of the Arab State (including Trans-Jordan) and of the Mandated Territories are likely to show substantial deficits. The Commission reject as impracticable the Royal Commission's recommendation for a direct subvention from the Jewish State to the Arab State. They think that, on economic grounds, a customs union between the States and the Mandated Territories is essential and they examine the possibility of finding the solution for the financial and economic problems of partition by means of a scheme based upon such a union. They consider that any such scheme would be inconsistent with the grant of fiscal independence to the Arab and Jewish States. Their conclusion is that, on a strict interpretation of their terms of reference, they have no alternative but to report that they are unable to recommend boundaries for the proposed areas which will afford a reasonable prospect of the eventual establishment of self-supporting Arab and Jewish States.

4. His Majesty's Government, after careful study of the Partition Commission's report, have reached the conclusion that this further examination has shown that the political, administrative and financial difficulties involved in the pro-

posal to create independent Arab and Jewish States inside Palestine are so great that this solution of the problem is impracticable.

5. His Majesty's Government will therefore continue their responsibility for the government of the whole of Palestine. They are now faced with the problem of finding alternative means of meeting the needs of the difficult situation described by the Royal Commission which will be consistent with their obligations to the Arabs and the Jews. His Majesty's Government believe that it is possible to find these alternative means. They have already given much thought to the problem in the light of the reports of the Royal Commission and of the Partition Commission. It is clear that the surest foundation for peace and progress in Palestine would be an understanding between the Arabs and the Jews, and His Majesty's Government are prepared in the first instance to make a determined effort to promote such an understanding. With this end in view, they propose immediately to invite representatives of the Palestinian Arabs and of neighbouring States on the one hand and of the Jewish Agency on the other, to confer with them as soon as possible in London regarding future policy, including the question of immigration into Palestine. As regards the representation of the Palestinian Arabs, His Majesty's Government must reserve the right to refuse to receive those leaders whom they regard as responsible for the campaign of assassination and violence.

6. His Majesty's Government hope that these discussions in London may help to promote agreement as to future policy regarding Palestine. They attach great importance, however, to a decision being reached at an early date. Therefore, if the London discussions should not produce agreement within a reasonable period of time, they will take their own decision in the light of their examination of the problem and of the discussions in London, and announce the policy which they propose to pursue.

7. In considering and settling their policy His Majesty's Government will keep constantly in mind the international character of the Mandate with which they have been entrusted and their obligations in that respect.

The White Paper of 1939

After the failure of the partition scheme and a subsequent attempt to work out an agreed solution at a Conference in London (February–March, 1939), the British government announced its new policy in a White Paper published on May 17, 1939. The Arab demands were largely met: Jewish immigration was to continue at a maximum rate of 15,000 for another five years. After that it was to cease altogether unless the Arabs would accept it. Purchase of land by Jews would be prohibited in some areas, restricted in others. Jewish reaction was bitterly hostile (Document 18), but the Arab leaders also rejected the White Paper: according to their demands, Palestine was to become an Arab state immediately, no more Jewish immigrants were to enter the country, the status of every Jew who had immigrated since 1918 was to be reviewed.

May 17, 1939

In the Statement on Palestine, issued on 9th November, 1938, His Majesty's Government announced their intention to invite representatives of the Arabs of Palestine, of certain neighbouring countries and of the Jewish Agency to confer with them in London regarding future policy. It was their sincere hope that, as a result of full, free and frank discussion, some understanding might be reached. Conferences recently took place with Arab and Jewish delegations, lasting for a period of several weeks, and served the purpose of a complete exchange of views between British Ministers and the Arab and Jewish representatives. In the light of the discussions as well as of the situation in Palestine and of the Reports of the Royal Commission and the Partition Commission, certain proposals were formulated by His Majesty's Government and were laid before the Arab and Jewish delegations as the basis of an agreed settlement. Neither the Arab nor the Jewish delegation felt able to accept these proposals, and the conferences therefore did not result in an agreement. Accordingly His Majesty's Government are free to formulate their own policy, and after careful consideration they have decided to adhere generally to the proposals which were finally submitted to, and discussed with, the Arab and Jewish delegations.

2. The Mandate for Palestine, the terms of which were confirmed by the Council of the League of Nations in 1922, has governed the policy of successive British Governments for nearly 20 years. It embodies the Balfour Declaration and imposes on the Mandatory four main obligations. These obligations are set out in Article 2, 6 and 13 of the Mandate. There is no dispute regarding the interpretation of one of these obligations, that touching the protection of and access to the Holy Places and religious building or sites. The other three main obligations are generally as follows:—

(i) To place the country under such political, administrative and economic conditions as will secure the establishment in Palestine of a national home for the Jewish people, to facilitate Jewish immigration under suitable conditions, and to encourage, in co-operation with the Jewish Agency, close settlement by Jews on the land.

(ii) To safeguard the civil and religious rights of all the inhabitants of Palestine irrespective of race and religion, and, whilst facilitating Jewish immigration and settlement, to ensure that the rights and position of other sections of the population are not prejudiced.

(iii) To place the country under such political, administrative and economic conditions as will secure the development of self-governing institutions.

3. The Royal Commission and previous Commissions of Enquiry have drawn attention to the ambiguity of certain expressions in the Mandate, such as the expression "a national home for the Jewish people", and they have found in this ambiguity and the resulting uncertainty as to the objectives of policy a fundamental cause of unrest and hostility between Arabs and Jews. His Majesty's Government are convinced that in the interests of the peace and well-being of the whole people of Palestine a clear definition of policy and objectives is essential. The proposal of partition recommended by the Royal Commission would have afforded such clarity, but the establishment of self-supporting independent Arab and Jewish States within Palestine has been found to be impracticable. It has therefore been necessary for His Majesty's Government to devise an alternative policy which will, consistently with their obligations to Arabs and Jews, meet the needs of the situation in Palestine. Their views and proposals are set forth below under the three heads, (I) The Constitution, (II) Immigration, and (III) Land.

I.—THE CONSTITUTION

4. It has been urged that the expression "a national home for the Jewish people" offered a prospect that Palestine might in due course become a Jewish State or Commonwealth. His Majesty's Government do not wish to contest the view, which was expressed by the Royal Commission, that the Zionist leaders at the time of the issue of the Balfour Declaration recognised that an ultimate Jewish State was not precluded by the terms of the Declaration. But, with the Royal Commission, His Majesty's Government believe that the framers of the Mandate in which the Balfour Declaration was embodied could not have intended that Palestine should be converted into a Jewish State against the will of the Arab population of the country. That Palestine was not to be converted into a Jewish State might be held to be implied in the passage from the Command Paper of 1922 which reads as follows:—

"Unauthorized statements have been made to the effect that the purpose in view is to create a wholly Jewish Palestine. Phrases have been used such as that 'Palestine is to become as Jewish as England is English.' His Majesty's Government regard any such expectation as impracticable and have no such aim in view. Nor have they at any time contemplated . . . . the disappearance or the subordination of the Arabic population, language or culture in Palestine. They would draw attention to the fact that the terms of the (Balfour) Declaration referred to do not contemplate that Palestine as a whole should be converted into a Jewish National Home, but that such a Home should be founded *in Palestine.*"

But this statement has not removed doubts, and His Majesty's Government therefore now declare unequivocally that it is not part of their policy that Palestine should become a Jewish State. They would indeed regard it as contrary to their obligations to the Arabs under the Mandate, as well as to the assurances which have been given to the Arab people in the past, that the Arab population of Palestine should be made the subjects of a Jewish State against their will.

5. The nature of the Jewish National Home in Palestine was further described in the Command Paper of 1922 as follows:

"During the last two or three generations the Jews have re-created in Palestine a community, now numbering 80,000, of whom about one-fourth are farmers or workers upon the land. This community has its own political organs; an elected assembly for the direction of its domestic concerns; elected councils in the towns; and an organisation for the control of its schools. It has its elected Chief Rabbinate and Rabbinical Council for the direction of its religious affairs. Its business is conducted in Hebrew as a vernacular language, and a Hebrew press serves its needs. It has its distinctive intellectual life and displays considerable economic activity. This community, then, with its town and country population, its political, religious and social organisations, its own language, its own customs, its own life, has in fact 'national' characteristics. When it is asked what is meant by the development of the Jewish National Home in Palestine, it may be answered that it is not the imposition of a Jewish nationality upon the inhabitants of Palestine as a whole, but the further development of the existing Jewish community, with the assistance of Jews in other parts of the world, in order that it may become a centre in which the Jewish people as a whole may take, on grounds of religion and race, an interest and a pride. But in order that this community should have the best prospect of free development and provide a full opportunity for the Jewish people to display its capacities, it is essential that it should know that it is in Palestine as of right and not on sufferance. That is the reason why it is necessary that the existence of a Jewish National Home in Palestine should be internationally guaranteed, and that it should be formally recognised to rest upon ancient historic connection."

6. His Majesty's Government adhere to this interpretation of the Declaration of 1917 and regard it as an authoritative and comprehensive description of the character of the Jewish National Home in Palestine. It envisaged the further development of the existing Jewish community with the assistance of Jews in other parts of the world. Evidence that His Majesty's Government have been carrying out their obligation in this respect is to be found in the facts that, since the statement of 1922 was published, more than 300,000 Jews have immigrated to Palestine, and that the population of the National Home has risen to some 450,000, or approaching a third of the entire population of the country. Nor has the Jewish community failed to take full advantage of the opportunities given to it. The growth of the Jewish National Home and its achievements in many fields are a remarkable constructive effort which must command the admiration of the world and must be, in particular, a source of pride to the Jewish people.

7. In the recent discussions the Arab delegations have re-

peated the contention that Palestine was included within the area in which Sir Henry McMahon, on behalf of the British Government, in October, 1915, undertook to recognise and support Arab independence. The validity of this claim, based on the terms of the correspondence which passed between Sir Henry McMahon and the Sharif of Mecca, was thoroughly and carefully investigated by British and Arab representatives during the recent conferences in London. Their Report, which has been published, states that both the Arab and the British representatives endeavoured to understand the point of view of the other party but that they were unable to reach agreement upon an interpretation of the correspondence. There is no need to summarize here the arguments presented by each side. His Majesty's Government regret the misunderstandings which have arisen as regards some of the phrases used. For their part they can only adhere, for the reasons given by their representatives in the Report, to the view that the whole of Palestine west of Jordan was excluded from Sir Henry Mc-Mahon's pledge, and they therefore cannot agree that the McMahon correspondence forms a just basis for the claim that Palestine should be converted into an Arab State.

8. His Majesty's Government are charged as the Mandatory authority "to secure the development of self-governing institutions" in Palestine. Apart from this specific obligation, they would regard it as contrary to the whole spirit of the Mandate system that the population of Palestine should remain forever under Mandatory tutelage. It is proper that the people of the country should as early as possible enjoy the rights of self-government which are exercised by the people of neighbouring countries. His Majesty's Government are unable at present to foresee the exact constitutional forms which government in Palestine will eventually take, but their objective is self-government, and they desire to see established ultimately an independent Palestine State. It should be a State in which the two peoples in Palestine, Arabs and Jews, share authority in government in such a way that the essential interests of each are secured.

9. The establishment of an independent State and the complete relinquishment of Mandatory control in Palestine would require such relations between the Arabs and the Jews as would make good government possible. Moreover, the growth of self-governing institutions in Palestine, as in other countries, must be an evolutionary process. A transitional period will be required before independence is achieved, throughout

which ultimate responsibility for the Government of the country will be retained by His Majesty's Government as the Mandatory authority, while the people of the country are taking an increasing share in the Government, and understanding and co-operation amongst them are growing. It will be the constant endeavour of His Majesty's Government to promote good relations between the Arabs and the Jews.

10. In the light of these considerations His Majesty's Government make the following declaration of their intentions regarding the future government of Palestine:—

(1) The objective of His Majesty's Government is the establishment within ten years of an independent Palestine State in such treaty relations with the United Kingdom as will provide satisfactorily for the commercial and strategic requirements of both countries in the future. The proposal for the establishment of the independent State would involve consultation with the Council of the League of Nations with a view to the termination of the Mandate.

(2) The independent State should be one in which Arabs and Jews share in government in such a way as to ensure that the essential interests of each community are safeguarded.

(3) The establishment of the independent State will be preceded by a transitional period throughout which His Majesty's Government will retain responsibility for the government of the country. During the transitional period the people of Palestine will be given an increasing part in the government of their country. Both sections of the population will have an opportunity to participate in the machinery of government, and the process will be carried on whether or not they both avail themselves of it.

(4) As soon as peace and order have been sufficiently restored in Palestine steps will be taken to carry out this policy of giving the people of Palestine as increasing part in the government of their country, the objective being to place Palestinians in charge of all the Departments of Government, with the assistance of British advisers and subject to the control of the High Commissioner. With this object in view His Majesty's Government will be prepared immediately to arrange that Palestinians shall be placed in charge of certain Departments, with British advisers. The Palestinian heads of Departments will sit on the Executive Council which advises the High Commissioner. Arab and Jewish representatives will be invited to serve as heads of Departments approximately in proportion to their respective populations. The number of

Palestinians in charge of Departments will be increased as circumstances permit until all heads of Departments are Palestinians, exercising the administrative and advisory functions which are at present performed by British officials. When that stage is reached consideration will be given to the question of converting the Executive Council into a Council of Ministers with a consequential change in the status and functions of the Palestinian heads of Departments.

(5) His Majesty's Government make no proposals at this stage regarding the establishment of an elective legislature. Nevertheless they would regard this as an appropriate constitutional development, and, should public opinion in Palestine hereafter show itself in favour of such a development, they will be prepared, provided that local conditions permit, to establish the necessary machinery.

(6) At the end of five years from the restoration of peace and order, an appropriate body representative of the people of Palestine and of His Majesty's Government will be set up to review the working of the constitutional arrangements during the transitional period and to consider and make recommendations regarding the constitution of the independent Palestine State.

(7) His Majesty's Government will require to be satisfied that in the treaty contemplated by sub-paragraph (1) or in the constitution contemplated by sub-paragraph (6) adequate provision has been made for:—

(*a*) the security of, and freedom of access to, the Holy Places, and the protection of the interests and property of the various religious bodies.

(*b*) the protection of the different communities in Palestine in accordance with the obligations of His Majesty's Government to both Arabs and Jews and for the special position in Palestine of the Jewish National Home.

(*c*) such requirements to meet the strategic situation as may be regarded as necessary by His Majesty's Government in the light of the circumstances then existing.

His Majesty's Government will also require to be satisfied that the interests of certain foreign countries in Palestine, for the preservation of which they are at present responsible, are adequately safeguarded.

(8) His Majesty's Government will do everything in their power to create conditions which will enable the independent Palestine State to come into being within ten years. If, at the end of ten years, it appears to His Majesty's Government that,

contrary to their hope, circumstances require the postponement of the establishment of the independent State, they will
consult with representatives of the people of Palestine, the
Council of the League of Nations and the neighbouring Arab
States before deciding on such a postponement. If His Majesty's Government come to the conclusion that postponement
is unavoidable, they will invite the co-operation of these
parties in framing plans for the future with a view to achieving the desired objective at the earliest possible date.

11. During the transitional period steps will be taken to
increase the powers and responsibilities of municipal corpora-
tions and local councils.

II.—IMMIGRATION

12. Under Article 6 of the Mandate, the Administration of
Palestine, "while ensuring that the rights and position of other
sections of the population are not prejudiced," is required to
"facilitate Jewish immigration under suitable conditions." Beyond this, the extent to which Jewish immigration into Palestine is to be permitted is nowhere defined in the Mandate.
But in the Command Paper of 1922 it was laid down that for
the fulfilment of the policy of establishing a Jewish National
Home

"it is necessary that the Jewish community in Palestine
should be able to increase its numbers by immigration. This
immigration cannot be so great in volume as to exceed whatever may be the economic capacity of the country at the time
to absorb new arrivals. It is essential to ensure that the immigrants should not be a burden upon the people of Palestine
as a whole, and that they should not deprive any section of
the present population of their employment."

In practice, from that date onwards until recent times, the
economic absorptive capacity of the country has been treated
as the sole limiting factor, and in the letter which Mr. Ramsay
MacDonald, as Prime Minister, sent to Dr. Weizmann in
February 1931 it was laid down as a matter of policy that
economic absorptive capacity was the sole criterion. This interpretation has been supported by resolutions of the Permanent Mandates Commission. But His Majesty's Government
do not read either the Statement of Policy of 1922 or the
letter of 1931 as implying that the Mandate requires them,
for all time and in all circumstances, to facilitate the immigration of Jews into Palestine subject only to consideration of the
country's economic absorptive capacity. Nor do they find any-

thing in the Mandate or in subsequent Statements of Policy to support the view that the establishment of a Jewish National Home in Palestine cannot be effected unless immigration is allowed to continue indefinitely. If immigration has an adverse effect on the economic position in the country, it should clearly be restricted; and equally, if it has a seriously damaging effect on the political position in the country, that is a factor that should not be ignored. Although it is not difficult to contend that the large number of Jewish immigrants who have been admitted so far have been absorbed economically, the fear of the Arabs that this influx will continue indefinitely until the Jewish population is in a position to dominate them has produced consequences which are extremely grave for Jews and Arabs alike and for the peace and prosperity of Palestine. The lamentable disturbances of the past three years are only the latest and most sustained manifestation of this intense Arab apprehension. The methods employed by Arab terrorists against fellow-Arabs and Jews alike must receive unqualified condemnation. But it cannot be denied that fear of indefinite Jewish immigration is widespread amongst the Arab population and that this fear has made possible disturbances which have given a serious setback to economic progress, depleted the Palestine exchequer, rendered life and property insecure, and produced a bitterness between the Arab and Jewish populations which is deplorable between citizens of the same country. If in these circumstances immigration is continued up to the economic absorptive capacity of the country, regardless of all other considerations, a fatal enmity between the two peoples will be perpetuated, and the situation in Palestine may become a permanent source of friction amongst all peoples in the Near and Middle East. His Majesty's Government cannot take the view that either their obligations under the Mandate, or considerations of common sense and justice, require that they should ignore these circumstances in framing immigration policy.

13. In the view of the Royal Commission the association of the policy of the Balfour Declaration with the Mandate system implied the belief that Arab hostility to the former would sooner or later be overcome. It has been the hope of British Governments ever since the Balfour Declaration was issued that in time the Arab population, recognizing the advantages to be derived from Jewish settlement and development in Palestine, would become reconciled to the further growth of the Jewish National Home. This hope has not been

fulfilled. The alternatives before His Majesty's Government are either (i) to seek to expand the Jewish National Home indefinitely by immigration, against the strongly expressed will of the Arab people of the country; or (ii) to permit further expansion of the Jewish National Home by immigration only if the Arabs are prepared to acquiesce in it. The former policy means rule by force. Apart from other considerations, such a policy seems to His Majesty's Government to be contrary to the whole spirit of Article 22 of the Covenant of the League of Nations, as well as to their specific obligations to the Arabs in the Palestine Mandate. Moreover, the relations between the Arabs and the Jews in Palestine must be based sooner or later on mutual tolerance and goodwill; the peace, security and progress of the Jewish National Home itself require this. Therefore His Majesty's Government, after earnest consideration, and taking into account the extent to which the growth of the Jewish National Home has been facilitated over the last twenty years, have decided that the time has come to adopt in principle the second of the alternatives referred to above.

14. It has been urged that all further Jewish immigration into Palestine should be stopped forthwith. His Majesty's Government cannot accept such a proposal. It would damage the whole of the financial and economic system of Palestine and thus affect adversely the interests of Arabs and Jews alike. Moreover, in the view of His Majesty's Government, abruptly to stop further immigration would be unjust to the Jewish National Home. But, above all, His Majesty's Government are conscious of the present unhappy plight of large numbers of Jews who seek a refuge from certain European countries, and they believe that Palestine can and should make a further contribution to the solution of this pressing world problem. In all these circumstances, they believe that they will be acting consistently with their Mandatory obligations to both Arabs and Jews, and in the manner best calculated to serve the interests of the whole people of Palestine, by adopting the following proposals regarding immigration:—

(1) Jewish immigration during the next five years will be at a rate which, if economic absorptive capacity permits, will bring the Jewish population up to approximately one-third of the total population of the country. Taking into account the expected natural increase of the Arab and Jewish populations, and the number of illegal Jewish immigrants now in the country, this would allow of the admission, as from the beginning of April this year, of some 75,000 immigrants over the next

five years. These immigrants would, subject to the criterion of economic absorptive capacity, be admitted as follows:—

(*a*) For each of the next five years a quota of 10,000 Jewish immigrants will be allowed on the understanding that a shortage in any one year may be added to the quotas for subsequent years, within the five-year period, if economic absorptive capacity permits.

(*b*) In addition, as a contribution towards the solution of the Jewish refugee problem, 25,000 refugees will be admitted as soon as the High Commissioner is satisfied that adequate provision for their maintenance is ensured, special consideration being given to refugee children and dependants.

(2) The existing machinery for ascertaining economic absorptive capacity will be retained, and the High Commissioner will have the ultimate responsibility for deciding the limits of economic capacity. Before each periodic decision is taken, Jewish and Arab representatives will be consulted.

(3) After the period of five years no further Jewish immigration will be permitted unless the Arabs of Palestine are prepared to acquiesce in it.

(4) His Majesty's Government are determined to check illegal immigration, and further preventive measures are being adopted. The numbers of any Jewish illegal immigrants who, despite these measures, may succeed in coming into the country and cannot be deported will be deducted from the yearly quotas.

15. His Majesty's Government are satisfied that, when the immigration over five years which is now contemplated has taken place, they will not be justified in facilitating, nor will they be under any obligation to facilitate, the further development of the Jewish National Home by immigration regardless of the wishes of the Arab population.

III.—LAND

16. The Administration of Palestine is required, under Article 6 of the Mandate, "while ensuring that the rights and position of other sections of the population are not prejudiced," to encourage "close settlement by Jews on the land," and no restriction has been imposed hitherto on the transfer of land from Arabs to Jews. The Reports of several expert Commissions have indicated that, owing to the natural growth of the Arab population and the steady sale in recent years of Arab land to Jews, there is now in certain areas no room for

further transfers of Arab land, whilst in some other areas such transfers of land must be restricted if Arab cultivators are to maintain their existing standard of life and a considerable landless Arab population is not soon to be created. In these circumstances, the High Commissioner will be given general powers to prohibit and regulate transfers of land. These powers will date from the publication of this statement of policy and the High Commissioner will retain them throughout the transitional period.

17. The policy of the Government will be directed towards the development of the land and the improvement, where possible, of methods of cultivation. In the light of such development it will be open to the High Commissioner, should he be satisfied that the "rights and position" of the Arab population will be duly preserved, to review and modify any orders passed relating to the prohibition or restriction of the transfer of land.

18. In framing these proposals His Majesty's Government have sincerely endeavoured to act in strict accordance with their obligations under the Mandate to both the Arabs and the Jews. The vagueness of the phrases employed in some instances to describe these obligations has led to controversy and has made the task of interpretation difficult. His Majesty's Government cannot hope to satisfy the partisans of one party or the other in such controversy as the Mandate has aroused. Their purpose is to be just as between the two peoples in Palestine whose destinies in that country have been affected by the great events of recent years, and who, since they live side by side, must learn to practice mutual tolerance, goodwill and co-operation. In looking to the future, His Majesty's Government are not blind to the fact that some events of the past make the task of creating these relations difficult; but they are encouraged by the knowledge that at many times and in many places in Palestine during recent years the Arab and Jewish inhabitants have lived in friendship together. Each community has much to contribute to the welfare of their common land, and each must earnestly desire peace in which to assist in increasing the well-being of the whole people of the country. The responsibility which falls on them, no less than upon His Majesty's Government, to co-operate together to ensure peace is all the more solemn because their country is revered by many millions of Moslems, Jews and Christians throughout the world who pray for peace in Palestine and for the happiness of her people.

Document 18

The Zionist Reaction to the White Paper

*Statement by the Jewish Agency
for Palestine (1939)*

1. The new policy for Palestine laid down by the Mandatory
in the White Paper now issued denies to the Jewish people the
right to rebuild their national home in their ancestral country.
It transfers the authority over Palestine to the present Arab
majority and puts the Jewish population at the mercy of that
majority. It decrees the stoppage of Jewish immigration as
soon as the Jews form a third of the total population. It puts
up a territorial ghetto for Jews in their own homeland.

2. The Jewish people regard this policy as a breach of faith
and a surrender to Arab terrorism. It delivers Britain's
friends into the hands of those who are biting her and must
lead to a complete breach between Jews and Arabs which
will banish every prospect of peace in Palestine. It is a policy
in which the Jewish people will not acquiesce. The new regime
now announced will be devoid of any moral basis and contrary to international law. Such a regime can only be established and maintained by force.

3. The Royal Commission invoked by the White Paper
indicated the perils of such a policy, saying it was convinced
that an Arab Government would mean the frustration of all
their (Jews') efforts and ideals and would convert the national
home into one more cramped and dangerous ghetto. It seems
only too probable that the Jews would fight rather than submit to Arab rule. And repressing a Jewish rebellion against
British policy would be as unpleasant a task as the repression
of the Arab rebellion has been. The Government has disregarded this warning.

4. The Jewish people have no quarrel with the Arab people. Jewish work in Palestine has not had an adverse effect
upon the life and progress of the Arab people. The Arabs are
not landless or homeless as are the Jews. They are not in need
of emigration. Jewish colonization has benefited Palestine and
all its inhabitants. Insofar as the Balfour Declaration contributed to British victory in the Great War, it contributed
also, as was pointed out by the Royal Commission, to the
liberation of the Arab peoples. The Jewish people has shown

its will to peace even during the years of disturbances. It has not given way to temptation and has not retaliated to Arab violence. But neither have the Jews submitted to terror nor will they submit to it even after the Mandatory has decided to reward the terrorists by surrendering the Jewish National Home.

5. It is in the darkest hour of Jewish history that the British Government proposes to deprive the Jews of their last hope and to close the road back to their Homeland. It is a cruel blow, doubly cruel because it comes from the government of a great nation which has extended a helping hand to the Jews, and whose position must rest on foundations of moral authority and international good faith. This blow will not subdue the Jewish people. The historic bond between the people and the land of Israel cannot be broken. The Jews will never accept the closing to them of the gates of Palestine nor let their national home be converted into a ghetto. The Jewish pioneers who, during the past three generations, have shown their strength in the upbuilding of a derelict country, will from now on display the same strength in defending Jewish immigration, the Jewish home and Jewish freedom.

Document 19

Towards a Jewish State:
The Biltmore Program (1942)

During a visit to the United States by David Ben Gurion, Chairman of the Executive of the Jewish Agency, Zionist policy was reformulated. At a conference at the Biltmore Hotel in New York, in May 1942, the establishment of a Jewish state was envisaged to open the doors of Palestine to Jewish refugees escaping from Nazi terror and to lay the foundations for the establishment of a Jewish majority.

Declaration Adopted by the Extraordinary Zionist Conference, Biltmore Hotel, New York City, May 11, 1942

1. American Zionists assembled in this Extraordinary Conference reaffirm their unequivocal devotion to the cause of democratic freedom and international justice to which the people of the United States, allied with the other United

Nations, have dedicated themselves, and give expression to their faith in the ultimate victory of humanity and justice over lawlessness and brute force.

2. This Conference offers a message of hope and encouragement to their fellow Jews in the Ghettos and concentration camps of Hitler-dominated Europe and prays that their hour of liberation may not be far distant.

3. The Conference sends its warmest greetings to the Jewish Agency Executive in Jerusalem, to the Va'ad Leumi, and to the whole Yishuv in Palestine, and expresses its profound admiration for their steadfastness and achievements in the face of peril and great difficulties. The Jewish men and women in field and factory, and the thousands of Jewish soldiers of Palestine in the Near East who have acquitted themselves with honor and distinction in Greece, Ethiopia, Syria, Libya and on other battlefields, have shown themselves worthy of their people and ready to assume the rights and responsibilities of nationhood.

4. In our generation, and in particular in the course of the past twenty years, the Jewish people have awakened and transformed their ancient homeland; from 50,000 at the end of the last war their numbers have increased to more than 500,000. They have made the waste places to bear fruit and the desert to blossom. Their pioneering achievements in agriculture and in industry, embodying new patterns of cooperative endeavor, have written a notable page in the history of colonization.

5. In the new values thus created, their Arab neighbors in Palestine have shared. The Jewish people in its own work of national redemption welcomes the economic, agricultural and national development of the Arab peoples and states. The Conference reaffirms the stand previously adopted at Congresses of the World Zionist Organization, expressing the readiness and the desire of the Jewish people for full cooperation with their Arab neighbors.

6. The Conference calls for the fulfilment of the original purpose of the Balfour Declaration and the Mandate which *"recognizing the historical connection of the Jewish people with Palestine"* was to afford them the opportunity, as stated by President Wilson, to found there a Jewish Commonwealth.

The Conference affirms its unalterable rejection of the White Paper of May 1939 and denies its moral or legal validity. The White Paper seeks to limit, and in fact to nullify

Jewish rights to immigration and settlement in Palestine, and, as stated by Mr. Winston Churchill in the House of Commons in May 1939, constitutes "a breach and repudiation of the Balfour Declaration." The policy of the White Paper is cruel and indefensible in its denial of sanctuary to Jews fleeing from Nazi persecution; and at a time when Palestine has become a focal point in the war front of the United Nations, and Palestine Jewry must provide all available manpower for farm and factory and camp, it is in direct conflict with the interests of the allied war effort.

7. In the struggle against the forces of aggression and tyranny, of which Jews were the earliest victims, and which now menace the Jewish National Home, recognition must be given to the right of the Jews of Palestine to play their full part in the war effort and in the defense of their country, through a Jewish military force fighting under its own flag and under the high command of the United Nations.

8. The Conference declares that the new world order that will follow victory cannot be established on foundations of peace, justice and equality, unless the problem of Jewish homelessness is finally solved.

The Conference urges that the gates of Palestine be opened; that the Jewish Agency be vested with control of immigration into Palestine and with the necessary authority for upbuilding the country, including the development of its unoccupied and uncultivated lands; and that Palestine be established as a Jewish Commonwealth integrated in the structure of the new democratic world.

Then and only then will the age-old wrong to the Jewish people be righted.

Document 20

Adolf Hitler, Zionism and the Arab Cause*

Haj Amin al Husaini, the most influential leader of Palestinian Arabs, lived in Germany during the Second World War. He met Hitler, Ribbentrop and other Nazi leaders on various occasions and attempted to coordinate Nazi and Arab policies in the Middle East.

* *Documents on German Foreign Policy 1918-45*, Series D, Vol. XIII, London, 1964, pp. 881 ff.

BERLIN, NOVEMBER 30, 1941.

Record of the Conversation Between the Führer and the Grand Mufti of Jerusalem on November 28, 1941, in the Presence of Reich Foreign Minister and Minister Grobba in Berlin

The Grand Mufti began by thanking the Führer for the great honor he had bestowed by receiving him. He wished to seize the opportunity to convey to the Führer of the Greater German Reich, admired by the entire Arab world, his thanks for the sympathy which he had always shown for the Arab and especially the Palestinian cause, and to which he had given clear expression in his public speeches. The Arab countries were firmly convinced that Germany would win the war and that the Arab cause would then prosper. The Arabs were Germany's natural friends because they had the same enemies as had Germany, namely the English, the Jews, and the Communists. They were therefore prepared to cooperate with Germany with all their hearts and stood ready to participate in the war, not only negatively by the commission of acts of sabotage and the instigation of revolutions, but also positively by the formation of an Arab Legion. The Arabs could be more useful to Germany as allies than might be apparent at first glance, both for geographical reasons and because of the suffering inflicted upon them by the English and the Jews. Furthermore, they had had close relations with all Moslem nations, of which they could make use in behalf of the common cause. The Arab Legion would be quite easy to raise. An appeal by the Mufti to the Arab countries and the prisoners of Arab, Algerian, Tunisian, and Moroccan nationality in Germany would produce a great number of volunteers eager to fight. Of Germany's victory the Arab world was firmly convinced, not only because the Reich possessed a large army, brave soldiers, and military leaders of genius, but also because the Almighty could never award the victory to an unjust cause.

In this struggle, the Arabs were striving for the independence and unity of Palestine, Syria, and Iraq. They had the fullest confidence in the Führer and looked to his hand for the balm on their wounds which had been inflicted upon them by the enemies of Germany.

The Mufti then mentioned the letter he had received from Germany, which stated that Germany was holding no Arab territories and understood and recognized the aspirations to independence and freedom of the Arabs, just as she supported the elimination of the Jewish national home.

A public declaration in this sense would be very useful for its propagandistic effect on the Arab peoples at this moment. It would rouse the Arabs from their momentary lethargy and give them new courage. It would also ease the Mufti's work of secretly organizing the Arabs against the moment when they could strike. At the same time, he could give the assurance that the Arabs would in strict discipline patiently wait for the right moment and only strike upon an order from Berlin.

With regard to the events in Iraq, the Mufti observed that the Arabs in that country certainly had by no means been incited by Germany to attack England, but solely had acted in reaction to a direct English assault upon their honor.

The Turks, he believed, would welcome the establishment of an Arab government in the neighboring territories because they would prefer weaker Arab to strong European governments in the neighboring countries, and, being themselves a nation of 7 millions, they had moreover nothing to fear from the 1,700,000 Arabs inhabiting Syria, Transjordan, Iraq, and Palestine.

France likewise would have no objections to the unification plan because she had conceded independence to Syria as early as 1936 and had given her approval to the unification of Iraq and Syria under King Faisal as early as 1933.

In these circumstances he was renewing his request that the Führer make a public declaration so that the Arabs would not lose hope, which is so powerful a force in the life of nations. With such hope in their hearts the Arabs, as he had said, were willing to wait. They were not pressing for immediate realization of their aspirations; they could easily wait half a year or a whole year. But if they were not inspired with such a hope by a declaration of this sort, it could be expected that the English would be the gainers from it.

The Führer replied that Germany's fundamental attitude on these questions, as the Mufti himself had already stated, was clear. Germany stood for uncompromising war against the Jews. That naturally included active opposition to the Jewish national home in Palestine, which was nothing other than a center, in the form of a state, for the exercise of destructive influence by Jewish interests. Germany was also aware that the assertion that the Jews were carrying out the function of economic pioneers in Palestine was a lie. The work there was done only by the Arabs, not by the Jews. Germany was resolved, step by step, to ask one European nation after the other to solve its Jewish problem, and at the proper time direct a similar appeal to non-European nations as well.

Germany was at the present time engaged in a life and death struggle with two citadels of Jewish power: Great Britain and Soviet Russia. Theoretically there was a difference between England's capitalism and Soviet Russia's communism; actually, however, the Jews in both countries were pursuing a common goal. This was the decisive struggle; on the political plane, it presented itself in the main as a conflict between Germany and England, but ideologically it was a battle between National Socialism and the Jews. It went without saying that Germany would furnish positive and practical aid to the Arabs involved in the same struggle, because platonic promises were useless in a war for survival or destruction in which the Jews were able to mobilize all of England's power for their ends.

The aid to the Arabs would have to be material aid. Of how little help sympathies alone were in such a battle had been demonstrated plainly by the operation in Iraq, where circumstances had not permitted the rendering of really effective, practical aid. In spite of all the sympathies, German aid had not been sufficient and Iraq was overcome by the power of Britain, that is, the guardian of the Jews.

The Mufti could not but be aware, however, that the outcome of the struggle going on at present would also decide the fate of the Arab world. The Führer therefore had to think and speak coolly and deliberately, as a rational man and primarily as a soldier, as the leader of the German and allied armies. Everything of a nature to help in this titanic battle for the common cause, and thus also for the Arabs, would have to be done. Anything, however, that might contribute to weakening the military situation must be put aside, no matter how unpopular this move might be.

Germany was now engaged in very severe battles to force the gateway to the northern Caucasus region. The difficulties were mainly with regard to maintaining the supply, which was most difficult as a result of the destruction of railroads and highways as well as of the oncoming winter. If at such a moment, the Führer were to raise the problem of Syria in a declaration, those elements in France which were under de Gaulle's influence would receive new strength. They would interpret the Führer's declaration as an intention to break up France's colonial empire and appeal to their fellow country-men that they should rather make common cause with the English to try to save what still could be saved. A German declaration regarding Syria would in France be understood to refer to the French colonies in general, and that would at the present time create new troubles in western Europe, which means that a portion of the German armed forces would be immobilized in the west and no longer be available for the campaign in the east.

The Führer then made the following statement to the Mufti, enjoining him to lock it in the uttermost depths of his heart:

1. He (the Führer) would carry on the battle to the total destruction of the Judeo-Communist empire in Europe.

2. At some moment which was impossible to set exactly today but which in any event was not distant, the German armies would in the course of this struggle reach the southern exit from Caucasia.

3. As soon as this had happened, the Führer would on his own give the Arab world the assurance that its hour of liberation had arrived. Germany's objective would then be solely the destruction of the Jewish element residing in the Arab sphere under the protection of British power. In that hour the Mufti would be the most authoritative spokesman for the Arab world. It would then be his task to set off the Arab operations which he had secretly prepared. When that time had come, Germany could also be indifferent to French reaction to such a declaration.

Once Germany had forced open the road to Iran and Iraq through Rostov, it would be also the beginning of the end of the British world empire. He (the Führer) hoped that the coming year would make it possible for Germany to thrust open the Caucasian gate to the Middle East. For the good of their common cause, it would be better if the Arab proclamation were put off for a few more months than if Germany were to create difficulties for herself without being able thereby to help the Arabs.

He (the Führer) fully appreciated the eagerness of the Arabs for a public declaration of the sort requested by the Grand Mufti. But he would beg him to consider that he (the Führer) himself was the Chief of State of the German Reich for 5 long years during which he was unable to make to his own homeland the announcement of its liberation. He had to wait with that until the announcement could be made on the basis of a situation brought about by the force of arms that the Anschluss had been carried out.

The moment that Germany's tank divisions and air squadrons had made their appearance south of the Caucasus, the public appeal requested by the Grand Mufti could go out to the Arab world.

The Grand Mufti replied that it was his view that everything would come to pass just as the Führer had indicated. He was fully reassured and satisfied by the words which he had heard from the Chief of the German State. He asked, however, whether it would not be possible, secretly at least, to enter into an agreement with Germany of the kind he had just outlined for the Führer.

The Führer replied that he had just now given the Grand Mufti precisely that confidential declaration.

The Grand Mufti thanked him for it and stated in conclusion that he was taking his leave from the Führer in full confidence and with reiterated thanks for the interest shown in the Arab cause.

SCHMIDT

Documents 21–23

The Anglo–American Committee of Inquiry—1946

An Anglo-American Inquiry Committee was appointed in November, 1945, to examine the status of the Jews in former Axis-occupied countries and to find out how many were impelled by their conditions to migrate. Britain, weakened by the war, found itself under growing pressure from Jews and Arabs alike and the Labor Government decided, therefore, to invite the United States to participate in finding a solution. The Report of the Committee was published on May 1, 1945 (Document 21). President Truman welcomed its recommendation that the immigration and land laws of the 1939 White Paper were to be rescinded. Prime Minister Attlee, on the other hand, declared that the report would have to be "considered as a whole in all its implications." Arab reaction was hostile

(Document 22); the Arab League announced that Arabs would not stand by with their arms folded. The Ihud (Association) group led by Dr. J. L. Magnes and Professor M. Buber (who submitted Document 23 to the Committee), favored a bi-national solution, equal political rights for Arabs and Jews, and a Federative Union of Palestine and the neighboring countries. Ihud found little support among the Jewish Community. It had, in the beginning, a few Arab sympathizers, but some of them were assassinated by supporters of the Mufti and the others dropped out.

Document 21

Recommendations and Comments

THE EUROPEAN PROBLEM

Recommendation No. 1. We have to report that such information as we received about countries other than Palestine gave no hope of substantial assistance in finding homes for Jews wishing or impelled to leave Europe.

But Palestine alone cannot meet the emigration needs of the Jewish victims of Nazi and Fascist persecution; the whole world shares responsibility for them and indeed for the resettlement of all "displaced persons."

We therefore recommend that our Governments together, and in association with other countries, should endeavor immediately to find new homes for all such "displaced persons," irrespective of creed or nationality, whose ties with their former communities have been irreparably broken.

Though emigration will solve the problems of some victims of persecution, the overwhelming majority, including a considerable number of Jews, will continue to live in Europe. We recommend therefore that our Governments endeavor to secure that immediate effect is given to the provision of the United Nations Charter calling for "universal respect for, and observation of, human rights and fundamental freedoms for all without distinction as to race, sex, language or religion." *Comment.* In recommending that our Governments, in association with other countries, should endeavor to find new homes for "displaced persons," we do not suggest that any country should be asked to make a permanent change in its immigration policy. The conditions which we have seen in Europe are unprecedented and so unlikely to arise again that we are convinced that special provision could and should be made in existing immigration laws to meet this unique and peculiarly distressing situation. Furthermore, we believe that much could be accomplished—particularly in regard to those "displaced persons," including Jews, who have relatives in countries outside Europe—by a relaxation of administrative regulations.

Our investigations have led us to believe that a considerable number of Jews will continue to live in most European countries. In our view the mass emigration of all European Jews would be of service neither to the Jews themselves nor to Europe. Every effort should be made to enable the Jews to rebuild their shattered communities, while permitting those Jews who wish to do so to emigrate. In order to achieve this, restitution of Jewish property should be effected as soon as possible. Our investigations showed us that the Governments chiefly concerned had for the most part already passed legislation to this end. A real obstacle, however, to individual restitution is that the attempt to give effect to this legislation is frequently a cause of active anti-Semitism. We suggest that, for the reconstruction of the Jewish communities, restitution of their corporate property, either through reparations payments or through other means, is of the first importance.

Nazi occupation has left behind it a legacy of anti-Semitism. This cannot be combatted by legislation alone. The only really effective antidotes are the enforcement by each Government of guaranteed civil liberties and equal rights, a program of education in the positive principles of democracy, the sanction of a strong world public opinion—combined with economic recovery and stability.

REFUGEE IMMIGRATION INTO PALESTINE

Recommendation No. 2. We recommend (a) that 100,000 certificates be authorized immediately for the admission into Palestine of Jews who have been the victims of Nazi and Fascist persecution; (b) that these certificates be awarded as far as possible in 1946 and that actual immigration be pushed forward as rapidly as conditions will permit.

Comment. The number of Jewish survivors of Nazi and Fascist persecution with whom we have to deal far exceeds 100,000: indeed there are more than that number in Germany,

Austria and Italy alone. Although nearly a year has passed
since their liberation, the majority of those in Germany and
Austria are still living in assembly centers, the so-called
"camps," island communities in the midst of those at whose
hands they suffered so much.

In their interests and in the interests of Europe, the centers
should be closed and their camp life ended. Most of them
have cogent reasons for wishing to leave Europe. Many are
the sole survivors of their families and few have any ties
binding them to the countries in which they used to live.

Since the end of hostilities, little has been done to provide
for their resettlement elsewhere. Immigration laws and restrictions bar their entry to most countries and much time must
pass before such laws and restrictions can be altered and
effect given to the alterations.

Some can go to countries where they have relatives; others
may secure inclusion in certain quotas. Their number is com-
paratively small.

We know of no country to which the great majority can
go in the immediate future other than Palestine. Furthermore,
that is where almost all of them want to go. There they are
sure that they will receive a welcome denied them elsewhere.
There they hope to enjoy peace and rebuild their lives.

We believe it is essential that they should be given an
opportunity to do so at the earliest possible time. Furthermore,
we have the assurances of the leaders of the Jewish Agency
that they will be supported and cared for.

We recommend the authorization and issue of 100,000
certificates for these reasons and because we feel that their
immediate issue will have a most salutary effect upon the
whole situation.

In the awarding of these certificates priority should, as
far as possible, be given to those in the centers and to those
liberated in Germany and Austria who are no longer in the
centers but remain in those countries. We do not desire
that other Jewish victims who wish or will be impelled by their
circumstances to leave the countries where they now are or
that those who fled from persecution before the outbreak of
war should be excluded. We appreciate that there will be
difficulty in deciding questions of priority, but none the less
we urge that so far as possible such a system should be adhered to, and that, in applying it, primary consideration
should be given to the aged and infirm, to the very young
and also to skilled workmen whose services will be needed

for many months on work rendered necessary by the large influx.

It should be made clear that no advantage in the obtaining of a certificate is to be gained by migrating from one country to another or by entering Palestine illegally.

Receiving so large a number will be a heavy burden on Palestine. We feel sure that the authorities will shoulder it and that they will have the full cooperation of the Jewish Agency.

Difficult problems will confront those responsible for organizing and carrying out the movement. The many organizations —public and private—working in Europe will certainly render all the aid they can; we mention UNRRA especially. Cooperation by all throughout is necessary.

We are sure that the Government of the United States, which has shown such keen interest in this matter, will participate vigorously and generously with the Government of Great Britain in its fulfillment. There are many ways in which help can be given.

Those who have opposed the admission of these unfortunate people into Palestine should know that we have fully considered all that they have put before us. We hope that they will look upon the situation again, that they will appreciate the considerations which have led us to our conclusion, and that above all, if they cannot see their way to help, at least they will not make the position of these sufferers more difficult.

PRINCIPLES OF GOVERNMENT: NO ARAB, NO JEWISH STATE

Recommendation No. 3. In order to dispose, once and for all, of the exclusive claims of Jews and Arabs to Palestine, we regard it as essential that a clear statement of the following principles should be made:

(I) That Jew shall not dominate Arab and Arab shall not dominate Jew in Palestine. (II) That Palestine shall be neither a Jewish state nor an Arab state. (III) That the form of government ultimately to be established, shall, under international guarantees, fully protect and preserve the interests in the Holy Land of Christendom and of the Moslem and Jewish faiths.

Thus Palestine must ultimately become a state which guards the rights and interests of Moslems, Jews and Christians alike and accords to the inhabitants, as a whole, the fullest

measure of self-government consistent with the three paramount principles set forth above.

Comment. Throughout the long and bloody struggle of Jew
and Arab for dominance in Palestine, each crying fiercely:
"This land is mine"—except for the brief reference in the
Report of the Royal Commission (Hereinafter referred to as
the Peel Report) and the little evidence, written and oral, that
we received on this point—the great interest of the Christian
world in Palestine has been completely overlooked, glossed
over or brushed aside.

We therefore emphatically declare that Palestine is a Holy
Land, sacred to Christian, to Jew and to Moslem alike; and
because it is a Holy Land, Palestine is not, and can never
become, a land which any race or religion can justly claim
as its very own.

We further, in the same emphatic way, affirm that the fact
that it is the Holy Land sets Palestine completely apart from
other lands and dedicates it to the precepts and practices of the
brotherhood of man, not those of narrow nationalism.

For another reason, in the light of its long history, and
particularly its history of the last thirty years, Palestine cannot
be regarded as either a purely Arab or a purely Jewish land.

The Jews have a historic connection with the country. The
Jewish National Home, though embodying a minority of the
population, is today a reality established under international
guarantee. It has a right to continued existence, protection and
development.

Yet Palestine is not, and never can be a purely Jewish land.
It lies at the crossroads of the Arab world. Its Arab population, descended from long-time inhabitants of the area, rightly
look upon Palestine as their homeland.

It is, therefore, neither just nor practicable that Palestine
should become either an Arab state, in which an Arab
majority would control the destiny of a Jewish minority, or
a Jewish state, in which a Jewish majority would control that
of an Arab minority. In neither case would minority guarantees afford adequate protection for the subordinated group.

A Palestinian put the matter thus: "In the hearts of us Jews
there has always been a fear that some day this country would
be turned into an Arab state and the Arabs would rule over
us. This fear has at times reached the proportions of terror
. . . Now this same feeling of fear has started up in the hearts
of Arabs . . . fear lest the Jews acquire the ascendancy and
rule over them."

Palestine, then, must be established as a country in which the legitimate national aspirations of both Jews and Arabs can be reconciled without either side fearing the ascendancy of the other. In our view this cannot be done under any form of constitution in which a mere numerical majority is decisive, since it is precisely the struggle for a numerical majority which bedevils Arab-Jewish relations. To ensure genuine self-government for both the Arab and the Jewish communities, this struggle must be made purposeless by the constitution itself.

MANDATE AND UNITED NATIONS TRUSTEESHIP

Recommendation No. 4. We have reached the conclusion that the hostility between Jews and Arabs and, in particular, the determination of each to achieve domination, if necessary by violence, make it almost certain that, now and for some time to come, any attempt to establish either an independent Palestinian state or independent Palestinian states would result in civil strife such as might threaten the peace of the world. We therefore recommend that, until this hostility disappears, the Government of Palestine be continued as at present under mandate pending the execution of a trusteeship agreement under the United Nations.

Comment. We recognize that in view of the powerful forces both Arab and Jewish, operating from outside Palestine, the task of Great Britain, as mandatory, has not been easy. The Peel Commission declared in 1937 that the mandate was unworkable, and the Permanent Mandates Commission of the League of Nations thereupon pointed out that it became almost unworkable once it was publicly declared to be so by such a body. Two years later the British Government, having come to the conclusion that the alternative of partition proposed by the Peel Commission was also unworkable, announced their intention of taking steps to terminate the mandate by establishment of an independent Palestine state.

Our recommendations are based on what we believe at this stage to be as fair a measure of justice to all as we can find in view of what has gone before and of all that has been done. We recognize that they are not in accord with the claims of either party, and furthermore that they involve a departure from the recent policy of the mandatory.

We recognize that, if they are adopted, they will involve a long period of trusteeship, which will mean a very heavy burden for any single Government to undertake, a burden which would be lightened if the difficulties were appreciated and the trustee had the support of other members of the United Nations.

EQUALITY OF STANDARDS

Recommendation No. 5. Looking toward a form of ultimate self-government consistent with the three principles laid down in Recommendation No. 3, we recommend that the mandatory or trustee should proclaim the principle that Arab economic, educational and political advancement in Palestine is of equal importance with that of the Jews; and should at once prepare measures designed to bridge the gap which now exists and raise the Arab standard of living to that of the Jews; and to bring the two peoples to a full appreciation of their common interest and common destiny in the land where both belong.

Comment. Our examination of conditions in Palestine led us to the conclusion that one of the chief causes of friction is the great disparity between the Jewish and Arab standards of living. Even under conditions of war, which brought considerable financial benefits to the Arabs, this disparity has not been appreciably reduced. Only by a deliberate and carefully planned policy on the part of the mandatory can the Arab standard of living be raised to that of the Jews. In stressing the need for such a policy we would particularly call attention to the discrepancies between the social services, including hospitals, available in Palestine for Jews and Arabs.

SOCIAL AID

We fully recognize that the Jewish social services are financed to a very great extent by the Jewish community in Palestine, with the assistance of outside Jewish organizations; and we would stress that nothing should be done which would bring these social services down to the level of those provided for the Arabs, or halt the constant improvements now being made in them.

We suggest that consideration be given to the advisability of encouraging the formation by the Arabs of an Arab community on the lines of the Jewish community which now largely controls and finances Jewish social services. The Arabs will have to rely, to a far greater extent than the Jews, on financial aid from the Government. But the Jews of Palestine should accept the necessity that taxation, raised from

both Jews and Arabs, will have to be spent very largely on
the Arabs in order to bridge the gap which now exists between
the standard of living of the two peoples.

FURTHER IMMIGRATION POLICY

Recommendation No. 6. We recommend that pending the
early reference to the United Nations and the execution of
a trusteeship agreement, the mandatory should administer
Palestine according to the mandate, which declares, with
regard to immigration, that "the administration of Palestine,
while insuring that the rights and position of other sections
of the population are not prejudiced, shall facilitate Jewish
immigration under suitable conditions."
Comment. We have recommended the admission of 100,000
immigrants, victims of Nazi persecution, as soon as possible.
We now deal with the position after the admission of that
number. We cannot look far into the future. We cannot construct a yardstick for annual immigration. Until a trusteeship
agreement is executed it is our clear opinion that Palestine
should be administered in accordance with the terms of the
mandate quoted above.

Further than that we cannot go in the form of a recommendation. In this disordered world speculation as to the economic
position of any country a few years ahead would be a hazardous proceeding. It is particularly difficult to predict what,
after a few years have passed, will be the economic and
political condition of Palestine. We hope that the present
friction and turbulence will soon die away and be replaced
by an era of peace, absent so long from the Holy Land; that
the Jew and Arab will soon realize that collaboration is to
their mutual advantage, but no one can say how long this will
take.

The possibility of the country sustaining a largely increased
population at a decent standard of living depends largely on
whether or not plans referred to in Recommendation No. 8
can be brought to fruition.

The Peel Commission stated that political as well as
economic considerations have to be taken into account in
regard to immigration, and recommended a "political high
level" of 12,000 a year. We cannot recommend the fixing of
a minimum or of a maximum for annual immigration in the
future. There are too many uncertain factors.

We desire, however, to state certain considerations which

we agree should be taken into account in determining what number of immigrants there should be in any period. It is the right of every independent nation to determine in the interests of its people the number of immigrants to be admitted to its lands. Similarly it must, we think, be conceded that it should be the right of the Government of Palestine to decide, having regard to the well-being of all the people of Palestine, the number of immigrants to be admitted within any given period.

In Palestine there is the Jewish National Home, created in consequence of the Balfour Declaration. Some may think that that declaration was wrong and should not have been made; some that it was a conception on a grand scale and that effect can be given to one of the most daring and significant colonization plans in history. Controversy as to which view is right is fruitless. The national home is there. Its roots are deep in the soil of Palestine. It cannot be argued out of existence; neither can the achievements of the Jewish pioneers.

The Government of Palestine in having regard to the well-being of all the people of Palestine cannot ignore the interests of so large a section of the population. It cannot ignore the achievements of the last quarter of a century. No Government of Palestine doing its duty to the people of that land can fail to do its best not only to maintain the national home but also to foster its proper development and such development must, in our view, involve immigration.

The well-being of all the people of Palestine, be they Jews, Arabs or neither, must be the governing consideration. We reject the view that there shall be no further Jewish immigration into Palestine without Arab acquiescence, a view which would result in the Arab dominating the Jew. We also reject the insistent Jewish demand that forced Jewish immigration must proceed apace in order to produce as quickly as possible a Jewish majority and a Jewish State. The well-being of the Jews must not be subordinated to that of the Arabs; nor that of the Arabs to the Jews. The well-being of both, the economic situation of Palestine as a whole, the degree of execution of plans for further development, all have to be carefully considered in deciding the number of immigrants for any particular period.

Palestine is a land sacred to three faiths and must not become the land of any one of them to the exclusion of the others, and Jewish immigration for the development of the national home must not become a policy of discrimination against other immigrants. Any person, therefore, who desires and is qualified under applicable laws to enter Palestine must not be refused admission or subjected to discrimination on the ground that he is not a Jew. All provisions respecting immigration must be drawn, executed and applied with that principle always firmly in mind.

Further, while we recognize that any Jew who enters Palestine in accordance with its laws is there of right, we expressly disapprove of the position taken in some Jewish quarters that Palestine has in some way been ceded or granted as their state to the Jews of the world, that every Jew everywhere is, merely because he is a Jew, a citizen of Palestine and therefore can enter Palestine as of right without regard to conditions imposed by the Government upon entry and that therefore there can be no illegal immigration of Jews into Palestine. We declare and affirm that any immigrant Jew who enters Palestine contrary to its laws is an illegal immigrant.

[Recommendations 7-9 deal with land policy, economic development, and education. Ed.]

Document 22

*The Arab Case for Palestine: Evidence Submitted
by the Arab Office, Jerusalem, to the
Anglo–American Committee of Inquiry,
March, 1946*

The Problem of Palestine

1. The whole Arab people is unalterably opposed to the attempt to impose Jewish immigration and settlement upon it, and ultimately to establish a Jewish State in Palestine. Its opposition is based primarily upon right. The Arabs of Palestine are descendants of the indigenous inhabitants of the country, who have been in occupation of it since the beginning of history; they cannot agree that it is right to subject an indigenous population against its will to alien immigrants, whose claim is based upon a historical connection which ceased effectively many centuries ago. Moreover they form the majority of the population; as such they cannot submit to a policy of immigration which if pursued for long will turn them from a majority into a minority in an alien state; and they claim the democratic right of a majority to make its own decisions in matters of urgent national concern. . . .

2. In addition to the question of right, the Arabs oppose the

claims of political Zionism because of the effects which
Zionist settlement has already had upon their situation and is
likely to have to an even greater extent in the future. Negatively, it has diverted the whole course of their national development. Geographically Palestine is part of Syria; its indigenous inhabitants belong to the Syrian branch of the Arab
family of nations; all their culture and tradition link them to
the other Arab peoples; and until 1917 Palestine formed
part of the Ottoman Empire which included also several
of the other Arab countries. The presence and claims of the
Zionists, and the support given them by certain Western
Powers have resulted in Palestine being cut off from the other
Arab countries and subjected to a regime, administrative,
legal, fiscal and educational, different from that of the
sister-countries. Quite apart from the inconvenience to individuals and the dislocation of trade which this separation has
caused, it has prevented Palestine participating fully in the
general development of the Arab world.

First, while the other Arab countries have attained or are
near to the attainment of self-government and full membership
of the U.N.O., Palestine is still under Mandate and has taken
no step towards self-government; not only are there no representative institutions, but no Palestinian can rise to the
higher ranks of the administration. This is inacceptable on
grounds of principle, and also because of its evil consequence.
It is a hardship to individual Palestinians whose opportunities
of responsibility are thus curtailed; and it is demoralizing to
the population to live under a government which has no basis
in their consent and to which they can feel no attachment
or loyalty.

Secondly, while the other Arab countries are working
through the Arab League to strengthen their ties and co-
ordinate their policies, Palestine (although her Arab inhabitants are formally represented in the League's Council)
cannot participate fully in this movement so long as she has
no indigenous government; thus the chasm between the
administrative system and the institutions of Palestine and
those of the neighbouring countries is growing, and her
traditional Arab character is being weakened.

Thirdly, while the other Arab countries have succeeded in
or are on the way to achieving a satisfactory definition of
their relations with the Western Powers and with the world-
community, expressed in their treaties with Great Britain
and other Powers and their membership of the United Nations

Organization, Palestine has not yet been able to establish any definite status for herself in the world, and her international destiny is still obscure.

3.   All these evils are due entirely to the presence of the Zionists and the support given to them by certain of the Powers; there is no doubt that had it not been for that, Arab Palestine would by now be a self-governing member of the U.N.O. and the Arab League. Moreover, in addition to the obstacles which Zionism has thus placed in the way of Palestine's development, the presence of the Zionists gives rise to various positive evils which will increase if Zionist immigration continues.

The entry of incessant waves of immigrants prevents normal economic and social development and causes constant dislocation of the country's life; in so far as it reacts upon prices and values and makes the whole economy dependent upon the constant inflow of capital from abroad it may even in certain circumstances lead to economic disaster. It is bound moreover to arouse continuous political unrest and prevent the establishment of that political stability on which the prosperity and health of the country depend. This unrest is likely to increase in frequency and violence as the Jews come nearer to being the majority and the Arabs a minority.

Even if economic and social equilibrium is re-established, it will be to the detriment of the Arabs. The superior capital resources at the disposal of the Jews, their greater experience of modern economic technique and the existence of a deliberate policy of expansion and domination have already gone far toward giving them the economic mastery of Palestine. The biggest concessionary companies are in their hands; they possess a large proportion of the total cultivable land, and an even larger one of the land in the highest category of fertility; and the land they possess is mostly inalienable to non-Jews. The continuance of land-purchase and immigration, taken together with the refusal of Jews to employ Arabs on their lands or in their enterprises and the great increase in the Arab population, will create a situation in which the Arab population is pushed to the margin of cultivation and a landless proletariat, rural and urban, comes into existence. This evil can be palliated but not cured by attempts at increasing the absorptive capacity or the industrial production of Palestine; the possibility of such improvements is limited, they would take a long time to carry out, and would scarcely do more than keep pace with the rapid growth of the Arab population; moreover in present circumstances they would be used primarily for the benefit of the Jews and thus might increase the disparity between the two communities.

Nor is the evil economic only. Zionism is essentially a political movement, aiming at the creation of a state: immigration, land-purchase and economic expansion are only aspects of a general political strategy. If Zionism succeeds in its aim, the Arabs will become a minority in their own country; a minority which can hope for no more than a minor share in the government, for the state is to be a Jewish state, and which will find itself not only deprived of that international status which the other Arab countries possess but cut off from living contact with the Arab world of which it is an integral part.

It should not be forgotten too that Palestine contains places holy to Moslems and Christians, and neither Arab Moslems nor Arab Christians would willingly see such places subjected to the ultimate control of a Jewish Government.

4. These dangers would be serious enough at any time, but are particularly so in this age, when the first task of the awakening Arab nation is to come to terms with the West; to define its relationship with the Western Powers and with the westernized world community on a basis of equality and mutual respect, and to adapt what is best in Western civilization to the needs of its own genius. Zionist policy is one of the greatest obstacles to the achievement of this task: both because Zionism represents to the Arabs one side of the Western spirit and because of the support given to it by some of the Western Powers. In fact Zionism has became in Arab eyes a test of Western intentions towards them. So long as the attempt of the Zionists to impose a Jewish state upon the inhabitants of Palestine is supported by some or all of the Western Governments, so long will it bé difficult if not impossible for the Arabs to establish a satisfactory relationship with the Western world and its civilization, and they will tend to turn away from the West in political hostility and spiritual isolation; this will be disastrous both for the Arabs themselves and for those Western nations which have dealings with them.

5. There are no benefits obtained or to be expected from Zionism commensurate with its evils and its dangers. The alleged social and economic benefits are much less than is claimed. The increase in the Arab population is not primarily due to Zionist immigration, and in any case would not neces-

sarily be a sign of prosperity. The rise in money wages and
earnings is largely illusory, being offset by the rise in the cost
of living. In so far as real wages and the standard of living
have risen, this is primarily an expression of a general trend
common to all Middle Eastern countries. The inflow of capital
has gone largely to raising money prices and real estate
values. The whole economy is dangerously dependent upon
the citrus industry. The benefits derived from the establishment of industries and the exploitation of the country's few
natural resources have been largely neutralized by the failure
of Jewish enterprises to employ Arabs.

The Zionist contention that their social organizations provide health and social services for the Arab population is
exaggerated; only a minute proportion of the Arabs, for example, are looked after by Jewish health organizations. Even if
true it would prove nothing except that the Government was
neglecting its responsibilities in regard to the welfare of the
population. Arab voluntary social organizations have grown
up independently of Jewish bodies and without help from
them. Even in so far as social and economic benefits have
come to the Arabs from Zionist settlement, it remains true
on the one hand that they are more than counter-balanced by
the dangers of that settlement, and on the other that they are
only incidental and are in no way necessary for the progress
of the Arab people. The main stimulus to Arab economic and
social progress does not come from the example or assistance
of the Zionists but from the natural tendency of the whole
Middle Eastern areas, from the work of the Government
and above all from the newly awakened will to progress of
the Arabs themselves. The Arabs may have started later than
the Jews on the road of modern social and economic organization, but they are now fully awake and are progressing fast.
This is shown in the economic sphere for example by the continued development of the Arab citrus industry and financial
organizations, in the social sphere by the growth of the labour
movement and the new Land Development Scheme.

If any proof were needed of this, it could be found in the
progress made during the last three decades by the neighbouring countries. None of the Arab countries is stagnant today:
even without the example and capital of the Zionists, they are
building up industries, improving methods and extending the
scope of agriculture, establishing systems of public education
and increasing the amenities of life. In some countries and
spheres the progress has been greater than among the Arabs

of Palestine, and in all of them it is healthier and more normal.

The Zionists claim further that they are acting as mediators of Western civilization to the Middle East. Even if their claim were true, the services they were rendering would be incidental only: the Arab world has been in direct touch with the West for a hundred years, and has its own reawakened cultural movement, and thus it has no need of a mediator. Moreover the claim is untrue: so long as Jewish cultural life in Palestine expresses itself through the medium of the Hebrew language, its influence on the surrounding world is bound to be negligible; in fact, Arab culture today is almost wholly uninfluenced by the Jews, and practically no Arabs take part in the work of Jewish cultural or educational institutions. In a deeper sense the presence of the Zionists is even an obstacle to the understanding of Western civilization, in so far as it more than any other factor is tending to induce in the Arabs an unsympathetic attitude towards the West and all its works.

6. Opposition to the policy of the Zionists is shared by all sections of the Palestinian Arab people. It is not confined to the towns people but is universal among the rural population, who stand to suffer most from the gradual alienation of the most fertile land to the Jewish National Fund. It is felt not only by the landowners and middle class but by the working population, both for national reasons and for reasons of their own. It is not an invention of the educated class; if that class have seen the danger more clearly and sooner than others, and if they have assumed the leadership of the opposition, that is no more than their duty and function.

Moreover not only the Arab Moslem majority are opposed to Zionism but also and equally the Arab Christian minority who reject Zionism both because they share to the full in the national sentiments of other Arabs and because as Christians they cannot accept that their Holy Places should be subject to Jewish control, and cannot understand how any Christian nation could accept it.

7. The sentiments of the Palestinian Arabs are fully shared by the other Arab countries, both by their Government and their peoples. Their support has shown itself in many ways: in Pan-Arab Conferences, in the moral and material support given by the whole Arab world to the revolt of 1936-39, in the diplomatic activities of Arab Governments, and most recently in the formation of the Arab League, which has

taken the defense of Palestine as one of its main objectives. The members of the Arab League are now taking active measures to prevent the alienation of Arab lands to the Zionists and Jewish domination of the economic life of the Middle East. . . .

8. In the Arab view, any solution of the problem created by Zionist aspirations must satisfy certain conditions:

(i) It must recognize the right of the indigenous inhabitants of Palestine to continue in occupation of the country and to preserve its traditional character.

(ii) It must recognize that questions like immigration which affect the whole nature and destiny of the country, should be decided in accordance with democratic principles by the will of the population.

(iii) It must accept the principle that the only way by which the will of the population can be expressed is through the establishment of responsible representative government. (The Arabs find something inconsistent in the attitude of Zionists who demand the establishment of a free democratic commonwealth in Palestine and then hasten to add that this should not take place until the Jews are in a majority.)

(iv) This representative Government should be based upon the principle of absolute equality of all citizens irrespective of race and religion.

(v) The form of Government should be such as to make possible the development of a spirit of loyalty and cohesion among all elements of the community, which will override all sectional attachments. In other words it should be a Government which the whole community could regard as their own, which should be rooted in their consent and have a moral claim upon their obedience.

(vi) The settlement should recognize the fact that by geography and history Palestine is inescapably part of the Arab world; that the only alternative to its being part of the Arab world and accepting the implications of its position is complete isolation, which would be disastrous from every point of view; and that whether they like it or not the Jews in Palestine are dependent upon the goodwill of the Arabs.

(vii) The settlement should be such as to make possible a satisfactory definition within the framework of U.N.O. of the relations between Palestine and the Western Powers who possess interests in the country.

(viii) The settlement should take into account that Zionism is essentially a political movement aiming at the creation of a

Jewish state and should therefore avoid making any concession which might encourage Zionists in the hope that this aim can be achieved in any circumstances.

9. In accordance with these principles, the Arabs urge the establishment in Palestine of a democratic government representative of all sections of the population on a level of absolute equality; the termination of the Mandate once the Government has been established; and the entry of Palestine into the United Nations Organization as a full member of the working community.

Pending the establishment of a representative Government, all further Jewish immigration should be stopped, in pursuance of the principle that a decision on so important a matter should only be taken with the consent of the inhabitants of the country and that until representative institutions are established there is no way of determining consent. Strict measures should also continue to be taken to check illegal immigration. Once a Palestinian state has come into existence, if any section of the population favours a policy of further immigration it will be able to press its case in accordance with normal democratic procedure; but in this as in other matters the minority must abide by the decision of the majority.

Similarly, all further transfer of land from Arabs to Jews should be prohibited prior to the creation of self-governing institutions. The Land Transfer Regulations should be made more stringent and extended to the whole area of the country, and severer measures be taken to prevent infringement of them. Here again once self-government exists matters concerning land will be decided in the normal democratic manner.

10. The Arabs are irrevocably opposed to political Zionism, but in no way hostile to the Jews as such nor to their Jewish fellow-citizens of Palestine. Those Jews who have already entered Palestine, and who have obtained or shall obtain Palestinian citizenship by due legal process will be full citizens of the Palestinian state, enjoying full civil and political rights and a fair share in government and administration. There is no question of their being thrust into the position of a "minority" in the bad sense of a closed community, which dwells apart from the main stream of the State's life and which exists by sufferance of the majority. They will be given the opportunity of belonging to and helping to mould the full community of the Palestinian state, joined to the Arabs by links of interest and goodwill, not the goodwill of the strong to the powerless, but of one citizen to another.

It is to be hoped that in course of time the exclusiveness of the Jews will be neutralized by the development of loyalty to the state and the emergence of new groupings which cut across communal divisions. This however will take time; and during the transitional period the Arabs recognize the need for giving special consideration to the peculiar position and the needs of the Jews. No attempt would be made to interfere with their communal organization, their personal status or their religious observances. Their schools and cultural institutions would be left to operate unchecked except for that general control which all governments exercise over education. In the districts in which they are most closely settled they would possess municipal autonomy and Hebrew would be an official language of administration, justice and education.

11. The Palestinian State would be an Arab state not (as should be clear from the preceding paragraph) in any narrow racial sense, nor in the sense that non-Arabs should be placed in a position of inferiority, but because the form and policy of its government would be based on a recognition of two facts: first that the majority of the citizens are Arabs, and secondly that Palestine is part of the Arab world and has no future except through close co-operation with the other Arab states. Thus among the main objects of the Government would be to preserve and enrich the country's Arab heritage, and to draw closer the relations between Palestine and the other Arab countries. The Cairo Pact of March, 1945, provided for the representation of Palestine on the Council of the Arab League even before its independence should be a reality; once it was really self-governing, it would participate fully in all the work of the League, in the cultural and economic no less than the political sphere. This would be of benefit to the Jewish no less than the Arab citizens of Palestine, since it would ensure those good relations with the Arab world without which their economic development would be impossible.

12. The state would apply as soon as possible for admission into U.N.O., and would of course be prepared to bear its full share of the burdens of establishing a world security-system. It would willingly place at the disposal of the Security Council whatever bases or other facilities were required, provided those bases were really used for the purpose for which they were intended and not in order to interfere in the internal affairs of the country, and provided also Palestine and the other Arab states were adequately represented on the controlling body.

The state would recognize also the world's interest in the maintenance of a satisfactory regime for the Moslem, Christian and Jewish Holy Places. In the Arab view however the need for such a regime does not involve foreign interference in or control of Palestine; no opportunity should be given to Great Powers to use the Holy Places as instruments of policy. The Holy Places can be most satisfactorily and appropriately guarded by a Government representative of the inhabitants, who include adherents of all three faiths and have every interest in preserving the holy character of their country.

Nor in the Arab view would any sort of foreign interference or control be justified by the need to protect the Christian minorities. The Christians are Arabs, who belong fully to the national community and share fully in its struggle. They would have all the rights and duties of citizens of a Palestinian state, and would continue to have their own communal organizations and institutions. They themselves would ask for no more, having learnt from the example of other Middle Eastern countries the dangers of an illusory foreign "protection" of minorities.

13. In economic and social matters the Government of Palestine would follow a progressive policy with the aim of raising the standard of living and increasing the welfare of all sections of the population, and using the country's natural resources in the way most beneficial to all. Its first task naturally would be to improve the condition of the Arab peasants and thus to bridge the economic and social gulf which at present divides the two communities. Industry would be encouraged, but only in so far as its economic basis was sound and as part of a general policy of economic development for the whole Arab world; commercial and financial ties with the other Arab countries would so far as possible be strengthened, and tariffs decreased or abolished.

14. The Arabs believe that no other proposals would satisfy the conditions of a just and lasting settlement. In their view there are insuperable objections of principle or of practice to all other suggested solutions of the problem.

(1) The idea of partition and the establishment of a Jewish state in a part of Palestine is inadmissible for the same reasons of principle as the idea of establishing a Jewish state in the whole country. If it is unjust to the Arabs to impose a Jewish state on the whole of Palestine, it is equally unjust to impose it in any part of the country. Moreover, as the Wood-

head Commission showed, there are grave practical difficulties in the way of partition; commerce would be strangled, communications dislocated and the public finances upset. It would also be impossible to devise frontiers which did not leave a large Arab minority in the Jewish state. This minority would not willingly accept its subjection to the Zionists, and it would not allow itself to be transferred to the Arab state. Moreover, partition would not satisfy the Zionists. It cannot be too often repeated that Zionism is a political movement aiming at the domination at least of the whole of Palestine; to give it a foothold in part of Palestine would be to encourage it to press for more and to provide it with a base for its activities. Because of this, because of the pressure of population and in order to escape from its isolation it would inevitably be thrown into enmity with the surrounding Arab states and this enmity would disturb the stability of the whole Middle East.

(2) Another proposal is for the establishment of a bi-national state, based upon political parity, in Palestine and its incorporation into a Syrian or Arab Federation. The Arabs would reject this as denying the majority its normal position and rights. There are also serious practical objections to the idea of a bi-national state, which cannot˙exist unless there is a strong sense of unity and common interest overriding the differences between the two parties. Morover, the point made in regard to the previous suggestion may be repeated here: this scheme would in no way satisfy the Zionists, it would simply encourage them to hope for more and improve their chances of obtaining it. . . .

Document 23

*The Case for a Bi-national State**

The Arab Contention

The Arabs say that "the existence of the Jewish National Home, whatever its size, bars the way to the attainment by the Arabs of Palestine of the same national status as that attained, or soon to be attained, by all the other Arabs of Asia" (Royal Commission, p. 307). That is so. And they ask if they are not as fit for self-government as the Arabs of other countries. They are.

* Reprinted from M. Buber and J. L. Magnes, *Arab-Jewish Unity*. London: Victor Gollancz Ltd., 1947.

Arab Concessions

But the whole history of Palestine shows that it just has not been made for uni-national sovereign independence. This is an inescapable fact which no one can disregard. Although the Arabs cannot have a uni-national independent Arab Palestine, they can enjoy independence in a bi-national Palestine together with their Jewish fellow-citizens. This will afford them a maximum of national freedom. What the bi-national State will take away from them is sovereign independence in Palestine. There are other Arab States with sovereign independence. But we contend that the sovereign independence of tiny Palestine, whether it be Jewish sovereignty or Arab sovereignty, is a questionable good in this post-war period, when even great States must relinquish something of their sovereignty and seek union, if the world is not to perish. We contend that for this Holy Land the idea of a bi-national Palestine is at least as inspiring as that of an Arab sovereign Palestine or a Jewish sovereign Palestine.

Jewish Concessions

On the other hand, the bi-national Palestine would deprive the Jews of their one chance of a Jewish State. But this bi-national Palestine would be the one State in the world where they would be a constituent nation, i.e. an equal nationality within the body politic, and not a minority as everywhere else. The absence of a Jewish State would make more difficult direct access by the Jewish people to U.N.O. To compensate for this, some form should be devised for giving the Jewish people a recognised place within the structure of the United Nations Organisation.

Nevertheless, the concessions the Jews would have to make on these matters are, we think, more far-reaching than the concessions the Arabs of Palestine would have to make. But the hard facts of the situation are that this is not a Jewish land and it is not an Arab land—it is the Holy Land, a bi-national country—and it is in the light of such hard facts that the problem must be approached.

The Advantages of a Bi-national Palestine

Before proceeding to outline our suggestions as to the political structure of the bi-national Palestine, we should like finally to point out some of the advantages of bi-nationalism based on parity in a country which has two nationalities.

FAILURE OF MINORITY GUARANTEES

1. The breakdown of the minority guarantees provided for in the Versailles Peace treaties is proof that in a bi-national country the only safeguard for a minority is equality with the majority. There is no prospect of peace in a country where there is a dominant people and a subordinate people. The single nation-State is a proper form for a country where there is but one legally recognised nationality, as, for example, the United States. But in countries with more than one recognised nationality—and they are numerous in Europe and in Asia—bitterness is engendered among the minority because the civil service, the military, the economic key positions, foreign affairs, are in the hands of the ruling class of the majority nation. Parity in a multi-national country is the only just relationship between the peoples.

SWITZERLAND

2. The multi-national state is an effective method of affording full protection for the national languages, cultures and institutions of each nationality. That there can be full cultural autonomy combined with full allegiance to the multi-national political state is proven in Switzerland's history for more than 100 years. The Swiss are divided by language, religion and culture; nor do the linguistic and religious groupings coincide in the various cantons. Yet all of these divergencies have not been obstacles to political unity. This is a newer form of democracy which is as important for multi-national states as the more familiar form of democracy is for uni-national states. The Swiss example is most relevant to Palestine, although there are, of course, many points of difference.

OTHER MULTI-NATIONAL COUNTRIES

The Soviet Union is a newer example of a multi-national State. The new Yugoslav State is an attempt at multi-national federalism. Professor Seton Watson outlines a bi-national solution of the age-long problem of Transylvania. Roumanian domination, Hungarian domination, partition had all been tried without success.

Bi-nationalism a High Ideal

3. In many senses the multi-national state represents a higher, more modern and more hopeful ideal than the uni-national sovereign independent State. The old way of having a major people and a minor people in a State of various nationalities is reactionary. The progressive conception is parity among the peoples of the multi-national State. The way of peace in the world to-day and tomorrow is through federation, union. Dividing up the world into tiny nationalistic sovereign units has not been the success the advocates of self-determination had hoped for at the end of the First World War. (Cobban, *National Self-Determination.*) The peoples who have been placed by fate or by history in the same country have warred with one another for domination throughout the centuries. The majority have tried to make the State homogeneous through keeping down the minority nationalities. The federal multi-national State, based on the parity of the nationalities, is a most hopeful way of enabling them to retain their national identity, and yet of coalescing in a larger political framework. It results in separate nationalities, yet a single citizenship. This is a noble goal to which the youth of multi-national countries can be taught to give their enthusiasm and their energies. It is a modern challenge to the intelligence and the moral qualities of the peoples constituting multi-national lands.

Documents 24–25

The United Nations Takes Over

British Foreign Secretary Ernest Bevin announced on February 14, 1947, that His Majesty's Government had decided to refer the Palestine problem to the United Nations. Tension inside Palestine had risen, illegal Jewish immigration continued, there was growing restiveness in the Arab countries: Palestine, Bevin said, could not be so divided as to create two viable states, since the Arabs would never agree to it, the Mandate could not be administered in its present form, and Britain was going to ask the United Nations how it could be amended.

The United Nations set up a U.N. Special Committee on Palestine (U.N.S.C.O.P.) composed of representatives of eleven member states. Its report and recommendations were published on August 31, 1947 (Document 24). The Jewish Agency occepted the partition plan as the "indispensable minimum," the Arab governments and the Arab Higher Executive rejected it. On November 29, 1947, the U.N. General Assembly endorsed the partition plan by a vote of thirty-three to thirteen (Document 25). The two-thirds majority included the United States and the Soviet Union but not Britain.

Document 24

Summary of the Report of U.N.S.C.O.P.
(U.N. Special Committee on Palestine)

August 31, 1947

(a) GENERAL RECOMMENDATIONS
OF THE COMMITTEE

The eleven unanimously-adopted resolutions of the Committee were:

That the Mandate should be terminated and Palestine granted independence at the earliest practicable date (recommendations I and II);

That there should be a short transitional period preceding the granting of independence to Palestine during which the authority responsible for administering Palestine should be responsible to the United Nations (recommendations III and IV);

That the sacred character of the Holy Places and the rights of religious communities in Palestine should be preserved and stipulations concerning them inserted in the constitution of any state or states to be created and that a system should be found for settling impartially any disputes involving religious rights (recommendation V);

That the General Assembly should take steps to see that the problem of distressed European Jews should be dealt with as a matter of urgency so as to alleviate their plight and the Palestine problem (recommendation VI);

That the constitution of the new state or states should be fundamentally democratic and should contain guarantees for the respect of human rights and fundamental freedoms and for the protection of minorities (recommendation VII);

That the undertakings contained in the Charter whereby states are to settle their disputes by peaceful means and to refrain from the threat or use of force in international relations in any way inconsistent with the purposes of the United Nations should be incorporated in the constitutional provisions applying to Palestine (recommendation VIII);

That the economic unity of Palestine should be preserved (recommendation IX);

That states whose nationals had enjoyed in Palestine privileges and immunities of foreigners, including those formerly enjoyed by capitulation or usage in the Ottoman Empire, should be invited to renounce any rights pertaining to them (recommendation X);

That the General Assembly should appeal to the peoples of Palestine to cooperate with the United Nations in its efforts to settle the situation there and exert every effort to put an end to acts of violence (recommendation XI);

In addition to these eleven unanimously approved recommendations, the Special Committee, with two members (Uruguay and Guatemala) dissenting, and one member recording no opinion, also approved the following twelfth recommendation:

"*Recommendation XII. The Jewish Problem in General*

"It is recommended that

"In the appraisal of the Palestine question, it be accepted as incontrovertible that any solution for Palestine cannot be considered as a solution of the Jewish problem in general."

(b) Majority Proposal: Plan of Partition with Economic Union

According to the plan of the majority (the representatives of Canada, Czechoslovakia, Guatemala, Netherlands, Peru, Sweden and Uruguay), Palestine was to be constituted into an Arab State, a Jewish State and the City of Jerusalem. The Arab and the Jewish States would become independent after a transitional period of two years beginning on September 1, 1947. Before their independence could be recognized, however, they must adopt a constitution in line with the pertinent recommendations of the Committee and make to the United Nations a declaration containing certain guarantees, and sign a treaty by which a system of economic collaboration would be established and the economic union of Palestine created.

The plan provided, *inter alia,* that during the transitional period, the United Kingdom would carry on the administration of Palestine under the auspices of the United Nations and on such conditions and under such supervision as the United Kingdom and the United Nations might agree upon. During this period a stated number of Jewish immigrants was to be admitted. Constituent Assemblies were to be elected by the populations of the areas which were to comprise the Arab and Jewish States, respectively, and were to draw up the constitutions of the States.

These constitutions were to provide for the establishment in each State of a legislative body elected by universal suffrage and by secret ballot on the basis of proportional representation and an executive body responsible to the legislature. They would also contain various guarantees, e.g., for the protection of the Holy Places and religious buildings and sites, and of religious and minority rights.

The Constituent Assembly in each State would appoint a provisional government empowered to make the declaration and sign the Treaty of Economic Union, after which the independence of the State would be recognized. The Declaration would contain provisions for the protection of the Holy Places and religious buildings and sites and for religious and minority rights. It would also contain provisions regarding citizenship.

A treaty would be entered into between the two States, which would contain provisions to establish the economic union of Palestine and to provide for other matters of common interest. A Joint Economic Board would be established consisting of representatives of the two States and members appointed by the Economic and Social Council of the United Nations to organize and administer the objectives of the Economic Union.

The City of Jerusalem would be placed, after the transitional period, under the International Trusteeship System by means of a Trusteeship Agreement, which would designate the United Nations as the Administering Authority. The plan contained recommended boundaries for the city and provisions concerning the governor and the police force.

The plan also proposed boundaries for both the Arab and Jewish States.

(c) MINORITY PROPOSAL:
PLAN OF A FEDERAL STATE

Three U.N.S.C.O.P. members (the representatives of India, Iran and Yugoslavia) proposed an independent federal state. This plan provided, *inter alia,* that an independent federal state of Palestine would be created following a transitional period not exceeding three years, during which responsibility for administering Palestine and preparing it for independence would be entrusted to an authority to be decided by the General Assembly.

The independent federal state would comprise an Arab State and a Jewish State. Jerusalem would be its capital.

During the transitional period a Constituent Assembly would be elected by popular vote and convened by the administering authority on the basis of electoral provisions which would ensure the fullest representation of the population.

The Constituent Assembly would draw up the constitution of the federal state, which was to contain, *inter alia,* the following provisions:

The federal state would comprise a federal government and governments of the Arab and Jewish States, respectively.

Full authority would be vested in the federal government with regard to national defence, foreign relations, immigration, currency, taxation for federal purposes, foreign and inter-state waterways, transport and communications, copyrights and patents.

The Arab and Jewish States would enjoy full powers of local self-government and would have authority over education, taxation for local purposes, the right of residence, commercial licenses, land permits, grazing rights, inter-state migration, settlement, police, punishment of crime, social institutions and services, public housing, public health, local roads, agriculture and local industries.

The organs of government would include a head of state, an executive body, a representative federal legislative body composed of two chambers, and a federal court. The executive would be responsible to the legislative body.

Election to one chamber of the federal legislative body would be on the basis of proportional representation of the population as a whole, and to the other on the basis of equal representation of the Arab and Jewish citizens of Palestine. Legislation would be enacted when approved by majority votes in both chambers; in the event of disagreement between the two chambers, the issue would be submitted to an arbitral body of five members including not less than two Arabs and two Jews.

The federal court would be the final court of appeal regarding constitutional matters. Its members who would include not less than four Arabs and three Jews, would be elected by both chambers of the federal legislative body.

The constitution was to guarantee equal rights for all minorities and fundamental human rights and freedoms. It would guarantee, *inter alia,* free access to the Holy Places and protect religious interests.

The constitution would provide for an undertaking to settle international disputes by peaceful means.

There would be a single Palestinian nationality and citizen ship.

The constitution would provide for equitable participation of representatives of both communities in delegations to international conferences.

A permanent international body was to be set up for the supervision and protection of the Holy Places, to be composed of three representatives designated by the United Nations and one representative of each of the recognized faiths having an interest in the matter, as might be determined by the United Nations.

For a period of three years from the beginning of the transitional period Jewish immigration would be permitted into the Jewish State in such numbers as not to exceed its absorptive capacity, and having due regard for the rights of the existing population within that State and their anticipated natural rate of increase. An international commission, composed of three Arab, three Jewish and three United Nations representatives, would be appointed to estimate the absorptive capacity of the Jewish State. The commission would cease to exist at the end of the three-year period mentioned above.

The minority plan also laid down the boundaries of the proposed Arab and Jewish areas of the federal state.

Document 25

U.N. General Assembly Resolution on the Future Government of Palestine (Partition Resolution)

November 29, 1947

The General Assembly,

Having met in special session at the request of the mandatory Power to constitute and instruct a special committee to prepare for the consideration of the question of the future government of Palestine at the second regular session;

Having constituted a Special Committee and instructed it to investigate all questions and issues relevant to the problem of Palestine, and to prepare proposals for the solution of the problem, and

Having received and examined the report of the Special Committee (document A/364) including a number of unanimous recommendations and a plan of partition with economic union approved by the majority of the Special Committee,

Considers that the present situation in Palestine is one which is likely to impair the general welfare and friendly relations among nations;

Takes note of the declaration by the mandatory Power that it plans to complete its evacuation of Palestine by 1 August 1948;

Recommends to the United Kingdom, as the mandatory Power for Palestine, and to all other Members of the United Nations the adoption and implementation, with regard to the future government of Palestine, of the Plan of Partition with Economic Union set out below;

Requests that

(a) The Security Council take the necessary measures as provided for in the plan for its implementation;

(b) The Security Council consider, if circumstances during the transitional period require such consideration, whether the situation in Palestine constitutes a threat to the peace. If it decides that such a threat exists, and in order to maintain international peace and security, the Security Council should supplement the authorization of the General Assembly by taking measures, under Article 39 and 41 of the Charter, to empower the United Nations Commission, as provided in this resolution, to exercise in Palestine the functions which are assigned to it by this resolution;

(c) The Security Council determine as a threat to the peace, breach of the peace or act of aggression, in accordance with Article 39 of the Charter, any attempt to alter by force the settlement envisaged by this resolution;

(d) The Trusteeship Council be informed of the responsibilities envisaged for it in this plan;

Calls upon the inhabitants of Palestine to take such steps as may be necessary on their part to put this plan into effect;

Appeals to all Governments and all peoples to refrain from taking any action which might hamper or delay the carrying out of these recommendations, and

Authorizes the Secretary-General to reimburse travel and subsistence expenses of the members of the commission referred to in Part I, Section B, paragraph 1 below, on such basis and in such form as he may determine most appropriate in the circumstances, and to provide the Commission with the necessary staff to assist in carrying out the functions assigned to the Commission by the General Assembly.

Plan of Partition with Economic Union
Part I—Future Constitution and Government of Palestine

A. Termination of Mandate Partition and Independence

1. The Mandate for Palestine shall terminate as soon as possible but in any case not later than 1 August 1948.

2. The armed forces of the mandatory Power shall be progressively withdrawn from Palestine, the withdrawal to be completed as soon as possible but in any case not later than 1 August 1948.

The mandatory Power shall advise the Commission, as far in advance as possible, of its intention to terminate the Mandate and to evacuate each area.

The mandatory Power shall use its best endeavours to ensure that an area situated in the territory of the Jewish State, including a seaport and hinterland adequate to provide facilities for a substantial immigration, shall be evacuated at the earliest possible date and in any event not later than 1 February 1948.

3. Independent Arab and Jewish States and the Special International Regime for the City of Jerusalem, set forth in part III of this plan, shall come into existence in Palestine two months after the evacuation of the armed forces of the mandatory Power has been completed but in any case not later than 1 October 1948. The boundaries of the Arab State, the Jewish State, and the City of Jerusalem shall be described in parts II and III below.

4. The period between the adoption by the General Assembly of its recommendation on the question of Palestine and the establishment of the independence of the Arab and Jewish States shall be a transitional period.

B. STEPS PREPARATORY TO INDEPENDENCE

1. A Commission shall be set up consisting of one representative of each of five Member States. The Members represented on the Commission shall be elected by the General Assembly on as broad a basis, geographically and otherwise, as possible.

2. The administration of Palestine shall, as the mandatory Power withdraws its armed forces, be progressively turned over to the Commission, which shall act in conformity with the recommendations of the General Assembly, under the guidance of the Security Council. The mandatory Power shall to the fullest possible extent co-ordinate its plans for withdrawal with the plans of the Commission to take over and administer areas which have been evacuated.

In the discharge of this administrative responsibility the Commission shall have authority to issue necessary regulations and take other measures as required.

The mandatory Power shall not take any action to prevent, obstruct or delay the implementation by the Commission of the measures recommended by the General Assembly.

3. On its arrival in Palestine the Commission shall proceed to carry out measures for the establishment of the frontiers of the Arab and Jewish States and the City of Jerusalem in accordance with the general lines of the recommendations of the General Assembly on the partition of Palestine. Nevertheless, the boundaries as described in part II of this plan are to be modified in such a way that village areas as a rule will not be divided by state boundaries unless pressing reasons make that necessary.

4. The Commission, after consultation with the democratic parties and other public organizations of the Arab and Jewish

States, shall select and establish in each State as rapidly as possible a Provisional Council of Government. The activities of both the Arab and Jewish Provisional Councils of Government shall be carried out under the general direction of the Commission.

If by 1 April 1948 a Provisional Council of Government cannot be selected for either of the States, or, if selected, cannot carry out its functions, the Commission shall communicate that fact to the Security Council for such action with respect to that State as the Security Council may deem proper, and to the Secretary-General for communication to the Members of the United Nations.

5. Subject to the provisions of these recommendations, during the transitional period the Provisional Councils of Government, acting under the Commission, shall have full authority in the areas under their control, including authority over matters of immigration and land regulation.

6. The Provisional Council of Government of each State, acting under the Commission, shall progressively receive from the Commission full responsibility for the administration of that State in the period between the termination of the Mandate and the establishment of the State's independence.

7. The Commission shall instruct the Provisional Councils of Government of both the Arab and Jewish States, after their formation, to proceed to the establishment of administrative organs of government, central and local.

8. The Provisional Council of Government of each State shall, within the shortest time possible, recruit an armed militia from the residents of that State, sufficient in number to maintain internal order and to prevent frontier clashes.

This armed militia in each State shall, for operational purposes, be under the command of Jewish or Arab officers resident in that State, but general political and military control, including the choice of the militia's High Command, shall be exercised by the Commission.

9. The Provisional Council of Government of each State shall, not later than two months after the withdrawal of the armed forces of the mandatory Power, hold elections to the Constituent Assembly which shall be conducted on democratic lines.

The election regulations in each State shall be drawn up by the Provisional Council of Government and approved by the Commission.

Qualified voters for each State for this election shall be

persons over eighteen years of age who are: (*a*) Palestinian citizens residing in that State and (*b*) Arabs and Jews residing in the State, although not Palestinian citizens, who, before voting, have signed a notice of intention to become citizens of such State.

Arabs and Jews residing in the City of Jerusalem who have signed a notice of intention to become citizens, the Arabs of the Arab State and the Jews of the Jewish State, shall be entitled to vote in the Arab and Jewish States respectively.

Women may vote and be elected to the Constituent Assemblies.

During the transitional period no Jew shall be permitted to establish residence in the area of the proposed Arab State, and no Arab shall be permitted to establish residence in the area of the proposed Jewish State, except by special leave of the Commission.

10. The Constituent Assembly of each State shall draft a democratic constitution for its State and choose a provisional government to succeed the Provisional Council of Government appointed by the Commission. The constitutions of the States shall embody chapters 1 and 2 of the Declaration provided for in section C below and include *inter alia* provisions for:

(*a*) Establishing in each State a legislative body elected by universal suffrage and by secret ballot on the basis of proportional representation, and an executive body responsible to the legislature;

(*b*) Settling all international disputes in which the State may be involved by peaceful means in such a manner that international peace and security, and justice, are not endangered;

(*c*) Accepting the obligation of the State to refrain in its international relations from the threat or use of force against the territorial integrity or political independence of any State, or in any other manner inconsistent with the purposes of the United Nations;

(*d*) Guaranteeing to all persons equal and non-discriminatory rights in civil, political, economic and religious matters and the enjoyment of human rights and fundamental freedoms, including freedom of religion, language, speech and publication, education, assembly and association;

(*e*) Preserving freedom of transit and visit for all residents and citizens of the other State in Palestine and the City of Jerusalem, subject to considerations of national security, provided that each State shall control residence within its borders.

11. The Commission shall appoint a preparatory economic commission of three members to make whatever arrangements are possible for economic co-operation, with a view to establishing, as soon as practicable, the Economic Union and the Joint Economic Board, as provided in section D below.

12. During the period between the adoption of the recommendations on the question of Palestine by the General Assembly and the termination of the Mandate, the mandatory Power in Palestine shall maintain full responsibility for administration in areas from which it has not withdrawn its armed forces. The Commission shall assist the mandatory Power in the carrying out of these functions. Similarly the mandatory Power shall co-operate with the Commission in the execution of its functions.

13. With a view to ensuring that there shall be continuity in the functioning of administrative services and that, on the withdrawal of the armed forces of the mandatory Power, the whole administration shall be in charge of the Provisional Councils and the Joint Economic Board, respectively, acting under the Commission, there shall be a progressive transfer, from the mandatory Power to the Commission, of responsibility for all the functions of government, including that of maintaining law and order in the areas from which the forces of the mandatory Power have been withdrawn.

14. The Commission shall be guided in its activities by the recommendations of the General Assembly and by such instructions as the Security Council may consider necessary to issue.

The measures taken by the Commission, within the recommendations of the General Assembly, shall become immediately effective unless the Commission has previously received contrary instructions from the Security Council.

The Commission shall render periodic monthly progress reports, or more frequently if desirable, to the Security Council.

15. The Commission shall make its final report to the next regular session of the General Assembly and to the Security Council simultaneously.

C. DECLARATION

A declaration shall be made to the United Nations by the provisional government of each proposed State before independence. It shall contain *inter alia* the following clauses:

General Provision

The stipulations contained in the declaration are recognized as fundamental laws of the State and no law, regulation or official action shall conflict or interfere with these stipulations, nor shall any law, regulation or official action prevail over them.

Chapter 1.—Holy Places, Religious Buildings and Sites

1. Existing rights in respect of Holy Places and religious buildings or sites shall not be denied or impaired.

2. In so far as Holy Places are concerned, the liberty of access, visit and transit shall be guaranteed, in conformity with existing rights, to all residents and citizens of the other State and of the City of Jerusalem, as well as to aliens, without distinction as to nationality, subject to requirements of national security, public order and decorum.

Similarly, freedom of worship shall be guaranteed in conformity with existing rights, subject to the maintenance of public order and decorum.

3. Holy Places and religious buildings or sites shall be preserved. No act shall be permitted which may in any way impair their sacred character. If at any time it appears to the Government that any particular Holy Place, religious building or site is in need of urgent repair, the Government may call upon the community or communities concerned to carry out such repair. The Government may carry it out itself at the expense of the community or communities concerned if no action is taken within a reasonable time.

4. No taxation shall be levied in respect of any Holy Place, religious building or site which was exempt from taxation on the date of the creation of the State.

No change in the incidence of such taxation shall be made which would either discriminate between the owners or occupiers of Holy Places, religious buildings or sites, or would place such owners or occupiers in a position less favourable in relation to the general incidence of taxation than existed at the time of the adoption of the Assembly's recommendation.

5. The Governor of the City of Jerusalem shall have the right to determine whether the provisions of the Constitution of the State in relation to Holy Places, religious buildings and sits within the borders of the State and the religious rights appertaining thereto, are being properly applied and respected,

and to make decisions on the basis of existing rights in cases of disputes which may arise between the different religious communities or the rites of a religious community with respect to such places, buildings and sites. He shall receive full co-operation and such privileges and immunities as are necessary for the exercise of his functions in the State.

Chapter 2.—Religious and Minority Rights

1. Freedom of conscience and the free exercise of all forms of worship, subject only to the maintenance of public order and morals, shall be ensured to all.

2. No discrimination of any kind shall be made between the inhabitants on the ground of race, religion, language or sex.

3. All persons within the jurisdiction of the State shall be entitled to equal protection of the laws.

4. The family law and personal status of the various minorities and their religious interests, including endowments, shall be respected.

5. Except as may be required for the maintenance of public order and good government, no measure shall be taken to obstruct or interfere with the enterprise of religious or charitable bodies of all faiths or to discriminate against any representative or member of these bodies on the ground of his religion or nationality.

6. The State shall ensure adequate primary and secondary education for the Arab and Jewish minority, respectively, in its own language and its cultural traditions.

The right of each community to maintain its own schools for the education of its own members in its own language, while conforming to such educational requirements of a general nature as the State may impose, shall not be denied or impaired. Foreign educational establishments shall continue their activity on the basis of their existing rights.

7. No restriction shall be imposed on the free use by any citizen of the State of any language in private intercourse, in commerce, in religion, in the Press or in publications of any kind, or at public meetings.[1]

8. No expropriation of land owned by an Arab in the Jew-

---

[1] The following stipulation shall be added to the declaration concerning the Jewish State: "In the Jewish State adequate facilities shall be given to Arabic-speaking citizens for the use of their language, either orally or in writing, in the legislature, before the Courts and in the administration."

ish State (by a Jew in the Arab State)[2] shall be allowed except for public purposes. In all cases of expropriation full compensation as fixed by the Supreme Court shall be paid previous to dispossession.

Chapter 3.—Citizenship, International Conventions and Financial Obligations

1. *Citizenship.* Palestinian citizens residing in Palestine outside the City of Jerusalem, as well as Arabs and Jews who, not holding Palestinian citizenship, reside in Palestine outside the City of Jerusalem shall, upon the recognition of independence, become citizens of the State in which they are resident and enjoy full civil and political rights. Persons over the age of eighteen years may opt, within one year from the date of recognition of independence of the State in which they reside, for citizenship of the other State, providing that no Arab residing in the area of the proposed Arab State shall have the right to opt for citizenship in the proposed Jewish State and no Jews residing in the proposed Jewish State shall have the right to opt for citizenship in the proposed Arab State. The exercise of this right of option will be taken to include the wives and children under eighteen years of age of persons so opting.

Arabs residing in the area of the proposed Jewish State and Jews residing in the area of the proposed Arab State who have signed a notice of intention to opt for citizenship of the other State shall be eligible to vote in the elections to the Constituent Assembly of that State, but not in the elections to the Constituent Assembly of the State in which they reside.

2. *International conventions.* (*a*) The State shall be bound by all the international agreements and conventions, both general and special, to which Palestine has become a party. Subject to any right of denunciation provided for therein, such agreements and conventions shall be respected by the State throughout the period for which they were concluded.

(*b*) Any dispute about the applicability and continued validity of international conventions or treaties signed or adhered to by the mandatory Power on behalf of Palestine shall be referred to the International Court of Justice in accordance with the provisions of the Statute of the Court.

3. *Financial obligations.* (*a*) The State shall respect and fulfil all financial obligations of whatever nature assumed on

[2] In the declaration concerning the Arab State, the words "by an Arab in the Jewish State" should be replaced by the words "by a Jew in the Arab State."

behalf of Palestine by the mandatory Power during the exercise of the Mandate and recognized by the State. This provision includes the right of public servants to pensions, compensation or gratuities.

(*b*) These obligations shall be fulfilled through participation in the Joint Economic Board in respect of those obligations applicable to Palestine as a whole, and individually in respect of those applicable to, and fairly apportionable between, the States.

(*c*) A Court of Claims, affiliated with the Joint Economic Board, and composed of one member appointed by the United Nations, one representative of the United Kingdom and one representative of the State concerned, should be established. Any dispute between the United Kingdom and the States respecting claims not recognized by the latter should be referred to that Court.

(*d*) Commercial concessions granted in respect of any part of Palestine prior to the adoption of the resolution by the General Assembly shall continue to be valid according to their terms, unless modified by agreement between the concession-holder and the State.

[Section D has been deleted: "Economic Union and Transit." Part II of the Resolution deals with the borders of the new State; Part III with "Capitulations." Ed.]

PART III

Israel and the Arab World
1948-1967

Part III of the Reader extends from the establishment of the State of Israel in May, 1948 to the aftermath of the third Arab–Israeli war in 1967. The United Nations resolution about the partition of Palestine was bitterly resented by the Palestinian Arabs and their supporters in the neighboring countries who tried to prevent with the force of arms the establishment of a Zionist state by the "Jewish usurpers." This attempt failed and Israel, as a result, seized areas beyond those defined in the U.N. resolution. The armistice of 1949 did not restore peace; an Arab refugee problem came into being, guerrilla attacks, Israel retaliation and Arab blockage of the Suez Canal and the Gulf of Aqaba led to the second and third Arab–Israeli Wars.

State of Israel Proclamation of Independence

The Proclamation of Independence was published by the Provisional State Council in Tel Aviv on May 14, 1948. The Provisional State Council was the forerunner of the Knesset, the Israeli parliament. The British Mandate was terminated the following day and regular armed forces of Transjordan, Egypt, Syria and other Arab countries entered Palestine.

The Land of Israel was the birthplace of the Jewish people. Here their spiritual, religious and national identity was formed. Here they achieved independence and created a culture of national and universal significance. Here they wrote and gave the Bible to the world.

Exiled from the Land of Israel the Jewish people remained faithful to it in all the countries of their dispersion, never ceasing to pray and hope for their return and the restoration of their national freedom.

Impelled by this historic association, Jews strove throughout the centuries to go back to the land of their fathers and regain their statehood. In recent decades they returned in their masses. They reclaimed the wilderness, revived their language, built cities and villages, and established a vigorous and ever-growing community, with its own economic and cultural life. They sought peace, yet were prepared to defend themselves. They brought the blessings of progress to all inhabitants of the country and looked forward to sovereign independence.

In the year 1897 the First Zionist Congress, inspired by

Theodor Herzl's vision of the Jewish State, proclaimed the right of the Jewish people to national revival in their own country.

This right was acknowledged by the Balfour Declaration of November 2, 1917, and re-affirmed by the Mandate of the League of Nations, which gave explicit international recognition to the historic connection of the Jewish people with Palestine and their right to reconstitute their National Home.

The recent holocaust, which engulfed millions of Jews in Europe, proved anew the need to solve the problem of the homelessness and lack of independence of the Jewish people by means of the re-establishment of the Jewish State, which would open the gates to all Jews and endow the Jewish people with equality of status among the family of nations.

The survivors of the disastrous slaughter in Europe, and also Jews from other lands, have not desisted from their efforts to reach Eretz-Yisrael, in face of difficulties, obstacles and perils; and have not ceased to urge their right to a life of dignity, freedom and honest toil in their ancestral land.

In the second World War the Jewish people in Palestine made their full contribution to the struggle of the freedom-loving nations against the Nazi evil. The sacrifices of their soldiers and their war effort gained them the right to rank with the nations which founded the United Nations.

On November 29, 1947, the General Assembly of the United Nations adopted a Resolution requiring the establishment of a Jewish State in Palestine. The General Assembly called upon the inhabitants of the country to take all the necessary steps on their part to put the plan into effect. This recognition by the United Nations of the right of the Jewish people to establish their independent State is unassailable.

It is the natural right of the Jewish people to lead, as do all other nations, an independent existence in its sovereign State.

ACCORDINGLY WE, the members of the National Council, representing the Jewish people in Palestine and the World Zionist Movement, are met together in solemn assembly to-day, the day of termination of the British Mandate for Palestine; and by virtue of the natural and historic right of the Jewish people and of the Resolution of the General Assembly of the United Nations.

WE HEREBY PROCLAIM the establishment of the Jewish State in Palestine, to be called Medinath Yisrael (The State of Israel).

WE HEREBY DECLARE that, as from the termination of the Mandate at midnight, the 14th-15th May, 1948, and pending the setting up of the duly elected bodies of the State in accordance with a Constitution, to be drawn up by the Constituent Assembly not later than the 1st October, 1948, the National Council shall act as the Provisional State Council, and that the National Administration shall constitute the Provisional Government of the Jewish State, which shall be known as Israel.

THE STATE OF ISRAEL will be open to the immigration of Jews from all countries of their dispersion; will promote the development of the country for the benefit of all its inhabitants; will be based on the principles of liberty, justice and peace as conceived by the Prophets of Israel; will uphold the full social and political equality of all its citizens, without distinction of religion, race, or sex; will guarantee freedom of religion, conscience, education and culture; will safeguard the Holy Places of all religions; and will loyally uphold the principles of the United Nations Charter.

THE STATE OF ISRAEL will be ready to co-operate with the organs and representatives of the United Nations in the implementation of the Resolution of the Assembly of November 29, 1947, and will take steps to bring about the Economic Union over the whole of Palestine.

We appeal to the United Nations to assist the Jewish people in the building of its State and to admit Israel into the family of nations.

In the midst of wanton aggression, we yet call upon the Arab inhabitants of the State of Israel to preserve the ways of peace and play their part in the development of the State, on the basis of full and equal citizenship and due representation in all its bodies and institutions—provisional and permanent.

We extend our hand in peace and neighbourliness to all the neighbouring states and their peoples, and invite them to co-operate with the independent Jewish nation for the common good of all. The State of Israel is prepared to make its contribution to the progress of the Middle East as a whole.

Our call goes out to the Jewish people all over the world to rally to our side in the task of immigration and development, and to stand by us in the great struggle for the fulfilment of the dream of generations for the redemption of Israel.

With trust in the Rock of Israel, we set our hand to this Declaration, at this Session of the Provisional State Council, on the soil of the Homeland, in the city of Tel-Aviv, on this Sabbath eve, the fifth of Iyar, 5708, the fourteenth of May, 1948.

Document 27

The Law of Return

The "Law of Return" was passed unanimously by the Knesset on July 5, 1950 and written into the State Legislation.

The Law of Return states:

1. Every Jew has the right to immigrate to the country.
2. (a) Immigration shall be on the basis of immigration visas.
   (b) Immigrant visas shall be issued to any Jew expressing a desire to settle in Israel, except if the Minister of Immigration is satisfied that the applicant:
      (i) acts against the Jewish nation; or
      (ii) may threaten the public health or State security.
3. (a) A Jew who comes to Israel and after his arrival expresses a desire to settle there may, while in Israel, obtain an immigrant certificate.
   (b) The exceptions listed in Article 2 (b) shall apply also with respect to the issue of an immigrant certificate, but a person shall not be regarded as a threat to public health as a result of an illness that he contracts after his arrival in Israel.
4. Every Jew who migrated to the country before this law goes into effect, and every Jew who was born in the country either before or after the law is effective enjoys the same status as any person who migrated on the basis of this law.
5. The Minister of Immigration is delegated to enforce this law and he may enact regulations in connection with its implementation and for the issue of immigrant visas and immigrant certificates.

Document 28

The Manifesto of the United Arab
Republic (Preamble)

The manifesto concerning the principles to govern the new Federal State of the United Arab Republic was published in April 1963. It was prepared in connection with an abortive attempt to establish federal union in the Arab world. Signed by Gamal Abdel Nasser and the presidents of Iraq and Syria, it is of interest mainly in view of the reference to Palestine.

In the name of the Merciful Compassionate God,
In the name of the Almighty God,
The three delegations representing the United Arab Republic, Syria and Iraq met in Cairo and in response to the will of the Arab people in the three regions and the great Arab fatherland, brotherly talks began between the three delegations on Saturday, April 6, and ended on Wednesday, April 17, 1963.

The delegations in all their discussions were inspired by faith that Arab unity was an inevitable aim deriving its principles from the oneness of language bearing culture and thought, common history-making sentiment and conscience, common national struggle deciding and defining destiny, common spiritual values stemming from Divine messages and common social and economic understanding based on liberty and socialism.

The delegations were guided by the will of the masses of the Arab peoples, demanding unity, struggling to attain it and sacrificing in its defence, and realising that the hard core of the union is to be formed by the unification of the parts of the homeland which have acquired their freedom and independence and in which nationalist, progressive governments have emerged with the determination to destroy the alliance of feudalism, capital, reaction and imperialism, and to liberate the working forces of the people in order to join them in alliance and to express their genuine will.

The revolution of July 23 was a historical turning point at which the Arab people in Egypt, discovering their identity and regaining their free will, set out on their quest for freedom, Arabism and union. The revolution of the 14th of Ramadan (February 8) illuminated the true Arab face of Iraq, and the path leading it to the horizons of unity, envisaged by the zealous elements of the July 14 revolution. The revolution of March 8 put Syria back into the line of the union destroyed by the setback of reactionary secession, having destroyed all the obstacles which the reactionaries and imperialism had determinedly put up in the path of union.

The three Revolutions thus met which affirmed again that unity is a revolutionary action deriving its conceptions from the people's faith, its power from their will, and its objectives from their aspirations for freedom and socialism.

Unity is a revolution—a revolution because it is popular, a revolution because it is progressive, and a revolution because it is a powerful tide in the current of civilisation.

Unity is especially a revolution because it is profoundly connected with the Palestine cause and with the national duty to liberate that country. It was the disaster of Palestine that revealed the conspiracy of the reactionary classes and exposed the treacheries of the hired regional parties and their denial of the people's objectives and aspirations. It was the disaster of Palestine that showed the weakness and backwardness of the economic and social systems that prevailed in the country, released the revolutionary energies of our people and awakened the spirit of revolt against imperialism, injustice, poverty and underdevelopment. It was the disaster of Palestine that clearly indicated the path of salvation, the path of unity, freedom and socialism. This was kept in mind by the delegations during their talks. If unity is a sacred objective, it is also the instrument of the popular struggle and its means to achieve its major objectives of freedom and security in liberating all the parts of the Arab homeland and in establishing a society of sufficiency and justice, a society of socialism, in continuing the revolutionary tide without deviation or relapse and its extension to embrace the greater Arab homeland, and in contributing to the progress of human civilisation and consolidation of world peace.

It was unanimously agreed that unity between the three regions would be based, as required by the Arab people, on the principles of democracy and socialism, would be a real and strong unity which would consider the regional circumstances to consolidate the ties of unity on a basis of practical understanding, not ignore the reasons for partitioning and separation, and make the power of each region a power for the Federal State of the Arab Nation, and make the Federal State a power for each of its regions as well as for the whole Arab Nation.

Document 29

The Draft Constitution of the "Palestine Liberation Organisation"

The charter of the Palestine Liberation Organisation (PLO) was prepared under Egyptian auspices following an agreement at the Arab Summit Conference in 1963 by Ahmed Shukairy, a lawyer born in Palestine who represented Saudi Arabia and later Syria in the U.N. and ultimately became President of the PLO. The role of the PLO on the eve of the Arab-Israeli war was later criticized in the Arab capitals and Shukairy forced to resign in December 1967.

1. In accordance with this constitution, an organisation known as "The Palestine Liberation Organisation" shall be formed, and shall launch its responsibilities in accordance with the principles of the National Charter and clauses of this constitution.

2. All the Palestinians are natural members in the Liberation Organisation exercising their duty in the liberation of their homeland in accordance with their abilities and efficiency.

3. The Palestinian people shall form the larger base for this Organisation; and the Organisation, after its creation, shall work closely and constantly with the Palestine people for the sake of their organisation and mobilisation so they may be able to assume their responsibility in the liberation of their country.

4. Until suitable conditions are available for holding free general elections among all the Palestinians and in all the countries in which they reside, the Liberation Organisation shall be set up in accordance with the rules set in this constitution.

5. Measures listed in this constitution shall be taken for the convocation of a Palestinian General Assembly in which shall be represented all Palestinian factions, emigrants and residents, including organisations, societies, unions, trade unions and representatives of (Palestinian) public opinions of various

ideological trends; this assembly shall be called 'The National Assembly of the Palestine Liberation Organisation.'

6. In preparation and facilitation of work of the assembly, the Palestinian representative at the Arab League (i.e., Ahmed Shukairy), shall, after holding consultations with various Palestinian factions, form:

a)—A Preparatory Committee in every Arab country hosting a minimum of 10,000 Palestinians; the mission of each one of these committees is to prepare lists according to which Palestinian candidates in the respective Arab country will be chosen as members of the assembly; these committees shall also prepare studies and proposals which may help the assembly carry out its work; these studies and proposals shall be presented to the Coordination Committee listed below.

b)—A Coordination Committee, with headquarters in Jerusalem; the mission of this committee shall be to issue invitations to the assembly, adopt all necessary measures for the holding of the assembly, and coordinate all proposals and studies as well as lists of candidates to the assembly, as specified in the clause above; also the committee shall prepare a provisional agenda—or as a whole, undertake all that is required for the holding and success of the assembly in the execution of its mission.

7. The National Assembly shall be held once every two years; its venue rotates between Jerusalem and Gaza; the National Assembly shall meet for the first time on May 14, 1964, in the city of Jerusalem.

8. To facilitate its work, the Assembly shall form the following committees:

a)—The Political Committee: shall be in charge of studying the political sides of the Palestine question in the Arab and international fields.

b)—The Charter By-laws and Lists Committee: shall consider the National Charter as well as the various by-laws and lists required by the Organisation in the execution of its duties.

c)—The Financial Committee: shall formulate a complete plan for the National Palestinian Fund required for financing the Organisation.

d)—Information Committee: shall work out a complete scheme for information and offices to be established in various parts of the world.

e)—The Juridical Committee: shall study the various legal aspects of the Palestine question, be it in relation to principles of International Law, U.N. Charter, or international documents pertaining to the Palestine question.

f)—Proposals and Nomination Committee: shall coordinate proposals and nominations submitted to the Assembly.

g)—Awakening Committee: shall study ways and means for the up-bringing of the new generations both ideologically and spiritually so they may serve their country and work for the liberation of their homeland.

h)—The National Organisation Committee: shall lay down general plans pertaining to trade unions, federations, sports organisations and scouts groups; this is in accordance with rules and laws in effect in Arab countries.

9. The National Assembly shall have a Presidency Office composed of the president, two vice presidents, a secretary, and a secretary general; these officers shall be elected by the National Assembly when it meets.

10. These (above-listed eight committees) shall submit their reports and recommendations to the National Assembly which, in turn, shall discuss them and issu• the necessary resolutions.

11. The National Assembly shall have an executive apparatus to be called 'The Executive Committee of the Liberation Organisation' which shall practice all responsibilities of the Liberation Organisation in accordance with the general plans and resolutions issued by the National Assembly.

12. The Executive Committee shall be formed of fifteen members elected by the National Assembly; the Committee shall in its turn elect a President, two Vice Presidents and a Secretary General.

13. The Executive Committee can be called to a meeting in the time and place decided by the President, or by a proposal submitted by five members of the Committee.

14. The President of the Executive Committee shall represent the Palestinians at the Arab League; therefore, his office shall be in Cairo since the Arab League Headquarters is there.

15. The Executive Committee shall establish the following departments:

a)—Department of Political and Information Affairs.

b)—Department of the National Fund.

c)—Department of General Affairs.

Each one of these departments shall have a Director General and the needed number of employees. Duties of each one of these departments shall be defined by special by-laws pre-pared by the Executive Committee.

16. The Executive Committee has the right of calling the National Assembly to meet in a place and time it specifies; it has the right also to call to a meeting any committee of the National Assembly to study certain subjects.

17. The Executive Committee shall have a consultative council to be known as 'The Shura (Consultative) Council'; the Executive Committee shall select the president and members of this council from people of opinion and prestige among the Palestinians; prerogatives of the Consultative Council are in matters proposed to it by the Executive Committee.

18. The Arab states shall avail the sons of Palestine the opportunity of enlisting in their regular armies on the widest scale possible.

19. Private Palestinian contingents shall be formed in accordance with the military needs and plans decided by the Unified Arab Military Command in agreement and cooperation with the concerned Arab states.

20. A Fund, to be known as 'The National Palestinian Fund', shall be established to finance operations of the Executive Committee: the Fund shall have a Board of Directors whose members shall be elected by the National Assembly.

21. Sources of the Fund are to be from:

a)—Fixed taxes levied on Palestinians and collected in accordance with special laws.

b)—Financial assistance offered by the Arab governments and people.

c)—A 'Liberation Stamp' to be issued by the Arab states and be used in postal and other transactions.

d)—Donations on national occasions.

e)—Loans and assistance given by the Arabs or by friendly nations.

22. Committees, to be known as 'Support Palestine Committees', shall be established in Arab and friendly countries to collect donations and to support the Liberation Organisation.

23. The Executive Committee shall have the right to issue by-laws for fulfillment of provisions of this constitution.

24. This draft constitution shall be submitted to the National Assembly for consideration; what is ratified of it cannot be changed except by a two-thirds majority of the National Assembly.

Document 30

United Nations General Assembly
Resolution on the Internationalization
of Jerusalem

This U.N. Resolution (No. 303[IV]) and the following one (Document 31—Resolution 619[VII]) are among those most frequently quoted in the discussions about the Arab-Israeli conflict.

December 9, 1949

The General Assembly,

Having regard to its resolution 181 (II) of 29 November 1947 and 194 (III) of 11 December 1948,

Having studied the reports of the United Nations Conciliation Commission for Palestine set up under the latter resolution,

I. Decides

In relation to Jerusalem,

Believing that the principles underlying its previous resolutions concerning this matter, and in particular its resolution of 29 November 1947, represent a just and equitable settlement of the question,

1. To restate, therefore, its intention that Jerusalem should be placed under a permanent international regime, which should envisage appropriate guarantees for the protection of the Holy Places, both within and outside Jerusalem and to confirm specifically the following provisions of General Assembly resolution 181 (II):

(1) The City of Jerusalem shall be established as a *corpus separatum* under a special international régime and shall be administered by the United Nations; (2) The Trusteeship Council shall be designated to discharge the responsibilities of the Administering Authority . . . ; and (3) The City of Jerusalem shall include the present municipality of Jerusalem plus the surrounding villages and towns, the most eastern of which shall be Abu Dis; the most southern, Bethlehem; the most western, Ein Karim (including also the built-up area of Motsa); and the most northern, Shu'fat, as indicated on the attached sketch-map; (*map not reproduced: Ed.*)

2. To request for this purpose that the Trusteeship Council at its next session, whether special or regular, complete the

preparation of the Statute of Jerusalem, omitting the now inapplicable provisions, such as articles 32 and 39, and, without prejudice to the fundamental principles of the international régime for Jerusalem set forth in General Assembly resolution 181 (II) introducing therein amendments in the direction of its greater democratization, approve the Statute, and proceed immediately with its implementation. The Trusteeship Council shall not allow any actions taken by any interested Government or Governments to divert it from adopting and implementing the Statute of Jerusalem;

II. Calls upon the States concerned, to make formal undertakings, at an early date and in the light of their obligations as Members of the United Nations, that they will approach these matters with good will, and be guided by the terms of the present resolution.

Document 31

U.N. Security Council Resolution Concerning Restrictions on the Passage of Ships through the Suez Canal

September 1, 1951

THE SECURITY COUNCIL

1. *Recalling* that in its resolution of 11 August 1949 (S/1376) relating to the conclusion of Armistice Agreements between Israel and the neighbouring Arab States, it drew attention to the pledges, in these Agreements "against any further acts of hostility between the Parties";

2. *Recalling* further that in its resolution of 17 November 1950 (S/1907) it reminded the States concerned that the Armistice Agreements to which they were parties contemplated "the return of permanent peace in Palestine," and therefore urged them and the other States in the area to take all such steps as would lead to the settlement of the issues between them;

3. *Noting* the report of the Chief of Staff of the Truce Supervision Organization to the Security Council of 12 June 1951 (S/2194);

4. *Further noting* that the Chief of Staff of the Truce Supervision Organization recalled the statement of the senior Egyptian delegate in Rhodes on 13 January 1949, to the effect that his delegation was "inspired with every spirit of co-operation, conciliation and a sincere desire to restore peace

in Palestine," and that the Egyptian Government has not complied with the earnest plea of the Chief of Staff made to the Egyptian delegate on 12 June 1951, that it desist from the present practice of interfering with the passage through the Suez Canal of goods destined for Israel;

5. *Considering* that since the Armistice regime, which has been in existence for nearly two and a half years, is of a permanent character, neither party can reasonably assert that it is actively a belligerent or requires to exercise the right of visit, search, and seizure for any legitimate purpose of self-defence;

6. *Finds* that the maintenance of the practice mentioned in paragraph 4 above is inconsistent with the objectives of a peaceful settlement between the parties and the establishment of a permanent peace in Palestine set forth in the Armistice Agreement;

7. *Finds further* that such practice is an abuse of the exercise of the right of visit, search and seizure;

8. *Further finds* that that practice cannot in the prevailing circumstances be justified on the ground that it is necessary for self-defence;

9. *And further noting* that the restrictions on the passage of goods through the Suez Canal to Israel ports are denying to nations at no time connected with the conflict in Palestine valuable supplies required for their economic reconstruction, and that these restrictions together with sanctions applied by Egypt to certain ships which have visited Israel ports represent unjustified interference with the rights of nations to navigate the seas and to trade freely with one another, including the Arab States and Israel;

10. *Calls upon* Egypt to terminate the restrictions on the passage of international commercial shipping and goods through the Suez Canal wherever bound and to cease all interference with such shipping beyond that essential to the safety of shipping in the Canal itself and to the observance of international conventions in force.

Document 32

President Nasser on Zionism and Israel

The following excerpts are from Nasser's "The Philosophy of the Revolution," and speeches on various occasions between 1960 and 1963. Nasser served as an army officer in the Palestine War of 1948. The liberation of Palestine has been one of the chief planks of his political program, but there have been conflicting statements as to whether there was a definitive plan for the liberation. On several occasions, he announced that his army would soon be ready to enter Palestine on "a carpet of blood," on others that the time was not ripe yet.

As far as I am concerned I remember that the first elements of Arab consciousness began to filter into my mind as a student in secondary schools, wherefrom I went out with my fellow schoolboys on strike on December 2nd of every year as a protest against the Balfour Declaration whereby England gave the Jews a national home usurped unjustly from its legal owners.

When I asked myself at that time why I left my school enthusiastically and why I was angry for this land which I never saw I could not find an answer except the echoes of sentiment. Later a form of comprehension of this subject began when I was a cadet in the Military College studying the Palestine campaigns in particular and the history and conditions of this region in general which rendered it, throughout the last century, an easy prey ravaged by the claws of a pack of hungry beasts.

My comprehension began to be clearer as the foundation of its facts stood out when I began to study, as a student in the Staff College, the Palestine campaign and the problems of the Mediterranean in greater detail.

And when the Palestine crisis loomed on the horizon I was firmly convinced that the fighting in Palestine was not fighting on foreign territory. Nor was it inspired by sentiment. It was a duty imposed by self-defense.

Address by President
Gamal Abdel Nasser in Aleppo
(February 17, 1960)

Yesterday, the elderly Foreign Minister of Israel threatened the U.A.R. and said that Israel would not tolerate the ban on Israeli ships transiting the Suez Canal.

I would like to tell her and her master, Ben Gurion, as well as the Israeli people, that Israeli ships and cargoes will not, under any circumstances, transit the Canal.

Once these cargoes arrive in Port-Said or in any other port in the U.A.R. they become the property of the people of Palestine against whom Zionism and imperialism have conspired.

Eleven years after this tragedy, the people of Palestine have not changed. They, and we, are working for the restoration of their rights in their homeland. The rights of the people of Palestine are Arab rights above all. We feel it is our sacred duty to regain those rights for the people of Palestine.

By this unity which is binding you and the power of Arab unity and Arab nationalism, we can march along the road of freedom and liberation in order to get back the usurped rights of the Palestine Arabs.

Speech by President Gamal Abdel Nasser at a Mass Rally of the Youth Organisations in Damascus (October 18, 1960)

Now for the Palestinian issue. Wherever I have been in this or the Southern Region I hear the strong call for the liberation of this Arab territory of Palestine, and I would like to tell you, Brethren, that all that we are now doing is just a part of the battle for Palestine. Once we are fully emancipated from the shackles of colonialism and the intrigues of colonialist agents, we shall take a further step forward towards the liberation of Palestine.

When we have brought our armed forces to full strength and made our own armaments we will take another step forward towards the liberation of Palestine, and when we have manufactured jet aircraft and tanks we will embark upon the final stage of this liberation.

Address by President Gamal Abdel Nasser on the 11th Anniversary of the Revolution at the Republican Square, Cairo (July 22, 1963)

Work and readiness are the only means to protect the Arab's right in Palestine.

Arab unity is our hope of liberating Palestine and restoring the rights of the people of Palestine.

Arab unity is a sort of preparation, a human and national preparation as well as a preparation with weapons and plans in all fields. It is not enough to deliver speeches declaring that we would liberate Palestine and liberate it just on paper for political consumption. As I said before, we do not have any defined plan for the liberation of Palestine. I mention this because I find it my duty to say it. But we have a plan to be implemented in case of any Israeli aggression against us or against any Arab country.

In this case, we know well what to do. We have to be prepared. We have a plan for this preparation and for the unification of the Arab world which is the only means to protect the Arab land and safeguard Arab Nationalism.

God be with you and may his peace and mercy be upon you.

Speech Delivered by President Gamal Abdel Nasser at Alexandria on the Return of Another Contingent of U.A.R. Troops in Yemen (August 11, 1963)

The Armed Forces are getting ready for the restoration of the rights of the Palestine people because the Palestine battle was a smear on the entire Arab nation. No one can forget the shame brought by the battle of 1948. The rights of the Palestine people must be restored. Therefore, we must get ready to face Israel and Zionism as well as Imperialism which stands behind them.

Document 33

Ahmed Shukairy: The Palestine Refugees

Excerpts from a speech at the United Nations by Shukairy in 1958 when serving as a member of the Saudi Arabian mission.

The Five Principles

Having portrayed the refugees' problem against its lengthy background of United Nations' action, of the Conciliation Commission and the relief Agency, we come to the crucial question. What is next? What is the solution?

In my submission, this is the question which must engage our attention and call for our action; and I shall endeavor to answer the question in a manner devoid of any decoration.

For when the destiny of a whole people is involved, when the fundamental human rights are in question, and lastly when the peace of the world is at stake, there should be no fineness in our approach. The need calls for plain talking characterized with frankness, and sharp frankness indeed.

It is for these reasons that it becomes our duty to answer the question in all the candour under our command. In this spirit, Mr. Chairman, I propose now to deal with three matters: The solution of the problem, the fundamental principles of the solution, and the measures and sanctions to implement the solution.

Beginning with the fundamental principle of the solution, I must reiterate, even to the point of redundance, that these fundamental principles constitute the only basis for the solution to the refugee question. No matter how we view the problem, no solution can offer a chance for a peaceful settlement unless it takes full cognizance of the following five principles:

FIRST: The *de facto* situation created by Israel is entirely unacceptable as a basis for the solution of the Palestine problem in general, or the refugee question in particular. This *de facto* situation is the *fait accompli* of military action that does not vest rights non existing, or divest rights already existing.

SECOND: The rights of the refugees to their homes and homeland are not related to, or in any way dependent upon, the consent or refusal of Israel. These rights are natural, inherent and self-existing. They are not bestowed even by the United Nations, let alone Israel. They cannot be denied even by the United Nations, let alone Israel. They are vested in the refugees; they reside with the refugees. Thus, consent or no consent, these rights are theirs imprescriptible, irresistible and indivisible.

THIRD: Resettlement, reintegration, rehabilitation or any similar projects, no matter what their connotation may be, are not a solution by themselves. They should be planned or implemented not as aims, but merely as a means to meet the legitimate aspirations of the refugees and to the extent of giving effect to their inherent right to their homeland.

FOURTH: The relief program of the refugees is no solution to the problem, neither is it a substitute, no matter for how long it is continued. It is a humanitarian measure having no political implications.

FIFTH: Works projects, and self-support programs are not a solution; nor a solution to avoid the solution. Self-supporting or dependent, a refugee remains a refugee and his status remains an international problem until it is finally and satisfactorily solved.

To recast such a background has become the more necessary after we heard yesterday the statement on behalf of the United States. The Distinguished Representative of the United States, in his outline of the background of the refugee question, has omitted certain truths entirely, related half truths on certain aspects and finally arrived at wrongful conclusions on the substance of the problem.

As to the termination of the mandate of the Agency in favor of a better system as implied in the statement of the United States, we have serious misgivings of paramount nature. I must assure the Distinguished Representative of the United States that no Arab State, and no refugee, to use the words of the Distinguished Representative of the United States, feels it "best to let matters ride as in the past." To the refugees, continuation of relief is a source of great humiliation. To the Arab Governments it is a source of distress. If "some" feel differently, I assure the Distinguished Representative of the United States, it is not the Arabs anyhow. These refugees who are costing you 7 cents a day per head, have properties, revenues, fortunes in their homeland. The minute they lay hand on their properties they will be the first to thank you and plead the discontinuation of relief. It is only then that the U. N. responsibility ends, but not before.

I must, therefore, make it quite clear to the Committee in general and to the Distinguished Representative of the United States in particular, that we shall resist any attempt which directly or indirectly reduces in any degree the right of the refugees to repatriation. At a later stage of the debate, I will show the flaw in the reasoning underlying the position of the United States on the question. I simply wish to say here and now that any measure that might be in the direction of even scratching the right to repatriation or absolving the United Nations from its responsibility will be resisted in the Committee and in the Arab World.

With these five principles in mind, I can turn now to the solution of the problem. Here I would say that we need not look for a solution. The solution is there. It is repatriation and nothing but repatriation. It is the only solution that does not dishonour, but certainly does honour the Charter. It is the only solution that does not defeat, but rather does endorse the resolution of the United Nations. It is the only solution that does not defame the bill of human rights, but surely gives it a worthy fame. Lastly, it is the only solution that constitutes an investment of peace, and an asset of confidence in this organization.

After all, repatriation is one of those principles that cannot be questioned by the United Nations. It does not stand by our acceptance, nor does it lapse by our non-acceptance. To borrow a legal term, repatriation is a right *In Rem,* that can be exercised against the whole world, if need be. It springs from the right to a homeland, which is not subject to waiver, surrender, or compensation. Compensation is one remedy open for individual property rights, but a homeland does not submit to compensation even for the most precious possessions of this planet, and indeed the whole universe with all its fabulous riches. This is no exaggeration, unless I exaggerate your feelings towards your respective homelands.

Document 34

Erskine Childers: The Other Exodus*

Erskine Childers, an Irish journalist has published articles bitterly critical of Israeli policies. The present article was originally published in the London weekly *The Spectator* (May 12, 1961) and provoked a great deal of controversy. Childers, the grandson of a well known Irish patriot and writer, also worked for the British Broadcasting Corporation and subsequently became a leading official in Irish television.

The Palestine Arab refugees wait, and multiply, and are debated at the United Nations. In thirteen years, their numbers have increased from 650,000 to 1,145,000. Most of them survive only on rations from the U.N. agency, UNRWA. Their subsistence has already cost L.S. 110,000,000. Each year, UNRWA has to plead at New York for the funds to carry on, against widespread and especially Western lack of sympathy. There is one reason for this impatience: the attitude created towards these refugees by Israeli argument. For over ten years, Israeli spokesmen have claimed that:

> Unless we understand how this problem was caused we cannot rightly judge how it should be solved. . . . The re-

* Reprinted by permission of *The Spectator* Limited.

sponsibility of the Arab Governments is threefold. Theirs is the initiative for its creation. Theirs is the onus for its endurance. Above all—theirs is the capacity for its solution.

(Abba Eban to the U.N. 1957).

In this inquiry, I propose only briefly to examine the last two of these three claims. The last, about a "solution," is that if the Arab host governments were willing, they could resettle the refugees quite easily outside Palestine—where, as Israel claims and as President Kennedy's 1960 election platform also had it, "there is room and opportunity for them." This is not even remotely true. UNRWA's new chief, Dr. John Davis, has now bluntly and bravely warned against "facile assumptions that it rests with the host governments to solve the problem . . . the simple truth is that the jobs . . . do not exist today within the host countries." Nor can the jobs be created, Dr. Davis reports, because most of the refugees are unskilled peasants—precisely the host countries' worst problem among their own rapidly expanding populations.

These Arabs, in short, are displaced persons in the fullest, most tragic meaning of the term—an economic truth cruelly different from the myth. But there is also the political myth, and it too has been soothing our highly pragmatic Western conscience for thirteen years. This is the Israeli charge, solemnly made every year and then reproduced around the world, that these refugees are—to quote a character in Leon Uris's *Exodus*—"kept caged like animals in suffering as a deliberate political weapon."

This, again, Dr. Davis has now bravely called a "misconception." The reality here is that the refugees themselves fanatically oppose any resettlement outside Palestine. UNRWA even had to persuade them that concrete huts, even in the U.N. camps, replacing their squalid tents and hovels, would not be the thin end of a resettlement wedge. Unlike other refugees, these refuse to move; they insist on going home.

Why? The answer, I believe, lies in the third of the three issues Israel argues—in the cause itself of the mass exodus. The very fact that cause is argued by both sides is significant. Israel claims that the Arabs left because they were ordered to, and deliberately incited into panic, by their own leaders who wanted the field cleared for the 1948 war. It is also argued that there would today be no Arab refugees if the Arab States had not attacked the new Jewish State on May 15, 1948 (though 800,000 had already fled before that date).

The Arabs charge that their people were evicted at bayonet-point and by panic deliberately incited by the Zionists.

Examining every official Israeli statement about the Arab exodus, I was struck by the fact that no primary evidence of evacuation orders was ever produced. The charge, Israel claimed, was "documented"; but where were the documents? There had allegedly been Arab radio broadcasts ordering the evacuation; but no dates, names of stations, or texts of messages were ever cited. In Israel in 1958, as a guest of the Foreign Office and therefore doubly hopeful of serious assistance, I asked to be shown the proofs, I was assured they existed, and was promised them. None had been offered when I left, but I was again assured. I asked to have the material sent on to me. I am still waiting.

While in Israel, however, I met Dr. Leo Kohn, professor of political science at Hebrew University and an ambassador-rank adviser to the Israeli Foreign Office. He had written one of the first official pamphlets on the Arab refugees. I asked him for concrete evidence of the Arab evacuation orders. Agitatedly, Dr. Kohn replied: "Evidence? Evidence? What more could you want than this?" and he took up his own pamphlet. "Look at this 'Economist' report," and he pointed to a quotation. "You will surely not suggest that the 'Economist' is a Zionist journal?"

The quotation is one of about five that appear in every Israeli speech and pamphlet, and are in turn used by every sympathetic analysis. It seemed very impressive: it referred to the exodus from Haifa, and to an Arab broadcast order as one major reason for that exodus.

I decided to turn up the relevant (October 2) 1948 issue of the 'Economist.' The passage that has literally gone around the world was certainly there, but I had already noticed one curious word in it. This was a description of the massacre at Deir Yassin as an "incident." No impartial observer of Palestine in 1948 calls what happened at this avowedly non-belligerent, unarmed Arab village in April, 1948, an "incident"—any more than Lidice is called an "incident." Over 250 old men, women and children were deliberately butchered, stripped and mutilated or thrown into a well, by men of the Zionist Irgun Zvai Leumi.

Seen in its place in the full 'Economist' article, it was at once clear that Dr. Kohn's quotation was a second-hand account, inserted as that of an eye-witness at Haifa, by the journal's own correspondent who had not been in that city at the time. And in the rest of the same article, written by the Economist correspondent himself, but never quoted by Israel, the second great wave of refugees were described as "all destitute, as the Jewish troops gave them an hour in which to quit, but simultaneously requisitioned all transport."

It was now essential to check all other, even secondary, Israeli "evidence." Another stock quotation down the years has been that, supposedly, of the Greek-Catholic Archbishop of Galilee. For example, Israel's Abba Eban told the U.N. Special Political Committee in 1957 that the Archbishop had "fully confirmed" that the Arabs were urged to flee by their own leaders.

I wrote to His Grace, asking for his evidence of such orders. I hold signed letters from him, with permission to publish, in which he has categorically denied ever alleging Arab evacuation orders; he states that no such orders were ever given. He says that his name has been abused for years; and that the Arabs fled through panic and forcible eviction by Jewish troops.

As none of the other stock quotations in Israeli propaganda are worth comment, I next decided to test the undocumented charge that the Arab evacuation orders were broadcast by Arab radio—which could be done thoroughly because the BBC monitored all Middle Eastern broadcasts throughout 1948. The records, and companion ones by a U.S. monitoring unit, can be seen at the British Museum.

There was not a single order, or appeal, or suggestion about evacuation from Palestine from any Arab radio station, inside or outside Palestine, in 1948. There is repeated monitored record of Arab appeals, even flat orders, to the civilians of Palestine to stay put. To select only two examples: on April 4, as the first great wave of flight began, Damascus Radio broadcast an appeal to everyone to stay at their homes and jobs. On April 24, with the exodus now a flood, Palestine Arab leaders warned that:

> Certain elements and Jewish agents are spreading defeatist news to creats chaos and panic among the peaceful population. Some cowards are deserting their houses, villages or cities. . . . Zionist agents and corrupt cowards will be severely punished (Al-Inqaz, the Arab Liberation Radio, at 12.00 hours).

Even Jewish broadcasts (in Hebrew) mentioned such Arab appeals to stay put. Zionist newspapers in Palestine reported the same: none so much as hinted at any Arab evacuation orders.

The fact is that Israel's official charges, which have vitally influenced the last ten years of Western thought about the refugees, are demonstrably and totally hollow. And from this alone, suspicion is justified. Why make such charges at all? On the face of it, this mass exodus might have been entirely the result of "normal" panic and wartime dislocation.

We need not even touch upon Arab evidence that panic was quite deliberately incited. The evidence is there, on the Zionist record. For example, on March 27, four days before the big offensive against Arab centres by the official Zionist (Haganah) forces, the Irgun's radio unit broadcast in Arabic. Irgun, a terrorist organisation like the Stern Gang, was officially disowned by Ben Gurion and the Haganah. Yet just four days before the Haganah offensive Irgun warned "Arabs in urban agglomerations" that typhus, cholera and similar diseases would break out "heavily" among them "in April and May."

The effect may be imagined. Two weeks later, it was this same Irgun, apparently so solicitous of Arab welfare, that butchered the people of Deir Yassin. Irgun then called a press conference to announce the deed; paraded other captured Arabs through Jewish quarters of Jerusalem to be spat upon; then released them to tell their kin of the experience. Arthur Koestler called the "bloodbath" of Deir Yassin "the psychologically decisive factor in this spectacular exodus." But this was only Irgun, it may be said. Is there evidence that official Zionist forces—the Haganah under Ben Gurion and the Jewish Agency—were inciting panic? An Israeli Government pamphlet of 1958 states that "the Jews tried, by every means open to them, to stop the Arab evacuation" (this same 1958 pamphlet has diluted Deir Yassin to "the one and only instance of Jewish high-handed (sic) action in this war").

There is one recorded instance of such an appeal. It is beyond dispute even by Arabs, that in Haifa the late gentle Mayor, Shabeitai Levi, with the tears streaming down his face, implored the city's Arabs to stay. But elsewhere in Haifa, Arthur Koestler wrote in his book that Haganah loudspeaker vans and the Haganah radio promised that city's Arabs escort to "Arab territory," and "hinted at terrible consequences if their warning were disregarded." There are many witnesses of this loudspeaker method elsewhere. In Jerusalem the Arabic warning from the vans was, "The road to Jericho is open!

Fly from Jerusalem before you are all killed!" (Meyer Levin in *Jerusalem Embattled*). Bertha Vester, a Christian missionary, reported that another theme was, "Unless you leave your homes, the fate of Deir Yassin will be your fate." The Haganah radio station also broadcast, in Arabic, repeated news of Arabs fleeing "in terror and fear" from named places.

Still, however, we have plumbed this exodus only so far as panic is concerned. There are U.N. and Economist reports of forcible expulsion, which is something else. How much evidence is there for this? And were only the "unofficial" Irgun and Stern forces responsible? This is what Nathan Chofshi, one of the original Jewish pioneers in Palestine, wrote in an ashamed rebuttal of an American Zionist rabbi's charges of evacuation orders:

> If Rabbi Kaplan really wanted to know what happened, we old Jewish settlers in Palestine who witnessed the fight could tell him how and in what manner we, Jews, forced the Arabs to leave cities and villages . . . some of them were driven out by force of arms; others were made to leave by deceit, lying and false promises. It is enough to cite the cities of Jaffa, Lydda, Ramleh, Beersheba, Acre from among numberless others. (in 'Jewish Newsletter,' New York, February 9, 1959).

Were official Zionist troops involved at any of these places? I propose to select, for the sake of brevity, only the Lydda-Ramleh area. It was about the exodus from this area, among others, that the Economist reported. "Jewish troops gave them an hour to quit."

In their latest book, which has been publicly endorsed by Ben Gurion, Jon Kimche and his brother devoted considerable detail to the Zionist offensive against Lydda and Ramleh. It was undertaken by official Israeli forces under Yigael Alon. And the immediately responsible officer was Moshe Dayan, commander of the 1956 Sinai attack, now a Cabinet Minister. Kimche has described how, on July 11, 1948, Dayan with his columns:

> . . . drove at full speed into Lydda, shooting up the town and creating confusion and a degree of terror among the population . . . its Arab population of 30,000 either fled or were herded on the road to Ramallah. The next day Ramleh also surrendered and its Arab population suffered the same fate. Both towns were sacked by the victorious Israelis.

Ramallah, on the road to which these particular Arabs—numbering over 60,000 from this one area alone—were

herded, was up in the Judean hills, outside Zionist-held territory. The "road to Jericho," which Arabs in Jerusalem were
warned to take, brought them into the Jordan Valley. Some
85,000 are still there in one U.N. camp alone, under the
Mount of Temptation. The Arab population of Acre, mentioned by Chofshi, exceeded 45,000: Acre was attacked by
official Zionist troops.

From this analysis of only some of the sources of the Arab
exodus, then, it is clear beyond all doubt that official Zionist
forces were responsible for expulsion of thousands upon
thousands of Arabs, and for deliberate incitement to panic.
Seen from the viewpoint of the Arab refugees themselves,
little more would need to be said. And needless to say, even
those Arabs expelled or who fled through "unofficially" incited panic can hardly be asked to look differently on the
Israeli Government today. It pays former Irgunists and Stern-
ists the same war pensions as former Haganah troops; its
denial of expulsion is total.

But is it conceivable that Ben Gurion and his colleagues
could have deliberately contemplated an "emptying" of Palestine? That a motive existed is beyond doubt. The U.N. partition scheme had in no way solved the "Arab problem" that
a Jewish State would face. It would have given Zionism what
its leaders publicly called the "irreducible minimum" of
territory in a Palestine they claimed should entirely belong
to them. And we know that the official Zionist movement had
in fact no intention of accepting the U.N. territorial award.
Six weeks before the British Mandate ended, before the Israeli
State was proclaimed, and before the Arab States sent in their
armies, an all-out Zionist military offensive was launched.
Later, Ben Gurion publicly said of this offensive:

> As fighting spread, the (Arab) exodus was joined by
> Bedouin and fellahin (peasants), but not the remotest Jewish
> homestead was abandoned and nothing a tottering (British)
> administration could unkindly do stopped us from reaching
> our goal on May 14, 1948, in a State made larger and Jewish
> by the Haganah (cf. Rebirth and Destiny of Israel).

The Jewish State envisaged by the U.N. would have contained a 45 per cent Arab population: the extra territory
attacked by the Zionists before May 14 would have increased
that ratio—for example, by more than 80,000 Arabs in Jaffa
alone. But it was not just a question of numbers. The Arabs
owned and occupied far too much of the territory's productive

and social facilities to enable anything like the mass Jewish immigration of which Zionists dreamed.

What this meant in terms of motive can be seen in the statistics that followed the Arab exodus. More than 80 per cent, of the entire land area of Israel is land abandoned by the Arab refugees. Nearly a quarter of all the standing buildings in Israel had been occupied by those Arabs. Ten thousand shops, stores and other firms inside new Israel had been Arab. Half of all the citrus fruit holdings in the new State had belonged to the Arabs now made refugees. By 1954, more than one-third of the entire Jewish population of Israel was living on "absentee property"—most of it now "absorbed" into the Israeli economy, and unilaterally sequestered by Israeli legislation against a "global" compensation offer.

It is, then, little wonder that old Chaim Weizmann, Israel's first President, described the Arab exodus as a "miraculous simplification of Israel's tasks." But was it "miraculous"? Unexpected? In no way part of combined military and economic planning of nascent Israel's leaders?

We come to perhaps the most grave evidence of all. The mass exodus began in April, 1948. By June, the U.N. Mediator was fully seized of it. He formally demanded a statement of policy from the new Israeli Government about the refugees. At first, he could get no satisfaction. Then, in an official letter dated: August 1, 1948, Israeli's Foreign Minister replied.

It was only four months since the first waves of flight; only eleven weeks since Israel had been proclaimed, ostensibly calling on the Arabs to "play their part in the development of the State." And it was at this time that a Government since claiming that this whole exodus was unexpected and despite its implorings, formally denied the refugees the right of return. Israel did not merely plead "security," but told the United Nations:

> On the economic side, the reintegration of the returning Arabs into normal life, and even their mere sustenance, would present an insuperable problem. The difficulties of accommodation, employment, and ordinary livelihood would be insuperable.

The case rests. This is not the place to discuss a "solution," and no summary conclusion is needed, save perhaps to recall the words of an official Israeli spokesman, though in rather different import:

Unless we understand how this problem was caused, we cannot rightly judge how it should be solved.

The Arabs of Palestine now enter their fourteenth year of exile. If you go among them in the hills of Judea, they will take you by the arm to a crest of land and point downwards, across the rusty skeins of barbed wire. "Can you see it—over there beside those trees? That is my home."

It is shaming beyond all brief descriptions to move among these million people, as a Westerner. It is shaming for many Jews, and some speak out as Nathan Chofshi has bravely done:

> We came and turned the native Arabs into tragic refugees. And still we dare to slander and malign them, to besmirch their name. Instead of being deeply ashamed of what we did and trying to undo some of the evil we committed . . . we justify our terrible acts and even attempt to glorify them.

Document 35

Abba Eban: The Refugee Problem

Excerpts from a speech (Nov. 17, 1958) by the Chief Israeli representative to the United Nations who subsequently became Foreign Minister of Israel.

How Was the Refugee Problem Caused?

AGGRESSION BY ARAB STATES CREATED REFUGEE PROBLEM

The Arab refugee problem was caused by a war of aggression, launched by the Arab States against Israel in 1947 and 1948. Let there be no mistake. If there had been no war against Israel, with its consequent harvest of bloodshed, misery, panic and flight, there would be no problem of Arab refugees today. Once you determine the responsibility for that war, you have determined the responsibility for the refugee problem. Nothing in the history of our generation is clearer or less controversial than the initiative of Arab governments for the conflict out of which the refugee tragedy emerged. The historic origins of that conflict are clearly defined by the confessions of Arab governments themselves:

"This will be a war of extermination," declared the Secretary General of the Arab League speaking for the governments of six Arab States; "It will be a momentous massacre to be spoken of like the Mongolian massacre and the Crusades."

Palestine Arabs Urged to Flee by Arab Leaders

The assault began on the last day of November 1947. From then until the expiration of the British Mandate in May 1948 the Arab States, in concert with Palestine Arab leaders, plunged the land into turmoil and chaos. On the day of Israel's Declaration of Independence, on May 14, 1948, the armed forces of Egypt, Jordan, Syria, Lebanon and Iraq, supported by contingents from Saudi Arabia and the Yemen, crossed their frontiers and marched against Israel. The perils which then confronted our community; the danger which darkened every life and home; the successful repulse of the assault and the emergence of Israel into the life of the world community are all chapters of past history, gone but not forgotten. But the traces of that conflict still remain deeply inscribed upon our region's life. Caught up in the havoc and tension of war; demoralized by the flight of their leaders; urged on by irresponsible promises that they would return to inherit the spoils of Israel's destruction—hundreds of thousands of Arabs sought the shelter of Arab lands. A survey by an international body in 1957 described these violent events in the following terms:

"As early as the first months of 1948 the Arab League issued orders exhorting the people to seek a temporary refuge in neighboring countries, later to return to their abodes in the wake of the victorious Arab armies and obtain their share of abandoned Jewish property" (Research Group for European Migration Problems Bulletin, Vol. V—No. 1, 1957, p. 10).

Contemporary statements by Arab leaders fully confirm this version. On 16 August 1948 Msgr. George Hakim, the Greek Catholic Archbishop of Galilee, recalled:

"The refugees had been confident that their absence from Palestine would not last long; that they would return within a few days—within a week or two; their leaders had promised them that the Arab armies would crush the 'Zionist gangs' very quickly and that there would be no need for panic or fear of a long exile."

A month later on September 15, 1948, Mr. Emile Ghoury who had been the Secretary of the Arab Higher Committee at the time of the Arab invasion of Israel declared:

> "I do not want to impugn anyone but only to help the refugees. The fact that there are these refugees is the direct consequence of the action of the Arab States in opposing partition and the Jewish State. The Arab States agreed upon this policy unanimously and they must share in the solution of the problem."

MISERY IS RESULT OF UNLAWFUL RESORT TO FORCE BY ARABS

No less compelling than these avowals by Arab leaders are the judgments of United Nations organs. In April 1948, when the flight of the refugees was in full swing, the United Nations Palestine Commission inscribed its verdict on the tablets of history:

> "Arab opposition to the plan of the Assembly of 29 November 1947 has taken the form of organized efforts by strong Arab elements, both inside and outside Palestine, to prevent its implementation and to thwart its objectives by threats and acts of violence, including repeated armed incursions into Palestine territory. The Commission has had to report to the Security Council that powerful Arab interests, both inside and outside Palestine, are defying the resolution of the General Assembly and are engaged in a deliberate effort to alter by force the settlement envisaged therein."

This is a description of the events between November 1947 and May 1948 when the Arab exodus began. Months later, when the tide of battle rolled away, its consequences of bereavement, devastation and panic were left behind. At the General Assembly meetings in 1948 the United Nations Acting Mediator recorded a grave international judgment:

> "The Arab States had forcibly opposed the existence of the Jewish State in Palestine in direct opposition to the wishes of two-thirds of the members of the Assembly. Nevertheless their armed intervention proved useless. The (Mediator's) report was based solely on the fact that the Arab States had no right to resort to force and that the United Nations should exert its authority to prevent such a use of force."

The significance of the Arab assault upon Israel by five neighboring States had been reflected in a letter addressed by the Secretary General of the United Nations to representatives of the permanent members of the Security Council on 16 May 1948:—

"The Egyptian Government," wrote the Secretary-General, "has declared in a cablegram to the President of the Security Council on 15 May that Egyptian armed forces have entered Palestine and it has engaged in 'armed intervention' in that country. On 16 May I received a cablegram from the Arab League making similar statements on behalf of the Arab States. I consider it my duty to emphasize to you that *this is the first time since the adoption of the Charter that Member States have openly declared that they have engaged in armed intervention outside their own territory.*"

ARAB GOVERNMENTS MUST ACCEPT RESPONSIBILITY

These are only a few of the documents which set out the responsibility of the Arab Governments for the warfare of which the refugees are the main surviving victims. Even after a full decade it is difficult to sit here with equanimity and listen to Arab representatives disengaging themselves from any responsibility for the travail and anguish which they caused. I recall this history not for the purpose of recrimination, but because of its direct bearing on the Committee's discussion. Should not the representatives of Arab States, as the authors of this tragedy, come here in a mood of humility and repentance rather than in shrill and negative indignation? Since these governments have, by acts of policy, created this tragic problem, *does it not follow that the world community has an unimpeachable right to claim their full assistance in its solution?* How can governments create a vast humanitarian problem by their action—then wash their hands of all responsibility for its alleviation? The claim of the world community on the cooperation of Arab governments is all the more compelling when we reflect that these States, in their vast lands, command all the resources and conditions which would enable them to liberate the refugees from their plight, in full dignity and freedom.

With this history in mind the Committee should not find it difficult to reject the assertion that the guilt for the refugee problem lies with the United Nations itself. The refugee problem was not created by the General Assembly's recommendation for the establishment of Israel. It was created by the attempts of Arab governments to destroy that recommendation by force. The crisis arose not as Arab spokesmen have said because the United Nations adopted a resolution eleven years ago; it arose because Arab governments attacked that resolution by force. If the United Nations proposal had been peacefully accepted, there would be no refugee problem today hanging as a cloud upon the tense horizons of the Middle East.

The next question is—why has the problem endured?

Why Does the Refugee Problem Endure?

REFUGEE PROBLEM CANNOT BE SOLVED BY REPATRIATION

In his statement to the Committee on November 10, 1958, the representative of the United States said:

> "In our view it is not good enough consciously to perpetuate for over a decade the dependent status of nearly a million refugees."

Other speakers in this debate have echoed a similar sense of frustration.

Apart from the question of its origin, the perpetuation of this refugee problem is an unnatural event, running against the whole course of experience and precedent. Since the end of the Second World War, problems affecting forty million refugees have confronted Governments in various parts of the world. In no case, except that of the Arab refugees, amounting to less than two percent of the whole, has the international community shown constant responsibility and provided lavish aid. In every other case a solution has been found by the integration of refugees into their host countries. Nine million Koreans; 900,000 refugees from the conflict in Viet Nam; 8½ million Hindus and Sikhs leaving Pakistan for India; 6½ million Moslems fleeing India to Pakistan; 700,000 Chinese refugees in Hong Kong; 13 million Germans from the Sudetenland, Poland and other East European States reaching West and East Germany; thousands of Turkish refugees from Bulgaria; 440,000 Finns separated from their homeland by a change of frontier; 450,000 refugees from Arab lands arrived destitute in Israel; and an equal number converging on Israel from the remnants of the Jewish holocaust in Europe—these form the tragic procession of the world's refugee population in the past two decades. *In every case but that of the Arab refugees now in Arab lands the countries in which the refugees sought shelter have facilitated their integration.* In this case alone has integration been obstructed.

The paradox is the more astonishing when we reflect that the kinship of language, religion, social background and national sentiment existing between the Arab refugees and their Arab host countries has been at least as intimate as those existing between any other host countries and any other refugee groups. It is impossible to escape the conclusion that the integration of Arab refugees into the life of the Arab world is an objectively feasible process which has been resisted for political reasons.

In a learned study on refugee problems published by the Carnegie Endowment for International Peace in November 1957 under the title "Century of the Homeless Man" Dr. Elfan Rees, Advisor on Refugees to the World Council of Churches, sums up the international experience in the following terms:

> "No large scale refugee problem has ever been solved by repatriation, and there are certainly no grounds for believing that this particular problem can be so solved. Nothing can bring it about except wars which in our time would leave nothing to go back to. War has never solved a refugee problem and it is not in the books that a modern war would."

ARAB LEADERS BLOCK SOLUTION FOR POLITICAL REASONS

Those words should be compared with Mr. Shukairy's peroration, in which he seems to look forward to a settlement of the refugee problem by a war launched for the extinction of Israel's independence. Such a war, whose result would not be that envisaged by Mr. Shukairy, would be more likely to create new refugee problems than to solve the existing ones.

Dr. Rees' Report continues:

> "This then is not a case of a refugee rejecting a particular solution but of the international community having to reject it as dangerous and impossible. It is time this was done with more frankness and force than has been used hitherto. Until it is—real danger remains, and these refugee problems will be unnecessarily perpetuated by the rejection of other and viable solutions."

The Carnegie Endowment publication concludes:

> "The facts we must face force us to the conclusion that for most of the world refugees the only solution is integration where they are."

Another important study on refugee problems carried out last year has been published by the Research Group for European Migration. This study reaches the following grave conclusion:

"The official attitude of the (Arab) host countries is well known. It is one of seeking to prevent any sort of adaptation and integration because the refugees are seen as a political means of pressure to get Israel wiped off the map or to get the greatest possible number of concessions."

It is painfully evident that this refugee problem has been artificially maintained for political motives against all the economic, social and cultural forces which, had they been allowed free play, would have brought about a solution.

Recent years have witnessed a great expansion of economic potentialities in the Middle East. The revenues of the oil bearing countries have opened up great opportunities of work and development, into which the refugees by virtue of their linguistic and national background could fit without any sense of dislocation. The expansion in the areas of Arab sovereignty has also created opportunities of employment which did not exist in the days of colonial tutelage. There cannot be any doubt that if free movement had been granted to the refugees there would have been a spontaneous absorption of thousands of them into these expanded Arab economies. It is precisely this that Arab Governments have obstructed. In his report to the Eighth session of the General Assembly the Director of UNRWA describes Arab policies on free movement in a highly significant passage:

"The full benefit of the spread of this large capital investment (in Arab countries) will be felt only if restrictions on the movement of refugees are withdrawn. This is a measure which was proposed in the original three-year plan but little has been done so far to give effect to it. Such freedom of movement would enable refugees to take full advantage of the opportunities for work arising in countries such as Iraq, Saudi Arabia and the Persian Gulf Sheikhdoms where economic development has already taken place."

There has, of course, been some movement of refugees into the new labor opportunities of the region. The force of economic attraction has sometimes prevailed. But these potentialities can only be fully realized if political resistance to integration is overcome. There are broad opportunities in the Arab world for refugees to build new lives; but the governments concerned have so far sought to debar refugees from using them. In the survey published by the Carnegie Endowment the obstructive record of Arab governments is set out in graphic words:

"The history of UNRWA has been a clinical study in frustration. No Agency has been better led or more devoutly served but the organized intransigence of the refugees and the calculated indifference of the Arab States concerned have brought all its plans to nought. By chicanery it is feeding the dead, by political pressure it is feeding non-refugees, its relief supplies have been subjected in some instances to import duty, its personnel policies are grossly interfered with and its 'constructive measures,' necessarily requiring the concurrence of governments, have been pigeon-holed. The net result is that relief is being provided in 1957 to refugees who could have been rehabilitated in 1951 with 'home and jobs,' without prejudice to their just claims."

In a survey on "Social Forces in the Middle East 1956," Dr. Channing B. Richardson of Hamilton University writes:

"Towards UNRWA the attitudes of the Arab Governments vary between suspicion and obstruction. It cannot be denied that the outside observer gains the impression that the Arab governments have no great desire to solve the refugee problem."

In June, 1957 the Chairman of the Near Eastern Sub-Committee of the United States Senate Foreign Relations Committee reported at the end of an illuminating survey:

"The fact is that the Arab States have for ten years used the Palestine refugees as political hostages in their struggle with Israel. While Arab delegates in the United Nations have condemned the plight of their brothers in the refugee camps nothing has been done to assist them in a practical way lest political leverage against Israel be lost."

450,000 JEWISH REFUGEES FROM ARAB LANDS ABSORBED BY ISRAEL

The failure or refusal of Arab governments to achieve a permanent economic integration of refugees in their huge lands appears all the more remarkable when we contrast it with the achievements of other countries when confronted by the challenge and opportunity of absorbing their kinsmen into their midst. Israel with her small territory, her meager water resources and her hardpressed finances, has found homes, work and citizenship in the past ten years for nearly a million newcomers arriving in destitution no less acute than those of Arab refugees. These refugees from Arab lands left their homes, property and jobs behind. Their standards of physique and nutrition were in many cases pathetically low. They have had to undergo processes of adaptation to a social, linguistic and national ethos far removed from any that they had known before. Thus, integration in this case has been far more arduous than it would be for Arab refugees in Arab lands, where no such differences exist between the society and culture of the host country and those with which the refugees are already familiar. If Israel in these conditions could assimilate nearly one million refugees—450,000 of them from Arab lands—how much more easily could the vast Arab world find a home for a similar number of Arab refugees if only the same impulse of kinship asserted itself.

This is concisely described in the report published by the Carnegie Endowment:

"There is another aspect of the Middle East refugee problem that is also frequently ignored. It is necessary to remember that concurrently with the perpetuation of the Arab refugee problem more than 400,000 Jews have been forced to leave their homes in Iraq, the Yemen, and North Africa. They have not been counted as refugees because they were readily and immediately received as new immigrants into Israel. Nevertheless they were forced to leave their traditional homes against their will and to abandon, in the process, all that they possessed. The latest addition to their number are the 20,000 Jews for whom life has become impossible in Egypt. Fifteen thousand of them have sought asylum in Israel while the remainder are in Europe seeking other solutions to their problem."

Nor is this an isolated example of what can be achieved by Governments in circumstances much less favorable than those which the Arab States command. Less than two weeks ago the representative of Finland, in the Third Committee of this Assembly, gave the following moving account of what a small country can achieve in refugee integration:

"In 1944 the 3,300,000 people who lived within the present boundaries of Finland had to receive in a couple of weeks' time around 440,000 displaced persons, all Finnish citizens who had left their homesteads after the new frontier line had cut off some 13 percent of our territory from the rest of Finland. . . .

> As in 1944 practically no emigration of the displaced persons was possible and none of them could be sent back to their earlier home region, complete integration was the only solution. It was an extremely heavy economic burden taking into consideration that there was no international aid, that the reparation of war destruction and the payment of war indemnities all came simultaneously and that the displaced persons came practically empty handed."

I will not ask the Committee to consider the other numerous precedents. Enough has been said to prove the crucial point that there is no objective difficulty in solving such problems provided the will for a solution exists.

Indeed, compared with other problems, the Arab refugee problem is one of the easiest to solve.

REFUGEES CLOSELY AKIN TO ARABS IN HOST COUNTRIES

The Research Group for European Migration points out in its report (pps. 25-26) that

> "The Palestine refugees have the closest possible affinities of national sentiment, language, religion and social organization with the Arab host countries and the standard of living of the majority of the refugee population is little different from those of the inhabitants of the countries that have given them refuge or will do so in the future."

The same point is made in the report of a Special Study Commission to the Near East and Africa despatched by the Committee on Foreign Affairs of the United States House of Representatives, the source of a great proportion of U.N. relief funds:

> "Unlike refugees in other parts of the world the Palestine refugees are no different in language and social organization from the other Arabs. Resettlement therefore would be in familiar environment. If the local governments are unwilling to tackle the problem except on their own terms there is little incentive for outside governments to continue financial support. Original humanitarian impulse which led to the creation and perpetuation of UNRWA is gradually being perverted into a political weapon." (May 19, 1958).

REGIONAL ECONOMIC DEVELOPMENT BLOCKED BY ARAB GOVERNMENTS

Most of the recent literature describes Arab resistance to integration by two methods—political opposition to integration; and careful scrutiny of UNRWA's activities to ensure that they do not develop into permanent solutions. The policy of obstruction however also has a third heading. I refer to the rejection of economic development proposals which seemed to hold the promise of a refugee solution. The thinking behind these plans was simple but imaginative. The international community was willing to create special opportunities of livelihood by irrigating new areas of land, establishing new farms or, in some cases, new village communities with industrial as well as agricultural activity. Refugees were to be placed into these newly created labor opportunities. The result would be a reduction of the number of refugees receiving relief and progress towards lightening the international burden.

None of these schemes has won Arab acceptance. Many of them have been rejected precisely because their implementation would help solve the refugee problem. A typical and spectacular instance is to be found in the long negotiations conducted between 1953 and 1956 on a project for the coordinated use of the Jordan and Yarmuk Rivers. Israel was prepared, despite certain disavowal—indeed is still prepared— to cooperate in this plan. Ambassador Eric Johnston has summed up his experience in the following words:

"Between 1953 and 1956, at the request of President Eisenhower, I undertook to negotiate with these States a comprehensive Jordan Valley development plan that would have provided for the irrigation of some 225,000 acres. . . . After two years of discussion, technical experts of Israel, Jordan, Lebanon and Syria agreed upon every important detail of a unified Jordan plan. But in October 1956 it was rejected for political reasons at a meeting of the Arab League. . . . Three years have passed and no agreement has yet been reached on developing the Jordan. Every year a billion cubic meters of precious water still roll down the ancient stream, wasted, to the Dead Sea."

ARAB GOVERMENTS PREFER REFUGEE STATUS QUO

In the light of these experiences it cannot be doubted that Arab Governments have been determined that the refugees shall remain refugees; and that the aim of wrecking any alternative to "repatriation" has been pursued by these governments with an ingenuity worthy of a better cause. With an international agency working for integration; with millions of dollars expended every year to move refugees away from a life of dependence, the Arab governments have brought us to a point where there are more refugees on United Nations rolls than ever before.

How to Solve the Arab Refugee Problem

RESETTLEMENT AMONG HOST COUNTRIES THE ONLY SOLUTION

Any discussion of this problem revolves around the two themes of resettlement, and what is called "repatriation." There is a growing skepticism about the feasibility of repatriation. These hundreds of thousands of Arab refugees are now in Arab lands on the soil of their kinsmen. They have been nourished for ten years on one single theme—hatred of Israel; refusal to recognize Israel's sovereignty; resentment against Israel's existence; the dream of securing Israel's extinction. All these implacable sentiments found expression in the address by the representative of Saudi Arabia.

REPATRIATION A THREAT TO SECURITY

Repatriation would mean that hundreds of thousands of people would be introduced into a State whose existence they oppose, whose flag they despise and whose destruction they are resolved to seek. The refugees are all Arabs; and the countries in which they find themselves are Arab countries. Yet the advocates of repatriation contend that these Arab refugees should be settled in a non-Arab country, in the only social and cultural environment which is alien to their background and tradition. The Arab refugees are to be uprooted from the soil of nations to which they are akin and loyal—and placed in a State to which they are alien and hostile. Israel, whose sovereignty and safety are already assailed by the States surrounding her, is invited to add to its perils by the influx from hostile territories of masses of people steeped in the hatred of her existence. All this is to happen in a region where the Arab nations possess unlimited opportunities for resettling their kinsmen, and in which Israel has already contributed to a solution of the refugee problems of Asia and Africa by receiving 450,000 refugees from Arab lands among its immigrants.

Surely the Committee will not find it difficult to understand why this solution finds such little favor. In discussing the rights and duties of individuals let us not forget the rights and duties of States. Israel is a small sovereign State whose primary preoccupation is that of its safety. It cannot in conscience entertain a solution which would involve its own disruption, and bring misery and disillusionment to refugees who have surely suffered enough from false hopes and vain illusions. While every State is entitled to respect for its security needs, Israel is surely unique in the acuteness of the threats which surround her. No other State on the face of the globe is surrounded, as we are, by hostile neighbors who openly avow its destruction. To suggest that in addition to facing external perils from the north, south and east, we should import a massive quantity of hatred and rancor into our midst is to demand something beyond prudence or reason.

ARAB COUNTRIES TRUE 'PATRIA' FOR ARAB REFUGEES

There are three other considerations which must be placed on the scale against repatriation. First the word itself is not accurately used in this context. Transplanting an Arab refugee from an Arab land to a non-Arab land is not really "repatriation." "Patria" is not a mere geographical concept. Resettlement of a refugee in Israel would be not repatriation, but alienation from Arab society; a true repatriation of an Arab refugee would be a process which brought him into union with people who share his conditions of language and heritage, his impulses of national loyalty and cultural identity.

Second, the validity of the "repatriation" concept is further undermined when we examine the structure of the refugee population. More than 50% of the Arab refugees are under 15 years of age. This means that at the time of Israel's establishment many of those, if born at all at that time, were under 5 years of age. We thus reach the striking fact that a majority of the refugee population can have no conscious memory of Israel at all.

Thirdly those who speak of repatriation to Israel might not always be aware of the measure of existing integration of refugees into countries of their present residence. In the Kingdom of Jordan, refugees have full citizenship and participate fully in the Government of the country. They are entitled to vote and be elected to the Jordanian parliament. Indeed many of them hold high rank in the government of the kingdom. Thousands of refugees are enrolled in the Jordanian army and its National Guard. It is, to say the least, eccentric to suggest that people who are citizens of another land and are actually or potentially enrolled in the armed forces of a country at war with Israel are simultaneously endowed with an optional right of Israel citizenship.

In the Syrian region of Egypt refugees have not been granted citizenship; but by virtue of a law of July 1956, their status is, to a large degree, assimilated to that of citizens. This is especially so in respect of the right to work and to establish commercial enterprises. According to the law of July 1956, refugees are subject to compulsory military service in the Syrian army. Here again, to adduce an unconditional right "repatriation" would signify that those who are citizens of a state foreign and hostile to Israel have a simultaneous right to be regarded as Israel citizens! Is there any state represented here which would acknowledge a right of entry to those who having left its shores have become the citizens of a foreign and hostile state, and have taken military service under Governments which proclaim a state of war against it?

This is merely a striking example of the sharp paradox which we enter if we try to reconcile the slogan of "repatriation" with the actual context, the hard facts of Arab Israel relations.

I do not believe it necessary to speak at any length on the point that resettlement in Arab countries is free from all the disadvantages which adhere to "repatriation." Every condition which has ever contributed to a solution of refugee problems by integration is present in this case. With its expanse of territory, its great rivers, its resources of mineral wealth, its accessibility to international aid, the Arab world is easily capable of absorbing an additional population, not only without danger to itself, but with actual reinforcement of its security and welfare. . . .

Document 36

Golda Meir: A Call for Disarmament

From an address by the then Israeli Foreign Minister before the U.N. General Assembly on October 9, 1962.

The small and new countries, emerging into a world of armed camps, suffer twofold. Our immediate aim is rapid development, but since the danger of war still looms over every dispute, we are constantly burdened with defense expenditures to the detriment of our development needs. We too quickly learn the bitter lesson that those who threaten others must be deterred by some equilibrium, and let not those whose declared policy is to attack their neighbour cry out in mock indignation when the latter seeks some means of defense.

My Government rejects war as a means of settling disputes. From the day that the State of Israel was established, my Government has called for settling all outstanding differences by direct negotiations.

We do not rest content with calling upon the Great Powers to find a way to disarmament, and to settle outstanding problems by negotiation and conciliation between them. We are prepared to put this into practice in the dispute in which we are involved with our neighbours. As we have done in the past, we call again upon the Arab States to agree to complete disarmament with mutual inspection, covering all types of weapons, and to accept that method of direct negotiations as the only means for solving all differences between them and Israel . . .

There are many that are misled by two fallacies regarding the Middle East. The first is that it is an Arab region. In fact there are in it more non-Arabs than Arabs—Moslems, Christians and Jews. This composite pattern of peoples of various faiths and cultures has always been the pattern of the Middle East, each people with its historic continuity, past, present and future.

The second fallacy is that all would be well in that region if it were not for the tension between the Arab States and Israel. I would be the last to underrate the difficulties and dangers which arise from that conflict. But this is only one source of tension in a part of the world which is, unhappily, the scene of so much political instability, economic and social backwardness, rivalry and friction between different countries and regions and the pressures of the cold war. Anyone who follows the affairs of the Middle East knows that during this last year the focus of trouble in the area has been the bitter struggles within the Arab world which have made of the Arab League no longer even a façade of unity.

Israel longs for the day when the political independence and territorial integrity of every single State in the area—Arab and non-Arab—will be assured and when we can all concentrate on the welfare of our people. When I refer to the turmoil in the Arab world, it is because we are a Middle Eastern country and therefore affected by all that affects the peace of our area.

As far as the Israel-Arab dispute itself is concerned, it is well to see clearly what is the basic problem. It is the denial by the Arab States of Israel's right to exist. If this attitude were to change, and if the Arab States and Israel were to discuss their differences at the conference table in a frank and open manner, I am positive that solutions could be found on all the specific issues.

Year after year Israel has come on this rostrum with one demand—peace between it and its Arab neighbours. May I say here that we were grateful to the distinguished Deputy Foreign Minister of Ghana when he drew our attention again to the important statement of President Nkrumah during the 15th General Assembly, in which he called for recognition of the political realities in the Middle East and for insurance against non-aggression. We are entirely in agreement with that view.

The Arab denial of Israel's right of existence has a direct bearing on the distressing refugee problem. We are willing, and always have been willing, to discuss with the Arab Governments what can best be done to secure the future of the refugees in the light of the political and economic realities in the region. But a natural solution to the problem is frustrated by the Arab dream of destroying Israel and openly-proclaimed Arab intention of using the refugees for this purpose.

This design has been openly propagated even from the rostrum of this Assembly. This small spot of land, in which the Jewish people have revived their ancient home and nationhood, must again be wrested from them and they again be scattered to the four corners of the earth. Our neighbours have tried to achieve this by various means, open or guerilla warfare, economic boycott, propaganda and threats.

Negotiations and conciliation are proclaimed from this rostrum as the method to solve all other problems in the world except this one, which must, according to these spokesmen, be resolved by force. For every other nation, they claim co-existence, practised in peace. For Israel, non-existence, to be achieved by war. This doctrine not only runs counter to the basic principles of the United Nations Charter; its acceptance strikes at the very roots of our organization.

The world of today is overwhelmed by ideological disputes, international conflicts and economic controversies. In face of this situation, the basic concepts of the Charter, on the eschewing of force, on the unremitting search for peace, on international co-operation, on negotiation as the means to solve problems, have gained a new depth and significance. As long as negotiation is sought, there is hope. Those who rule out negotiation in the Middle East, those who year after year engage in sterile and stereotyped speeches of hostility, should know that their attitude is irrelevant to the basic theme of the international community and can have no echo in an organization which has proclaimed peace to be synonymous with human survival: that they are assaulting the foundations of human progress.

The policy of the Israel Government has been and continues to be peace. It is peace, not only for the world, but also between us and our neighbours. We believe in co-existence and co-operation everywhere and we shall do everything in our power towards that end . . .

Despite all the speeches which we have heard from Arab representatives, we are convinced that for us and for our neighbours the day must come when we shall live in amity and co-operation. Then will the entire Middle East become a region where the tens of millions of people will dwell in peace and then will its economic potentialities and rich cultural heritage achieve fulfilment. This Israel believes and towards this end we shall devote all our efforts.

Document 37

Fayez A. Sayegh: Zionist Colonialism in Palestine

This statement is from a booklet published in Beirut in 1965 by a leading spokesman of the Palestinian refugees maintaining that the Liberation of Palestine from the Zionist usurpers was the only possible solution of the problem.

In 1948, the Palestinian Arab people was forcibly dispossessed. Most Palestinians were evicted from their country. Their unyielding resistance and their costly sacrifices over three decades had failed to avert the national catastrophe.

But those sacrifices were not in vain. For they safeguarded the Palestinian national rights and underscored the legitimacy of the Arabs' claim to their national heritage. Rights undefended are rights surrendered. Unopposed and acquiesced in, usurpation is legitimized by default. For forfeiture of its patrimony, the Palestinian generation of the Inter-War era will be indicted by the Palestinian generations to come. It lost indeed—but not without fighting. It was dislodged indeed—but not for want of the will to defend its heritage.

Nor has the people of Palestine retroactively bestowed undeserved legitimacy upon the Zionist colonization of Palestine by recognizing the *fait accompli* after the fact. Many have been the self-appointed counselors of "realism", urging upon Palestinians acknowledgement of the new *status quo* in Palestine and acceptance of their exile "in good grace"; and many have been the lucrative offers of economic aid for "resettlement" and "rehabilitation" outside Palestine. But the people which had remained for thirty years undaunted by the combined power of British Imperialism and Zionist Colonialism, and which subsequently refused to allow the seizure of its land and the dispersal of its body to conquer its soul also, knew very well how to resist those siren-calls.

The Zionist settler-state, therefore, has remained a usurper, lacking even the semblance of legitimacy—because the people of Palestine has remained loyal to its heritage and faithful to its rights . . .

The people of Palestine, notwithstanding all its travails and misfortunes, still has undiminished faith in its future.

And the people of Palestine knows that the pathway to that future is the liberation of its homeland.

It was in this belief that the Palestinian people—after sixteen years of dispersion and exile, during which it had reposed its faith in its return to its country in world conscience and international public opinion, in the United Nations, and/or in the Arab states—chose at last to seize the initiative. In 1964, it reasserted its corporate personality by creating the Palestine Liberation Organization.

Only in the liberation of Palestine, spearheaded by Palestinians prepared to pay the price, can the supreme sacrifices of past generations of Palestinians be vindicated, and the visions and hopes of living Palestinians be transformed into reality.

Documents 38–42

Towards the Third Round

The Arab-Israeli conflict again escalated with the Egyptian decision in mid-May, 1967 to concentrate troops in Sinai and the announcement that the Straits of Tiran would be closed to Israeli shipping. In his speech on May 25, Nasser said that "under no circumstances" would he allow the Israeli flag to pass the Straits. On the day after: "Recently we felt we are strong enough, that if we were to enter a battle with Israel, with God's help, we could triumph" (Document 39). On the 29th: "The issue now at hand is not the Gulf of Aqabah but the rights of the Palestinian people" (Document 41). Meanwhile Hassanain Haykal, Egypt's leading spokesman, had explained (on May 26— Document 40) why a war with Israel was inevitable. On June 9, after the Egyptian defeat, Nasser announced his resignation (Document 42), but several hours after, following demonstrations in Cairo, withdrew it. The summing up of the war and its pre-history as Nasser saw it, appears in Part IV of this Reader (page 197).

Document 38

Nasser's Speech at UAR Advanced Air Headquarters, May 25, 1967

The entire country looks up to you today. The entire Arab nation supports you. It is clear that in these circumstances the entire people support you completely and consider the armed forces as their hope today. It is also a fact that the entire Arab nation supports our armed forces in the current situation through which the entire Arab nation is passing.

What I wish to say is that we are now in 1967 and not in 1956 after the tripartite aggression. A great deal was said then and all the secrets revealed had a double interpretation. Israel, its commanders and rulers, boasted a great deal after 1956. I have read every word written about the 1956 events and I also know exactly what happened in 1956.

On the night of 29th October 1956 the Israeli aggression against us began. Fighting began on 30th October. We received the Anglo-French ultimatum which asked us to withdraw several miles west of the Suez Canal. On 31st October the Anglo-French attack on us began. The air raids began at sunset on 31st October. At the same time all our forces in Sinai were withdrawn completely to inside Egypt.

Thus in 1956 we did not have an opportunity to fight Israel. We decided to withdraw before the actual fighting with Israel began. Despite our decision to withdraw Israel was unable to occupy any of our positions except after we left them. Yet Israel created a major uproar, boasted and said a great deal about the Sinai campaign and the Sinai battle. Everyone of you knows all the rubbish that was said. They probably believed what they said themselves.

Today, more than 10 years after Suez all the secrets have been exposed. The most important secret concerns when they brought Ben Gurion to France to employ him as a dog for imperialism, to begin the operation. Ben Gurion refused to undertake anything unless he was given a written guarantee that they would protect him from the Egyptian bombers and the Egyptian Air Force. All this is now no longer secret. The entire world knows. It was on this basis that France sent fighter aircraft to Ben Gurion, and it was also on this basis that Britain pledged to Ben Gurion to bomb Egyptian airfields within 24 hours after the aggression began.

This goes to show how much they took into account the Egyptian forces. Ben Gurion himself said he had to think about the Haifa-Jerusalem-Tel Aviv triangle, which holds one-third of Israel's population. He could not attack Egypt out of fear of the Egyptian air force and bombers. At that time we had a few Ilyushin bombers. We had just acquired them to arm ourselves. Today we have many Ilyushins and other aircraft. There is a great difference between yesterday and today, between 1956 and 1967. Why do I say all this? I say it because we are in a confrontation with Israel. Israel today is not backed by Britain and France as was the case in 1956. It has the United States supporting it and supplying it with arms. But the world cannot again accept the plotting which took place in 1956.

Israel has been clamouring since 1956. They spoke of Israel's competence and high standard of training. It was backed in this by the West and the Western press. They capitalised on the Sinai campaign where no fighting actually took place because we withdrew to confront Britain and France.

Today we have a chance to prove the fact. We have, indeed, a chance to make the world see matters in their true perspective. We are now face to face with Israel. In recent days Israel has been making aggressive threats and boasting. On 12th May a very impertinent statement was made. Anyone reading this statement must believe that these people are so boastful and deceitful that one simply cannot remain silent.

The statement said that the Israeli commanders announced they would carry out military operations against Syria in order to occupy Damascus and overthrow the Syrian Government. On the same day the Israeli Premier, Eshkol, made a very threatening statement against Syria. At the same time the commentaries said that Israel believed that Egypt could not make a move because it was bogged down in Yemen.

Of course they say that we are bogged down in Yemen and have problems there. We are in Yemen but they seem to have believed the lies they have been saying all these years about our being in Yemen. It is very possible that the Israelis themselves believed such lies. We are capable of carrying out our duties in Yemen and at the same time doing our national duty here in Egypt, both in defending our borders and in attacking if Israel attacks any Arab country.

On 13th May we received accurate information that Israel was concentrating on the Syrian border huge armed forces of about 11 to 13 brigades. These forces were divided into two fronts, one south of Lake Tiberias and the other north of the Lake. The decision made by Israel at this time was to carry out an attack against Syria starting on 17th May. On 14th May we took action, discussed the matter and contacted our Syrian brothers. The Syrians also had this information. Based on the information Lt-Gen. Mahmud Fawzi left for Syria to co-ordinate matters. We told them that we had decided that if Syria was attacked Egypt would enter the battle right from the start. This was the situation on 14th May; forces began to move in the direction of Sinai to take up their normal positions.

News agencies reported yesterday that these military movements must have been the result of a previously well laid plan. I say that the sequence of events determined the plan. We had no plan prior to 13th May because we believed that Israel would not have dared to make such an impertinent statement.

On 16th May we requested the withdrawal of the United Nations Emergency Force [UNEF] in a letter from Lt-Gen. Mahmud Fawzi. We requested the complete withdrawal of the UNEF. A major world wide campaign, led by the United States, Britain and Canada, began opposing the withdrawal of the UNEF from Egypt. Thus we felt that attempts were being made to turn the UNEF into a force serving neo-imperialism. It is obvious that the UNEF entered Egypt with our approval and therefore cannot continue to stay in Egypt except with our approval. Until yesterday a great deal was said about the UNEF. A campaign is also being mounted against the UN Secretary-General because he made a faithful and honest decision and could not surrender to the pressure brought to bear upon him by the United States, Britain and Canada to make the UNEF an instrument for implementing imperialism's plans.

It is quite natural, and I say this quite frankly, that had the UNEF ignored its basic task and turned to working for the aims of imperialism we would have regarded it as a hostile force and forcibly disarmed it. We are definitely capable of doing such a job. I say this now not to discredit the UNEF but to those who have neo-imperialist ideas and who want the UN to achieve their neo-imperialist aims—that there is not a single nation which respects itself and enjoys full sovereignty which could accept these methods in any shape or form. At the same time I say that the UNEF has honourably and faithfully carried out its duties. The UN Secretary-General refused to succumb to pressure. He issued immediate orders to the UNEF to withdraw. Consequently we praise the UNEF which has stayed 10 years in our country serving peace. And when they left—at a time when we found that the neo-imperialist force wanted to divert them from their basic task—we gave them a cheerful send-off and saluted them.

Our forces are now in Sinai and we are fully mobilised both in Gaza and Sinai. We notice that there is a great deal of talk about peace these days. Peace, peace, international peace, international security, UN intervention, and so on and so forth, all appears daily in the press. Why is it that no one spoke about peace, the UN and security when on 12th May the Israeli premier and the Israeli commanders made their statements that they would occupy Damascus, overthrow the Syrian regime, strike vigorously at Syria, and occupy a part of Syria? It was obvious that the press approved of the statements made by the Israeli premier and commanders.

There is talk about peace now. What peace? If there is a true desire for peace we say that we also work for peace. But does peace mean ignoring the rights of the Palestinian people because of the passage of time? Does peace mean that we should concede our rights because of the passage of time? Nowadays they speak about a UN presence in the region for the sake of peace. Does a UN presence in the region for peace mean that we should close our eyes to everything? The UN has adopted a number of resolutions in favour of the Palestinian people. Israel has implemented none of these resolutions. This brought no reaction from the UN.

Today US Senators, members of the House of Representatives, the press and the entire world speak in favour of Israel, of the Jews. But nothing is said in the Arabs' favour. The UN resolutions which favour the Arabs have not been implemented. What does this mean? No one is speaking in the Arabs' favour. How does the UN stand with regard to the Palestinian people? How does it stand with regard to the rights of the Palestinian people? How does it stand with regard to the tragedy which has continued since 1948? Talk of peace is heard only when Israel is in danger. But when Arab rights and the rights of the Palestinian people are lost, no one speaks about peace, rights, or anything like this.

It is clear, therefore, than an alliance exists between the Western powers, chiefly represented by the United States and Britain, with Israel. There is a political alliance. This political alliance prompts the Western powers to give military equipment to Israel. Yesterday and the day before yesterday the entire world was speaking about Sharm ash-Shaykh, navigation in the Gulf of Aqabah, and Eilat Port. This morning I heard the BBC say that in 1956 Abd an-Nasir promised to open the Gulf of Aqabah.

Of course, this is not true. It was copied from a British paper called the 'Daily Mail.' No such thing happened. Abd an-Nasir would never forfeit any UAR right. As I said, we would never give away a grain of sand from our soil or our country.

The armed forces' responsibility is now yours. The armed forces yesterday occupied Sharm ash-Shaykh. What does this mean? It is affirmation of our rights and our sovereignty over the Gulf of Aqabah which constitutes Egyptian territorial waters. Under no circumstances will we allow the Israeli flag to pass through the Gulf of Aqabah.

The Jews threaten war. We tell them you are welcome, we are ready for war. Our armed forces and all our people are ready for war, but under no circumstances will we abandon any of our rights. This water is ours. War might be an opportunity for the Jews, for Israel and Rabin, to test their forces against ours and to see that what they wrote about the 1956 battle and the occupation of Sinai was all a lot of nonsense.

With all this there is imperialism, Israel and reaction. Reaction casts doubt on everything and so does the Islamic alliance. We all know that the Islamic alliance is now represented by three states: the Kingdom of Saudi Arabia, the Kingdom of Jordan and Iran. They are saying that the purpose of the Islamic alliance is to reunite the Muslim against Israel. I would like the Islamic alliance to serve the Palestine question in only one way—by preventing the supply of oil to Israel. The oil which now reaches Israel, which reaches Eilat, comes from some of the Islamic alliance states. It goes to Eilat from Iran. Who then is supplying Israel with oil? The Islamic alliance—Iran, an Islamic alliance state. Such is the Islamic alliance. It is an imperialist alliance and this means it sides with Zionism because Zionism is the main ally of imperialism.

The Arab world, which is now mobilised to the highest degree, knows all this. It knows how to deal with the imperialist agents, the allies of Zionism and the fifth column.

They say they want to co-ordinate their plans with us. We cannot co-ordinate our plans in any way with Islamic alliance members because it would mean giving our plans to the Jews and to Israel. This is a vital battle. When we said that we were ready for the battle we meant that we would surely fight if Syria or any other Arab state was subjected to aggression.

The armed forces are now everywhere. The army and all the forces are now mobilised and so are the people. They are all behind you, praying for you day and night and believing that you are the pride of their nation, of the Arab nation. This is the feeling of the Arab people in Egypt and outside Egypt. We are confident that you will honour the trust. Everyone of us is ready to die and not give away a grain of his country's sand. This for us is the greatest honour. It is the greatest honour for us to defend our country. We are not scared by the imperialist, Zionist or reactionary campaigns. We are independent and we know the taste of freedom. We have built a strong national army and achieved our aims. We are building our country. There is currently a propaganda campaign, a psychological campaign, and a campaign of doubt against us. We leave all this behind us and follow the course of duty and victory. May God be with you.

Document 39

Nasser's Speech to Arab Trade Unionists,
May 26, 1967

Thank you for this initiative. You have provided me with an opportunity to see you. I have actually heard your speeches and resolutions, there is nothing to add during this meeting to what you have already said. You, the Arab workers' federation, represent the biggest force in the Arab world.

We can achieve much by Arab actions, which is a main part of our battle. We must develop and build our countries to face the challenge of our enemies. The Arab world now is very different from what it was 10 days ago. Israel is also different from what it was 10 days ago. Despair has never found its way into Arab hearts and never will. The Arabs insist on their rights and are determined to regain the rights of the Palestinian people. The Arabs must accomplish this set intention and this aim. The first elements of this aim appeared in the test of Syria and Egypt in facing the Israeli threat. I believe that this test was a major starting point and basis from which to achieve complete cohesion in the Arab world. What we see today in the masses of the Arab people everywhere is their desire to fight. The Arab people want to regain the rights of the people of Palestine.

For several years, many people have raised doubts about our intentions towards Palestine. But talk is easy and action is difficult, very difficult. We emerged wounded from the 1956 battle. Britain, Israel and France attacked us then. We sustained heavy losses in 1956. Later, union was achieved. The 1961 secession occurred when we had only just got completely together and had barely begun to stand firmly on our feet.

Later the Yemeni revolution broke out. We considered it our duty to rescue our brothers, simply because of the principles and ideals which we advocated and still advocate.

We were waiting for the day when we would be fully prepared and confident of being able to adopt strong measures if we were to enter the battle with Israel. I say nothing aimlessly. One day two years ago, I stood up to say that we have no plan to liberate Palestine and that revolutionary action is our only course to liberate Palestine. I spoke at the summit conferences. The summit conferences were meant to prepare the Arab states to defend themselves.

Recently we felt we are strong enough, that if we were to enter a battle with Israel, with God's help, we could triumph. On this basis, we decided to take actual steps.

A great deal has been said in the past about the UN Emergency Force (UNEF). Many people blamed us for UNEF's presence. We were not strong enough. Should we have listened to them, or rather built and trained our Army while UNEF still existed? I said once that we could tell UNEF to leave within half an hour. Once we were fully prepared we could ask UNEF to leave. And this is what actually happened.

The same thing happened with regard to Sharm al Shaykh. We were also attacked on this score by some Arabs. Taking Sharm al Shaykh meant confrontation with Israel. Taking such action also meant that we were ready to enter a general war with Israel. It was not a separate operation. Therefore we had to take this fact into consideration when moving to Sharm al Shaykh. The present operation was mounted on this basis.

Actually I was authorised by the [Arab Socialist Union's] Supreme Executive Committee to implement this plan at the right time. The right time came when Syria was threatened with aggression. We sent reconnaissance aircraft over Israel. Not a single brigade was stationed opposite us on the Israeli side of the border. All Israeli brigades were confronting Syria. All but four brigades have now moved south to confront Egypt. Those four are still on the border with Syria. We are confident that once we have entered the battle we will triumph, God willing.

With regard to military plans, there is complete co-ordination of military action between us and Syria. We will operate as one army fighting a single battle for the sake of a common objective—the objective of the Arab nation.

The problem today is not just Israel, but also those behind it. If Israel embarks on an aggression against Syria or Egypt the battle against Israel will be a general one and not confined to one spot on the Syrian or Egyptian borders. The battle will be a general one and our basic objective will be to destroy Israel. I probably could not have said such things five or even three years ago. If I had said such things and had been unable to carry them out my words would have been empty and worthless.

Today, some 11 years after 1956, I say such things because I am confident. I know what we have here in Egypt and what

Syria has. I also know that other states—Iraq, for instance, has sent its troops to Syria; Algeria will send troops; Kuwait also will send troops. They will send armoured and infantry units. This is Arab power. This is the true resurrection of the Arab nation, which at one time was probably in despair.

Today people must know the reality of the Arab world. What is Israel? Israel today is the United States. The United States is the chief defender of Israel. As for Britain, I consider it America's lackey. Britain does not have an independent policy. Wilson always follows Johnson's steps and says what he wants him to say. All Western countries take Israel's view.

The Gulf of Aqabah was a closed waterway prior to 1956. We used to search British, US, French and all other ships. After the tripartite aggression—and we all know the tripartite plot—we left the area to UNEF which came here under a UN resolution to make possible the withdrawal of Britain, France and Israel. The Israelis say they opened the maritime route. I say they told lies and believed their own lies. We withdrew because the British and the French attacked us. This battle was never between us and Israel alone.

I have recently been with the armed forces. All the armed forces are ready for a battle face to face between the Arabs and Israel. Those behind Israel are also welcome.

We must know and learn a big lesson today. We must actually see that in its hypocrisy and in its talks with the Arabs, the United States sides with Israel 100 per cent and is partial in favour of Israel. Why is Britain biased towards Israel? The West is on Israel's side. Gen. de Gaulle's personality caused him to remain impartial on this question and not to toe the US or the British line; France therefore did not take sides with Israel.

The Soviet Union's attitude was great and splendid. It supported the Arabs and the Arab nation. It went to the extent of stating that, together with the Arabs and the Arab nation, it would resist any interference or aggression.

Today every Arab knows foes and friends. If we do not learn who our enemies and our friends are, Israel will always be able to benefit from this behaviour. It is clear that the United States is an enemy of the Arab because it is completely biased in favour of Israel. It is also clear that Britain is an enemy of the Arabs because she, too, is completely biased in favour of Israel. On this basis we must treat our enemies and those who side with our enemies as our actual

enemies. We can accord them such treatment. In fact we are
not states without status. We are states of status, occupying
an important place in the world. Our states have thousands of
years of civilisation behind them—7,000 years of civilisation.
Indeed, we can do much; we can expose the hypocrisy—the
hypocrisy of our enemies if they try to persuade us that they
wish to serve our interests. The United States seeks to serve
only Israel's interests. Britain also seeks to serve only Israel's
interests.

The question is not one of international law. Why all this
uproar because of the closure of the Gulf of Aqabah? When
Eshkol and Rabin threatened Syria, nobody spoke about peace
or threats to peace. They actually hate the progressive regime
in Syria. The United States, Britain and reaction—which is
the friend of the United States and Britain—do not favour
the national progressive regime in Syria. Israel, of course,
shares their feelings. Israel is an ally of the United States and
Britain. When Israel threatened Syria, they kept quiet and
accepted what it said. But when we exercise one of our legitimate rights, as we always do, they turn the world upside down
and speak about threats to peace and about a crisis in the
Middle East. They fabricate these matters and threaten us
with war.

We shall not relinquish our rights. We shall not concede
our right in the Gulf of Aqabah. Today, the people of Egypt,
the Syrian Army, and the Egyptian Army comprise one front.
We want the entire front surrounding Israel to become one
front. We want this. Naturally there are obstacles at present.
Of course, Wasfi at-Tall is a spy for the Americans and the
British. We cannot co-operate with these spies in any form,
because the battle is one of destiny and the spies have no
place in this battle. We want the front to become one united
front around Israel. We will not relinquish the rights of the
people of Palestine, as I have said before. I was told at the
time that I might have to wait 70 years. During the crusader's
occupation, the Arabs waited 70 years before a suitable opportunity arose and they drove away the crusaders. Some
people commented that Abd an-Nasir said we should shelve
the Palestinian question for 70 years. I do not mean exactly
70 years, but I say that as a people with an ancient civilisation,
as an Arab people, we are determined that the Palestine
question will not be liquidated or forgotten. The whole question then, is the proper time to achieve our aims. We are
preparing ourselves constantly.

You are the hope of the Arab nation and its vanguard. As workers, you are actually building the Arab nation. The quicker we build, the quicker we will be able to achieve our aim. I thank you for your visit and wish you every success. Please convey my greetings and best wishes to the Arab workers in every Arab country.

Document 40

Hassanain Haykal: An Armed Clash with Israel Is Inevitable—Why?

Al Ahram, May 26, 1967.

It is extremely difficult to write about current events, particularly when such events are as swift and violent as a hurricane. But it is easy to write about what has already happened, to give an account and analysis of facts. It is also safe to write about what could take place in the future, because the future is boundless. Tomorrow never comes because every day has a tomorrow. The real problem is to speak about what is taking place while it happens. Then every interpretation may endure only a few minutes or even seconds.

There are two considerations which make the problem even more difficult: the topic is one of destiny and life, and there is the need for rational, intelligent writing without indulging in a long composition or platitudes.

What I am going to say after this introduction will in fact be no more than a collection of observations which I think are important at present. The first observation is that I believe an armed clash between the UAR and Israel is inevitable. This armed clash could occur at any moment, at any place along the line of confrontation between the Egyptian forces and the enemy Israeli forces—on land, air or sea along the area extending from Gaza in the North to the Gulf of Aqabah at Sharm ash-Shaykh in the South. But why do I emphasise this in such a manner? There are many reasons, particularly the psychological factor and its effect on the balance of power in the Middle East.

Passage through the Gulf of Aqabah is economically important to Israel at a time when it is suffering the symptoms a man has on waking up after a long, boisterous and drunken party. The fountains of German reparations are drying up. Israel has also drained the sources of contributions and gifts. Although emergency sources will emerge as a result of the present crisis, particularly with the help of Western propaganda trumpets, people in the West, at least many of them, are getting tired of an entity which has been unable to lead a normal life, like a child who does not want to grow up, who cannot depend on himself and does not want to take on any responsibility. Israel is suffering from an economic crisis. There are over 100,000 unemployed, nearly one quarter of Israel's manpower. The new blow had added to the economic plight. Israel attached great importance to its trade with East Africa and Asia. This trade depended on one route: the Red Sea via the Gulf of Aqabah, to Eilat. There were many projects for enlarging the port of Eilat, which at present can handle 400,000 tons a year. In addition, there were the oil lines. Israel has built two pipelines to carry Iranian oil from Eilat to the Haifa oil refinery. Israel has also dreamed of digging a canal from Eilat to Ashdod to compete with or replace the Suez Canal.

In my personal opinion all these important economic matters and questions are not the decisive factor which will influence or dictate the Israeli reaction to the closure of the Gulf of Aqabah. The decisive factor in my opinion is the psychological factor. The economic aspect swings back and forth between yes and no. From this aspect the challenge of war can be either accepted or put off. But the psychological factor cannot swing back and forth. From this aspect there is one answer: Yes. It is in the light of the compelling psychological factor that the needs of security, of survival itself, make acceptance of the challenge of war inevitable.

One thing is clear: The closure of the Gulf of Aqabah to Israeli navigation and the ban on the import of strategic goods, even when carried by non-Israeli ships, means first and last that the Arab nation represented by the UAR has succeeded for the first time, *vis-à-vis* Israel, in changing by force a *fait accompli* imposed on it by force. This is the essence of the problem, regardless of the complications surrounding it and future contingencies.

As for the complications, we can find in the past ample justification for Arab resistance. We could say that the British mandate in Palestine had sold Palestine to Zionism in accordance with a resolution adopted by the League of Nations. This is true. We could say that the UN betrayed Palestine, and this is true. We could say Arab reaction from the Jordanian King Abdullah to the Saudi King Faysal connived at the plot against Palestine, and this is true. We could say about the Gulf of Aqabah that in 1956 imperialism, represented by the British and French forces, imposed a *fait accompli* during this period from autumn 1956 to spring 1967. It was imperialist not Israeli arms which imposed this *fait accompli*. We could say all this is seeking to justify Arab resistance. But the naked and rocky truth which remains after all this is that the accomplished fact was aggressively imposed by force. The Arabs did not have the force to resist the accomplished fact, let alone to change it by force and to impose a substitute consistent with their rights and interests.

As for the contingencies which may be precipitated by this new development, I do not think I need go into detail.

Israel has built its existence, security and future on force. The prevalent philosophy of its rulers has been that the Arab quakes before the forbidding glance, and that nothing deters him but fear. Thus Israeli intimidation reached its peak. Provocation went beyond tolerable bounds. But all of this, from the Israeli point of view, had the psychological aim of convincing the Arabs that Israel could do anything and that the Arabs could do nothing; that Israel was omnipotent and could impose any accomplished fact, while the Arabs were weak and had to accept any accomplished fact. Despite the error and danger in this Israeli philosophy—because two or even three million Israelis cannot by military force or by myth dominate a sea of 80 million Arabs—this philosophy remained a conviction deeply embedded in Israeli thinking, planning and action for many disturbing years, without any Arab challenge capable of restoring matters to their proper perspective.

Now this is the first time the Arabs have challenged Israel in an attempt to change an accomplished fact by force and to replace it by force with an alternative accomplished fact consistent with their rights and interests. The opening of the Gulf of Aqabah to Israel was an accomplished fact imposed by the force of imperialist arms. This week the closure of the Gulf of Aqabah to Israel was an alternative accomplished fact imposed and now being protected by the force of Arab arms. To Israel this is the most dangerous aspect of the current situation . . . Therefore it is not a matter of the Gulf of Aqabah but of something bigger. It is the whole philosophy of Israeli security. It is the philosophy on which Israeli existence has pivoted since its birth and on which it will pivot in the future.

Hence I say that Israel must resort to arms. Therefore I

say that an armed clash between UAR and the Israeli enemy is inevitable.

As from now, we must expect the enemy to deal us the first blow in the battle. But as we wait for that first blow, we should try to minimise its effect as much as possible. The second blow will then follow. But this will be the blow we will deliver against the enemy in retaliation and deterrence. It will be the most effective blow we can possibly deal. Why do I say this now? My point of view is as follows:

When one studies the strategy of the Egyptian action of the 10 great days from 14th to 23rd May in which the positions and balance in the Middle East changed, one will immediately perceive two factors which at first sight may appear contradictory: The first factor: Egypt was ready and prepared. The second factor: the Egyptian action was a complete surprise, even to Egypt in so far as it was a reaction to a specific situation, namely, Israel's threat to and readiness to invade Syria.

By analysing the first factor in the strategy of the Egyptian action during the 10 great days which changed the positions and balance in the Middle East we find that there are roots extending from the spring of 1967 back to the time when the UAR called for the Arab summit conferences. The first summit conference was convened in January 1964. The first item submitted by the UAR to that conference was the Jordan headwaters. At that time the anti-Egyptian Western propaganda which was backed by the reactionary elements sought, discreetly at times but most of the time shamelessly, to hamper Egyptian policy at that time by two propaganda themes: (1) that Egypt's whole aim in the summit conferences policy was to settle the Yemeni issue with Saudi Arabia; (2) that when Egypt called for the summit conferences it wanted to abandon the responsibility of action for Palestine, in accordance with the traditional method which says that when you face a problem for which you cannot find a solution the only way to bury and get rid of it is to form a commission to discuss and study it. All this, of course, was untrue, since Egypt at the time imagined that the Arab summit conferences could draw up the policy of the liberation battle and could prepare for it. Egypt wanted unified action to be the front of a broad movement which might have world-wide political influence serving the strategy of battle. Besides, unified Arab action might be beneficial in providing possibilities for defending Arab countries which at that time did not have reassuring defences. At the same time Egypt believed that when the time came for earnest action, loyalty and fidelity to the trust dictated that it should primarily depend on itself.

Accordingly the summit conferences were a broad front suitable for world-wide political influence. It was also possible for them to help strengthen the defence of Arab countries surrounding Israel. Behind this broad front and the consolidation of the other Arab countries surrounding Israel Egypt could prepare and mobilise its own effective forces.

The remainder of the story of the summit conferences is known and I do not propose to repeat it. It ended in utter failure because of Arab reactionary rancour, and because reaction had greater hatred for Arab social progress than for the Israeli enemy, which wants to humiliate all the Arabs whatever their social views. The broad front for unified Arab action therefore collapsed with the failure of the summit conferences. The possibilities of strengthening the defence of the other Arab countries surrounding Israel did not sufficiently materialise as they should have done. Egypt was unable to control all those circumstances but it was able to control the third objective, namely, to prepare and mobilise its effective forces.

Anti-Egyptian Western propaganda, backed by the Arab reactionary elements, continued to attack Egypt fiercely. The attack went to the length of spreading the belief that the entire Egyptian Army had perished in Yemen, had been scattered into aimless groups, and that the remainder had been killed, wounded or captured. Similarly it was said that the Egyptian economy was collapsing and could not stand on its feet, let alone bear the weight of any bold venture and carry on with it. But Egypt knew the truth and was confident that the truth would appear to the entire Arab nation one day when the time was ripe for serious action.

Egypt, then, was prepared and ready. This is the first fact about the strategy of Egyptian action during the 10 great days.

I will now come to the second factor in the crisis. This factor is that the Egyptian action was a complete surprise. It appears, and it is now almost certain, that the forces hostile to Egypt, that is imperialism, Arab reaction and Israel, had come in the end to believe their own propaganda. People sometimes fall prey to the lies they themselves fabricate. Something of that sort must certainly have happened, otherwise Israel would not have persisted in its threats against Syria and gone to the length of the cry of 'March on Damas-

cus.' It must have felt certain that there would be no decisive
Egyptian reaction, because there were insufficient forces for
any initiative or retaliatory action.

It was this Israeli threat to Syria and information confirming it concerning intentions and plans that precipitated the
emergency situation to which Egypt had to react immediately,
even though it came as a surprise to it. There was preparation
and mobilisation of the effective Egyptian forces. There was
national consciousness and abidance by its principles. There
was creative leadership. What I mean to say is that Egypt was
not prepared for this specific contingency but was prepared
for all contingencies including such a one.

Now, to turn to the march of events during the 10 great
days which changed the situation and the balance of the
Middle East. Events began to move. One calculated and effective step followed another: the decision was taken to implement the joint defence agreement with Syria—this is the
decision which Lt-Gen. Muhammad Fawzi, the Chief of Staff
of the Egyptian Armed Forces, carried on the five-hour visit
to Damascus. Then followed the message addressed by Lt-Gen.
Muhammad Fawzi to the Commander of the UN Emergency
Force to withdraw his forces from the Egyptian borders with
Israel. The Egyptian Armed Forces then, without waiting,
actually began occupying all the border positions. The Foreign
Minister Mahmud Riyad then sent his message to the UN
Secretary-General U Thant on the withdrawal and evacuation
of the Emergency Forces in the UAR and Gaza. Then followed the advance on Sharm al Shaykh, the entrance to the
Gulf of Aqabah; the order was issued to close the Gulf of
Aqabah to Israeli shipping and to strategic goods for Israel
even if transported aboard non-Israeli ships; and all the US
initiatives were rejected. All these actions were backed by a
massive, ready force enjoying a morale brimming over with
a fighting spirit the like of which the Middle East has never
seen.

Two results were thus achieved, that is to say: (1) The
plan against Syria collapsed; the invasion of Syria became
impossible because all of the enemy forces streamed into the
South to confront the Egyptian concentration. (2) The accomplished fact which the British-French invasion, and not
the Israeli Army, had imposed in 1956 to the benefit of Israel,
was changed.

In other words the strategy of this stage achieved its first
objective by frustrating the plot to invade Syria, and more-

over, it achieved another longed-for and precious objective: the return of the armed forces to direct confrontation with Israel and the closing once again of the door to the Gulf of Aqabah in Israel's face.

Is this, then, the end of the matter? I would answer that I have explained—or rather tried to explain—with the first observation in this inquiry that the problem has not ended but rather has hardly begun. This is because I am confident that for many reasons, chiefly the psychological, Israel cannot accept or remain indifferent to what has taken place. In my opinion it simply cannot do so. This means, and that is what I intend to say in the second observation of this inquiry that the next move is up to Israel. Israel has to reply now. It has to deal a blow. We have to be ready for it, as I said, to minimise its effect as much as possible. Then it will be our turn to deal the second blow, which we will deliver with the utmost possible effectiveness.

In short, Egypt has exercised its power and achieved the objectives of this stage without resorting to arms so far. But Israel has no alternative but to use arms if it wants to exercise power. This means that the logic of the fearful confrontation now taking place between Egypt, which is fortified by the might of the masses of the Arab nation, and Israel, which is fortified by the illusion of American might, dictates that Egypt, after all it has now succeeded in achieving must wait, even though it has to wait for a blow. This is necessitated also by the sound conduct of the battle, particularly from the international point of view. Let Israel begin. Let our second blow then be ready. Let it be a knockout.

Document 41

Nasser's Speech to National Assembly Members on May 29, 1967

Brothers, when Brother Anwar as Sadat informed me of your decision to meet me I told him that I myself was prepared to call on you at the National Assembly, but he said you were determined to come. I therefore responded to this and I thank you heartily for your consideration.

I was naturally not surprised by the law which Brother Anwar as Sadat read because I was notified of it before I came here. However, I wish to thank you very much for your feelings and for the powers given me. I did not ask for such powers because I felt that you and I were as one, that we could co-operate and work for the sublime interest of this country giving a great example of unselfishness and of work for the welfare of all. Thanks be to God, for four years now the National Assembly has been working and has given great examples. We have given great examples in co-operation and unselfishness and in placing before us the sublime and highest objective—the interest of this nation.

I am proud of this resolution and law. I promise you that I will use it only when necessary. I will, however, send all the laws to you. Thank you once again. The great gesture of moral support represented by this law is very valuable to my spirit and heart. I heartily thank you for this feeling and this initiative.

The circumstances through which we are now passing are in fact difficult ones because we are not only confronting Israel but also those who created Israel and who are behind Israel. We are confronting Israel and the West as well—the West, which created Israel and which despised us Arabs and which ignored us before and since 1948. They had no regard whatsoever for our feelings, our hopes in life, or our rights. The West completely ignored us, and the Arab nation was unable to check the West's course.

Then came the events of 1956—the Suez battle. We all know what happened in 1956. When we rose to demand our rights. Britain, France and Israel opposed us, and we were faced with the tripartite aggression. We resisted, however, and proclaimed that we would fight to the last drop of our blood. God gave us success and God's victory was great.

Subsequently we were able to rise and to build. Now, 11 years after 1956, we are restoring things to what they were in 1956. This is from the material aspect. In my opinion this material aspect is only a small part, whereas the spiritual aspect is the great side of the issue. The spiritual aspect involves the renaissance of the Arab nation, the revival of the Palestine question, and the restoration of confidence to every Arab and to every Palestinian. This is on the basis that if we are able to restore conditions to what they were before 1956 God will surely help and urge us to restore the situation to what it was in 1948 [prolonged applause].

Brothers, the revolt, upheaval and commotion which we now see taking place in every Arab country are not only because we have returned to the Gulf of Aqabah or rid ourselves of the UNEF, but because we have restored Arab honour and renewed Arab hopes.

Israel used to boast a great deal, and the Western powers, headed by the United States and Britain, used to ignore and even despise us and consider us of no value. But now that the time has come—and I have already said in the past that we will decide the time and place and not allow them to decide—we must be ready for triumph and not for a recurrence of the 1948 comedies. We shall triumph, God willing.

Preparations have already been made. We are now ready to confront Israel. They have claimed many things about the 1956 Suez war, but no one believed them after the secrets of the 1956 collusion were uncovered—that mean collusion in which Israel took part. Now we are ready for the confrontation. We are now ready to deal with the entire Palestine question.

The issue now at hand is not the Gulf of Aqabah, the Straits of Tiran, or the withdrawal of the UNEF, but the rights of the Palestine people. It is the aggression which took place in Palestine in 1948 with the collaboration of Britain and the United States. It is the expulsion of the Arabs from Palestine, the usurpation of their rights, and the plunder of their property. It is the disavowal of all the UN resolutions in favour of the Palestinian people.

The issue today is far more serious than they say. They want to confine the issue to the Straits of Tiran, the UNEF and the right of passage. We demand the full rights of the Palestinian people. We say this out of our belief that Arab rights cannot be squandered because the Arabs throughout the Arab world are demanding these Arab rights.

We are not afraid of the United States and its threats, of Britain and her threats, or of the entire Western world and its partiality to Israel. The United States and Britain are partial to Israel and give no consideration to the Arabs, to the entire Arab nation. Why? Because we have made them believe that we cannot distinguish between friend and foe. We must make them know that we know who our foes are and who our friends are and treat them accordingly.

If the United States and Britain are partial to Israel, we must say that our enemy is not only Israel but also the United States and Britain and treat them as such. If the Western Powers disavow our rights and ridicule and despise us, we Arabs must teach them to respect us and take us seriously. Otherwise all our talk about Palestine, the Palestine people, and Palestinian rights will be null and void and of no consequence. We must treat enemies as enemies and friends as friends.

I said yesterday that the States that champion freedom and peace have supported us. I spoke of the support given us by India, Pakistan, Afghanistan, Yugoslavia, Malaysia, the Chinese People's Republic and the Asian and African States.

After my statements yesterday I met the War Minister Shams Badran and learned from him what took place in Moscow. I wish to tell you today that the Soviet Union is a friendly Power and stands by us as a friend. In all our dealings with the Soviet Union—and I have been dealing with the USSR since 1955—it has not made a single request of us. The USSR has never interfered in our policy or internal affairs. This is the USSR as we have always known it. In fact, it is we who have made urgent requests of the USSR. Last year we asked for wheat and they sent it to us. When I also asked for all kinds of arms they gave them to us. When I met Shams Badran yesterday he handed me a message from the Soviet Premier Kosygin saying that the USSR supported us in this battle and would not allow any Power to intervene until matters were restored to what they were in 1956.

Brothers, we must distinguish between friend and foe, friend and hypocrite. We must be able to tell who is making requests, who has ulterior motives, and who is applying economic pressure. We must also know those who offer their friendship to us for no other reason than a desire for freedom and peace.

In the name of the UAR people, I thank the people of the USSR for their great attitude, which is the attitude of a real friend. This is the kind of attitude we expect. I said yesterday that we had not requested the USSR or any other state to intervene, because we really want to avoid any confrontation which might lead to a world war and also because we really work for peace and advocate world peace. When we voiced the policy of non-alignment, our chief aim was world peace.

Brothers, we will work for world peace with all the power at our disposal, but we will also hold tenaciously to our rights with all the power at our disposal. This is our course. On this occasion, I address myself to our brothers in Aden and say: Although occupied with this battle, we have not forgotten you. We are with you. We have not forgotten the struggle of Aden and the occupied South for liberation. Aden and the occupied South must be liberated and colonialism

must end. We are with them; present matters have not taken
our minds from Aden.

I thank you for taking the trouble to pay this visit. Moreover, your presence is an honour to the Qubbah Palace, and I
am pleased to have met you. Peace be with you.

Document 42

Nasser's Resignation Broadcast, June 9, 1967

Brothers, at times of triumph and tribulation, in the sweet
hours and bitter hours, we have become accustomed to sit
together to discuss things, to speak frankly of facts, believing
that only in this way can we always find the right path however difficult circumstances may be.

We cannot hide from ourselves the fact that we have met
with a grave setback in the last few days, but I am confident
that we all can and, in a short time, will overcome our
difficult situation, although this calls for much patience and
wisdom as well as moral courage and ability to work on our
part. Before that, brothers, we need to cast a glance back
over past events so that we shall be able to follow developments and the line of our march leading to the present conditions.

All of us know how the crisis started in the Middle East.
At the beginning of last May there was an enemy plan for
the invasion of Syria and the statements by his politicians and
all his military leaders openly said so. There was plenty of
evidence concerning the plan. Sources of our Syrian brothers
were categorical on this and our own reliable information
confirmed it. Add to this the fact that our friends in the Soviet
Union warned the parliamentary delegation, which was on
a visit to Moscow, at the beginning of last month, that there
was a premeditated plan against Syria. We considered it our
duty not to accept this silently. This was the duty of Arab
brotherhood, it was also the duty of national security. Whoever starts with Syria will finish with Egypt.

Our armed forces moved to our frontiers with a competence
which the enemy acknowledged even before our friends.
Several steps followed. There was the withdrawal of the
United Nations Emergency Force and the return of our forces
to the Sharm al Shaykh post, the controlling point in the
Straits of Tiran, which had been used by the Israeli enemy
as one of the after-effects of the tripartite aggression against

us in 1956. The enemy's flag passing in front of our forces was intolerable, apart from other reasons connected with the dearest aspirations of the Arab nation.

Accurate calculations were made of the enemy's strength and showed us that our armed forces, at the level of equipment and training which they had reached, were capable of repelling the enemy and deterring him. We realised that the possibility of an armed clash existed and accepted the risk.

Before us were several factors—national, Arab and international. A message from the US President Lyndon Johnson was handed to our Ambassador in Washington 26th May asking us to show self-restraint and not to be the first to fire, or else we should have to face grave consequences. On the very same night, the Soviet Ambassador asked to have an urgent meeting with me at 05.30 [as broadcast] after midnight. He informed me of an urgent request from the Soviet Government not to be the first to open fire.

In the morning of last Monday, 5th June, the enemy struck. If we say now it was a stronger blow than we had expected, we must say at the same time, and with complete certainty that it was bigger than the potential at his disposal. It became very clear from the first moment that there were other powers behind the enemy—they came to settle their accounts with the Arab national movement. Indeed, there were surprises worthy of note:

(1) The enemy, whom we were expecting from the east and north, came from the west—a fact which clearly showed that facilities exceeding his own capacity and his calculated strength had been made available to him.

(2) The enemy covered at one go all military and civilian airfields in the UAR. This means that he was relying on some force other than his own normal strength to protect his skies against any retaliatory action from our side. The enemy was also leaving other Arab fronts to be tackled with outside assistance which he had been able to obtain.

(3) There is clear evidence of imperialist collusion with the enemy—an imperialist collusion, trying to benefit from the lesson of the open collusion of 1956, by resorting this time to abject and wicked concealment. Nevertheless, what is now established is that American and British aircraft carriers were off the shores of the enemy helping his war effort. Also, British aircraft raided, in broad daylight, positions on the Syrian and Egyptian fronts, in addition to operations by a

number of American aircraft reconnoitering some of our positions. The inevitable result of this was that our land forces, fighting most violent and brave battles in the open desert, found themselves at the difficult time without adequate air cover in face of the decisive superiority of the enemy air forces. Indeed it can be said without emotion or exaggeration, that the enemy was operating with an air force three times stronger than his normal force.

The same conditions were faced by the forces of the Jordanian Army, fighting a brave battle under the leadership of King Husayn who—let me say for the sake of truth and honesty—adopted an excellent stand; and I admit that my heart was bleeding while I was following the battles of his heroic Arab Army in Jerusalem and other parts of the West Bank on the night when the enemy and his plotting forces massed no less than 400 aircraft over the Jordanian front.

There were other honourable and marvellous efforts. The Algerian people, under their great leader Hawwari Bumedien, gave without reservation and without stinting for the battle. The people of Iraq and their faithful leader Abd ar-Rahman Arif gave without reservation or stinting for the battle. The Syrian Army fought heroically, consolidated by the forces of the great Syrian people and under the leadership of their national Government. The peoples and governments of Sudan, Kuwait, Yemen, Lebanon, Tunisia and Morocco adopted honourable stands. All the peoples of the Arab nation, without exception, adopted a stand of manhood and dignity all along the Arab homeland; a stand of resolution and determination that Arab right shall not be lost, shall not be humiliated, and that the war in its defence is advancing, regardless of sacrifice and setbacks, on the road of the sure and inevitable victory. There were also great nations outside the Arab homeland who gave us invaluable moral support.

But the plot, and we must say this with the courage of men, was bigger and fiercer. The enemy's main concentration was on the Egyptian front which he attacked with all his main force of armoured vehicles and infantry, supported by air supremacy the dimensions of which I have outlined for you. The nature of the desert did not permit a full defence especially, in face of the enemy's air supremacy. I realised that the armed battle might not go in our favour. I, with others, tried to use all sources of Arab strength. Arab oil came in to play its part. The Suez Canal came in to play its part. A great role is still reserved for general Arab action. I am fully confident that it will measure up to its task. Our Armed Forces in Sinai were obliged to evacuate the first line of defence. They fought fearful tank and air battles on the second line of defence.

We then responded to the cease-fire resolution, in view of assurances contained in the latest Soviet draft resolution, to the Security Council, as well as French statements to the effect that no one must reap any territorial expansion from the recent aggression, and in view of world public opinion, especially in Asia and Africa, which appreciates our position and feels the ugliness of the forces of international domination which pounced on us.

We now have several urgent tasks before us. The first is to remove the traces of this aggression against us and to stand by the Arab nation resolutely and firmly; despite the setback, the Arab nation, with all its potential and resources, is in a position to insist on the removal of the traces of the aggression.

The second task is to learn the lesson of the setback. In this connection there are three vital facts, (1) The elimination of imperialism in the Arab world will leave Israel with its own intrinsic power; yet, whatever the circumstances, however long it may take, the Arab intrinsic power is greater and more effective. (2) Redirecting Arab interests in the service of Arab rights is an essential safeguard: the American Sixth Fleet moved with Arab oil, and there are Arab bases, placed forcibly and against the will of the peoples, in the service of aggression. (3) The situation now demands a united word from the entire Arab nation; this, in the present circumstances, is irreplaceable guarantee.

Now we arrive at an important point in this heartsearching by asking ourselves: does this mean that we do not bear responsibility for the consequences of the setback? I tell you truthfully and despite any factors on which I might have based my attitude during the crisis, that I am ready to bear the whole responsibility. I have taken a decision in which I want you all to help me. I have decided to give up completely and finally every official post and every political role and return to the ranks of the masses and do my duty with them like every other citizen.

The forces of imperialism imagine that Jamal Abd al-Nasser is their enemy. I want it to be clear to them that their enemy is the entire Arab nation, not just Jamal Abd al-Nasser. The forces hostile to the Arab national movement try to portray this movement as an empire of Abd al-Nasser. This is not true, because the aspiration for Arab unity began before Abd al-Nasser and will remain after Abd al-Nasser. I always used to tell you that the nation remains, and that the individual—whatever his role and however great his contribution to the causes of his homeland—is only a tool of the popular will, and not its creator.

In accordance with Article 110 of the Provisional Constitution promulgated in March 1964 I have entrusted my colleague, friend and brother Zakariya Muhiedin with taking over the point of President and carrying out the constitutional provisions on this point. After this decision, I place all I have at his disposal in dealing with the grave situation through which our people are passing.

In doing this I am not liquidating the revolution—indeed the revolution is not the monopoly of any one generation of revolutionaries. I take pride in the brothers of this generation of revolutionaries. It has brought to pass the evacuation of British imperialism, has won the independence of Egypt and defined its Arab personality, and has combated the policy of spheres of influence in the Arab world; it has led the social revolution and created a deep transformation in the Egyptian reality by establishing the people's control over the sources of their wealth and the result of Arab action; it recovered the Suez Canal and laid down the foundation of industrial upsurge in Egypt; it built the High Dam to bring fertile greenness to the barren desert; it laid down a power network over the whole of the north of the Nile Valley; it made oil resources gush out after a long wait. More important still, it gave the leadership of political action to the alliance of the people's working forces, the constant source of renewed leaderships carrying the banners of Egyptian and Arab struggle through its successive stages, building socialism, succeeding and triumphing.

I have unlimited faith in this alliance as the leader of national action: the peasants, the workers, the soldiers, the intellectuals and national capital. Its unity and cohesion and creative response within the framework of this unity are capable of creating—through work, serious work, difficult work, as I have said more than once—colossal miracles for this country in order to be a strength for itself, for its Arab nation, for the movement of national revolution and for world peace based on justice.

The sacrifices made by our people and their burning spirit

during the crisis and the glorious pages of heroism written by the officers and soldiers of our armed forces with their blood will remain an unquenchable torch in our history and a great inspiration for the future and its great hopes. The people were splendid as usual, noble as their nature, believing, sincere and loyal. The members of our armed forces were an honourable example of Arab man in every age and every place. They defended the grains of sand in the desert to the last drop of their blood. In the air, they were, despite enemy supremacy, legends of dedication and sacrifice, of courage and willingness to perform the duty in the best way.

This is an hour for action; not an hour for sorrow. It is a situation calling for ideals and not for selfishness or personal feelings. All my heart is with you, and I want all your hearts to be with me. May God be with us all, a hope in our hearts, a light and guidance. Peace and the blessing of God be with you.

PART IV

Views and Comments:
The Arab-Israeli Conflict
Today and Tomorrow

This section of the Reader presents a selection of Israeli and Arab views about the prospects of war and peace in the Middle East as expressed since the war of 1967, as well as the analysis and/or the opinions of outside observers. Three wars in twenty years have not brought a solution of the conflict any nearer; a renewal of fighting at some future date is again thought likely as no substantial progress has been made in the attempts to mediate between the two sides. There is, moreover, the distinct danger of big power involvement, and, as a result, the transformation of a local conflict into a world crisis.

"The Most Severe Crisis"

Nasser's Revolution Anniversary Speech at Cairo University, July 23, 1967.*

Brother compatriots, the 15th anniversary of the revolution of 23rd July 1952 comes while we are living through a crisis. We will not be exaggerating if we say that this is the most severe crisis we have faced in the history of our revolutionary work.

At no time has our work been easy. We have always had to face all kinds of political, economic, and military dangers. Every victory we have achieved came after difficulties and hardships which we bore patiently.

To carry out the revolution of 23rd July was not an easy job for our people after 70 years of British occupation. For 70 years the British, in collaboration with the feudalists and the capitalists, ruled this country with the backing of 80,000 British soldiers in the Suez Canal zone. Nor was our people's resistance to the policy of pacts and zones of influence which others tried to impose on us an easy job at a time when the national liberation movement had not attained the present level of independence and non-subservience.

Moreover, our people's acceptance of the challenge to build the High Dam was not an easy job in the face of the arrogance of the United States, which thought that by withdrawing a Western offer to finance the High Dam it could harm the Egyptian economy and reveal our people as incapable of assuming the responsibility of executing such a project, which is unequalled anywhere in the world. In fact by its arrogance

---

* This speech was delivered on the fifteenth anniversary of the Egyptian revolution, on July 23, 1967 at Cairo University It is the most detailed survey from the Arab point of view of the events leading to the Arab–Israeli war.

the United States wanted our people to lose confidence in themselves and to overthrow our revolutionary regime.

Nor was our people's endurance of the horrors of the Suez war an easy job. In 1956 our people were attacked by three states, two of which were big Powers. The aggression has utilised the base that imperialism had established in the heart of the Arab homeland to threaten and terrorise this homeland, once overtly and the second time covertly.

Our people's progress in the field of socialist reconstruction, self-reliance and justice and their attempt to increase national wealth through the enormous process of industrialisation; reclamation of vast lands; electrification of the entire country; restoration of all foreign interests; elimination of monopolism, capitalism, and feudalism; redistribution of land; provision for education, health and social security services; and the participation of the workers in the profits and administration of firms —all this, brothers, was not an easy job in this country where foreign and feudalist interests once dominated the national resources. It was not an easy job in the heart of this Arab world which was dominated by foreign and feudalist interests. Whatever happens in our country has its repercussions in our entire Arab world whether we like it or not.

Our people's acceptance of the responsibilities of Arab solidarity, the common struggle and of destiny was not an easy job. In exercising these responsibilities we resisted the attempt to invade Syria in 1957, accepted the consequences of unity and secession, supported the revolution in Iraq in 1958, supported the Algerian revolution from 1954 to 1962, and backed the Yemeni revolution and the revolution in South Arabia. The latest problem we have confronted and are still confronting is the attempt to invade Syria.

Brothers, our work has never been easy. The road of the struggle is strewn with dangers, the way to glory with sacrifices, and the way to great hopes with great sacrifices. Should the peoples fail to take this course they would face rigidity and backwardness. They would take no chances and would not face life—the sweet and bitter. Those who do not shoulder responsibilities have no right to entertain hopes. Those who do not take chances become the prisoner of fear itself because of their fear. This is not the quality of vigorous peoples; it is not their nature or their course.

I have said that the crisis we now face is one of the severest we have faced in the history of our revolutionary action for more than one reason. For one thing, this crisis which we are confronting, although it is not the gravest and most difficult we have faced, certainly marks the highest degree of hypocrisy and meanness we have encountered. Imperialism—we must admit this—has benefited from all its encounters with us and with the other peoples who have frequently been exposed to its assaults. This time imperialism did not face us overtly as it did in 1956. But imperialism made an effort—and we must admit that it was skilful—to conceal its role and hide its collusion. In the end perhaps imperialism left nothing to incriminate it but its fingerprints. But this is one thing and catching imperialism redhanded as we did in 1956 is something else.

For another thing, this is perhaps the first revolution anniversary that has found our homeland in the midst of a savage conspiracy. Despite their courage and insistence on confronting it, our people undoubtedly at the same time are experiencing deep sorrow and severe pain.

Brothers, perhaps Almighty God wanted to test us to judge whether we deserve what we have achieved, whether we are able to protect our achievements, and whether we have the courage to be patient and stand firm against affliction. Brothers, perhaps Almighty God also wanted to give us a lesson to teach us what we had not learned, to remind us of some things we might have forgotten, and to cleanse our souls of the blemishes that have affected us and the shortcomings that we must avoid [applause] as we build our new society. Whatever the Almighty's will may be, we accept His test as our destiny. We are fully confident that He is with us: He will protect our struggle should we set out to struggle; grant us victory if we be determined to triumph and open the road to justice to us; endow us with victory if we be determined to be the victor; and open the road of justice to us if we be able to place ourselves on His right path.

Brother compatriots, I do not want to take you back to the circumstances which paved the way to this crisis. I explained some of these circumstances to you in my address to the nation on 9th June right after the setback. Also I realise, and we must all realise, that what happened has happened and there is no use wailing over the debris. Now it is more important to learn the lesson, overcome the setback, rise above it, and proceed triumphantly on our road towards the achievement of our aspirations.

But I do believe that we must ponder certain important matters so that we may all be able to achieve the highest degree of clarity. The first thing which should be clear to us all is that it was not we who started the crisis in the Middle East. We all know that this crisis began with Israel's attempt to invade Syria. It is quite clear to us all that in that attempt Israel was not working for itself alone but also for the forces which had got impatient with the Arab revolutionary movement.

The information we received about the invasion of Syria came from many sources. Our Syrian brothers had information that Israel had mobilised 18 brigades on their front. We confirmed this information. It became evident to us that Israel had mobilised no less than 13 brigades on the Syrian front. Our parliamentary delegation headed by Anwar as-Sadat was on a visit to Moscow, and our Soviet friends informed Anwar as-Sadat at that time that the invasion of Syria was imminent.

What were we to do? We could have remained silent, we could have waited, or we could have just issued statements and cables of support. But if this homeland had accepted such behaviour it would have meant that it was deserting its mission, its role and even its personality. There was a joint defence agreement between us and Syria. We do not consider our agreements with the peoples of our Arab nation or others merely ink on paper. To us these agreements are sacred, an honour and an obligation. Between us and Syria, between us and all Arab peoples there was and always will be something far greater and more lasting than agreements and treaties: faith in the common struggle and the common fate. Therefore it was imperative that we take concrete steps to face the danger threatening Syria, especially since the statements of Israeli political and military leaders at the time and their open threats to Syria—as reported in the press and frankly noted at the UN—left no room for anyone to doubt any information or to wait or hesitate.

The second question: when we decided to move, our actions led to certain practical results. First we asked for the withdrawal of the UN Emergency Force. Then we restored Egyptian sovereignty rights in the Gulf of Aqabah. This was one of the things our Arab brothers had always insisted on. It was natural that such steps had a great impact on the area and the world.

The third question: by moving and taking the initiative to repel the danger to Syria, we realised—particularly from an international point of view—that the question was whether we should strike first in an armed battle. Had we done this we would have exposed ourselves to very serious consequences, greater than we would have been able to tolerate. First we would have faced direct US military action against us on the pretext that we had fired the first bullet in the battle.

Here I should like to draw your attention to certain important points. The first is the US warnings. Perhaps you have read about these US warnings. President Johnson's adviser summoned our Ambassador in Washington at a late hour at night and told him that Israel had information that we were going to attack. The adviser said this would put us in a serious situation and urged us to exercise self-restraint. They also said they were telling Israel the same thing so that it would also exercise self-restraint. We also received messages from President Johnson referring to the UN and urging us to exercise self-restraint.

The second point—which perhaps I have discussed before —is that on the following day the Russian Ambassador asked to see me and conveyed to me a message from the Soviet Premier urging self-restraint. He informed me about a message he had sent to the Israeli Premier and said that any action on our part would expose the world to great danger.

The third point is that the entire international community was against the outbreak of war. President de Gaulle was clear when he said France would define its attitude on the basis of who fired the first shot.

The fourth point is that we were the victims of a diplomatic trick, a political deception in which we had not imagined a major Power would involve itself. This political trick was played by the United States. It was represented in the US President's speech, his appeals, his request that we co-operate with the UN Secretary-General, and his offer to send the Vice-President to discuss with us ways to save the entire world from this crisis. The UN Secretary-General came here and we co-operated with him to the maximum. The Secretary-General asked for a breathing-space with regard to the Gulf of Aqabah and we agreed to this. He said he wanted this breathing-space so that all concerned would have time to pause and deal with matters. The first thing we pointed out to him was that no Israeli ships would be allowed to pass through the Canal [sic], that no strategic shipments would be allowed to pass, and, in the meantime, we would not search any ships. We accepted this and considered it a proposal by the Secretary-General of the UN, providing a breathing-space for all to discuss the matter.

After that an envoy of the US President arrived here. The emissary suggested that a Vice-President go to the United States. I approved the idea on the understanding that the Vice-President would meet President Johnson and explain our attitude to him. Then I sent a letter to the US President telling him: We welcome the visit of the US Vice-President but at the same time I am prepared to send Vice-President Zakariya Muhiedin to Washington to meet you and explain the Arab view to you. Naturally, the next day I received the reply that they welcomed Zakariya Muhiedin's trip to Washington to meet the American President and they requested that we set a date. We set it for Tuesday 6th June, and we all know that the aggression began on 5th June.

What does this mean? It means that large-scale political and diplomatic activities were going on and it was right in the light of these activities to think that the explosion would not occur soon.

The fifth point: in spite of all this, we were not reassured about all these things. We knew that something was in the making and that it would not be long in coming. It was obvious that something was being planned against us. In fact, I had felt for two years that something would be prepared against us, since the cessation of US aid and America's warnings to us not to arm or enlarge our army, nor to follow a course of technical development, nor to seek military development.

When we concentrated our forces I estimated that the likelihood of war breaking out was 20 per cent. Before we closed the Gulf of Aqabah, we convened a meeting of the Higher Executive Committee at my home. We discussed the closure of the Gulf of Aqabah. That meeting took place on 22nd May. At that meeting I told them that the possibility of war was 50 per cent. At another meeting I said that the likelihood of war was 80 per cent. At our meeting of the Higher Executive Committee it was obvious that our action would be defensive, that we would attack only if aggression was launched against Syria, and that we would be on the alert. At that meeting no one spoke at all of attacking Israel. There was no intention at all that we would launch an offensive against Israel. As I explained earlier it was clear from all our analyses that any attack on Israel would expose us to great dangers. The foremost of these dangers would be an American attack on us in view of the statements America made saying that it guaranteed the borders of the states in this area. It was obvious to us that when America said it guaranteed the borders of the states in this area and would not tolerate any changes in this area, America did not at all mean the Arab states, but by this it meant Israel. It meant that if an aggression was carried out against Israel, America would implement the statement made by President Kennedy that America guaranteed all the borders in this area.

On these grounds there was no discussion at all of launching an attack on Israel. But our entire operation at the Joint Command was defensive. As we estimated at that time, our concentrations were a deterrent action so that Israel would not commit aggression against Syria.

On 23rd May we announced the closure of the Gulf of Aqabah to Israeli ships. Then came the political changes in Israel at the beginning of June. As we followed what was going on there, the probability of war became 100 per cent.

What does this mean? It means that we did not trust in the least all the political and diplomatic activities of the United States. We realised that something was being planned and that it would not take long.

On Friday 2nd June I personally went to the Armed Forces Supreme Command HQ. I participated at a meeting which was attended by all senior officers of the armed forces. At that meeting I gave my view before listening to theirs. I said at that meeting on Friday 2nd June that we must expect the enemy to strike a blow within 48 to 72 hours and no later on the basis of the indications of events and developments. I also said at that meeting that I expected the aggression to take place on Monday 5th June and the first blow to be struck at our Air Force. The Air Force commander was present at the meeting.

What does this mean? It means that we did not underestimate the situation as a result of all the diplomatic contacts, the dispatch of the UN Secretary-General, and Johnson's approval of a visit by Zakariya Muhiedin. It was quite clear on any political calculation that Israel was bound to take military action, especially after Iraqi forces had moved and Jordan had joined the joint defence agreements.

Question No. 6: After what has happened, we must faithfully and honourably admit that the military battle did not go as we had expected and hoped. It confirmed the proverb that precaution does not deter fate.

I do not wish now to talk about the causes, nor will I permit myself or this people, while the battle continues, to apportion blame. This is a matter for history and the struggle of our people. But I can say with satisfaction, good will and a conscience ready to give an account at any time that first and last the responsibility was mine. I said this in my address to the nation on 9th June, and I say it now and will continue to say it, bearing all the consequences and accepting any judgment of it. Actually this was why I decided to resign on 9th June. I wanted to take the responsibility and step down, and I wanted the enemies of the Egyptian people and the Arab nation to know that the issue is not Abd al-Nasser or Abd al-Nasser's ambitions, as they said. The Egyptian people's struggle began before Abd al-Nasser and will go on after Abd al-Nasser. The Arab nation sought its unity before Abd al-Nasser. I have said and will always say that I am not the leader of this people. The greatest honour I desire is to be their representative at a particular stage in their continuous struggle, a struggle not dependent on any individual.

Question No. 7, concerns the US role. A large part of the part played by the United States is still vague. We know only a little about this part. The secrets of the 1956 Suez war became known only last year—exactly 10 years after the war. Therefore, we shall not know the secrets of the 1967 war now. It will be some years before we know everything.

A large part of the US role in the recent aggression is still vague. But we already know a few things. We have already found the answers to several questions. What was behind the political and diplomatic part which the United States played before the battle? This role included the call for self-restraint, the threat that any action taken by us would expose the entire region to dangers, the proposal to send the US Vice-President to confer with us on the subject, the approval of Zakariya Muhiedin's trip to Washington to meet Johnson to confer on the subject and to try to reach a solution. All this took place before the aggression, before the battle.

It was a deception. We must ask: in whose interest was this deception? Certainly, it was in the interest of the imperialist-Israeli aggression. The deception was part of a US plan drawn up two years ago. The aim of this plan was to overthrow the free revolutionary regimes, which do not heed the words of the big Powers and refuse to be under anyone's influence.

What was behind the part played by the Sixth Fleet near our shores a few days before the war? How many arms were transported to Israel in the period from the outset of the crisis to the day of the aggression? How many aircraft reached Israel? How many volunteer pilots? How do we explain the huge air power which the enemy used on all Arab fronts? They attacked the Egyptian, Jordanian and Syrian fronts simultaneously. They also sent aircraft to attack Iraqi airports. On the evening of 7th June just before dawn, King Husayn contacted me by telephone saying that 400 aircraft were attacking the Jordanian front and were seen on his radar equipment. Where did these aircraft come from?

How do we explain the role of the US espionage ship *Liberty?* You have all read in the papers that an American ship named *Liberty* was near our territorial waters—probably in these waters—and that the Israelis thought it was an Egyptian warship and attacked it with torpedo boats. Some 34 officers and crew of this US ship were killed in this incident. For whom was the US ship with all its scientific equipment working? It was said that the ship was there to decode operational messages. It was also said that those messages were sent to the United States. Later it was said that the messages were sent to Israel. Messages can be radioed very rapidly. It was also said that those messages were sent to US Embassies in the area. What did the Americans do? When the Israelis hit them they pulled themselves together, hushed up the story, and went to Malta to repair the ship. Had we attacked the US ship, the Americans would have given us an ultimatum because we are neither an American colony nor an imperialist bridgehead. Nor are we in the US sphere of influence.

There is another question: why were there US aircraft over our front lines? On Wednesday 7th June two aircraft bearing US markings were seen over our lines. At first I did not believe it, but the information was certain. We then issued a statement saying that American aircraft had flown over our lines and over the front. We also said that we, therefore, believed the Americans were participating in the operation. We also spoke of the aircraft that were attacking Jordan and said that there had been a non-Israeli air attack on Jordan. We broadcast a statement including details about the two aircraft we had observed in flight.

In the evening I received a letter from President Johnson. He contacted the Soviet Head of State and requested him to send us a letter because at that time we did not have relations with him. He said it was true that there were two US aircraft over our lines, but they were going to the aid of the USS *Liberty* the spy ship.

The question arises: were there other US aircraft? A second question is: would they have made their admission had we not broadcast the statement? In fact, one asks oneself such questions about the things one knows.

What is the explanation of the US attitude at the UN and after the end of the operations? The US attitude at the UN after the operations was fully to endorse Israel's point of view. The US position at the UN was for unconditional surrender by the Arabs. This was the US position at the UN after the operations had ended. What does this mean?

There is an appalling difference between the two US attitudes—the attitude in 1956 when America was surprised by the tripartite aggression against us and the attitude in 1967 when America was not taken by surprise. In 1956 America was surprised by the tripartite aggression against us. In 1967, despite the letters and the agreement to send Zakariya Muhiedin, America was not surprised by the Israeli aggression against us. When America was surprised it stood steadfast against the aggression and demanded that it be halted and that the aggressive forces withdraw. But when America was not taken by surprise, it supported the aggression and brought pressure to bear on any State which America could influence in any way. The result was the failure of the UN as we have seen.

It is certain that America was not taken by surprise. Stories began to be told. These days American papers abound in news reports saying that the issue has provoked discussions at the highest levels in America. US papers and the American *Life* magazine said that Israel submitted to the US President the view that it should launch an attack, saying that it felt superior. US newspapers also say that the US President sought the views of the US Chief of Staff and the US Intelligence Director and that they agreed. Accordingly, Israel was allowed to launch the offensive and to perpetrate aggression. At the same time Israel obtained guarantees from the United States that should the Arabs enter Israel, the Sixth Fleet would intercept them and if Israel entered the Arab countries, America would support Israel. These stories were published in newspapers. The Israeli Premier Eshkol has thanked the US President for telling him: The Sixth Fleet is there for you and to help you. Eshkol replied in a soothing manner to the US President and told him: I am afraid that when we become exposed to danger, you will be busy with Vietnam or you may be spending the weekend at your Texas ranch. But the US President emphatically assured him that the Sixth Fleet would protect him should the Arabs cross the borders into Israel. These articles, statements and all these stories were published in the papers. Therefore, the USA was not surprised by the aggression. . . .

[The second part of the speech, which has been deleted here, was devoted to domestic problems. Ed.]

The Six Days War:

Abba Eban's Speech at the Special Assembly of the United Nations, June 19, 1967.*

Our Watchword Is 'Forward to Peace'

The subject of our discussion is the Middle East, its past agony and its future hope. We speak of a region whose destiny has profoundly affected the entire human experience. In the heart of that region, at the very centre of its geography and history, lives a very small nation called Israel. This nation gave birth to the currents of thought which have fashioned the life of the Mediterranean world and of vast regions beyond. It has now been re-established as the home and sanctuary of a people which has seen six million of its sons exterminated in the greatest catastrophe ever endured by a family of the human race.

In recent weeks the Middle East has passed through a crisis whose shadows darken the world. This crisis has many consequences but only one cause. Israel's rights to peace, security, sovereignty, economic development and maritime freedom—indeed its very right to exist—has been forcibly denied and aggressively attacked. This is the true origin of the tension which torments the Middle East. All the other elements of the conflict are the consequences of this single cause. There has been danger, there is still peril in the Middle East because Israel's existence, sovereignty and vital interests have been and are violently assailed.

The threat to Israel's existence, its peace, security, sovereignty and development has been directed against her in the

* Reprinted from *The Jerusalem Post*.

first instance by the neighbouring Arab states. But all the conditions of tension, all the impulses of aggression in the Middle
East have been aggravated by the policy of one of the Great
Powers which under our Charter bear primary responsibilities
for the maintenance of international peace and security. I
shall show how the Soviet Union has been unfaithful to that
trust. The burden of responsibility lies heavy upon her.

I come to this rostrum to speak for a united people which,
having faced danger to the national survival, is unshakably
resolved to resist any course which would renew the perils
from which it has emerged.

The General Assembly is chiefly pre-occupied by the situation against which Israel defended itself on the morning of
June 5. I shall invite every peace-loving state represented here
to ask itself how it woud have acted on that day if it faced
similar dangers. But if our discussion is to have any weight or
depth, we must understand that great events are not born in
a single instant of time. It is beyond all honest doubt that
between May 14 and June 5, Arab governments led and
directed by President Nasser, methodically prepared and
mounted an aggressive assault designed to bring about Israel's
immediate and total destruction. My authority for that conviction rests on the statements and actions of Arab governments themselves. There is every reason to believe what they
say and to observe what they do.

The Pattern of Aggression 1957–1967

During Israel's first decade, the intention to work for her
destruction by physical violence has always been part of the
official doctrine and policy of Arab states. But many members
of the United Nations hoped and believed that relative stability
would ensure from the arrangements discussed in the General
Assembly in March 1957. An attempt has been made to
inaugurate a period of non-belligerency and co-existence in
the relations between the UAR and Israel. A United Nations
emergency force was to separate the armies in Sinai and
Gaza. The Maritime Powers were to exercise free and innocent passage in the Gulf of Akaba and the Straits of Tiran.
Terrorist attacks against Israel were to cease. The Suez Canal
was to be opened to Israel shipping, as the Security Council
had decided six years before.

In March 1957, these hopes and expectations were endorsed
in the General Assembly by the United States, France, the

United Kingdom, Canada and other states in Europe, the Americas, Africa, Asia and Australia. These assurances, expressed with special solemnity by the four governments which I have mentioned, induced Israel to give up positions which she then held at Gaza and at the entrance to the Straits of Tiran and in Sinai. Non-belligerency, maritime freedom and immunity from terrorist attack were henceforth to be secured, not by Israel's own pressure but by the concerted will of the international community. Egypt expressed no opposition to these arrangements. Bright hopes for the future illuminated this hall ten years ago.

There were times during the past decade when it really seemed that a certain stability had been achieved. As we look back it becomes plain that the Arab governments regarded the 1957 arrangements merely as a breathing space enabling them to gather strength for a later assault. At the end of 1962, President Nasser began to prepare Arab opinion for an armed attack that was to take place within a few brief years. As his armaments grew his aggressive designs came more into light. On December 23, 1962, Nasser said:

'We feel that the soil of Palestine is the soil of Egypt, and of the whole Arab world. Why do we all mobilize? Because we feel that the land of Palestine is part of our land, and are ready to sacrifice ourselves for it.'

The present Foreign Minister of Egypt, Mahmoud Riad, echoed his master's voice:

'The sacred Arab struggle will not come to an end until Palestine is restored to its owners.'

In March 1963, the official Cairo radio continued the campaign of menace:

'Arab unity is taking shape towards the great goal—i.e. the triumphant return to Palestine with the banner of unity flying high in front of the holy Arab march.'

The newspaper Al-Gumhuriya published an official announcement on the same day:

'The noose around Israel's neck is tightening gradually . . . Israel is mightier than the empires which were vanquished in the Arab East and West . . . The Arab people will take possession of their full rights in their united homeland.'

Egypt is not a country in which the press utters views and opinions independently of the official will. There is thus significance in the statement of Al-Akhbar on April 4, 1963:

'The liquidation of Israel will not be realized through a declaration of war against Israel by Arab states, but *Arab unity and inter-Arab understanding will serve as a hangman's rope for Israel.*'

The Assembly will note that the imagery of a hangman's rope or of a tightening noose occurs frequently in the macabre vocabulary of Nasserism. He sees himself perpetually presiding over a scaffold. In June 1967 the metaphor of encirclement and strangulation was to come vividly to life, in Israel's hour of solitude and danger.

In February 1964 Nasser enunciated in simple terms what was to become his country's policy during the period of preparation:

'The possibilities of the future will be war with Israel. It is we who will dictate the time. It is we who will dictate the place.'

A similar chorus of threats arose during this period from other Arab capitals. President Aref of Iraq and President Ben-Bella of Algeria was especially emphatic and repetitive in their threat to liquidate Israel. The Syrian attitude was more ominous because it affected a neighbouring frontier. Syrian war propaganda has been particularly intense in the past few years. In 1964 the Syrian Defence Minister, General Abdulla Ziada, announced:

'The Syrian army stands as a mountain to crush Israel and demolish her. This army knows how to crush its enemies.'

Early last year Syria began to proclaim and carry out what it called a 'popular war' against Israel. The Syrian concept of 'popular war' expressed itself in the dispatch of trained terrorist groups into Israel territory to blow up installations and communication centres, to kill, maim, cripple and terrorise civilians in peaceful homes and farms. Sometimes the terrorists, trained in Syria, were dispatched through Jordan or Lebanon. The terrorist war was formally declared by President Al-Atassi on May 22, 1966, when he addressed soldiers on the Israel-Syrian front:

'We raise the slogan of the people's liberation war. We want total war with no limits, a war that will destroy the Zionist base.'

The Syrian Defence Minister, Hafiz Asad, said two days later:

> 'We say: We shall never call for, nor accept peace. We shall only accept war and the restoration of the usurped land. We have resolved to drench this land with our blood, to oust you, aggressors, and throw you into the sea for good. We must meet as soon as possible and fight a single liberation war on the level of the whole area against Israel, Imperialism and all the enemies of the people.'

Mr. President, from that day to this, not a week passed without Syrian officials adding to this turgid stream of invective and hate. From that day to this, there has not been a single month without terrorist acts, offensive to every impulse of human compassion and international civility, being directed from Syria against Israel citizens and territory. I would have no difficulty in filling the General Assembly's records with a thousand official statements by Arab leaders in the past two years announcing their intention to destroy Israel by diverse forms of organized physical violence. The Arab populations have been conditioned by their leaders to the anticipation of a total war, preceded by the constant harassment of the prospective victim.

Israel's Policy 1957–1967

From 1948 to this very day there has not been one statement by any Arab representative of a neighbouring Arab state indicating readiness to respect existing agreements or the permanent renunciation of force to recognize Israel's sovereign right of existence or to apply to Israel any of the central provisions of the United Nations Charter.

For some time Israel showed a stoic patience in her reaction to these words of menace. This was because the threats were not accompanied by a capacity to carry them into effect. But the inevitable result of this campaign of menace was the burden of a heavy race of arms. We strove to maintain an adequate deterrent strength and the decade beginning in March 1957 was not monopolized by security considerations alone. Behind the wall of a strong defence, with eyes vigilantly fixed on dangerous borders, we embarked on a constructive era in the national enterprise. These were years of swift expansion in our agriculture and industry, of intensive progress in the sciences and arts, of a widening international vocation, symbolized in the growth of strong links with the developing world. At the end of this first decade, Israel had established relations of commerce and culture with all the Americas, and with most of the countries of Western, Central and Eastern Europe. In her second decade she built constructive links with the emerging countries of the developing world with whom we are tied by a common aspiration to translate national freedom into creative economic growth and progress.

Fortified by friendships in all five continents, inspired by its role in the great drama of developments, intensely preoccupied by tasks of spiritual cooperation with kindred communities in various parts of the world, and in the efforts to assure the Jewish survival after the disastrous blows of Nazi oppressions, tenaciously involved in the development of original social ideas, Israel went on with its work. We could not concern ourselves exclusively with the torrent of hatred pouring in upon us from Arab governments. In the era of modern communication a nation is not entirely dependent on its regional context. The wide world is open to the voice of friendship. Arab hostility towards Israel became increasingly isolated, while our position in the international family became more deeply entrenched. Many in the world drew confidence from the fact that a very small nation could, by its exertion and example, rise to respected levels in social progress, scientific progress and the human arts, and so our policy was to deter the aggression of our neighbours so long as it was endurable, to resist it only when failure to resist would have invited its intensified renewal, to withstand Arab violence without being obsessed by it, and even to search patiently here and there for any glimmer of moderation and realism in the Arab mind. We also pursued the hope of bringing all the great powers to a harmonious policy in support of the security and sovereignty of Middle Eastern states. It was not easy to take this course. The sacrifice imposed upon our population by Arab violence was cumulative in its effects, but as it piled up month by month the toll of death and bereavement was heavy and in the last few years it was evident that this organized murder was directed by a central hand.

We were able to limit our response to this aggression so long as its own scope appeared to be limited. President Nasser seemed for some years to be accumulating inflammable material without an immediate desire to set it alight. He was heavily engaged in domination and conquest elsewhere. His speeches were strong against Israel, but his bullets, guns and poison gases were for the time being used to intimidate other

Arab states and to maintain a colonial war against the villagers of the Yemen and the peoples of the Arabian Peninsula.

But Israel's danger was great. The military build-up in Egypt proceeded at an intensive rate. It was designed to enable Egypt to press its war plans against Israel while maintaining its violent adventures elsewhere. In the face of these developments, Israel was forced to devote an increasing part of its resources to self-defence. With the declaration by Syria of the doctrine of a 'day by day military confrontation,' the situation in the Middle East grew darker. The Palestine Liberation Organization, the Palestine Liberation Army, the Unified Arab Command, the intensified expansion of military forces and equipment in Egypt, Syria, Lebanon, Jordan and more remote parts of the Arab continent—these were the signals of a growing danger to which we sought to alert the mind and conscience of the world.

The War Design, 1967

In three tense weeks between May 14, and June 5, Egypt, Syria and Jordan, assisted and incited by more distant Arab states, embarked on a policy of immediate and total aggression.

June 1967 was to be the month of decision. The 'final solution' was at hand.

There was no convincing motive for the aggressive design which was now unfolded. Egyptian and Soviet sources had claimed that a concentrated Israeli invasion of Syria was expected during the second or third week in May. No claim could be more frivolous or far-fetched. It is true that Syria was sending terrorists into Israel to lay mines on public roads and, on one occasion, to bombard the Israeli settlement at Manara from the Lebanese border. The accumulation of such actions had sometimes evoked Israeli responses always limited in scope and time. All that Syria had to do to ensure perfect tranquility on her frontier with Israel was to discourage the terrorist war. Not only did she not discourage these actions— she encouraged them, she gave them every moral and practical support. But the picture of Israeli troop concentrations in strength for an invasion of Syria was a monstrous fiction. Twice Syria refused to cooperate with suggestions by the U.N. authorities, and accepted by Israel, for a simultaneous and reciprocal inspection of the Israel-Syrian frontier. On one occasion the Soviet Ambassador complained to my Prime

Minister of heavy troop concentrations in the North of Israel. When invited to join the Prime Minister that very moment in a visit to any part of Israel which he would like to see, the distinguished envoy brusquely refused. The prospect of finding out the truth at first hand seemed to fill him with a profound disquiet. But by May 9, the Secretary-General of the United Nations from his own sources on the ground had ascertained that no Israeli troop concentration existed. This fact had been directly communicated to the Syrian and Egyptian Governments. The excuse had been shattered, but the allegations still remained. The steps which I now describe could not possibly have any motive or justification if an Israeli troop concentration, as both Egypt and Syria knew, did not exist. Indeed the Egyptian build-up ceased to be described by its authors as the result of any threat to Syria.

On May 14, Egyptian forces began to move into Sinai.

On May 16, the Egyptian Command ordered the United Nations Emergency Force to leave the border. The following morning the reason became clear. For on May 17, 1967, at 6 in the morning, Radio Cairo broadcast that Field-Marshal Amer had issued alert orders to the Egyptian armed forces. Nor did he mention Syria as the excuse. This announcement reads:

'1. The state of preparedness of the Egyptian armed forces will increase to the full level of preparedness for war, beginning 14.30 hours last Sunday.
2. Formations and units allocated in accordance with the operational plans will advance from their present locations to the designated positions.
3. The armed forces are to be in full preparedness to carry out any combat tasks on the Israel front in accordance with developments.'

On May 18, Egypt called for the total removal of the United Nations Emergency Force. The Secretary-General of the United Nations acceded to this request and moved to carry out, without reference to the Security Council or the General Assembly, without carrying out the procedures indicated by Secretary-General Hammerskjold in the event of a request for a withdrawal being made, without heeding the protesting voices of some of the permanent members of the Security Council and of the government at whose initiative the force had been established, without consulting Israel on the consequent prejudice to her military security and her vital maritime freedom, and without seeking such delay as would enable alternative measures to be concerted for preventing belligerency by sea and a dangerous confrontation of forces by land.

It is often said that United Nations procedures are painfully slow. This decision was disastrously swift. Its effect was to make Sinai safe for belligerency from North to South, to create a sudden disruption of the local security balance, and to leave an international maritime interest exposed to almost certain threat. I have already said that Israel's attitude to the peace-keeping functions of the United Nations has been traumatically affected by its experience. What is the use of a fire brigade which vanishes from the scene as soon as the first smoke and flames appear? Is it surprising that we are firmly resolved never again to allow a vital Israel interest and our very security to rest on such a fragile foundation?

The clouds now gathered thick and fast. Between May 14 and May 23, Egyptian concentrations in Sinai increased day by day. Israel took corresponding measures. In the absence of an agreement to the contrary it is, of course, legal for any state to place its armies wherever it chooses in its territory. It is equally true that nothing could be more uncongenial to the prospect of peace than to have large armies facing each other across a narrow space, with one of them clearly bent on an early assault. For the purpose of the concentration was not in doubt. On May 18, at 24.00 hours, the Cairo radio, Saut el-Arab, published the following order of the day by Abdul Mushin Murtagi, the General then commanding Sinai:

'The Egyptian forces have taken up positions in accordance with a definite plan.

'Our forces are definitely ready to carry the battle beyond the borders of Egypt.

'Morale is very high among the members of our armed forces because this is the day for which they have been waiting—to make a holy war in order to return the plundered land to its owners.

'In many meetings with army personnel they asked when the holy war would begin—the time has come to give them their wish.'

On May 21 General Amer gave the order to mobilize reserves. Now came the decisive step. All doubt that Egypt had decided upon immediate or early war was now dispelled. Appearing at an Air Force Base at 6 o'clock in the morning, President Nasser announced that he would blockade the Gulf of Akaba to Israeli ships, adding: 'The Jews threaten war and we say: by all means, we are ready for war.'

But the Jews were not threatening war. Prime Minister Eshkol was calling for a de-escalation of forces. Nasser treated this as a sign of weakness.

On May 25, Cairo Radio announced:

'The Arab people is firmly resolved to wipe Israel off the map and to restore the honour of the Arabs of Palestine.'

On the following day, May 26, Nasser spoke again:

'The Arab people wants to fight. We have been waiting for the right time when we will be completely ready. Recently we have felt that our strength has been sufficient and that if we make battle with Israel we shall be able, with the help of God, to conquer. Sharm e-Sheikh implies a confrontation with Israel. Taking this step makes it imperative that we be ready to undertake a total war with Israel.'

Writing in Al-Ahram, on May 26, Nasser's mouthpiece, Hasanein Heikal, wrote, with engaging realism:

'I consider that there is no alternative to armed conflict between the United Arab Republic and the Israeli enemy. This is the first time that the Arab challenge to Israel attempts to change an existing fact in order to impose a different fact in its place.'

On May 28, Nasser had a press conference. He was having them every day. He said:

'We will not accept any possibility of co-existence with Israel.'

And on the following day:

'If we have succeeded to restore the situation to what it was before 1956, there is no doubt that God will help us and will inspire us to restore the situation to what it was prior to 1948.'

There are various ways of threatening Israel's liquidation. Few ways could be clearer than this.

The troop concentrations and blockade were now to be accompanied by encirclement. The noose was to be fitted around the victim's neck. Other Arab states were closing the ring. On May 30 Nasser signed the Defence Agreement with Jordan, and described its purpose in these terms:

'The armies of Egypt, Jordan, Syria and Lebanon are stationed on the borders of Israel in order to face the challenge. Behind them stand the armies of Iraq, Algeria, Kuwait, Sudan and the whole of the Arab nation.

'This deed will astound the world. Today they will know that the Arabs are ready for the fray. The hour of decision has arrived.'

On June 4 Nasser made a statement on Cairo Radio after signing the protocol associating Iraq with the Egyptian-Jordanian Defence Pact. Here are his words:

'. . . We are facing you in the battle and are burning with desire for it to start, in order to obtain revenge. This will make the world realize what the Arabs are and what Israel is . . .'

Mr. President, Nothing has been more startling in recent weeks than to read discussions about who planned, who organized, who initiated, who wanted and who launched this war. Here we have a series of statements, mounting in crescendo from vague warning through open threat, to precise intention.

Here we have the vast mass of the Egyptian armies in Sinai with seven infantry and two armoured divisions, the greatest force ever assembled in that Peninsula in all its history. Here we have 40,000 regular Syrian troops poised to strike at the Jordan Valley from advantageous positions in the hills. Here we have the mobilized forces of Jordan, with their artillery and mortars trained on Israel's population centres in Jerusalem and along the vulnerable narrow coastal plain. Troops from Iraq, Kuwait and Algeria converge towards the battle-front at Egypt's behest. 900 tanks face Israel on the Sinai border, while 200 more are poised to strike the isolated town of Eilat at Israel's southern tip. The military dispositions tell their own story. The Northern Negev was to be invaded by armour and bombarded from the Gaza Strip. From May 27 onward, Egyptian air squadrons in Sinai were equipped with operation orders instructing them in detail on the manner in which Israeli airfields, pathetically few in number, were to be bombarded, thus exposing Israel's crowded cities to easy and merciless assault. Egyptian air sorties came in and out of Israel's southern desert to reconnoitre, inspect and prepare for the asault. An illicit blockade had cut Israel off from all her commerce with the eastern half of the world.

Blockade on Tiran Straits

Those who write this story in years to come will give a special place in their narrative to Nasser's blatant decision to close the Straits of Tiran in Israel's face. It is not difficult to understand why this outrage had a drastic impact. In 1957 the maritime nations, within the framework of the United Nations General Assembly, correctly enunciated the doctrine of free and innocent passage to the Straits. When that doctrine was proclaimed—and incidentally, not challenged by the Egyptian Representative at that time—it was little more than an abstract principle for the maritime world. For Israel it was a great but still unfulfilled prospect, it was not yet a reality. But during the ten years in which we and the other states of the maritime community have relied upon that doctrine and upon established usage, the principle had become a reality consecrated by hundreds of sailings under dozens of flags and the establishment of a whole complex of commerce and industry and communication. A new dimension has been added to the map of the world's communication. And on that dimension we have constructed Israel's bridge towards the friendly states of Asia and Africa, a network of relationships which is the chief pride of Israel in the second decade of its independence and on which its economic future depends.

All this, then, had grown up as an effective usage under the United Nations' flag. Does Mr. Nasser really think that he can come upon the scene in ten minutes and cancel the established legal usage and interests of ten years?

There was in his wanton act a quality of malice. For surely the closing of the Straits of Tiran gave no benefit whatever to Egypt except the perverse joy of inflicting injury on others. It was an anarchic act, because it showed a total disregard for the law of nations, the application of which in this specific case had not been challenged for ten years. And it was, in the literal sense, an act of arrogance, because there are other nations in Asia and East Africa that trade with the port of Eilat, as they have every right to do, through the Straits of Tiran and across the Gulf of Akaba. Other sovereign states from Japan to Ethiopia, from Thailand to Uganda, from Cambodia to Madagascar, have a sovereign right to decide for themselves whether they wish or do not wish to trade with Israel. These countries are not colonies of Cairo. They can trade with Israel or not trade with Israel as they wish, and

President Nasser is not the policeman of other African and Asian States.

Here then was a wanton intervention in the sovereign rights of other states in the eastern half of the world to decide for themselves whether or not they wish to establish trade relations with either or both of the two ports at the head of the Gulf of Akaba.

An Act of War

When we examine, then, the implications of this act, we have no cause to wonder that the international shock was great. There was another reason, too, for that shock. Blockades have traditionally been regarded, in the pre-Charter parlance, as acts of war. To blockade, after all, is to attempt strangulation—and sovereign states are entitled not to have their State strangled.

The blockade is by definition an act of war, imposed and enforced through violence.

Never in history have blockade and peace existed side by side. From May 24 onward, the question of who started the war or who fired the first shot became momentously irrelevant. There is no difference in civil law between murdering a man by slow strangulation or killing him by a shot in the head. From the moment at which the blockade was imposed, active hostilities had commenced and Israel owed Egypt nothing of her Charter rights. If a foreign power sought to close Odessa, or Copenhagen or Marseilles or New York Harbour by the use of force, what would happen? Would there be any discussion about who had fired the first shot? Would anyone ask whether aggression had begun? Less than a decade ago the Soviet Union proposed a draft resolution in the General Assembly on the question of defining aggression. The resolution reads:

'In an international conflict, that State shall be declared an attacker which first commits one of the following acts:
    a. Naval blockade of the coastal ports of another State.'

This act constituted in the Soviet view aggression as distinguished from other specific acts designated in the Soviet draft as indirect aggression. In this particular case the consequences of Nasser's action had been fully announced in advance. On March 1, 1967, my predecessor announced that:

'Interference, by armed force, with ships of the Israel flag exercising free and innocent passage in the Gulf of Akaba and through the Straits of Tiran, will be regarded by Israel as an attack entitling it to exercise its inherent right of self-defence under Article 51 of the United Nations Charter and to take all such measures as are necessary to ensure the free and innocent passage of its ships in the Gulf and in the Straits.'

The representative of France declared that any obstruction of free passage in the Straits or Gulf was contrary to international law 'entailing a possible resort to the measures authorized by Article 51 of the Charter.'

The United States, inside and outside of the United Nations, gave specific endorsement to Israel's right to invoke her inherent right of self-defence against any attempt to blockade the Gulf. Nasser was speaking with acute precision when he stated that Israel now faced the choice either between being choked to death in her southern maritime approaches or to await the death blow from Northern Sinai.

Nobody who lived through those days in Israel, between May 23 and June 5, will ever forget the air of doom that hovered over our country. Hemmed in by hostile armies ready to strike, affronted and beset by a flagrant act of war, bombarded day and night by predictions of her approaching extinction, forced into a total mobilization of all her manpower, her economy and commerce beating with feeble pulse, her main supplies of vital fuel choked by a belligerent act, Israel faced the greatest peril of her existence that she had known since her resistance against aggression 19 years before, at the hour of her birth. There was peril wherever she looked and she faced it in deepening solitude. On May 24 and on succeeding days, the Security Council conducted a desultory debate which sometimes reached a point of levity. The Soviet Representative asserted that he saw no reason for discussing the Middle Eastern situation at all. The Bulgarian delegate uttered these unbelievable words.

'At the present moment there is really no need for an urgent meeting of the Security Council.'

A crushing siege bore down upon us. Multitudes throughout the world trembled for Israel's fate. The single consolation lay in the surge of public opinion which rose up in Israel's defence. From Paris to Montevideo, from New York to Amsterdam, tens of thousands of persons of all ages, peoples and affiliations marched in horrified protest at the approaching stage of genocide. Writers and scientists, religious leaders, trade union movements and even the Communist parties in France, Holland, Switzerland, Norway, Austria and Finland asserted their view that Israel was a peace-loving State, whose peace was being wantonly denied. In the history of our generation it is difficult to think of any other hour in which progressive world opinion rallied in such tension and agony of spirit.

To understand the full depth of pain and shock, it is necessary to grasp the full significance of what Israel's danger meant. A small sovereign State had its existence threatened by lawless violence. The threat to Israel was a menace to the very foundations of the international order. The State thus threatened bore a name which stirred the deepest memories of civilized mankind and the people of the remnant of millions, who, in living memory had been wiped out by a dictatorship more powerful, through scarcely more malicious, than Nasser's Egypt. What Nasser had predicted, what he had worked for with undeflecting purpose, had come to pass—the noose was tightly drawn.

On the fateful morning of June 5, when Egyptian forces moved by air and land against Israel's western coast and southern territory, our country's choice was plain. The choice was to live or perish, to defend the national existence or to forfeit it for all time.

From these dire moments Israel emerged in five heroic days from awful peril to successful and glorious resistance. Alone, unaided, neither seeking nor receiving help, our nation rose in self-defence. So long as men cherish freedom, so long as small states strive for the dignity of existence, the exploits of Israel's armies will be told from one generation to another with the deepest pride. The Soviet Union has described our resistance as aggression and sought to have it condemned. We reject this accusation with all our might. Here was armed force employed in a just and righteous cause, as righteous as the defenders at Valley Forge, as just as the expulsion of Hitler's bombers from the British skies, as noble as the protection of Stalingrad against the Nazi hordes, so was the defence of Israel's security and existence against those who sought our nation's destruction.

What should be condemned is not Israel's action, but the attempt to condemn it. Never have freedom, honour, justice, national interest and international morality been so righteously protected. While fighting raged on the Egyptian-Israel frontier and on the Syrian front, we still hoped to contain the conflict. Jordan was given every chance to remain outside the struggle. Even after Jordan had bombarded and bombed Israel territory at several points we still proposed to the Jordanian monarch that he abstain from general hostilities. A message to this effect reached him several hours after the outbreak of hostilities on the southern front on June 5.

Jordan answered not with words but with shells. Artillery opened fire fiercely along the whole front with special emphasis on the Jerusalem area. Thus Jordan's responsibility for the second phase of the concerted aggression is established beyond doubt. This responsibility cannot fail to have its consequences in the peace settlement. As death and injury rained on the city, Jordan had become the source and origin of Jerusalem's fierce ordeal. The inhabitants of the city can never forget this fact, or fail to draw its conclusions.

Soviet Role in the Middle East Crisis

Mr. President, I have spoken of Israel's defence against the assaults of neighbouring states. This is not the entire story. Whatever happens in the Middle East for good or ill, for peace or conflict, is powerfully affected by what the Great Powers do or omit to do. When the Soviet Union initiates a discussion here, our gaze is inexorably drawn to the story of its role in recent Middle Eastern history. It is a sad and shocking story, it must be frankly told.

Since 1955 the Soviet Union has supplied the Arab States with 2,000 tanks, of which more than 1,000 have gone to Egypt. The Soviet Union has supplied the Arab States with 700 modern fighter aircraft and bombers, more recently with ground missiles, and Egypt alone has received from the U.S.S.R. 540 field guns, 130 medium guns, 200 120 mm mortars, anti-aircraft guns, 175 rocket launchers, 650 anti-tank guns, seven destroyers, a number of Luna M and SPKA 2 ground-to-ground missiles, 14 submarines and 46 torpedo boats of various types including missile-carrying boats. The Egyptian Army has been trained by Soviet experts. This has been attested to by Egyptian officers captured by Israel. Most of this equipment was supplied to the Arab States after the Cairo Summit Conference of Arab leaders in January 1964 had agreed on a specific programme for the destruction of Israel, after they had announced and hastened to fulfil this plan by accelerating their arms purchases from the Soviet

Union. The proportions of Soviet assistance are attested to by the startling fact that in Sinai alone the Egyptians abandoned equipment and offensive weapons of Soviet manufacture whose value is estimated at two billion dollars.

Together with the supply of offensive weapons, the Soviet Union has encouraged the military preparations of the Arab States.

Since 1961, the Soviet Union has assisted Egypt in its desire to conquer Israel. The great amount of offensive equipment supplied to the Arab States strengthens this assessment.

A Great Power which professes its devotion to peaceful settlement and the rights of states has for 14 years afflicted the Middle East with a headlong armaments race, with the paralysis of the United Nations as an instrument of security and against those who defend it.

The constant increase and escalation of Soviet armaments in Arab countries has driven Israel to a corresponding, though far smaller, procurement programme. Israel's arms purchases were precisely geared to the successive phases of Arab, and especially Egyptian, rearmament. On many occasions in recent months we and others have vainly sought to secure Soviet agreement for a reciprocal reduction of arms supplies in our region. These efforts have borne no fruit. The expenditure on social and economic progress of one half of what has been put into the purchase of Soviet arms would have been sufficient to redeem Egypt from its social and economic ills. A corresponding diversion of resources from military to social expenditure would have taken place in Israel. A viable balance of forces could have been achieved at a lower level of armaments, while our region could have moved forward to higher standards of human and social welfare. For Israel's attitude is clear. We should like to see the arms race slowed down. But if the race is joined, we are determined not to lose it. A fearful waste of economic energy in the Middle East is the direct result of the Soviet role in the constant stimulation of the race in arms.

It is clear from Arab sources that the Soviet Union has played a provocative role in spreading alarmist and incendiary reports of Israel intentions amongst Arab Governments.

On June 9 President Nasser said:

'Our friends in the U.S.S.R. warned the visiting parliamentary delegation in Moscow at the beginning of last month, that there exists a plan of attack against Syria.'

Similarly an announcement by Tass of May 23 states:

'The Foreign Affairs and Security Committee of the Knesset have accorded the Cabinet special powers to carry out war operations against Syria. Israeli forces concentrating on the Syrian border have been put in a state of alert for war. General mobilization has also been proclaimed in the country . . .'

There was not one word of truth in this story. But its diffusion in the Arab countries could only have an incendiary result.

Cairo Radio broadcast on May 28 (0500 hours) an address by Marshal Gretchko at a farewell party in honour of the former Egyptian Minister of Defence, Shams ed-Din Badran:

'The U.S.S.R., her armed forces, her people and Government will stand by the Arabs and will continue to encourage and support them. We are your faithful friends and we shall continue aiding you because this is the policy of the Soviet nation, its Party and Government. On behalf of the Ministry of Defence and in the name of the Soviet nation we wish you success and victory.'

This promise of military support came less than a week after the illicit closing of the Tiran Straits, an act which the U.S.S.R. has done nothing to condemn.

U.S.S.R. Attitudes at the U.N.

The U.S.S.R. has exercised her veto right in the Security Council five times. Each time a just and constructive judgment has been frustrated. On January 22, 1964, France, the United Kingdom and the United States presented a Draft Resolution to facilitate work on the West Bank of the River Jordan in the B'not Ya'akov Canal Project. The Soviet veto held up regional water development for several years. On March 29, 1954, a New Zealand resolution simply reiterating U.N. policy on blockade along the Suez Canal was frustrated by Soviet dissent. On August 19, 1963, a United Kingdom and United States Resolution on the murder of two Israelis at Almagor was denied adoption by Soviet opposition. On December 21, 1964, the U.S.S.R. vetoed a United Kingdom and United States Resolution on incidents at Tel Dan, including the shelling of Dan, Dafna and Sha'ar Yashuv. On November 2, 1966, Argentina, Japan, the Netherlands, New Zealand and Nigeria joined to express regret at 'infiltration from Syria and loss of human life caused by the incidents in October and November 1966.' This was one of the few resolutions sponsored by member-States from five continents.

The Soviet use of veto has had a dual effect. First, it prevented any resolution which an Arab State has opposed, from being adopted by the Council. Secondly, it has inhibited the Security Council from taking constructive action in disputes between an Arab State and Israel because of the certain knowledge that the veto would be applied in what was deemed to be the Arab interest. The consequences of the Soviet veto policy have been to deny Israel any possibility of just and equitable treatment in the Security Council, and to nullify the Council as a constructive factor in the affairs of the Middle East.

Does all this really add up to a constructive intervention by the U.S.S.R. in the Arab-Israel tension? The position becomes graver when we recall the unbridled invective against the Permanent Representative of Israel in the Security Council. In its words and in the letter to the Israel Government, the U.S.S.R. has formulated an obscene comparison between the Israel Defence Forces and the Hitlerite hordes which overran Europe in the Second World War. There is a flagrant breach of international morality and human decency in this comparison. Our nation never compromised with Hitler Germany. It never signed a pact with it as did the U.S.S.R. in 1939.

To associate the name of Israel with the accursed tyrant who engulfed the Jewish people in a tidal wave of slaughter is to violate every canon of elementary taste and fundamental truth.

In the light of this history, the General Assembly will easily understand Israel's reaction to the Soviet initiative in convening this Special Session for the purpose of condemning our country and recommending a withdrawal to the position that existed before June 5.

Your (the Soviet) Government's record in the stimulation of the arms race, in the paralysis of the Security Council, in the encouragement throughout the Arab World of unfounded suspicion concerning Israel's intentions, your constant refusal to say a single word of criticism at any time of declarations threatening the violent overthrow of Israel's sovereignty and existence—all this gravely undermines your claims to objectivity. You come here in our eyes not as a judge or as a prosecutor, but rather as a legitimate object of international criticism for the part that you have played in the sombre events which have brought our region to a point of explosive tension.

If the Soviet Union had made an equal distribution of the friendship amongst the peoples of the Middle East, if it had refrained from exploiting regional rancours and tensions for the purpose of its own global policy, if it had stood in even-handed devotion to the legitimate interests of all states, the crisis which now commands our attention and anxiety would never have occurred. To the charge of aggression I answer that Israel's resistance at the lowest ebb of its fortunes will resound across history, together with the uprising of our battered remnants in the Warsaw Ghetto, as a triumphant assertion of human freedom. From the dawn of its history the people now rebuilding a State in Israel has struggled often in desperate conditions against tyranny and aggression. Our action on June 5 falls nobly within that tradition. We have tried to show that even a small state and a small people have the right to live. I believe that we shall not be found alone in the assertion of that right, which is the very essence of the Charter of the United Nations. Similarly, the suggestion that everything goes back to where it was before the 5th of June is totally unacceptable. The General Assembly cannot ignore the fact that the Security Council, where the primary responsibility lay, has emphatically rejected such a course. It was not Israel, but Syria, Egypt and Jordan, who violently shattered the previous situation to smithereens. It cannot be recaptured. It is a fact of technology that it is easier to fly to the moon than to reconstruct a broken egg. The Security Council acted wisely in rejecting the backward step, advocated by the Soviet Union. To go back to the situation out of which the conflict arose would mean that all the conditions for renewed hostilities would be brought together again. I repeat what I said to the Security Council. Our watchword is not 'backward to belligerency' but 'forward to peace'.

What the Assembly should prescribe is not a formula for renewed hostilities, but a series of principles for the construction of a new future in the Middle East. With the cease-fire established, our progress must be not backward to an armistice regime which has collapsed under the weight of years and the brunt of hostility. History summons us forward to permanent peace and the peace that we envisage can only be elaborated in frank and lucid dialogue between Israel and each of the states which have participated in the attempt to overthrow her sovereignty and undermine her existence. We dare not be satisfied with intermediate arrangements which are neither war nor peace. Such patchwork ideas carry within themselves the seeds of future tragedy. Free from external pressures and interventions, imbued with a common love for a region which they are destined to share, the Arab and Jewish nations must now transcend their conflicts in dedication to a new Mediterranean future in concert with a renascent Europe and an Africa and Asia which have emerged at last to their independent role on the stage of history.

The Vision of Peace

In free negotiation with each of our neighbours we shall offer durable and just solutions redounding to our mutual advantage and honour. The Arab states can no longer be permitted to recognize Israel's existence only for the purpose of plotting its elimination. They have come face to face with us in conflict. Let them now come face to face with us in peace.

In peaceful conditions we could imagine communications running from Haifa to Beirut and Damascus in the north, to Amman and beyond in the east, and to Cairo in the south. The opening of these blocked arteries would stimulate the life, thought and commerce in the region beyond any level otherwise conceivable. Across the southern Negev, communication between the Nile Valley and the fertile crescent could be resumed without any change in political jurisdiction. What is now often described as a wedge between Arab lands would become a bridge. The Kingdom of Jordan, now cut off from its maritime outlet, could freely import and export its goods on the Israeli coast. On the Red Sea, cooperative action could expedite the port developments at Eilat and Akaba, which give Israel and Jordan their contact with a resurgent East Africa and a developing Asia.

The Middle East, lying athwart three continents, could become a busy centre of air communications, which are now impeded by boycotts and the necessity to take circuitous routes. Radio, telephone and postal communications, which now end abruptly in mid-air, would unite a divided region. The Middle East, with its historic monuments and scenic beauty, could attract a vast movement of travellers and pilgrims if existing impediments were removed. Resources which

lie across national frontiers—the minerals of the Dead Sea
and the phosphates of the Negev and the Arava—could be
developed in mutual interchange of technical knowledge. Economic cooperation in agricultural and industrial development
could lead to supranational arrangements like those which
mark the European community. The United Nations could
establish an economic commission for the Middle East, similar to the commissions now at work in Europe, Latin America and the Far East. The specialized agencies could intensify
their support of health and educational development with
greater efficiency if a regional harmony were attained. The
development of arid zones, the desalination of water and the
conquest of tropical disease are common interests of the entire region, congenial to a sharing of knowledge and experience.

In the institutions of scientific research and higher education of both sides of the frontiers, young Israelis and Arabs
could join in a mutual discourse of learning. The old prejudices could be replaced by a new comprehension and respect,
born of a reciprocal dialogue in the intellectual domain. In
such a Middle East, military budgets would spontaneously
find a less exacting point of equilibrium. Excessive sums devoted to security could be diverted to development projects.

Thus, in full respect of the region's diversity, an entirely
new story, never known or told before, would unfold across
the Eastern Mediterranean. For the first time in history, no
Mediterranean nation is in subjection. All are endowed with
sovereign freedom. The challenge now is to use this freedom
for creative growth. There is only one road to that end. It is
the road of recognition, of direct contact, of true cooperation.
It is the road of peaceful co-existence. This road, as the
ancient prophets of Israel foretold, leads to Jerusalem.

Jerusalem, now united after her tragic division, is no longer
an arena for gun emplacements and barbed wire. In our nation's long history there have been few hours more intensely
moving than the hour of our reunion with the Western Wall.
A people had come back to the cradle of its birth. It has renewed its link with the memories which that reunion evokes.
For 20 years there has not been free access by men of all
faiths to the shrines which they hold in unique reverence.
This access now exists. Israel is resolved to give effective expression, in cooperation with the world's great religions, to
the immunity and sanctity of all the Holy Places. The prospect

of a negotiated peace is less remote than it may seem. Israel waged her defensive struggle in pursuit of two objectives—security and peace. Peace and security, with their territorial, economic and demographic implications, can only be built by the free negotiation which is the true essence of sovereign responsibility. A call to the recent combatants to negotiate the conditions of their future co-existence is the only constructive course which this Assembly could take.

We ask the great powers to remove our tormented region from the scope of global rivalries, to summon its governments to build their common future themselves, to assist it, if they will, to develop social and cultural levels worthy of its past.

We ask the developing countries to support a dynamic and forward-looking policy and not to drag the new future back into the out-worn past.

To the small nations, which form the bulk of the international family, we offer the experience which teaches us that small communities can best secure their interests by maximal self-reliance. Nobody will help those who will not help themselves; we ask the small nations in the solidarity of our smallness, to help us stand firm against intimidation and threat such as those by which we are now assailed. We ask world opinion, which rallied to us in our plight, to accompany us faithfully in our new opportunity. We ask the United Nations, which was prevented from offering us security in our recent peril, to respect our independent quest for the peace and security which are the Charter's higher ends. We shall do what the Security Council decided should be done—and reject the course which the Security Council emphatically and wisely rejected. It may seem that Israel stands alone against numerous and powerful adversaries. But we have faith in the undying forces in our nation's history which have so often given the final victory to spirit over matter, to inner truth over mere quantity. We believe in the vigilance of history which has guarded our steps. The Guardian of Israel neither slumbers nor sleeps.

The Middle East, tired of wars, is ripe for a new emergence of human vitality. Let the opportunity not fall again from our hands.

The Right of Israel

By Yizhak Rabin*

Your Excellency, President of the State, Mr. Prime Minister, President of the Hebrew University, Rector of the University; Governors, Teachers, Ladies and Gentlemen:

I stand in awe before you, leaders of the generation, here in this venerable and impressive place overlooking Israel's eternal capital and the birth-place of our Nation's earliest history.

Together with other distinguished personalities who are no doubt worthy of this honour, you have chosen to do me great honour in conferring upon me the title of Doctor of Philosophy. Permit me to express to you here my feelings on this occasion. I regard myself, at this time, as a representative of the entire Israel Forces, of its thousands of officers and tens of thousands of soldiers who brought the State of Israel its victory in the six-day war. It may be asked why the University saw fit to grant the title of Honorary Doctor of Philosophy to a soldier in recognition of his martial activities. What is there in common to military activity and the academic world which represents civilisation and culture? What is there in common between those whose profession is violence and spiritual values? I, however, am honoured that through me you are expressing such deep appreciation to my comrades in arms and to the uniqueness of the Israel Defence Forces, which is no more than extension of the unique spirit of the entire Jewish People.

The world has recognised the fact that the Israel Defence Forces are different from other armies. Although its first task is the military task of ensuring security, the Israel Defence Forces undertakes numerous tasks of peace, tasks not of destruction but of construction and of the strengthening of the Nation's cultural and moral resources.

Our educational work has been praised widely and was given national recognition, when in 1966 it was granted the Israel Prize for Education, The Nahal, which combines military training and agricultural settlement, teachers in border villages contributing to social and cultural enrichment, these

---

* The text of an address by Rabin, formerly Israeli chief of staff and at present Israeli Ambassador in the United States, on the occasion of receiving an honorary doctorate from the Hebrew University, June 28, 1967.

are but a few small examples of the Israel Defence Forces'
uniqueness in this sphere.

However, today, the University has conferred this honorary
title on us in recognition of our Army's superiority of spirit
and morals as it was revealed in the heat of war, for we are
standing in this place by virtue of battle which though forced
upon us was forged into a victory astounding the world.

War is intrinsically harsh and cruel, bloody and tear-stained,
but particularly this war, which we have just undergone,
brought forth rare and magnificent instances of heroism and
courage, together with humane expressions of brotherhood,
comradeship, and spiritual greatness.

Whoever has not seen a tank crew continue its attack with
its commander killed and its vehicle badly damaged, whoever
has not seen sappers endangering their lives to extricate
wounded comrades from a minefield, whoever has not seen
the anxiety and the effort of the entire Air Force devoted to
rescuing a pilot who has fallen in enemy territory, cannot
know the meaning of devotion between comrades in arms.

The entire Nation was exalted and many wept upon hearing
the news of the capture of the Old City. Our Sabra Youth and
most certainly our soldiers do not tend to sentimentality and
shy away from revealing it in public. However, the strain of
battle, the anxiety which preceded it, and the sense of salvation and of direct participation of every soldier in the forging
of the heart of Jewish history cracked the shell of hardness
and shyness and released well-springs of excitement and spiritual emotion. The paratroopers, who conquered the Wailing
Wall, leaned on its stones and wept, and as a symbol this was
a rare occasion, almost unparalleled in human history. Such
phrases and cliches are not generally used in our Army but
this scene on the Temple Mount beyond the power of verbal
description revealed as though by a lightning flash deep truths.
And more than this, the joy of triumph seized the whole nation. Nevertheless we find more and more and more a strange
phenomenon among our fighters. Their joy is incomplete, and
more than a small portion of sorrow and shock prevails in
their festivities. And there are those who abstain from all cele-
bration. The warriors in the front lines saw with their own
eyes not only the glory of victory but the price of victory.
Their comrades who fell beside them bleeding. And I know
that even the terrible price which our enemies paid touched
the hearts of many of our men. It may be that the Jewish
People never learned and never accustomed itself to feel the

triumph of conquest and victory and therefore we receive it with mixed feelings.

The six-day war revealed many instances of heroism far beyond the single attack which dashes unthinkingly forward. In many places desperate and lengthy battles raged. In Rafiah, in El Arish, in Um Kataf, in Jerusalem, and in Ramat Hagollan, there, and in many other places, the soldiers of Israel were revealed as heroic in spirit, in courage, and in persistence which cannot leave anyone indifferent once he has seen this great and exalting human revelation. We speak a great deal of the few against the many. In this war perhaps for the first time since the Arab invasions of the spring of 1948 and the battles of Negba and Degania, units of the Israel Forces stood in all sectors, few against many. This means that relatively small units of our soldiers, often entered seemingly endless networks of fortification, surrounded by hundreds and thousands of enemy troops and faced with the task of forcing their way, hour after hour, in this jungle of dangers, even after the momentum of the first attack has passed and all that remains is the necessity of belief in our strength, the lack of alternative and the goal for which we are fighting, to summon up every spiritual resource in order to continue the fight to its very end.

Thus our armoured Forces broke through on all fronts, our paratroopers fought their way into Rafiah and Jerusalem, our sappers cleared minefields under enemy fire. The units which broke the enemy lines and came to their objectives after hours upon hours of struggle continuing on and on, while their comrades fell right and left and they continued forward, only forward. These soldiers were carried forward by spiritual values, by deep spiritual resources, far more than by their weapons or the technique of warfare.

We have always demanded the cream of our youth for the Israel Defence Forces when we coined the slogan 'Hatovim l'Tayis'—The Best to Flying, and this was a phrase which became a value. We meant not only technical and manual skills. We meant that if our airmen were to be capable of defeating the forces of four enemy countries within a few short hours, they must have moral values and human values.

Our airmen, who struck the enemies' planes so accurately that no one in the world understands how it was done and people seek technological explanations of secret weapons; our armoured troops who stood and beat the enemy even when their equipment was inferior to his; our soldiers in all various branches of the Israel Defence Forces who overcame our en-

emies everywhere, despite their superior numbers and forti-
fications; all these revealed not only coolness and courage in
battle but a burning faith in their righteousness, an understanding that only their personal stand against the greatest of
dangers could bring to their country and to their families
victory, and that if the victory was not theirs the alternative
was destruction.

Furthermore, in every sector our Forces' commanders, of
all ranks far outshone the enemies' commanders. Their understanding, their will, their ability to improvise, their care for
soldiers and above all, their leading troops into battle, these
are not matters of material or of technique. They have no
rational explanation, except in terms of a deep consciousness
of the moral justice of their fight.

All of this springs from the soul and leads back to the spirit.
Our warriors prevailed not by their weapons but by the consciousness of a mission, by a consciousness of righteousness,
by a deep love for their homeland and an understanding of
the difficult task laid upon them; to ensure the existence of our
people in its homeland, to protect, even at the price of their
lives, the right of the Nation of Israel to live in its own State,
free, independent and peaceful.

This Army, which I had the privilege of commanding
through these battles, came from the people and returns to
the people, to the people which rises in its hour of crisis and
overcomes all enemies by virtue of its moral values, its spiritual readiness in the hour of need.

As the representative of the Israel Defence Forces, and in
the name of everyone of its soldiers, I accept with pride your
recognition.

"We Shall Triumph"

**President Nasser's speech at the National
Congress of the Arab Socialist Union at
Cairo University, Cairo, July 23, 1968. (The
first part of the speech, which is omitted,
was devoted to questions of domestic policy.)**

The Middle East crisis: I do not want to go back to the
circumstances which led to the Middle East crisis. All the details are known, starting with the premeditated aggression
against Arab territory, to the imperialist collusion with the
Israeli enemy, to the 5th June setback and its serious and sad

results for our Arab nation. As you know, we lost the major part of our military power. We accepted the political solution experiment for several reasons. At that time we had no alternative to talking about a political solution; we had no armed forces to depend on. At the same time we are not advocates of war for the sake of war—not at all. If we can obtain our rights through political action, as happened in 1957, fine; if not, we have no alternative but to struggle for our rights and to liberate our land.

Furthermore, we want world public opinion to be on our side and really to know our position. At the same time, we must consider òur present friends and our possible friends before we consider our enemies. A major part of the battle is taking place on an international level and under the eyes of public opinion throughout the entire world, which wants to live in peace.

We realised from the beginning, as we were trying a political solution, that it was a difficult and thorny road because the enemy was drunk with victory. We know that the principle that what has been taken by force cannot be regained by anything but force is a sound and correct principle in all circumstances. But we tried sincerely and are still trying sincerely on a basis from which we do not deviate. This basis is clear and definite in UAR policy: no negotiations with Israel, no peace with Israel, no recognition of Israel, and no deals at the expense of Palestinian soil or the Palestinian people.

These are the foundations on which we proceeded in regard to solving the Middle East crisis peacefully. However, since 23rd November and until now, give and take has been going on with the UN representative. Have we achieved anything? We have achieved nothing. We co-operated to the maximum with the UN Secretary-General's representative. We accepted the Security Council resolution, but Israel did not.

No projects exist now for a peaceful solution, and it does not seem to me that there will be any in the future. We hear what the representative of the UN Secretary-General says, and we express our opinion on what we hear. So far our opinion has been clear.

With regard to a political solution, we will not in any way agree to give away one inch of Arab territory in any Arab country.

It is clear that Israel, which rejected the Security Council resolution, has many aims. The first is to achieve a political objective, because it won a military victory but did not achieve a political gain. Israel wants direct negotiations and wants a peace treaty signed. We reject this. Israel thus won a military victory but has so far been unable to achieve the political objective—signing a peace treaty with any of the Arab States surrounding it.

Therefore Israel will not withdraw. Why should it withdraw from the territory it occupied after achieving a crushing military victory? Israel, as they say, will remain in this territory hoping that conditions or regimes will be changed and replaced by regimes which will agree to the conclusion of a peace treaty with Israel [shouts of "God forbid" from audience].

How would the conditions change? Israel knows that the occupation burdens the hearts of all the sons of the Arab nation. Occupation represents fragmentation. Occupation is something out of the ordinary and is like a nightmare to all of us. Israel and the imperialist forces working behind it would be able to influence the domestic fronts and might be able to change the regimes and replace them with others which would agree to the conclusion of peace with Israel. As long as Israel knows that we have not yet attained a crushing offensive military strength, it will remain where it is, hoping to achieve political victory through a changing of regimes.

Israel continues to refuse the Security Council resolution. Israel refuses to discuss the Security Council resolution. Israel says: We will remain in our places along the cease-fire lines until you agree to negotiate with us and conclude a peace treaty. Naturally we counter this by rebuilding our armed forces. A year ago after the defeat, we had no armed forces. We now have armed forces which may be greater than those existing before the battle. We are working for the development of the armed forces in order to attain supremacy because our enemy is a cunning enemy backed by a force which gives him everything—money and arms.

After this, we shall discuss the possibilities of the military and political solutions. Because of its nature, the crisis cannot last long. We have been waiting for one year. Our area is a sensitive one. The status quo cannot be accepted. This status quo is against nature and creates a situation conducive to quick ignition and explosion at any time.

There exists a basic and principal commitment which is a question of life or death: the liberation of the land inch by inch if necessary even if one martyr must fall on every inch of land. That is clear. A war to regain a right is a legal war. However, we shall allow no one to provoke us. We shall decide, prepare and arrange things. This is a lengthy matter which demands our patience and endurance. We must be patient and stand fast in order to triumph and attain supremacy. Having attained supremacy, we shall triumph.

Life will be meaningless and worthless to us however, until every inch of Arab soil is liberated. To us the liberation of Arab soil represents an indivisible whole. In no circumstances is there an alternative to the departure of the occupation forces from all occupied territory. Prior to this departure, there can be no peace in the Middle East in any circumstances. If there is no peace in the Middle East, it is very doubtful that the repercussions will be restricted to borders of the Middle East.

We do not address ourselves to Israel alone but to the whole world. We have nothing to say as far as Israel is concerned. Israel's role has been exposed. Its role as a stooge of world imperialism and colonialism has been fully exposed. However, our talk today is addressed to the world, which is anxious for peace and adheres to peace. We add that peace in this part of the world will not be achieved by the mere elimination of the consequences of the 5th June aggression. Real peace should take into consideration the legal rights of the Palestinian people.

The third subject is the armed forces. When we study the causes of the defeat—I have studied the causes of the defeat and attended command meetings which discussed everything that took place—when we study the causes of the defeat, it becomes clear to us that there was no deficiency among the officers and soldiers. We must know this well. A mistake was made and it is painful to go back over its details.

Four-fifths of our forces did not encounter the enemy and had no opportunity to fight. They were placed in extremely bad conditions. It is not advantageous to talk now about the past except within the limits necessary to reassess matters and to benefit from the lessons of the battle. Our soldiers and officers who entered the battles proved that they could stand firm and die. The Egyptian soldier is a fighting soldier who does not fear death. I fought with the Egyptian peasant soldier in 1948 and saw how he welcomes death.

We should therefore be doing our soldiers and officers an injustice if we looked at them on the basis of what has taken place. The fact is that a very large part of the army did not enter battle. Each of us knows that during the withdrawal operation the hostile forces were finally able to inflict the heaviest losses on us. We have now learned and benefited from the lessons of the battle. We have compensated for much of the loss our armed forces suffered last year. As I said before, we have attained defence capability. We shall now strive to transform our army into a strong offensive army supplied with the most up-to-date weapons.

I witnessed an exercise before leaving for the Soviet Union. I saw our armed forces that participated in it. I can say that in the past year they achieved as much as five years of work. One can say that we now have capable armed forces. However it is all-essential that we understand that the officers and soldiers are doing a very difficult job. They are now working day and night. Every officer and NCO feels that the whole country is watching him and assigning him a duty which will determine our fate and future. Each of them feels that the nation is giving him the responsibility. They are therefore carrying out this duty. However, our armed forces must bide their time and be ready to take the opportunity to achieve what they are duty bound to achieve.

We, as a people, fully support our armed forces and have full faith in them because when the people lose confidence in their armed forces, they also lose confidence in themselves and in their destiny. The people must give to their armed forces because there is no alternative. It is my duty to say that the people have given. What have they given? They have given their sons. The best of their sons are now members of the armed forces. The soldiers and officers of the armed forces are our sons. The people feel and live with them constantly. The people feel that the armed forces are living under difficult psychological and physical conditions as a result of their hard work, great efforts, training and exhausting conditions. To live under such conditions day after day is painful to the soul and to our armed forces, who see the enemy on the other bank of the Canal.

The fourth question is my recent visit to the Soviet Union and to Yugoslavia. Brothers, I mainly went to thank the leaders and people of the Soviet Union for everything they have given us and to discuss the situation. However, there is a fact which we must realise and know: Had it not been for the Soviet Union, we would now find ourselves facing the enemy without any weapons and compelled to accept his conditions. The United States would not have given us a single round of ammunition. It has given us and will give us nothing, but it gives Israel everything from guns to aircraft and missiles.

In reality, we have so far paid not one millieme for the arms we obtained from the Soviet Union to equip our armed forces. Actually, were it a question of payment, we have no money to buy arms. We all know the situation. We took part of the Soviet weapons as a gift and concluded a contract for the remainder for which we shall pay in the future in long-term installments. Had it not been for the Soviet Union and its agreement to supply us with arms, we should now be in a position similar to our position a year ago. We should have no weapons and should be compelled to accept Israel's condition under its threat.

At the same time, there exists a question which we must fully realise and understand: Why does the Soviet Union give us all these things? Why? We have one common aim with the Soviet Union—to resist imperialism. We do not want foreign influence in our part of the world. For its part, the Soviet Union is most anxious to oppose imperialism and to liquidate the imperialist concentrations to the south of its borders. Our ideological and national interest is against imperialism; the Soviet Union's ideological interest and strategy are against imperialism. I wish to tell you frankly and clearly that the Soviet Union has never tried, not even in our most crucial times, to dictate conditions to us or to ask anything of us. On the contrary, it has always been we who have asked.

Naturally, I did not pay my recent visit to the Soviet Union to express gratitude only, but to ask for things as well. After expressing my gratitude, I asked for things and after asking, I told them that I was ashamed. Do you not want anything from us? We ask you for things. But they answered: We have nothing to ask of you. I am actually telling this to you and to history so we may know who our friends and enemies are.

We went on asking for hours but they did not make one request of us. Even when I told them I felt ashamed that we were making many demands while they had asked nothing of us—I wish they had a request which we could fulfil—I asked if they had nothing to ask of us. They told us: We take this stand on the basis of our ideology—the ideology of national liberation and the peoples' struggle. We have nothing to ask.

The Soviet Union did not try to dictate any conditions to us. In our constant dealings with it, the Soviet Union has not tried to dictate any conditions—not even when we differed and we differed with the Soviet Union in 1959. At that time there was agreement on the first stage of the High Dam, the first industrialisation agreement and the arms deal agreement. Despite this, despite the difference which reached such extent that it was published in the newspapers, no attempt was made to apply pressure and no word of threat was uttered by the Soviet Union. Sincerity prompts me to say this.

There is another point. This is the element of the Soviet Navy and its appearance in the Mediterranean. I say that the States of the region, all the liberated States in the region, welcome the appearance of the Soviet Navy in the Mediterranean Sea as an element to balance the US Sixth Fleet, which sought to turn the Mediterranean into an American sea. The Soviet Navy did not threaten us. The Sixth Fleet is a strategic reserve for Israel, according to the Israel Premier himself. When the US Navy leaves the Mediterranean, then those who wonder about the danger of the presence of the Soviet Navy will be able to speak and be heard.

On this occasion, I may make a quick reference to our attitude towards the United States. US policy has failed rapidly in this region. No one other than an obvious agent can openly declare friendship for the United States. The entire Arab world is aware of what the United States has done. We expected something different from the United States, or at least we did not expect all that has happened. However, that is the United States' business.

Giving arms to Israel while it is occupying Arab territory means that the United States supports Israel in the occupation of the Arab territory. Giving aircraft to Israel while it is occupying Arab territory means that the United States supports Israel in the occupation of the Arab territory. The complete US support for Israel at the United Nations and the adoption and defence of the Israeli point of view means that the United States supports Israel's occupation of the Arab territory. The US refusal to make a statement stipulating the need for the withdrawal of the Israeli forces to the positions they occupied before 5th June is proof that the United States supports Israel and, indeed, colludes with Israel in what it has done and is doing. Every member of the Arab nation is aware of this.

This matter is not confined to the Arab nation but also includes other States. Last year, it appeared that some CENTO member-States wanted to absolve themselves of CENTO, which was formerly called the Baghdad Pact. Yesterday we read that the Turkish students were throwing Sixth Fleet crews into the sea. Why? No sensible man in the United States asks himself why this has happened in the Arab world and in other States.

The United States, which possesses means of power that no other State has had the chance to possess throughout history or in our era, should really ask itself what the people want of it. The people want the United States to adopt an attitude based on justice, an attitude based on equality, for as a great Power the United States should also have great principles which reject aggression and occupation and in no circumstances agree to support the aggressor and give him arms.

I shall now refer to my visit to Yugoslavia. I visited Yugoslavia for a short time. Maybe we stayed two nights there. The purpose of the visit was to prove our appreciation for President Tito's visit to us last August. He decided to come in August, the warmest time, last year. Such a gesture on his part deserves great appreciation. President Tito is our friend. After the setback, he actually played a very great role everywhere and in all States against aggression, occupation and Israel's methods. At the same time we discussed the new conference of non-aligned States.

We shall now speak about the economic situation. Despite all the conditions of war, the Egyptian economic situation is sound in its entirety. Industry has obtained investments, new factories are being opened daily, and agricultural products are setting records. This does not mean that we have no economic problems. No. We have economic problems. We have problems in respect of hard currency, the balance of payments and investments required for development. We want to employ the largest number of people and therefore we need a large amount of money. However, despite these problems, the economy is proceeding on its course. There were hopes that economic pressure would make us hungry and would place us in a situation so that we could not import wheat or food. Now, one year later, we are able to stand fast. There is wheat, flour and corn. There are no crises involving supplies, all this despite the fact that we have made an unprecedented allocation for the defence budget this year—over £E300 million.

The next point I wish to discuss concerns youth and its role. Concern about youth is one of the most important phenomena in our homeland. We must develop this concern.

The worst thing that can happen to any country is to have its youth feel indifferent. We want our youth to be interested in everything. The condition of youth must be one of our most important subjects, because youth is the hope of the homeland. Young people participating in public affairs is a healthy sign and a guarantee of hope for the future. This is the reason for the concern about the representation of youth at this Congress.

We also believe that the university's positive participation in forming concepts is necessary. I have spoken, perhaps in this very hall, of this many times in past years. The university must be the stronghold protecting national social development and opening the way before it. I never cease to say that the guarantees for the future are the universities, concern about the universities, and democracy.

The next point is Arab action. The battle against the enemy must have priority over everything else. The battle demands a single Arab nation. Up to now we have been trying by all means to attain this aim.

A meeting was held at Khartoum. I have spoken previously about the Khartoum meeting and its importance. We called for another summit conference but did not insist on it and substituted bilateral co-ordination instead. We are not about to be side-tracked. Some have tried to drag us along, but we are not prepared to be dragged.

There is one battle which is absorbing all our efforts in preparing for it; we have no time for anything else. It is the battle against the enemy. Our attitude towards any Arab State depends on that State's attitude towards the battle. Naturally, some states have sent us forces, Sudan and Algeria for instance. Their forces are with us. Other Arab countries such as Iraq and Kuwait have forces with us too. Some States have helped us to resist economically and have adhered to the Arab support agreement such as Saudi Arabia, Libya and Kuwait. I believe that Arab action can progress day after day in spite of the slow rate of progress.

The next point concerns Palestinian fida'i activity. We are fully committed to offering all help to the Palestinian fida'i action. We consider that the Palestinian struggle last year was a big sign of change in the whole Arab situation. Not only we but the entire world senses this indication that the Palestinian people have risen to champion their own cause by themselves and to defend their rights by themselves.

The ninth point concerns psychological warfare. Psychological warfare means an attempt to arouse doubt about everything. Its aim is to strike at the domestic front. But attempts to cast suspicion are not new to us. As we have said, in 1957 there were 11 clandestine radios broadcasting against us. Attempts to arouse suspicions are useless so far as the masses of the Arab nation are concerned.

Suspicion campaigns act in various directions. Firstly, they try to distort the essential widescale diplomatic activity of the UAR and to depict it as accepting suspect plans. Of course, it is our duty to launch a diplomatic offensive and expose Israel throughout the world. Of course, psychological warfare is being used in an effort to depict this diplomatic offensive as acceptance of suspicious plans.

Psychological warfare also seeks to speak of the Soviet Union and holds that our relations with the USSR have expanded and become closer and that this will drive us into communism and embroil us in subservience. All of us know these points and I do not have to repeat them.

There is a big difference between co-operation and subservience. When we concluded the 1955 arms deal with the Soviet Union they said there was danger in the arms deal because it would drag us into subservience. They cited examples. When we began to conclude the High Dam agreement with the Soviet Union, they said Soviet experts would come to work at the High Dam and that this would lead to some sort of subservience. More than 5,000 Soviet experts came to the High Dam, but none of them interfered in our domestic affairs and none of them tried to convert any of the people of Aswan to communism. Nothing of the sort happened.

Today they are saying the same thing. For example, they say the Soviet experts in the Army mean domination of the army and subservience. I have said before that we asked the Soviet Union for these experts and that the Soviet Union was not receptive to giving us experts, saying it would expose us to attack. But in fact, after the 5th June events, anyone with insight who could evaluate things felt that we needed training and that we had a great deal to learn about war. Thus we asked for and got the military experts. They are helping us. We have, in fact, benefited from them; we have benefited from them in all fields.

What the psychological warfare suggested when we received arms in 1955 and when we concluded the High Dam agreement in 1960 may again be suggested this time.

Brothers, we feel that the entire Arab nation must feel

grateful to the Soviet Union. Had it not been for the Soviet Union, as I have already said, we should now find ourselves with no arms in the face of the Israeli militarism, which has been blinded by its victory of June 1967. Egypt's independence—and I say this to all people—is not for sale, is not for anyone to buy and is not for mortgage. This will continue to be the case. It is this attitude that has placed us in the difficult situations we are experiencing. Had we agreed to subservience, such as that represented by the Baghdad Pact which we were asked under threats to join, we should have accepted subservience some years ago, long ago and there would have been no need for us to wage all these battles. We have not accepted subservience, we will never accept it and for this reason we have been struggling and fighting for freedom, independence and the building of a free homeland and free citizens.

There has also been the psychological war—poisoned news. It was reported in recent dispatches that demonstrations had been started in Alexandria and that travellers were the source of this information. Our country is an open, not a closed, country. Our country is not a closed country—people can come and go. Thousands of people enter and leave our country every hour. These reports reflect a form of psychological war involving false reports to influence us and to prove that the domestic front is not strong and is not steadfast and, at the same time, to influence the domestic front and shake it so that imperialism, Israel and those who stand behind Israel can achieve their purpose.

Our enemies have succeeded in winning a military victory, but our country has not fallen, has not accepted defeat, but has decided to stand fast. They have applied economic pressure to us and, despite this pressure, we have not surrendered but have marched on. We have imposed restrictions on ourselves and have accepted these restrictions. Our enemies have failed to destroy us economically. Hence, there remains one thing for them to do—to strike at the domestic front and to break up the alliance of the people's working forces because if the domestic front collapses the hostile imperialist forces and Israel will achieve the aims they have so far been unable to achieve.

The 10th and last point is the inevitability of victory and the conditions for victory. Brothers, there is no alternative to victory for our nation. The nation is capable of achieving victory provided it mobilises its forces and benefits properly from its energy and conditions, and also if we can build up and safeguard our domestic front according to the needs of the battle. The domestic front is the pillar of the fighting front. We must expose, defeat and crush all enemy attempts to influence the domestic front.

Now comes your role, brothers, comrades in the struggle, and members of the ASU National Congress. You are the command of the alliance of the people's working forces. You are the more capable of cohesion with these forces. You are the more capable of guiding them through work, struggle, clarity and truth. The battle is all the people's battle. It is the battle for the people's lives, and all the people must participate in it. It must be a victory for life and for the people. May God grant you success. Peace be with you.

The Moment of Truth

Towards a Middle East Dialogue

By Cecil Hourani*

This essay is addressed to the educated classes in the Arab countries: to those who still participate actively in the political, social, and intellectual life of their countries, and to those who have been excluded forcibly or by their own free will. To all I trust it will have a message of hope. Destructive as much of my argument is, my aim is positive and constructive. On the understanding of our errors in the past may be built the new society of the future. I have no recrimination against states or individuals. Time and history will provide their own judgment. The moment is one for solidarity and mutual tolerance, and above all for a free discussion among ourselves. In a climate of honest self-criticism and free expression those truths may emerge which can lead us from our present disarray to a new vision of ourselves and the world we would like to build.

At this moment when the destiny of the Arab nation is being decided, it is the duty of every Arab thinker to witness to the truth as he sees it, without fear and without dissimulation.

* Cecil Hourani, who was for ten years an adviser to President Bourguiba of Tunisia, lives now in Beirut. His essay was originally published in *El Nahar*, Beirut, and appeared in English in *Encounter*, November, 1967.

For too long has the field of publicity and expression been left in the hands of professional demagogues, blackmailers, and semi-educated fanatics. Our silence on the one hand, their vociferation on the other, have led the Arab nation not merely to disaster, but to the brink of disintegration.

The primary condition of a redressment of this situation is to see things as they are, in all their brutal clarity: then to take action to change them in the light of the ideals and objectives we set ourselves. A victory over ourselves is more important than a physical defeat on the battlefield. Governments, states, régimes, frontiers, are all transient things, subject to fluctuations and fortune. What is important is that a people should survive, not as a mere agglomeration of individuals, but as a living, creative force in history. We can only survive by acting positively ourselves, not by reacting negatively to what others may do, or seek to do, to us.

History has given to the Arab nation in the 20th century a unique chance to return to the community of living creative forces in the world: a conjunction of international affairs which made possible the independence of all our territories; and the discovery of enormous wealth which with almost no effort on our part gives us the means to accomplish all we need to refashion our society and to raise it to prosperity and progress.

This unique chance we are now in danger of losing. Our sovereign and political liberty gives us the means to bring about our own destruction more easily than we can construct our future. Our very freedom implies dangers greater than existed when we were dependent. No one will now save us from the consequences of our own mistakes and follies, except ourselves. The fact that we inhabit certain territories in this world of strategic importance or material wealth is not a sufficient guarantee of our safety or survival. We can be driven from these territories, or lose control of these riches. We can commit suicide as a nation. And history will then judge us as a people who did not know how to use the chances which had been offered them, and condemn us to the fate we shall have deserved.

The most dramatic, but not the only, example of our weakness, and of our failure to recognise both our weakness and our strength, lies in our relationship with the Zionist movement and with the State of Israel.

We have been able neither to come to terms with them: nor to destroy them: nor even to contain them.

As a result of our failure to decide what position to adopt, or to take the necessary measures of self-defence, we have allowed Israel to usurp the whole of Palestine, and to occupy the most important strategic positions in the Near East.

While it is true that the Zionist movement did not develop wholly in relationship to the Arab world, but also in an international climate outside our control, nevertheless since the establishment of Israel in 1948, against our will, our struggle against that State has taken place within the framework of the international community, and largely within the United Nations Organisation. The frontiers established 'in 1948 as a result of the cease-fire were not wholly advantageous to Israel, because they set a territorial limit to Zionism.

The Arab objective, therefore, if we had thought clearly and calmly, should have been the *containment of Israel* within its boundaries as limited by *de facto* arrangements arrived at after two wars we had lost, rather than its conquest and destruction.

That we were unable to distinguish clearly between containment and conquest was due primarily to a psychological weakness in us: *that which we do not like we pretend does not exist*. Because we refused to recognise a situation which was distasteful to us, we were unable to define our own relationship to that situation, or to distinguish between what we would have liked ideally, and what we were capable of achieving in practice.

As a policy of containment, the moves of the U.A.R. until 5 June 1967 could have been successful. But it had implicit dangers, the greatest of which was that in the minds of those who were practising it, it could be at any moment transformed successfully into a policy of conquest. By this confusion in their own minds about their aims, and by their misjudgment of their own strength, the Arab Governments brought about the disaster of June 5. They also lost the battle of public opinion. By foolish and irresponsible statements they allowed themselves to appear as the aggressor instead of the victims. While they talked of war and conquest, Israel prepared it.

For years Israel had cultivated the image of herself as a small defenceless State surrounded by heavily-armed neighbours bent on destroying her. While in fact we were trying to contain her, some of our spokesmen, for home consumption, were exaggerating our military capacities and promising our

people conquests. This gave Israel a pretext for arming to the
teeth. The balance of power which Israel was trying to maintain was not one between Israel and Egypt, but between
Israel and all her neighbours combined. The higher technical
skills of the Israelis, and the integration of her armed forces
into her civilian population, combined with supplies of arms
qualitatively at least equal to those of the Arabs, in fact gave
her an advantage which we should have foreseen.

The greatest defeat, however, was not that on the battlefield
or in propaganda and public opinion, but that which our Governments inflicted on their own people: countless lives lost
uselessly; a great new exodus of refugees from their homes;
economic losses and misery not yet calculable; a new despair
and a new humiliation.

What greater proof of our capacities for self-deception and
moral cowardice than that Ahmed Shouqairi still sits with
our responsible leaders, or the claims of one Arab Head of
State that we were not defeated because we did not use our
full strength? Does not all this make one suspect that the
"final victory" of which some talk would be nothing less than
a *coup de grâce* delivered to the Arabs?

This is indeed our moment of truth: but some of our leaders
cannot make up their minds whether they want to be Torero
or Bull!

Another consequence of our unwillingness to accept as real
what we do not like is that *when reality catches up with us,
it is always too late*. At every *débâcle* we regret that we did
not accept a situation which no longer exists. In 1948 we
regretted that we had not accepted the 1947 U.N. plea for
partition. In May 1967 we were trying to go back to pre-Suez.
Today we would be happy—and are actually demanding
the U.N.—to go back to things as they were before 5 June.
From every defeat we reap a new regret and a new nostalgia,
but never seem to learn a new lesson.

Yet every human situation—except annihilation—contains
within it the seeds of its final reversal. Take for example
the creation of Israel in 1948. It is true that in relation to our
right to the total possession of Palestine this represented an
Arab loss: but there were also gains to us in what happened in
1948. We won independence for part of Palestine in place
of total dependence on the Mandatory Power before. Under
the Mandatory Régime, Jewish immigration and the expansion

of Zionism could have continued in the whole of Palestine: after 1948 Zionism was confined to a tiny territory which was strategically weak and scarcely viable economically. Had we consolidated the independence we had gained, we could have contained Israel, and with it World Zionism, for fifty years, after which Israel itself would have ceased to be a threat to us, and become just another Levantine state, part Jewish, part Arab, but overwhelmingly Oriental.

Instead of which, twenty years later, we have not only lost what remained of Arab Palestine: we have also helped Zionism to leap forward yet another stage in its dynamic progress towards full Jewish nationalism. The enormous material and moral support which the State of Israel received from Jewish citizens of other countries in the recent crisis shows that what extreme Zionists have always hoped, and moderate Jews always feared, is happening: namely the polarisation of Jewish nationalism around the State of Israel, and the progressive alienation of Jews from the societies in which they have been assimilated or at least accepted. The potential population of Israel is thus not the unborn generations in that country alone, but Jews from everywhere in the world.

Shall we in one, or ten, or twenty years, seek another "victory" like the one we have just gained, and lose the other side of the Jordan, the fertile plains of Jaulan and Hauran in Syria, and the Litani and Hasbani rivers in Lebanon? And shall we still have Ahmed Shouqairi with us to consecrate the final victory of stupidity over intelligence, of fanaticism over common sense, of dishonesty over truth?

The answer lies with us. What we do in reaction to the events of the last few weeks will determine the future of our people not for ten or twenty years, but for centuries. This time there can be no second chance. Either we continue on the same road that has led us to our present state, defeats, retreats, *débâcles,* and the rapid transformation of our settled urban and peasant populations in the Near East into a new nomadism: or we take positive measures to stop the process of disintegration, to limit the collapse, and to transform our military defeat into a political and a psychological victory.

What are these positive measures, and what are the psychological victories we may hope to gain?

We must first of all ask ourselves the question, what does victory mean in terms of our actual situation and our real strength? Does it mean victory over others—Israel, or the Anglo-Americans, or Western imperialism or international indifference, or all together? Does it mean we can impose our terms on others, draw frontiers as we want, dictate the conditions on which we agree to live with the rest of the world, and make others see us as we would like to see ourselves?

Our first effort must surely be to win a victory over ourselves: over defeatism on the one hand, extremism on the other. These two dangers are in fact intimately linked together. The real defeatists are not those who look facts in the face, accept them, and try to remedy the situation which brought them about, but those who refuse to do this, who deny facts, and who are thus preparing for new defeats.

The extremists are those who argue that our concepts were correct, but that we did not implement them seriously: and that therefore we should continue along the same path, but use more violent methods.

If however, our concepts were wrong, the use of the same methods even in a more violent form can only lead us to another defeat. It is therefore essential to re-think our basic ideas in terms of *reality,* rather than of wishes. What could we realistically hope to achieve?

Ourselves and Israel

I have pointed out the disastrous effects of not having formulated clearly in our minds the distinction between the containment and the conquest of Israel. The principal reason why we did not make this distinction, and imagined that we could at any moment switch from one to the other, was our failure to appreciate our own strength and weakness relatively to Israel and the rest of the world. We must therefore examine this question honestly and fearlessly.

1. The first basic truth we must face is that the Arabs as a whole do not yet have the scientific and technological skills, nor the general level of education among the masses, which make possible the waging of large-scale modern warfare. This is not merely a deduction from recent events: it is a statistically demonstrable fact. We do not have the educational facilities or standards at home, nor enough students abroad, to provide the General Staff, the officers, and the men capable of using modern weapons and modern methods. Nor do we have civilian populations sufficiently disciplined and educated

to collaborate with the armed forces and the civil authorities to the degree which modern warfare demands.

By not recognising this fact, our military leaders tried to fight the wrong kind of war. It is a classical accusation made against General Staffs that they use methods appropriate to the previous war. Our military thinkers and planners were trying to fight the next one. As a result our soldiers were not only unable to use the modern weapons that were placed in their hands: they were actually handicapped by them. Trapped in the tanks they could not manoeuvre, relying on the air support that never came, they fell easy victims to their enemies. And the material they had to abandon will be incorporated into the army of Israel, so that in fact we have helped to arm our opponents.

2. The second truth is that the rate of technological and scientific advance is so rapid in the modern world that even if in twenty years we can catch up with the military standards of today, we shall still be outdistanced by the Israelis, whose technological and scientific skills are the product not only of their own schools and research institutes, but of Jewish—and non-Jewish—talent throughout the world.

3. The third truth is that even if we had been able to defeat Israel militarily, we would have been deprived of the fruit of that victory by some of the Great Powers, who would have intervened to save Israel's political existence.

4. The fourth truth is that in twenty years, or even less, even if we succeed in bringing our scientific and technological skills to a point where we could wage a modern war, warfare itself will have taken on quite another aspect. The possession of nuclear weapons by smaller powers—including the Arab States and Israel—will offer a choice either of mutual annihilation or of international control: and in neither case shall we be able to get our own way on our own terms.

It is evident, therefore, that if we think primarily in terms of military power we shall be making a fundamental error. This does not mean that we should disarm. It does mean that we must re-appraise our own strength, and find a new relationship between military power on the one hand, and our political, economic, and geopolitical assets on the other.

What are the conclusions we should draw from these facts about our relationship to Israel? We must first of all realise that the immediate consequence of the present war has been to modify the strategic situation in favour of Israel, which has now reached more natural frontiers than she had before both for defence and attack. If therefore we try to rectify this situation by military force, we shall be in an even weaker position than we were in 1948, in 1956, or before 5 June 1967. And not only are we in a weaker position to attack: we are also less able to defend ourselves.

The conclusions to be drawn are two: in the first place, the resort to military force as a basic element in Arab policy towards Israel is an error. In the second place, our best chance of containing Israel lies in international pressures either within or outside the United Nations. These international pressures, of whatever nature, have, however, a price. What is the price we are prepared to pay, is a question I leave to later on.

If the balance of military power has now been seriously upset in favour of Israel, there are other aspects of the balance of power which remain in our favour. Some of these have always existed, though we have not used them properly: others spring from the defeat of 5 June itself, for in all situations lie the seeds of their reversal. In the first place, Israel's military victory was a limited one—limited by those territorial, geopolitical factors which make the physical conquest of the Arab world impossible. Military occupation is one thing, permanent conquest and domination quite another. In the second place, Israel's military victory was not a political one: it has not led her any nearer to that peace on her terms which she would like, or any nearer to the negotiating table with the Arabs. It has on the contrary brought against her a coalition of international pressures which never existed before, and liquidated the fruit of twenty years' work to win friends in Africa and Asia.

If military force is not the Arabs' best card, neither is it Israel's. By a military action far out of proportion to the immediate situation it had to face, Israel has brought into play other factors which in the long run may modify the situation within Israel in ways which their present leaders had never envisaged.

Firstly, let us suppose that international pressures do not succeed in forcing Israel to withdraw to her pre-5 June frontiers. By incorporating the Gaza Strip and the West Bank into her territory, the proportion of Arabs to Jews in Israel will be radically changed. The higher birth-rate of the Arabs will give them equality in numbers, then a majority, in a few years. And as the proportion of "Arab" Jews to European

Jews is also changing, the total population of Palestine will eventually, and before long, take on an oriental character. As we acquire some of their virtues, and they acquire some of our defects, the gap between Arab and Jew will narrow, and in fifty years could almost disappear.

Secondly, it is clear that the Zionist movement as a whole, and the Israeli leaders in particular, must now face a dramatic dilemma as a result of their *blitzkrieg* of 5 June. This dilemma is the following: If the Israeli Government accepts the Arabs within the territories she controls as full Israeli citizens, with equal civil and political rights, the concept of Israel which has hitherto been incorporated into her laws will have to be changed. Israel will no longer be a Jewish State, in which, as it does now, full citizenship requires not only membership of the Jewish religion, but Jewish ancestry. It will become a Jewish-Arab State in which nationality will be a function of residence or citizenship. Israel, in other words, as she has been since 1948, will no longer exist, and Palestine, with Arabs and Jews living together, will have been restored.

If, on the other hand, the Israeli authorities refuse to accept the Arabs as full citizens with equal civil and political rights, she will have on her hands a large population which she will be unable to liquidate or to govern.

It is the perception of this dilemma which is now leading some of the Israeli leaders to force the hands of the others and to try to have it both ways: to keep the territories they have conquered, and try to reduce the Arab population in numbers by encouraging their exodus across the Jordan. It is not difficult to foresee that the next step will be to encourage a new wave of Jewish immigration into Israel, to replace as many Arabs as possible in as short a period as possible.

If the extremists within Israel succeed in forcing the hand of the more reasonable, and getting the world Zionist movement to follow, then they will in fact make forever impossible their dream of an Arab-Jewish *rapprochement*. For the way in which the Arabs are ultimately going to judge the advantages of peace or war in their relations with Israel will depend on the way Israel treats the Arabs within its borders. If there is a genuine attempt to live together with the Arabs on terms of complete equality and within the same juropolitical framework, the way to an eventual conciliation between Israel, or Palestine, and the rest of the Arab world will have been opened. But if the Arabs are excluded from full citizenship, and reduced to the status of a colonised, dependent population, no peace will ever be possible, either inside or outside Palestine.

It is not difficult to draw logical conclusions about what Arab policy should be in the light of this situation, and of this dilemma which faces Israel. If the goals of Arab policy should be, as I have suggested, (1) the containment of Israel within whatever boundaries we can get international pressure to agree to and to stabilise, (2) the gradual transformation of Israel from a European-dominated "exclusive" Jewish State into a predominantly oriental Arab-Jewish State, then the problem of whether or not to make a formal "peace" becomes a secondary one. It will no longer be a question of principle on which no Arab leader can compromise: it becomes a question of expediency and efficacy. But there is no reason why we should accept the Israeli argument that peace can only be obtained by direct negotiations with them. Since the United Nations, or some other international group, will have to be a party to any attempt to stabilise frontiers, all our efforts to obtain a setlement can be canalised through that organisation. What we cannot afford is to have no policy at all: to be unable to support the conditions of war, and incapable of profiting from the advantages of peace.

The formulation of a consistent Arab policy towards Israel within the framework of the international community is thus perfectly possible and not difficult if we define both our aims and our methods. I have stated what these aims could be. As for the methods, a few are obvious, although others may also be found, and the way these methods are used will be up to the Arab negotiators to determine.

1. We should do all we can to secure the return to the frontiers as they were before 5 June 1967, not indeed as a final settlement but as a first step towards an arrangement in which the questions of frontiers, the rights of the refugees to return, and compensation will find a solution. The means we adopt to bring pressure on other powers to accept our point of view should be realistic, however: that is to say they should be capable of success, and they should not do us more harm than they can bring us benefits.

It is unlikely that we shall be able to achieve our objective without making some concessions. What these concessions might be, it is up to those governments who would have to make them to decide. But we should hope and insist that these governments would not act unilaterally, and thereby prejudice the outcome of any compromise they may accept.

2. In the event of our being unable to accept the terms on which a withdrawal from occupied territories is offered us, our second line of policy should be based on the principle that the forcible occupation of a territory involves a responsibility towards the inhabitants of that territory. We should not only bring the maximum international pressure to prevent Israel from expelling Arabs and expropriating their possessions in favour of new Jewish immigrants: we should bring the same international pressure on Israel to accord full political and civil rights to her Arab population, as well as the right of the Arab refugees to return. If all Palestine is re-united, there is no reason why any Palestinian should be prevented from returning to his country: not only the refugee masses now living in camps (old and new) should return: in addition all those Palestinians who have been able to find work and prosperity in the Arab countries should go back and help to rebuild the Palestine Arab community, and play their proper role in re-establishing the rights of the Arabs in their own country. The returning Arabs will not be a fifth column: one cannot be a fifth column in one's own country. The relations which the Palestinian Arabs within Palestine are then able or willing to establish with the Jews will be their own responsibility. The other Arab countries must help them by all means in their struggle to restore their rights and their human dignity: but the primary responsibility for their future will lie with the Palestinians themselves.

There remains one more question perhaps more important than any I have yet discussed, because in the long run it will determine our relations with the Jews and their relations with us. *The fate and the peace of the Near East should not be left to the initiative of Israel alone.* Even if Israel opts for the closed, exclusive type of society, and rejects the Arabs as fellow-citizens, *we should not do the same.* If there is no room in Israeli society for the Arabs, we should show that there is room in Arab society for the Jews. This has always been the pattern of our society, and the greatest victory of militant Zionism would be to get us to abandon it and to adopt their concept of the State. For in their hearts they know that a closed, exclusive, fanatic Israel can never co-exist with an open, liberal, and tolerant Arab society. There are Jews, however, in Israel and throughout the world who also reject the narrow vision and fanatical aims of some of their leaders, and who can be our allies in combating the introduction of racial nationalism into the Near East. Our greatest victory will be the day when the Jews in Palestine will prefer to live in an Arab society rather than in an Israeli one. It is up to us to make that possible.

Ourselves and the World

I have suggested that we formulate and try to implement a consistent Arab policy towards Israel within the framework of the international community, which means in effect the United Nations. But it is not only in the problem of Israel that the international community can be of service to us. In many of our foreign relations our numbers and our potential strength make the U.N. a suitable instrument of action. This implies, however, a correct appraisal of our strength and our weakness in the world.

Our greatest mistake in the past has been to overestimate our actual and to underestimate our potential strength. From this combination of misjudgments spring almost all the errors of our international behaviour. We have formulated and pursued policies we could not implement: we have neglected to practise policies which might have succeeded.

Nothing illustrates this truth better than the international policies we have adopted towards Israel. All our attempts to find military solutions have ended in failure, and led to subsequent political and diplomatic failures. On the other hand, our diplomatic, political and economic efforts have often met with success until we lost our advantages by pushing them too far, or not realising what these advantages were.

For example, the St. James's Conference in London in 1939 between the British Government and some of the Arab Governments led to the White Paper, which was in our favour, but which we rejected. In 1948 we secured the evacuation of British civil and military authorities from Palestine, but we did not take the necessary steps to take their place. In 1948 again, after our first unsuccessful war, we could have turned our military defeat into a limited political victory and confined Israel to an insignificant territory. Instead, we preferred our theoretical rights and principles to our real advantages. By

1967—and this was the basic cause of Israel's aggression on 5 June—we had succeeded in building up an economic situation in Jordan and most of the other Arab countries to a point where foreign investors were beginning to have serious doubts about putting money in Israel if that meant exclusion from Arab markets. We had also isolated Israel diplomatically in wide areas of international life. We lost all these advantages by failing to analyse the situation correctly. We did not perceive that the disparity between Israel's growing economic and diplomatic difficulties and her military strength would inevitably tempt her to restore the balance by a generalised rather than a localised military action. Instead of removing all possible pretexts for such an action we provided the pretexts they had difficulty in inventing themselves. . . .

The Arab Régimes

The greatest sources of weakness in the last twenty years has been the introduction into Arab political life of methods of government and of ideological slogans which are unsuitable and irrevelant to the actual conditions of the Arab countries. These methods and slogans have not only poisoned the relations between different Arab countries, they have also blinded some of their régimes to their real problems and their real interests.

The military régimes, for example, which have installed themselves in certain Arab countries since 1949 had their only justification in terms of the necessity of meeting external dangers. They have now given a public demonstration of their incompetence in war. What reason do we have to suppose that they are likely to be more successful in economic planning and development, in education, foreign affairs, finance, or culture?

Among the most harmful consequences of military régimes to the political, economic and social structure of the countries they have tried to govern is the exclusion from public life which they have deliberately or indirectly effected of vast numbers of educated and skilled citizens, who now languish idle either in their own countries, or in exile in others. This fact represents an enormous loss in terms of an investment in human resources going back at least forty years. The resulting poverty of technicians is felt not only in civilian affairs, but even in the armies themselves, so that it can reasonably be argued that the military régimes instead of strengthening their armed forces have in reality weakened them.

The introduction of ideological slogans and political and economic doctrines which derive from contexts radically different from those of the Arab countries has done even more harm to these countries both in their relations with each other and in their internal affairs. They have divided the Arab world into camps on issues which are not really relevant or along lines which do not make sense.

First of all, that between the so-called "progressive" or "revolutionary" and the "reactionary" or "conservative" régimes. It is interesting and significant that all those régimes which call themselves "progressive" are, in fact, military. What has led some of our leaders to adopt the language and imitate the style of movements and régimes with which they really have nothing in common? There are two basic reasons: the desire to find foreign allies and friends, and the need to seek popular support. Since most of the Arab countries have only recently emerged from Western domination or colonisation, it was natural for leaders seeking an easy popularity among the masses to align themselves with the enemies of the West in foreign policy, and to promise them economic and social welfare through "land reforms," "nationalisation," and other elements of the programme of certain socialist countries.

Except in Egypt, however, the "progressive" military régimes have not only failed to implement socialist programmes: they have actually lowered gross national products and seriously damaged the economic welfare of some sections of the population without improving that of others. Nor have they been able, or willing, to take those social and juridical measures which would have given a progressive character to their régimes, at least on paper. Not one of the "progressive" régimes, for example, has abolished polygamy. On the contrary, some of them have been trying to reintroduce a conservative interpretation of Islam into public life. And certain of the régimes which have been classified as "conservative" or "reactionary" have done much for their populations in terms of economic progress and social legislation.

Secondly, the attempt to identify Arab nationalism with the "progressive" as opposed to the "reactionary" régimes has led to a senseless and dangerous conflict between some of the

Arab Governments, just as it has inflamed and divided public opinion all over the Arab world. We must reject and resist the claim that any one régime or party or leader has a monopoly on Arab nationalism, and refuse to accept that differences of opinion or of interests provide an adequate basis for classifying régimes or individuals as genuine nationalists or traitors. The poisonous campaigns waged by the radio stations and the press in certain countries should be condemned, ignored, or ridiculed, and every pressure should be brought on those governments which utilise or permit them to put an end to this scandal of the Arab world.

The Real Problem

The introduction into Arab life of political and social doctrines which are not relevant to it at its present stage not only weakens the Arab countries by dividing them on irrelevant issues; it also diverts their attention from their real problems. The only valid distinction at this time between the Arab countries lies in the degree of their economic and social development, and in the resources they possess to promote their progress. The real difference is between the less- and the more-underdeveloped, and between the rich and the poor. There is no reason why we should anticipate the problems of more highly developed societies before we have reached the stage where these problems become real and demand solutions. There is no reason why we should adopt the language and the political forms of social and economic conflicts which are not relevant to our societies.

The most immediate and urgent problems which face nearly all the Arab countries are those involved in establishing the minimum conditions on which a modern society may eventually be built. While the nature of that society, and the social and economic content of the measures to be taken to bring it into existence must certainly be studied and discussed, and will certainly provide eventually the grounds for divergent opinions and political movements, we have not yet reached that stage. There is a wide area for action where interests are common and basic enough for us to ignore or at least to postpone questions which may divide us at a moment when we need to be united.

For some of the under-developed countries of the world the necessity of finding an outside source for the capital investments and the technical skills they lack forces them to an involvement in the ideological conflict and divisions of the more-developed world. No such necessity exists for the Arab world, which has all the material, and many of the human resources, which it needs. There is sufficient capital and liquidity to make us independent of outside financial help, and to promote our own economic and social progress provided we use our resources intelligently, and take a broad view of both the existing and the future needs of the Arab world as a whole. We have vast territories, enormous natural resources, and vital strategic positions. What we need is to exploit them in terms of today's and tomorrow's needs. Countries which are rich today may not be always: others which are poor today possess potentialities which may one day make them rich. The total human and natural resources of the Arab world must be studied and then exploited in the light of a general plan, a moving idea.

It is this great responsibility which now faces the educated classes in the Arab countries. They have a unique chance which is not given to many of the educated classes of more developed countries and societies, weighed down as they often are by traditions and already established patterns of life which do not give much scope to originality or to individual initiative. It is our good fortune to be born at a time when not only great tasks await us, but when the possibility of action is also present.

Instead of the sterile and irrelevant discussions, the bitter divisions and mutual suspicions which dominate our political and intellectual life, we should try to establish among ourselves an understanding, an agreement on principles, a mutual confidence which will make possible the action which must now be undertaken if the Arab world is to be saved from a rapid decline.

The Argument between Arabs and Jews

An Exchange between Arnold Toynbee and J. L. Talmon*

London, 3 July, 1967

Dear Professor Talmon,

I have just been staying with my son Philip and I have read your paper "For Total Peace in the Middle East" which Isaiah Berlin passed on to him. I believe, like you, that this is the moment for everyone of good will and good sense to make an all-out effort to get total, genuine, and lasting peace there. I believe there is a real opportunity for this, if we seize it now. I am just back from the United States, and, three weeks ago, I stuck my neck out by writing, for the United Press International, an article saying this, and making some concrete proposals for bringing it about. The United Press tell me that my article has been reproduced pretty widely in the U.S. press, so a copy of it may come into your hands some time, but, as there is no time to lose, I am writing to you now direct.

I feel a responsibility for doing anything I can to help towards getting a permanent peace now. I have a number of reasons. (1) I am British, so I have a share of responsibility for my country's past actions. (2) As a young man during the First World War, I was working as a "temporary Foreign Office clerk" on Middle Eastern affairs, particularly on British war-time commitments in the Middle East, so I know the history of these from the inside. (3) I am known as a Western spokesman for the Arab cause, and it is therefore just possible that what I say in public now might have some influence in the Arab World, though it is perhaps more likely that the Arabs might write me off with the verdict that I am no friend of theirs after all. Anyway, I believe that the truest act of friendship that any friend of either the Arabs or the Israelis can do for them at this moment is to try to help them to see that the facts make genuine peace a prime interest for both parties. (4) Being now an old man, with grandchildren, I feel what Johnson and Kosygin seem to have felt when they

---

* This exchange of letters between Professors Toynbee and Talmon, dated July 1967, appeared in *Encounter,* October 1967. PROFESSOR ARNOLD TOYNBEE, who refers to himself as "a Western spokesman for the Arab cause," is the author of many studies of Islamic history, politics, and culture. J. L. TAL- MON is Professor of Modern History at the Hebrew University of Jerusalem.

met. One's grandchildren symbolise for me, in a concrete way, all the future generations of the human race—70 million unborn generations who might be deprived, by our generation, of their right to life if we, in our time, were to stumble into an atomic third world war. (5) Thinking also in terms of the present, I want to see something done now which, besides saving the world from an enormous catastrophe, will reduce present human suffering in the Middle East to a minimum. I should have been as much horrified at genocide of Jews in the Middle East as I was horrified at it in Europe. I also think it very wrong to treat any people, living or unborn, as political pawns, instead of treating them as suffering human beings whose alleviation ought to have priority over any political considerations. In discussing the Arab states' policy with my Arab friends, I have always pointed out to them that West Germany's post-war policy towards refugees from Eastern Germany and from east of the Oder-Neisse line has not only been humane, but has paid dividends to Western Germany, economically and therefore also politically. Israelis should look ahead for their grandchildren.

Now about the facts that each side has to face and about practical possibilities for a settlement.

In your paper, you yourself, have put your finger on the fact that Israel has to face. A series of more and more sensational victories in successive wars does not, in itself, give Israel the vital thing that she wants and needs: that is, real peace with her Arab neighbours. So long as Israel has not mutually-agreed permanent frontiers, but only a military front, always smouldering and periodically flaring up into full-blown hostilities, Israel has to stay constantly on the alert and cannot concentrate her energies on her own internal development, which is, and always has been, her real objective. She has demonstrated now conclusively that, in war, she can always conquer more Arab territory without any foreign military aid; but, the more of this that she occupies, the more she will become militarily over-extended, and the larger the proportion of her limited and precious man-power she will have to keep unprofitably mobilised. The Arab World has the same passive military advantage as Russia and China have: there is virtually no end to it. So Israel's overriding interest is genuine peace; even the greatest military victories will be fruitless unless they can be converted into that.

The Arabs have to face the fact that Israel has come to

stay; that a three-times repeated experience has shown that they cannot defeat her; that the Soviet Union is not going to war with the United States for the Arabs' sake; and that, in the unlikely event of the Arabs becoming, one day, able to destroy Israel, the United States would not let this happen.

I need not dwell on your psychological analysis of the present-day Arab state of mind. It is masterly; you have shown a power of sympathetic understanding by which you have entered into it imaginatively. This is very important and very encouraging, because Israel, as the present victor, holds the initiative. The party that has suffered injustice and has been humiliated is the one that is the more sensitive and that therefore needs the more delicate handling. The Palestinian Arabs have suffered injustice. To put it simply, they have been made to pay for the genocide of Jews in Europe which was committed by Germans, not by Arabs. The Arabs as a whole have been humiliated, because, in the establishment, first of the Jewish National Home and then of the State of Israel, the Arabs have, as you point out, never been consulted. It has all been done over their heads. They have been treated as "natives," with no more than sub-human rights. For a people with a great, but no longer actual, historic past, this is infuriating. The present Arab and present Chinese states of mind have the same explanation.

So I would plead with Israel to make the first move towards achieving the total genuine and lasting peace which is the supreme common interest of Israel, the Palestinian Arab refugees, and the Arab states. For Israel publicly to make the first move would be magnanimous as well as far-sighted. I suggest that Israel should now propose that the two sides should make the following simultaneous declaration:

> "The Arab states and the Palestinian Arab people pledge themselves to recognise, *bona fide,* the existence of Israel with the intention of making a permanent peace with her, and they also guarantee to negotiate permanent frontiers with Israel on approximately the 1948 armistice lines. Israel pledges herself to accept these agreed frontiers *bona fide,* with the intention, on her side, of making permanent peace, and she also undertakes to take the initiative in bringing about a satisfactory permanent settlement of the problem of the 1948 refugees."[1]

[1] The repatriation of the 1967 refugees was taken for granted in this letter. Ed.

If both sides would give these reciprocal pledges in a formal agreement of the kind that used to be called "preliminaries of peace," this would open the way for a negotiated treaty about details, and then things that have so far been impossible would become possible, *e.g.*:

1. In the conversion of the 1948 armistice lines into permanent frontiers, there could be minor rectifications, so long as these offset each other fairly on balance.

2. There could be a mutual opening up of communications that are vital to both parties. Israel could be assured of a right of way not only through the Straits of Tiran but through the Suez Canal too. Egypt could be assured of a right of way, across Israel, to Lebanon, Syria, Jordan, and Saudi Arabia, thus removing the "Polish corridor" irritant of Israel's having split the Arab World in two by extending from the Mediterranean coast to the Gulf of Aqaba. Syria and Jordan could be given a free port at Haifa, with a right of way to it, and Jordan could be given a second one at Jaffa.

3. The 1948 Palestinian Arab refugees could (a) be given monetary compensation for the loss of their property situated in Israel; (b) be given an extra indemnity for having been forced, as innocent victims of the conflict between Israel and the Arab states, to spend twenty years as refugees; (c) be given the option of either returning to their former homes on condition of becoming loyal citizens of Israel (as the Galilaean Arabs have been during the present crisis) or else being settled on good land outside Israel; (d) a fund could be raised for the refugees' resettlement, whether inside Israel or outside it. I am sure the majority will opt for resettlement *outside* Israel; but for Israel to offer the choice of returning home (on condition of their becoming *bona fide* loyal Israeli citizens) is psychologically very important for producing a change of heart among the refugees. If Israel appealed to the world to help her raise a fund for these four purposes, money would pour in.

4. Water for irrigation: in the London *Times* a few days ago, there was an important letter from Edmund de Rothschild about this, followed up next day by a long and constructive article by a desalination expert. They make the point that, even though desalination has not yet been made possible at an economic price, it would pay the world to subsidise it for the use of Israel and Jordan. This would (a) make it no longer necessary to pay a pittance to the refugees; (b) in combination with the Jordan water, it would supply abundant water for *both* Israel *and* Jordan, and would therefore make it unnecessary for them to contend with each other over their respective shares of Jordan water.

The future of the Old City of Jerusalem is a question of special urgency and danger. It is of crucial importance that

Israel should not take unilateral action for annexing it. This would not be valid in international law; it could not be accepted by the United Nations; it would make genuine peace between Israel and the Arabs impossible; and it would arouse the whole Muslim World, and probably a large part of the Christian World too, not only against Israel, but against the Jews in general. It might seriously prejudice the diaspora's position in many countries.

Moreover, possession of the Temple area (the Muslims' Haram ash-Sherif) would be an embarrassment for Israel. She would have either to refrain from rebuilding the Temple or else she would have to demolish the Dome of the Rock and the Al Aksa Mosque, which would really be unthinkable. Of course, Israelis and all other Jews must have free access to the Wailing Wall. I like the Pope's proposal for an international trusteeship for the holy places of *all* religions in Palestine. But any change of sovereignty here would be most provocative unless it were freely negotiated in exchange for some equivalent *quid pro quo*. For instance, Jordan might conceivably say to Israel: "Cede to us the fields, now in Israel, that belong to villages on the Jordan side of the frontier, and then we will cede to you the south-west corner of the Old City of Jerusalem, up to the western face of the Wailing Wall." A bargain on these lines would be all right, but unilateral action by Israel would be disastrous.

Well, I am writing this to you, and am sending copies to Isaiah Berlin and to a friend of mine in Baltimore, Maryland, Rabbi Agus.

I am now an old man, and most of my treasure is therefore in future generations. This is why I care so much, and why I am writing this letter to you.

Please make any use of my letter that you think useful. I am not marking it "confidential."

> *Yours sincerely,*
> *Arnold Toynbee*

Jerusalem, 18 July 1967

Dear Professor Toynbee,

I expressed to you by wire my first deeply felt reaction to your letter as soon as I finished reading it. I wish to apologise to you now for the ten days delay in sending you the detailed reply which I promised in my telegram. This was the last week of term at our University, teaching having been resumed at the end of June, after the interruption caused by mobilisation and war. I had also wished to show your letter to friends at the University and to a few persons in government circles for their comments. Finally, I needed time to ponder over what you say and sort out my own thoughts in the light of the feelings and ideas which animate the people of Israel at this moment.

May I say at the outset that I have reason to claim that I voice the sentiments of most Israelis in the appreciation of the moral fervour and sense of urgency which motivate your letter. I speak however only for myself when I deal with your concrete proposals and offer my own suggestions. All the same, I know for certain that a very strong volume of Israeli opinion shares my views on the practical prospects of an Arab-Israeli settlement; and I do not think I exaggerate if I add that, given the proper response from the other side, the suggestions voiced in the second part of this letter may easily become acceptable to the vast majority of the people of Israel, and—Israel being a genuine democracy—to its government.

You list a number of reasons for your feeling of "responsibility for doing anything [you] can to help towards getting a permanent peace now." I would add one reason which you do not mention, but which to me outweighs perhaps all those enumerated by you, for in a sense it contains them all. I seemed to hear in your letter the voice of Arnold Toynbee who in the *Study of History* had been speaking to me not just as the architect of a colossal edifice, but, if I may say so, as a prophet who stands in awe before the mystery of Time and is engaged in a passionate quest for overriding purpose and redeeming significance in History. Some of us who are living in "permanent and anguished intimacy with the mystery of Jewish martyrdom and survival" could not help responding to these "Judaic" ingredients in your work, and therefore felt especially pained by what to us, Jews and Zionists, appeared as a failure to accord to Judaism and its contemporary mutation, Israel, their due place in your scheme of civilisations merging and falling, vast spiritual forces shaping and dissolving them, all that supposedly leading to some salvationist denouement in the end, but now suddenly faced by the mortal danger of total and meaningless destruction.

I welcome, therefore, most heartily your letter as some kind of opening to a friendly and fruitful dialogue. And it is not in any spirit of polemic or out of a wish to put into your mouth things which you did not say in your letter, but out of deep respect and genuine inner need, that I feel compelled to make these few, general comments before I come to your suggestions.

Zionism did not start with Hitler, and to us, therefore, the emergence of Israel could not be summed up in the statement that the Arabs "have been made to pay for the genocide of Jews in Europe which was commited by Germans, not by Arabs."

Just as we would not base our right to exist as an independent state in the Middle East solely on our right of conquest and demand of the Arabs simply to bow to that fact of nature (or history), so we could not possibly subordinate the immemorial aspiration of the Jewish people, admittedly much quickened by the rise of nationalism in the world at large, and made unbearably urgent by murderous persecution, to the exclusive resolve of the Arabs. Whatever the degree of our imaginative understanding of Arab resentment at not having been consulted on the Balfour Declaration and the Palestine Mandate and for having had their objections overridden by the UN and their armed resistance to partition (the solution contrived to meet a clash of rights) overpowered by the Jews in 1948; and whatever the measure of our embarrassed sympathy for the terrible plight of the Palestine refugees, we could not put into question the very basis of our existence.

It is probably too much to ask—in this fallen state of mankind—of a nationalist movement to see the point of the other side and to make concessions to it readily and altruistically. Many as may have been the Zionist sins of commission or omission in this respect, every one of their attempts at a compromise had all along been met by Arabs with the absolute and implacable refusal to recognise any Jewish claim. This was bound to lead to the half-despairing, half-defiant reaction that since nothing could be done with them, it had to be done in spite of and even against them. Arab intransigence has proved a disastrous policy to the Arab interests. Every crisis culminating in armed clash cost the Arabs more and more, and weakened their position still further, which again deepened Arab neurosis on the point of Israel.

Wounded pride of a race with glorious memories is not an ignoble feeling. But an obsessive sense of injury and self-pity are conducive to sterile self-centredness and stultifying misanthropy. Where would we Jews have been today, had we never ceased to remember all the scores and been reliving all the humiliations we had suffered at the hand of every possible nation with which we had come into contact throughout our long history? What would have happened to the persecuted and maltreated of our race, had we behaved like the Arab States towards the Arab refugees: "May they suffer and rot, for it is all the doing of the Jews, and we must not make it easier for the enemy, but should on the contrary keep that sore running." Is there any hope of breaking this vicious circle —the source of so much misery to the peoples of the Middle East, and now threatening to engulf the whole world in an unspeakable catastrophe?

A man greatly revered by both of us, my late teacher R. H. Tawney, wrote:

> It is the tragedy of a world where man must walk by sight that the discovery of the reconciling formula is always left to future generations, in which passion has cooled into curiosity, and the agonies of peoples have become the exercise in the schools. The devil who builds bridges does not span such chasms till much that is precious to mankind has vanished down them for ever.

Surely enough blood has flowed down the chasms for the reconciling formula to be evolved and accepted at last. It is infinitely sad that *homo sapiens* should be so slow-witted, and that his reason should be so dominated and twisted by irrational drives and intractable aversions that only an overwhelming shock and inexorable *faits accomplis* are able to make the sweet voice of reason heard.

I entirely agree with you that on the morrow of the third Arab-Israel war in twenty years, the most self-absorbed nationalists on both sides should be ripe for the acceptance of the fact that galling as it is not to be able to attain one's supreme goal in its undiminished totality, that is the way the jealous gods will it. It may be hard upon the Arabs impelled by a vision of a pan-Arab Empire from Iran to the Atlantic to find the Jews planted on the Eastern shore of the Mediterranean. But the war to the bitter end advocated by the extremists, while most unlikely to wipe out Israel, is sure to bring, at once, the Arab States under Soviet domination, with Russian "advisers" and "technicians" in every office and regiment: a strange consummation of the dream of an Islamic renaissance. Even those no longer very numerous Jews who are still capable of becoming intoxicated with verses on the vastness of the Kingdom promised by the Almighty to His children have to wake up to the fact that God has played them an unfair trick in putting so many Arabs on the banks of the Jordan and scattering so many more in the countries around. The Israelis may defeat them again and again, but only to find the promised "rest and inheritance" removed further and further, and themselves condemned to live by the sword instead of walking by the spirit, to be a Sparta and not the combination of Jerusalem and Athens—the fondest dream of the noblest among the prospects of Zionism.

There is in fact no need to persuade Israel of the desirability and necessity of peace. All the effort is required on the other side. As to the actual terms envisaged by Israel, these would be a function of Arab readiness to recognise Israel and make a genuine peace with her. The graver our fears, the stiffer the guarantees we think necessary for our survival and security; the greater the confidence the Arabs are able to inspire, the more lenient are our terms likely to be.

You single out two items as all-important and indeed all-embracing: refugees and frontiers.

Only yesterday I was deeply impressed by a person whom I was always inclined to consider something of an extremist exclaiming with heat, "But we should pawn all we have to the tenth generation to solve this terrible problem of Arab refugees!"

I feel sure that, on this, all but one of your suggestions would be met: monetary compensation, extra-indemnity, participation in an international fund for resettlement. The difficulty would frankly be the suggestion of an Israeli offer to the Arab refugees of 1948 of the choice of returning home. You consider this as more important for its symbolic significance by expressing the certainty that the "majority will opt for resettlement outside Israel." As you know, we have made such an offer to the 1967 refugees who, seized by panic (out of implacable hostility to Israel or out of a desire to be with their own next of kin) crossed to the East Bank of the Jordan during and since the recent hostilities. We do not know yet how many will avail themselves of the offer to return to the West Bank. While I can see the human and symbolic significance, indeed the duty, of allowing such an option to the recent refugees, I doubt whether there is a case for doing the same in regard to the refugees of twenty years ago. It would not only create very grave problems for Israel. It would also impose upon the refugees, transplanted into realities quite different from those they knew a generation ago, strains and stresses which they would be spared if resettled in an Arab land or overseas. This does not mean that we shall not be prepared, as we have been in the past, to allow reunion of families or make special consideration where warranted.

This world should become one and a fit place for men and women of different races and religions to live together. Yet I cannot help remembering to what extent precisely régimes which claim to be inspired by a universal creed, which subordinates racial peculiarity and national self-assertion to proletarian solidarity and universal brotherhood, have found no other solution to their nationalities problem but in the expulsion of millions of women and children, and in the annexation of vast territories to which their historic claim bears no comparison at all to the strength of the Jewish claim to Palestine. Even in such advanced and rich countries like Belgium and Canada racial conflict is assuming a virulence which baffles all observers. Incidentally, in absorbing some hundreds of thousands of Jewish immigrants or refugees from the Arab countries, Israel has carried out something of an exchange of populations.

As to the territorial terms, again, I and many like me hold the realistic opinion that territory densely populated by Arabs is not only not an asset to Israel, but a liability which even from the strategic point of view outweighs the supposed strategic advantages of what is called "more defensible frontiers." But there are reservations. Israel is entitled to security, and while I do not wish to be an annexationist, I could not consider the 1949 (you say by mistake 1948) armistice frontiers as sacrosanct, and would think rectifications for which you make an allowance in your letter to be justified and indeed indispensable on those trouble spots like the Syrian ridge, the Sinai border, the Straits of Tiran. But I hasten to add that if other effective guarantees for our security could be devised—by way of demilitarisation, international force (not one always exposed to be sent unilaterally packing), international government—I dare say there would not be any insistent pressure for far-reaching territorial changes. The Gaza strip cannot remain an Egyptian enclave.

Israel has repeatedly offered Jordan free access to Israeli ports on the Mediterranean, and although I cannot see the necessity for Syria, which has good ports of her own, of free access to Haifa, surely in an atmosphere of good neighbourly relations this request, like the question of a right of way for Egypt through Israeli Arab territory to the other Arab States, would not present an insurmountable obstacle. But for this, free passage for Israeli shipping through the Suez canal is a precondition.

The question of Jerusalem is a point *sui generis,* and on this our opinions are likely to differ. Of one thing I can assure you: there is no person or group of persons, of any standing in Israel, even among the ultra-orthodox, who would dream of rebuilding the Temple and destroying Muslim or other sanctuaries. The whole matter is not worth a moment of your anxiety. At the same time, public opinion in Israel is so unanimous and determined on the retention of Jerusalem that no government would survive a week if it showed signs of giving in on that. I invite the historian Arnold Toynbee to weigh the pros and cons of this issue in historical perspective and with the historian's detachment, difficult as it is to treat this loaded problem in that way.

If Israel is prepared, and indeed is most anxious, to submit all holy places to international administration and supervision exercised by the accredited representatives of the various religions, Christian and Muslim, with extra-territoriality guaranteed, why should there be all that fuss about sovereignty over the areas which do not contain any holy places? In what way was the Hashemite dynasty of Jordan, whose rule over Jordan resulted from a pure post-World War I accident and indeed a British embarrassment, a more trustworthy guardian than an Israeli government, which (as you hint) has hostages in all the Christian nations? The Jordanians have not left a single synagogue standing in Old Jerusalem and paved the road with tombstones from the ancient cemetery on the Mount of Olives. Are we not faced here with a residue of that unhappy, age-long special attitude to the nation of deicides, whose inferiority to Christendom (and Islam) must be made especially manifest, and the members of which must never be allowed to rule or command the members of the true and triumphant faith? Internationalisation? I seem to detect signs that the Vatican has by no means made up its mind on the desirability of a Jerusalem run by the UN, in which pagan, communist-atheist and Muslim, not to speak of Protestant powers, constitute the vast majority. Finally, may I recall the tremendous agitation against the incorpora-

tion of Rome, the capital of Christendom, the seat of the Holy
See, into the Kingdom of Italy in the 19th century. It requires
an effort of imagination today to visualise a situation in which
Rome is not the capital of Italy, but the free state of the Pope
or an international city.

This brings me to my last and most immediately practical
point: how to go about getting peace.

Like very many Israelis I fervently desire an early arrangement with King Hussein of Jordan. In order not to lose myself
in too sanguine illustrations I would say no more than that
this solution appears to me to be the least impossible of all
solutions talked of. The Israelis have genuine respect and a
sneaking affection for the brave little King, and one can
hear expressions of almost sympathetic regret that he should
have made the terrible blunder he did. Incidentally, the total
absence in Israel of any hatred or contempt for the Arabs
as such is best illustrated by the fact that the spate of songs
and poems of war and victory has not produced a single hate
hymn; and never has any note of abuse crept into radio or
press. There have been only minor cases of plunder which
received prompt punishment, although in the heat of firing
and sniping there seems to have been some unnecessary destruction of houses. The people left homeless were soon
provided with shelter. I believe it is our interest to come to
terms with Jordan and that Hussein stands to gain no less
than we from such a settlement which would return to him
most of the West Bank, except Jerusalem, its immediate
vicinity and a few strategic points elsewhere, while ensuring
to Jordanians some form of free access to Jerusalem and the
Holy places of Islam. I believe, like you, that the international
community, especially the West, would be enthusiastically
ready to offer very large sums and sponsor a joint international
venture, with Israel and Jordan as partners, designed to
resettle the refugees, execute those public works of irrigation
and desalination you mention, solving thereby not only the
refugee problem, but restoring Hussein to his former position.
A common stake in joint prosperity would thus be created.
Would Hussein dare to take such a step alone? Objectively
speaking, Egypt and Syria can afford not to conclude any
arrangement with Israel and play the part of the intransigent
patriots; Jordan just cannot exist without it. Hussein had
been for so long cruelly vilified and ill-used by the more
powerful Arab States. In the war he and his army have

acquitted themselves very honourably and the sacrifices made by them have been infinitely greater than those by other Arab States. So he has done more than his share to fight for Arab honour.

It is quite possible that once the shouting against Hussein for having come to terms with Israel had died down, the other Arab States would tire of their excitement and get down to their internal affairs and gradually slide into some modus vivendi, or even follow Hussein's example fairly soon.

Now I am going to stick out my neck with a good many Jews just as you in your words stuck out your neck with your Arabs. I dislike the idea of a separate little autonomous Arab State on the West Bank of Jordan which would be a camouflaged Israeli protectorate. Not only because I doubt its economic viability, am apprehensive of the crushing financial and administrative burden it is sure to impose upon Israel, fear its irredentism, and the grave security problems arising out of it. I recoil from the idea of Jews lording it over others. It is at variance with the image of Judaism I cherish, and the example of other nations makes me fear the dangers to the moral fibre, the psychological balance, and spiritual values lying in wait for a master race.

I pray that we shall not be compelled to assume that role, which may happen if an arrangement with Jordan proves impossible and the other Arab States refuse to establish peace with Israel.

You speak movingly of your grandchildren. I understand you well. I am a younger man and I have two small children. When I look into their eyes, I think of the million Jewish children whom the Nazis separated from their parents, starved to death and killed in the gas chambers. At such moments my heart goes out to all the children of the world, Arab, Vietnamese, and all others, and I feel like crying aloud: "Never, never again."

Yours sincerely,
J. L. Talmon

Palestine and Israel

By Albert Hourani*

At the heart of the Middle Eastern problem lies the problem of Palestine: the struggle of Palestinian Arabs and Jewish settlers for possession and mastery of the land. Now that the Powers have been drawn in and a local crisis has become a world-wide one, it is easy to forget the local causes of it; but it is dangerous, for unless they are treated the crisis may return.

The struggle of Arabs and Jews for Palestine cannot be explained by ancient religious hostility. Jews (and Christians) had always lived among the mainly Arab Muslim population of Palestine, and relations between them had usually been correct. But in the 1880s a new type of Jewish immigration began, mainly from Eastern Europe, inspired by the Zionist idea of a Jewish national home: this soon aroused the hostility of Ottoman officials and part of the population.

During its 30 years of rule, 1917-47, Britain bound itself by the Balfour Declaration and the Mandate to encourage the Jewish national home, subject to the rights of the existing population; immigration increased, particularly after the rise of Hitler, and Arab opposition became almost universal and drew in the surrounding Arab States.

This hostility sprang from the attempt to implant a new society in a land already occupied by an old one. When the settlers came they found a complete society already there: farmers, craftsmen and merchants, ancient towns and villages, religious institutions, a culture expressed in Arabic, a leadership which formed part of the Arab Ottoman *élite*. The aim of the newcomers was not to be absorbed into it but to create their own society with its farms and cities, institutions, Hebrew culture and political leaders.

In the age of European expansion, other such attempts were made to plant new societies amidst old ones. They always caused strain, but Zionist settlement in Palestine had special features. The new Jewish society, by the nature of the Zionist idea, was to be a complete and exclusive one. Its aim

---

* Albert Hourani is Director of the Middle Eastern Centre and fellow of St. Antony's College in Oxford. His article was first published in the *Observer*, (London), September 3, 1967. (Reprinted by permission of the *Observer* Foreign News Service.)

was to create a wholly Jewish economy: land bought by the Jewish National Fund became the inalienable property of the Jewish people and no non-Jew could ever be employed on it.

Zionist Idea

It is true, the Zionists bought their land. But in the Middle East political power and ownership of land have always gone together, and the Arabs were convinced that if the Jews had power they would seize the greater part of the land. That the Jews *would* take power became first a danger, then a certainty, as the Jewish population grew. Because of the nature of the Zionist idea, the new Jewish society was an expanding society, open to all who wished to come in. In 1922 Jews formed 13 per cent of the population of Palestine; in 1935, 28 per cent; in 1947, 33 per cent.

As numbers grew, the idea of a Jewish national home turned into that of a Jewish State, and this was unacceptable to the Arabs, not only because by the 1930s most of them were moved by the idea of an Arab State of which Palestine would be part, but because in a Jewish State they would have no choice (whatever guarantee the Mandate might contain) except between being a powerless minority and leaving their country.

Some Zionist leaders did indeed talk of a 'bi-national State,' but attempts at political agreement broke on the question of immigration. The Arabs wanted to preserve the Arab character of Palestine, and so wanted little or no Jewish immigration. The Zionists wanted to keep the doors of Palestine open, no matter what the form of government.

Here lay the dilemma of their policy: they wanted agreement with the Arabs and they wanted unlimited immigration, but they could not have both, and if forced to choose most of them would choose immigration.

The British, who were politically responsible, had no clear or stable policy on this matter. They had obligations to the Arabs and so opposed the idea of a Jewish State: they had obligations to the Zionists and so permitted immigration, not as much as the Jews wanted but enough to make a Jewish State possible. In 1948, unable to reach agreement with the two parties, they withdrew in circumstances which made fighting inevitable, and there happened what the Arabs had feared for so long.

The dynamic, exclusive, alien society which had grown up

among them seized power in the greater part of Palestine, with encouragement and help from some Western States, secured control of the land and brought in immigrants on a large scale; and two-thirds of the Arab inhabitants lost their lands and homes.

All wars create refugees, and after the armies have departed the peasants and merchants return to take up their lives again. Civilised Governments accept that they have a responsibility for those who live in the land they rule. But after the armistice agreements of 1949 Israel refused—with limited exceptions—to allow the Arab refugees to return. In a situation like this everything becomes political, and the Israelis made political use of the refugees.

Conquered Land

By refusing to consider the refugee problem except in the framework of a peace settlement with the surrounding Arab States, they linked together two matters which had no moral connection; for the return of the refugees was an obligation which they owed not to the surrounding Arab States but to the Palestinian Arabs themselves, as inhabitants of the land they had conquered. To make such a connection was the more tempting because Israel did not really wish the refugees to return. Even at a peace settlement it would only have offered to take back a small number; for what it wanted was to have the land without its inhabitants, so as to settle its own immigrants.

(This policy was made morally acceptable to Israelis and the outside world by the 'myth' that the Arabs left willingly under orders from their leaders. No more than the most tenuous evidence was produced for this, and, in fact, the flight of the Arabs presents no mystery. Some left for reasons of prudence, some from panic during the fighting, some were forced to go by the Israeli Army. What has happened this year throws some light on this. It is clear that no Arab Government ordered the Palestinians to leave this year, but a quarter of the inhabitants of the West Bank left in two months —and for the same reasons.)

Nothing could show more clearly that the basic dilemma of Zionist policy was still there. If it wanted land for immigrants, it was sensible to stop the return of the refugees. But if it wanted peace with the Arabs, then it was fatal.

After 1948, the first step to peace was that Israel should

recognise its responsibility to the Arabs who lived in its territory but had been displaced by the fighting. Only this could have set in motion a train of events leading towards peace; and only Israel, as victor and beneficiary of the war, could have taken the step. Israel never did so, and its attitude was accepted by the Western Powers. Every year the United Nations passed a resolution calling for the return or compensation of the refugees, but no one tried seriously to carry it out.

Shock of Exile

The assumption which underlay the attitude of Israel and the Western Powers was that sooner or later the refugees would melt away, absorbed into the surrounding Arab peoples, and then the problem of Palestine would cease to exist. But this was a false assumption. It was not a mass of individuals who fled in 1948, it was the greater part of a society. A common land and language, a common political fate, and the shock of exile created a Palestine Arab nation. After 1948 it lived scattered.

Allowing for natural increase, by the beginning of this year there must have been rather more than two million Palestinian Arabs: almost 400,000 in the Gaza Strip, 300,000 in Israel, 1,300,000 in Jordan, 150,000 each in Lebanon and Syria. About two-thirds of them were still registered refugees. Many of these had become wholly or partly self-supporting; if more had not, it was not (as was often said) because the host-countries did not wish them to be settled, but because the absorption of refugees depended on the pace of economic development, and this was bound to be slow in the early stages. In no country was their position satisfactory.

In Jordan they had full citizenship, but Palestinians and Transjordanians had not yet been welded into a complete unity, and positions of real power remained in Transjordanian hands; an intelligent policy of development created an economy into which some of them were absorbed, but the refugees formed a third of the whole population, and a country with such limited resources could not absorb so large a number in 20 years.

In Israel, their position was tolerable: they had civil and political rights, but fewer opportunities of higher education and skilled employment than Jews, they lived under a strict military control (until a relaxation in recent months), and were virtually shut out of the political community.

Thus the Palestinian Arabs remained in being as a nation which had lost almost everything but was determined to continue to exist: that is to say, to live with one another, and to live in Palestine. After 1948 this was the heart of the 'Palestine problem'; the *de facto* existence of Israel was not in serious danger, but what remained to be assured was the existence of the Palestinian nation. Its attitude to Israel was shared by the other Arab nations, for many reasons. The individual losses of the refugees were felt throughout Jordan, Syria and Lebanon, which belonged to the same geographical and historical unit as Palestine, and where almost every family had Palestinian connections.

More widespread still was a sense of human indignity, a feeling that in the eyes of Israel and the West the Arabs were surplus human beings, to be removed and dumped elsewhere to redress a wrong not they but Europe had done to the Jews. It seemed to most Arabs that Western Governments talked in one way about the rights of the Jews and in another about those of the Arabs. They often said that Israel was here to stay; they never said that the Palestinian Arab nation was here to stay. They talked in language of high principles and threats about Israel's right to free navigation; they used a milder language about the right of the refugees to return or compensation. Unwise statements by Arab spokesmen about throwing Israel into the sea were widely quoted and condemned; no one seemed to care that Israel had, in fact, thrown a large number of Arabs into the desert.

Together with this went an almost universal fear. So long as Israel remained open to all Jews who wished to immigrate, so long as it could maintain Western standards of technology and hope for wide support in Europe and America, there would be a danger of its expanding into the territory of the surrounding States. Sooner or later, most Arabs believed, Israel would absorb the rest of Palestine, and perhaps parts of southern Syria and Lebanon as well; for a second time the Palestinians would have to move out, and would find themselves walking down the road to Jericho or scrambling across the Jordan bridges.

Self-defeating

Whatever their differences on other matters, the Arab States were united in their attitude to Israel, and attracted the support—within limits—of most Afro-Asian and communist

States. But coalitions are fragile, in particular if they include States of unequal strength. The common object which brings them together becomes entangled with the separate interests and claims of each, and it was this which led the Arabs into statements and acts which were self-defeating. The essential point of their propaganda was justice for the Palestinian Arabs.

Before 1948 it had been possible to argue that a Jewish State should not be set up because this would be unjust to the Arabs; but once Israel had become a member of the UN, to talk in terms of its disappearance as a State was to embarrass allies and touch a sensitive spot in the European conscience. The official policy of the Arab States was not to destroy Israel but to return to the settlement of 1947-48 and a fulfilment of all the UN resolutions; but at the same time they insisted they were still in a state of active belligerence.

Extreme Terms

This was a dangerous policy for a weaker party to adopt towards a stronger: it gave Israel a license to attack whenever it could claim that its interests were in danger. Israel indeed always remained balanced between two policies: it wanted peace with the Arabs if it could obtain it on its own terms; but war with the Arabs might give it better frontiers.

An Arab policy based on inferior power but expressed in extreme terms played into Israel's hands. This was shown clearly in the events of May and June. For 10 years Egypt and Jordan had kept their frontiers with Israel quiet, and there is no reason to think they wanted a change. But the Syrian frontier was disturbed because of the difficult problem of the demilitarised zone.

Syria began supporting Palestinian activist groups; Israel replied, first by an unprovoked attack on Jordan, not Syria, then by threats which constituted a challenge to Egypt. Egypt replied by sending its Army to the frontier. In so doing Egypt acted as prisoner of the hopes it had aroused, but clearly it did not expect to fight. Egypt's acts were directed towards a political settlement, and its mistake was to think not that the Russians would support it more than they did, but that the Americans would restrain Israel more than they did —that the United States could or would force Israel to give Egypt a victory which might lead to further demands.

Israel called the Egyptian bluff in circumstances which

brought it the greatest possible support in the Western world, not only because of Egypt's bad relations with the US and Britain but because of foolish statements by Arab leaders skilfully used by Zionist propaganda.

The frightening wave of anti-Arab feeling which swept Europe and America in June is not the subject of this article. Ordinary people, Jews and non-Jews, certainly felt that Israel was threatened with destruction. It is more difficult to believe that the Israel Government thought so, knowing its own military strength and that it had a guarantee (implicit or formal) from the strongest Power in the world. However that may be, the defensive war soon became a 'defensive-offensive' one, and once more what the Palestinians had feared came true.

More Refugees

The Israeli victory has changed many things in the Middle East, but it has not changed the problem of Palestine. The Palestinian Arab people are still there, still in ruin and exile, still determined to exist. Perhaps two-thirds of them are now under Israeli rule; many more refugees have been created, and it is not certain that Israel will allow most of them to return; many who are not refugees have been ruined by the occupation of half Jordan; every individual Palestinian has now suffered or lost something because of Israel.

The attitude of the Palestinians towards Jordan may well have changed, and if the West Bank is returned Jordan may become a more solid and united State. But in spite of Israeli hopes and efforts, there is no reason to believe that the attitude of Palestinian Arabs towards Israel has changed, except to be hardened by new losses. The Arab States have more and not less reason to think of Israel as an expansionist State which, with the help or acquiescence of the US, may dominate politically and economically the region lying between Nile and Euphrates.

It seems not impossible that the Arab States will be persuaded to make a declaration of non-belligerence and the Israelis to withdraw from the conquered lands. Even so, the basic dilemma of Israeli policy remains. The Palestinian Arabs are the estranged neighbours with whom Israel must be reconciled if it is to become 'like all nations'; and it remains true, as it has been since 1948, that the first step towards a stable *modus vivendi* is one which only Israel can take—to accept its responsibility towards the indigenous people of the land it controls, and to grant the refugees the right of return or compensation.

In the long run it may be in Israel's interest to do this: only as a mixed State has it a chance of being accepted by its neighbours. But in the short run, the desire for security and for further immigration works against it. It seems more likely than not that Israel will do nothing. If so, it may stay in Gaza and the West Bank; part of the Arab population may be squeezed out; the rump of Jordan may be absorbed into some other State; and in a few more years the Palestinian Arab nation may rise once more to haunt Israel, this time inside as well as outside its frontiers.

Israel and the Arabs

By J. L. Talmon*

The Arab-Israeli dispute has become a world issue. This time the world has had a lucky escape, possibly thanks to the swiftness and completeness of the Israeli victory. No one can be sure of such good luck in the case of another round.

Who are the parties to the Israel-Arab conflict? Clearly not only the Jews of Israel on the one side, and the Palestine Arabs on the other. They are Israel—representing in some way world Jewry—and the Arab world acting on behalf of the Palestine Arabs.

To me, after reading Dr Hourani's article 'Palestine and Israel' in the *Observer* last week, the conflict illustrates that the view one takes on the particular rights and wrongs is determined by one's disposition towards the general case—recognition or non-recognition of an overriding right, a will to war or a will to peace.

But no one who believes and claims for his own people the right of national liberation and self-determination may decry Zionist settlement as 'imperialist invasion.' Nor must its significance be reduced to the dimensions of an asylum for a mob of refugees driven out by Hitler and then thrown upon the Arabs, who had no share in the persecution. It was only

* J. L. Talmon is Professor of Modern History at the Hebrew University, Jerusalem. His answer to Albert Hourani was published in the *Observer* (London), September 10, 1967 (Reprinted by permission of The Observer Foreign News Service.)

natural, once the urge for corporate self-expression in conditions of sovereign mastery over their own fate—the most potent and universal impulse in modern times—had seized the heirs of one of the most ancient peoples on earth, that the aspiration should rivet itself to their ancient home, where their identity was first evolved and where their distinct and so significant contribution to mankind's heritage was shaped.

Persecution

Millions of Europe's Jews were then overtaken by a wave of murderous persecutions without precedent. Literally hunted for their lives, they had no Government to appeal to for protection, no tribunal to turn to for redress—delivered into the hands of assassins on the sole condition that they would be put to death. This traumatic experience fired the Israelis with the desperate resolve to gain, in one place in the world, political sovereignty, without having to rely on the protection or help of others, and to fight for it to death.

On the plane of lesser urgency, the annihilation of that compact and vital Jewish civilisation in central and eastern Europe, coupled with the loss of cohesion in Jewish life in the remaining Diaspora, has left Israel as sole guarantor of the survival of the corporate identity of the Jews as a people. This explains the recent upsurge of first anguished and then proud solidarity with Israel in all parts of Jewry.

But what about the Arab rights and claims? I would classify myself as one of those Zionists who, though passionately convinced of the rightness of the Jewish case, are nevertheless made acutely uneasy by the thought of the Arabs. They can find no sustenance in ascribing to the Arabs some special dose of original sin and selfish greed, let alone inferiority. Dr Weizmann aptly described our position when he spoke of the Jewish-Arab conflict as a clash of rights, for which a solution could be found only on the lines of least injustice, and where no perfect justice was possible.

Dr Hourani seems to make the distinction between the Palestine Arabs as a mass of human beings and Palestinian Arab nationhood. On the sufferings of the former, I must confess I have no answer, no more than to the bafflingly cruel mystery why innocent people suffer and die when States engage in wars, nor to the chilling fact that there has not been a nation in history, including the mightiest Powers and

richest civilisations on earth, which has not established itself
through invading, subjugating, expelling, or indeed anni-
hilating vast native populations. Dr Hourani himself admits
that the situation of the Arabs under Israeli jurisdiction has
been tolerable.

Identity

Just as there is no justification for the claim that Israel is in
any way an obstacle to the flowering of an Arab renaissance
in the vast territories around Palestine, there is no ground
for maintaining that Palestinian Arab national identity and
culture have suffered mortal injury from the encroachment
of the Jews. The Arabs themselves had until recently been
vehemently denying the existence of such an entity as Palestine, insisting that the Holy Land was nothing but southern
Syria, as administratively it was under the Turks. There
has never been a distinct Arab-Palestinian culture, literature,
dialect or national consciousness. Although it is one of the
holy Muslim cities, Jerusalem has never played any role
comparable to Cairo, Damascus or Baghdad in Arab history.
And so, while the obliteration of Jewish Israel would make
the survival of the Jewish entity very problematic, even a
complete de-Arabisation of Palestine—which is hardly at
stake—would have no vital effect on the Arab totality nor, in
the last analysis, on even the aspiration towards permanent
Arab unity.

Admittedly, not much thought was given to the Palestine
Arabs before or at the end of the First World War. Britain,
which issued the Balfour Declaration of 1917, and the countries which endorsed the Mandate on Palestine in 1921, had
all been nurtured on biblical reminiscences of the eternal bond
between the children of Israel and their promised land. They
knew next to nothing of the Arabs, nor were they particularly
worried about the rights of the native populations of the partitioned Ottoman Empire—especially since the Arabs had
emerged after the First World War from centuries of Turkish
bondage with large self-governing territories, in comparison
with which what was promised to the Jews seemed so little.

For a fleeting moment it seemed also as if the Weizmann-
Faisal agreement might ensure a *modus vivendi* between the
diverse aspirations of the two races. Addicted to their idealis-
tic endeavour, so pathetically eager to turn the desert into

garden, the Jews would at first meet any argument about the Arabs with vague expressions of benevolence, quite sincerely disclaiming any wish to hurt them. They were passionately anxious to build up a normal integrated Jewish society and to disprove the slander of their detractors that they were made only for usury and commerce and not for labour and toil. They were also afraid of being put in the position of European planters in Asia and Africa, and so they insisted on employing only Jewish labour on the Jewish national land.

Then, in 1937, when the clash between Arabs and Jews became too acute, the Jews accepted the Royal (or Peel) Commission plan for partition, although by then the need for a refuge from antisemitic persecution was already desperately urgent. It was rejected uncompromisingly by the Arabs. The same happened in 1947—when the United Nations, with the United States and Russia acting as sponsors, resolved upon partition. The Arabs have never since tired of proclaiming a state of war against Israel. In violent and blood-curdling language they continued to voice their intention to wipe out Israel, and indeed its inhabitants. Survivors of Auschwitz could not be expected to treat such threats as mere rhetoric or figures of speech. Nor could they be blamed if they resolved to acts of war, when day in and day out it was not only dinned into their ears that a state of siege was on, but demonstrated to them in the form of infiltration, sabotage, murder and arson.

Intransigent

It was as if God had hardened the heart of Pharaoh: the more intransigent the form of Arab enmity toward Israel, the worse were the consequences for the Arabs themselves. The armed resistance of the Arab States to the UN plan created the refugee problem; the resumption of fighting after the first cease-fire resulted in the loss of more Arab territory; Arab sabotage on the one hand and alliance with Russia on the other only led to a strengthening of Israel's might; finally, this year, the attempt to strangle Israel brought the Arabs a most humiliating *débâcle*.

The armistice agreements concluded in 1949 between the new State of Israel and the Arab countries contained *prima facie* all the guarantees for peace, if not in form, at least in substance. They forbade hostile propaganda, acts of sabotage, operations by military or paramilitary formations, above all armed intrusions or incursions by Army detachments.

In a state of war no points of contact are possible. Hence the irrelevance of the empirical approach, so dear to Anglo-Saxon statesmanship, which sets its hopes on gradual, imperceptible sliding from a state of half-war, half-peace into a state of full peace, from contact and cooperation in small things—such as sharing the waters of the Jordan—to sustained neighbourly give-and-take in all spheres.

This is the context of the question of refugees. Acute as the problem is in terms of human suffering, and few Jews, sons of a nation of exiles and refugees, can be callously indifferent to this aspect of the problem, the state of war makes its solution quite impossible. The world is understandably deeply exercised by the plight of hundreds of thousands of refugees wasting away their lives in camps in pitiable conditions.

One often hears the well-intentioned opinion that this is the most serious obstacle to peace, and that if this tragedy were to be put out of the way, peace could easily be established. The Arabs themselves have never said that the return of the Arab refugees to Palestine was their condition for peace; quite the reverse. In October 1949 the Egyptian Foreign Minister said: 'It should be known and well understood that in demanding the return of the refugees to Palestine the Arabs mean their return as masters of their country and not as slaves. More clearly, they envisage the liquidation of Israel.' In a speech in 1964 President Nasser stated: 'There have been attempts to separate the issues and present them in an imaginary way, as if the question of Israel is just the problem of refugees, and that once this problem is solved the Palestine question would be solved and no trace would be left of it. The Israeli danger lies in the very existence of Israel and in what this State represents.'

If war was the objective, no one could blame the Israelis for believing that the demand for the readmission of refugees, or compensation for them, was motivated not just by the wish to see them restored to their homes, but by the desire to use them as an instrument, a Trojan horse, to disrupt Israel. Besides, the way to solve the refugee problem is surely not by revanchism. What Pandora's boxes would be opened if all nations whose members had been driven from their homes by armed hostilities were to resort to war to right the wrong or merely to wreak vengeance.

Immigrants

Israel has already absorbed in the last 20 years about 600,000 Jewish immigrants from the Arab countries. The Arab refugee problem is intractable, not because no solution can be found through their resettlement and absorption elsewhere in the Arab countries, but because of the implacable Arab refusal even to consider such a possibility lest this blunt the edge of the refugee issue as a political weapon. In fact, the refugee problem is not the sole or even the main obstacle to peace: it is the state of war that is the chief obstacle to the solution of the refugee problem. But Arabs would not, and perhaps could not, see that, because Israel has become to them an obsession, indeed a neurosis.

The Arabs are a proud race enamoured of the memories of their past glories. When they woke up so late from their long lethargy, they were, like all late-comers, in a great haste to recover their place in the sun. They were then faced by the inexorable facts of actual weakness, underdevelopment and vast misery. The combination of resentment towards the West and the envious desire to appropriate and utilise its achievements and levers of power, plus the frustrations encountered in the attempt to skip centuries of social and economic development, led Arabs to put all the blame on imperialism—although in comparative terms the brunt of imperialism was felt much more heavily by other races.

World support for Zionist settlement, for which Arab consent was neither sought nor obtained, and then the establishment of Israel, assumed in the eyes of Arab nationalism the dimensions of a mortal injury, especially as it came from the hands of the Jews, whom they had been accustomed to despise as second-class citizens and a non-martial race of infidels.

The Palestine issue has become the symbol and focus of all Arab frustrations. Their sense of grievance blinds them to the historic rights, the background of tragedy behind the Jewish aspirations, the ardour and high idealism motivating them and the genuine interest of the civilised world in the restoration of Jewish statehood.

The student of Arab opinion and Arab thought is often horrified to watch the growth of the anti-Israel obsession to the point of it having become the cornerstone of a kind of systematic Manichean metaphysic, with the Jew as devil incarnate.

The paramount task at present is to put an end to the general atmosphere of 'kill him before he kills you.' The Arabs threaten to kill the Jews; the Jews then feel they must forestall the Arabs; the Arabs are convinced the Jews are out to kill them off, and so when an armed clash occurs they start running; the Arabs swear bloody vengeance; the Jews insist on maximum guarantees. Any historian knows what a corroding effect this sense of a state of mortal emergency has on peace, morality and freedom. The Arabs are now, understandably, in a state of shock. But one believes one perceives wiser and more prudent counsels stirring among some of them, although for the time being these are too inhibited to come out into the open.

Israel is still more deeply divided. There are those who anxiously 'await a telephone call from King Hussein,' hoping for an arrangement with him whereby Jordan would receive back most of the West Bank, except some strategic points and of course, excepting Jerusalem, plus access to and possibly control over the Muslim holy places. These hopes also assume that world-wide financial support, combined with a substantial Israeli contribution—by way of compensation—would not only make the resettlement of refugees possible, but also put Hussein back on his feet, and create a network of joint, international sponsored ventures in the form of vast works for desalination, irrigation, and so on, for the benefit of all concerned.

There are the others who, pointing to Arab intransigence, claim to see in the triumph of Israel arms the hand of God. Such a chance occurs only once in history, they say. The present generation of Israelis has no right to barter away the promised inheritance, which belongs to all generations. There can be no retreat from the strategic frontiers, particularly on the Jordan, the heights of Golan, and the Suez Canal. (Others would be content with the demilitarisation of Sinai.) They insist on the sacrosanct character of the geopolitical entity that is Palestine.

Romantics

While the mystics and romantics are obsessed with the danger from outside, the moderate realists fear the enormous difficulties inside, arising out of the presence of a large compact territorial Arab minority. They are also beset by grave moral scruples and are apprehensive of world public opinion.

To this the former, among them a surprising number of declared leftists, retort by condemning their adversaries as men of small Zionist faith, who also lack confidence in the ability of Israel to treat an Arab minority humanely and well and to solve all the social and economic problems involved.

In the hopeless view they take of the Arab readiness to recognise the existence of Israel, the hawks of Israel are most likely to add fuel to the hawks in the Arab world. This paradoxical 'alliance' can be countered, and the vicious circle broken, only by an 'alliance' of the moderate realists on both sides. And I can only hope that my friend Hourani and men like him will heed this appeal to their moral obligation towards their own people and mankind in general.

The Origins of the Middle East Crisis[1]

By Hal Draper*

We have just seen War No. 3 in the tragedy known as the Israel-Arab conflict; and we find ourselves in the position of being unable to cheer for either side in this clash of chauvinisms. At this time I am going to devote myself mainly to the myths and illusions about the Israeli side of the story, for the simple reason that it is these myths and illusions that you mainly read and hear about.

It is not possible to understand what has happened merely by looking at what happened in the last couple of weeks. Behind War No. 3 is a closely connected chain of events and issues going far back. The main link in this chain is the story of a *nation that has been destroyed.*

That sounds like an echo of what we hear all around, viz. the threat of the Arab states to destroy the state of Israel

---

[1] This article is a somewhat condensed and edited version of a talk given in Berkeley shortly after the outbreak of the Third Arab-Israeli War, dealing with the historical background of the conflict but not with the current situation, which was discussed separately. Fully detailed documentation for the material contained here may be found in a book which has just been published, *Zionism, Israel and the Arabs: The Historical Background of the Middle East Tragedy* (Berkeley, 1967), edited by myself, comprising articles from the Independent Socialist press. Ed.

* Hal Draper is an editor of *New Politics* and author of "Berkeley: The New Student Revolt." His article appeared in *New Politics*, Winter, 1967 and is reprinted by permission of the author. An article in a similar vein by the late Isaac Deutscher ("On the Israel–Arab War") was published in the *New Left Review*, (London), July–August, 1967. It was answered in detail by Simha Flapan in *Temps Modernes*, (Paris), November, 1967.

—the threat which is the hallmark of Arab chauvinism. But while this is a threat, there *was* a nation that was destroyed in Palestine—already. It is this destroyed nation whose fate has been the crux of the Middle East tragedy, for its fate has been used and is being used as a football by each side.

When I was born, there was an Arab nation in Palestine, in whose midst Jews had lived for 2000 years in relative peace. Where is this nation now, and what has been done to it? The answer is at the heart of the program which we face now.

Today the leaders of the Arab states are saying, "We aim to destroy the nation which inhabits Palestine," and they are rightly denounced for this. But toward the end of the 19th century, a movement arose which did in fact set itself the aim of destroying the nation which inhabited Palestine then; and moreover it did so. That movement was the Zionist movement.

Everyone talks nowadays about "*the* Jews" and "*the* Arabs," with doubtful justice. There are Jews and Jews, as there are Arabs and Arabs; and right now I am talking not about "the Jews," but about the Zionist movement. Israel today is run by the old men of the world Zionist movement, and it is still the Zionist ideology which rules Israeli policy. The European survivors of Hitler's death camps are not the Jews who run Israel; their terrible fate has been a tool used by the men who run Israel, so that the crimes of the Nazis have been used to deflect the attention of world public opinion from the crimes committed in Palestine.

For present purposes, there are three things to understand about this Zionist ideology, which still rules the rulers of Israel. To present the first, I quote a typical example of anti-Semitic literature:

> The converted Jew remains a Jew, no matter how much he objects to it . . . Jews and Jewesses endeavor in vain to obliterate their descent through conversion or intermarriage with the Indo-Germanic and Mongolian races, for the Jewish type is indestructible. . . . Jewish noses cannot be reformed, and the black wavy hair of the Jews will not change through conversion into blond, nor can its curves be straightened out by constant combing.

There is more of the same where this comes from. Obviously from the Nazi commentary on the Nuremberg Laws, or from Streicher's *Stürmer,* or perhaps from Gerald L. K. Smith? Not at all: it is from a classic of Zionism, Moses Hess' *Rom und Jerusalem.* It is easily possible to quote pages and pages more of this same mystical blood-tribalism from the best Zionist sources, all sounding as if it came from the arsenal of the anti-Semites.

For Zionism is, first of all, a doctrine about a tribal blood-mystique which makes all Jews a single nation no matter where they live or how. It asserts that Jews are inevitably *aliens* everywhere, just as the anti-Semites say they are; and that anti-Semitism is correct in feeling this. This is the first element in Zionism.

Secondly: it follows that the Jews must reconstitute their "nation" in a state territory; but not just *any* state territory. In fact there is a point of view called "territorialism," as distinct from Zionism, which looked for the establishment of a Jewish nation in a land other than Palestine. But Zionism demands that the Jewish "nation" take over Palestine—only Palestine; and by Palestine it means the ancient Jewish state and its boundaries, *Eretz Isroel,* no less. This is what the tribal mystique demands.

Thirdly: the Zionist ideology dictates that this Jewish state must be set up not only by Jews who want to live in such a state. One of the tasks of the Zionist movement is to move *all* Jews, from all countries of the world, into Palestine, now Israel. In Zionist slang, this is called the "Ingathering of the Exiles;" for it is an article of basic faith that all Jews living outside this territory are living literally in exile, and always will merely be exiles, nothing else. It was not very many years ago that a writer in *Davar,* the organ of the Israeli ruling party, made the suggestion that a good way of uprooting all those American Jews who declined to go to Israel was to send a gang of anti-Semitic agitators there to make the ground hot under their feet so that they would move. This, of course, is not usually the course recommended on paper, as against persuasion. But how persuasion graduates into denunciation and arm-twisting was seen in the early fifties when David Ben-Gurion, on a visit to the U.S., denounced the Zionist Organization of America as traitors to Zionism because its leaders were not working actively to get the entire Jewish population of the U.S. to move to Israel. It must be understood (though American Zionists systematically obfuscate it to the best of their ability) that the Israeli leaders and world Zionist leaders sincerely believe in their mission to "ingather" *all* the Jews of the world to the state of Israel, and that they have devoted their lives to this mission.

The Zionists have always been fond of saying that they are tired of the Jews being a "peculiar people," that they have been "peculiar" long enough. They want (they say) the Jews to be a people like any other, and to have a state just like any other state. In Israel, I would tell you, they have succeeded notably in *this* aim: Israel more and more has become a state like any other state. In this stridently militarist Zionist state, the current of Jewish humanism which was one of the glories of the Jewish people from Maimonides to Spinoza and after, is today represented only by a minority—a minority whose voices are rarely heard abroad, and hardly at all in the U.S.; but it is this minority which represents the only Israel with whom one can identify.

Soon after the creation of Israel the press was full of enthusiastic reports by American Jewish tourists who went to Israel and came back to relate the wonders that they saw there (and there are many to see). One that I remember most vividly was a tourist who was quoted as follows in the course of his burbling: "Why, you walk around Tel Aviv, and you know what? Even the *policemen* are Jewish!" That's true, naturally. The cops are Jewish in Israel—and they are still cops. The militarists in Israel are Jewish—and they are militarists. And the people who destroyed the Arab Palestinian nation which I mentioned were, alas, also Jewish—though I do not believe that they will go down in the annals of history alongside Maimonides and Spinoza.

The destruction of that Palestinian nation went through four periods. The first period goes from the beginning of the Zionist movement up to World War I. This was a period of slow immigration of Jews into Palestine and of gradual land-buying. By the time it ended Jews constituted something under 10 percent of the population. Despite Zionism's profession that this was the thin edge of the wedge in its long-term aim to establish a Jewish state in the land inhabited by Arabs, it was not taken seriously enough to occasion much resistance until the second period, inaugurated by the 1917 Balfour Declaration.

It was in this period that British imperialism, taking over the area, started its decades-long policy of playing Zionists against Arabs in order to maintain its imperialist control. The Zionist leadership willingly and knowingly collaborated with the British. They knew that, at this stage, it was not they who could control the Arab people living in the land; only British imperialism could do it for them. To be sure, they were not *puppets* of the British: they were junior partners, in an enterprise in which each partner considered that it was using the other for its own ends.

This was also the period of the beginning of Arab nationalism, of an Arab national-liberation movement. This movement had every right to fight for liberation from Britain (or in other parts of the Middle East, from France). To supporters of Arab freedom, the Zionist movement could have appeared only as what it actually was: a partner of the European imperialists. It makes no difference whatsoever that the Zionists played this baneful role not out of love for Britain but in pursuit of their own expansion. The fact is that Britain used the Zionist tool to increase the number of Jewish settlers so as to play them off against the indigenous Arab population. Thus it was inevitable that Jewish immigration should appear to the Arabs as a tool of imperialist domination, for it was so.

It was therefore during the 1920s that, for pretty much the first time in Palestine, there began sporadic Arab attacks against Jewish settlers. On the one side, these were the first stirrings of an Arab national liberation movement, directed not only against the British but also against the allies of the British who were at hand, viz. Zionist infiltrators into the country. On the other hand—and here you get the typically tragic element in this story which goes through it from beginning to end—these stirrings took on strong overtones of the backward social and religious aims of the Arab movement; for progressive social elements were weak, working-class formations were incipient. But this hardly can change the fact that there was a legitimate nationalist movement under way.

The third period—which was to prove decisive to the outcome—came with the onset of the Nazis' anti-Jewish drive, first in Germany itself, and then in the course of World War II in the rest of Nazi-occupied Europe, up to the mass extermination campaign and its death camps. It should be added that, in the period immediately following the war, there was also the onset of Soviet anti-Semitism on a big scale, thereby boosting the impact of what had happened during the war.

This is the period that everyone knows about; some think it is all one has to know. But there is more to this than meets the myopic eye.

To be sure, for the Jewish remnant Europe represented

burning ground: they had to get out—somehow, somewhere, anywhere. This plight of the Jewish refugees—one of the most terrible in the history of man's bestiality to man—was what dramatically captured the sympathy of everyone decent in the world; it is this that is tied up in the public mind with the exodus to Palestine. This is entirely true as far as it goes; but one has to know something else too. *This terrible plight and this great world sympathy were not enough to open the gates of a single Western country to those Jewish refugees!*

During those years we Independent Socialists called for opening the doors of the United States to the Jewish victims of Hitlerism, those who were left. I can tell you that in this great "liberal" country, crawling with liberals, there was hardly an echo of such a notion, of opening the doors of *this* country to the poor Jews for whom everyone's heart bled—in print.

One reason for this is clear and can be easily documented. Morris Ernst, the famous civil liberties lawyer who was involved at the time, has told the story, among others: about how the leaders of the Zionist movement exerted all the influence they could muster to make sure that the U.S. did *not* open up immigration to these Jews—for the simple reason that they wanted to herd these same Jews to Palestine. This is what their Zionist ideology demanded. White Christian America was only too glad to go along with this "solution"! Who wanted a few hundred thousand miserable Jewish refugees coming into the country? Not our liberal Americans, who were so heart-stricken by Nazi brutality. Not the British, who took in an inconsequential token number. Nor anyone else. These Jewish victims were people on the planet without a visa. Liberals in this country, as elsewhere, had a convenient way of salving their tender consciences; all they had to do was parrot the line which the Zionists industriously provided them: "They want to go only to Palestine . . ."

Now there is no point in anyone's arguing to what extent this was really true or not, or of how many it was true, because no one ever gave them the chance to decide whether they wanted to go to Palestine or to some other country that was open to them. The doors were shut against them, with the help of the whole Zionist apparatus and of other "influential" Jews who were no more enthusiastic about "flooding" the country with poor Jews than their WASP neighbors. First it was made damned sure that Palestine was the only possible haven, and then they might possibly be asked where they wanted to go, as if they had a free choice! In my eyes, this is one of the basest crimes committed by the Zionist leadership.

In this way the Jewish survivors of the Hitlerite death camps were herded toward Palestine, to keep the U.S. and other countries from being contaminated by their presence (for some) or to make sure that they were properly "in-gathered" (for others). Of course, Palestine was not really open either, being still under the control of the British, but here at least the Zionist movement was willing to go all-out to crash the gates, with heavy financing from many an American Jew who himself had no sympathy for Zionism but could be convinced that Palestine was certainly a more suitable haven than New York.

This turn brought the Zionist movement into conflict with the same British imperialism whose junior partner it had been. The partners' paths now diverged. The Jewish refugees —fleeing from a horror behind them, and rejected on all sides—became the human material the Zionists needed to carry out the goal they had set a half century before: to dispossess the Arab nation of Palestine and install a Jewish state in its stead—and to do this with the sympathy of a good deal of the world.

The Palestinian Arabs, as well as their Arab neighbors, had a very simple comment to make on this situation: "Hitler's extermination program was a great crime, but why does that mean that *we* have to give up our land to the Jews? It is the world's problem, not just ours." I should like to see someone refute this.

We must note that by this time the Zionist movement had finally come out openly with its proclaimed intention of taking Palestine away as a Jewish state. This had been done in 1942, in the so-called "Biltmore Program." (Up to then, the Zionists had used doubletalk about a "Jewish homeland" to confuse the picture.) Now that the cards were on the table, there were even some Zionists—or at least people who considered themselves to be Zionists—who were outraged. It was around this time that the Ichud was founded in Palestine by Rabbi Judah Magnes. The idea of a bi-national state in Palestine was counterposed to the official Zionist program: instead of a "Jewish state" it meant a state in which both Jews and Arabs could live peacefully and tranquilly together; but it was rejected. Instead, the Zionists said, "We are going to take the whole country"; and they did.

Here I need only sketch how this happened. After a series of doubledealing maneuvers by the great powers (particularly the U.S., Britain and Russia) which it would take too long to go into, by 1947 the United Nations decided on a partition plan. There were to be two separate states in Palestine, a Jewish state and an Arab Palestinian state. By this time, there was indeed a Jewish majority in the territory assigned to the Jewish state—something like a 60% majority—and therefore one could feel that this majority had the right to invoke the right to self-determination. I might as well mention that, at that time (1948), I did myself believe and write that the Palestinian Jews had the *right* to make this mistaken choice (for, of course, a right exists only if it includes the right to make a mistake). I mention this only to make clear that I believed and wrote at that time that the attack on the new state of Israel by the Arab states was an aggression and a violation of the right to self-determination.

But at that moment Israel was still new-born, and there were different ways in which it could defend itself—in a progressive and democratic way, and in a racist and expansionist way. The answer to *that* historical question was not long in coming: it was given right away by the same Zionist leaders who were also the rulers of the new state power. From its first hour the Zionist power took the road of a reactionary and racist purge of the Arabs as such. At this point I am not talking about the foreign Arab states, but of the Arabs of Israel themselves, the great mass of whom never took up arms against Israel or aided the aggressors.

A new act in the Middle East tragedy begins here; although it is a crime smaller in magnitude than Hitler's against the Jews, it is still one of the most shameful in recent history. The Zionist rulers utilized the attack by the *foreign* Arab states to run the *Palestinian* Arabs off their land, by means of a series of laws and measures which were taken not only in 1948-49 but which went right on into the 1950s. The forty percent of the population which was Arab in the partitioned territory was reduced to about 10 percent in the new state of Israel. Immense proportions of Arab-owned land were simply robbed from them, by "legal" means. By 1954 over one-third of the Jewish population then in Israel was settled on land that had been stolen from the Palestinian Arabs. And the Arab state of Palestine which had been created by the partition never came into existence; by the end of the war, five sections of it had been grabbed by Israel and were never given up, and the West Jordan area was incorporated into the state of Jordan.

Thus the Arab nation of Palestine was destroyed, except as a discriminated-against remnant in Israel, and even the truncated Arab state of Palestine set up by partition was destroyed. I am entirely willing to denounce anyone who wants to destroy any existing state, including Israel; but some thought should be given to this recent history by those who are willing to denounce *only* the threat to destroy Israel.

The great land robbery of the Israeli Arabs was the despoiling of a whole people. It was carried out in various ways, but generally speaking the pattern was this: any Arab who had left his village during the war for any reason whatsoever was declared an "absentee" and his land was taken away by Zionist agencies. The Zionist myth has it that all these Palestinian Arabs left at the behest of the foreign Arab invaders and in cahoots with them. This is a big lie. There was a war on, and even if they *fled from* the Arab invaders and in fear of them, and even if they fled only to a neighboring village, they became "absentees." They also fled from the British; they not only fled from the invading Arabs but also fled from the Zionist troops—the Haganah and the Irgun. This was especially true after the massacre at Deir Yassin.

Deir Yassin was the name of an Arab village in Palestine, whose people were outstandingly *hostile* to the Arab invaders. In 1948 a battalion of the Irgun (the right-wing Zionist force) attacked the village. There were no armed men in the village, and no arms. Purely for terroristic purposes, the Irgun sacked the village and massacred 250 men, women and children. One hundred and fifty bodies were thrown down a well; 90 were left scattered around. This massacre was deliberately directed by the Irgun against a village known to be *friendly* to the Jews, as an example. Although the dirty job was done by the Irgun, the official-Zionist Haganah knew of the planned attack; immediately afterward the Irgun, instead of being pilloried in horror by the Zionist movement, was welcomed by the Haganah into a new pact of collaboration. (The Irgun's leader, Beigin, by the way, was taken into the Israeli cabinet along with General Dayan just before the outbreak of the recent Third War.)

Of course, the Irgun was able to show the way to the Haganah because it was semi-fascist; but the Haganah leaders learned fast. Before the First War had ended the Haganah too was attacking and ousting unarmed and non-belligerent

Arab villagers, although naturally not as brutally as the Irgun (since they were democrats and "socialists"). Especially after the Deir Yassin massacre, it was only necessary that any troops show up, and the Arab peasants got out of the way, as anyone else would do. They thus became "absentees," and their land was taken away by a series of laws over the next several years. *All* of the Zionist parties, from "left" to right, sanctioned this robbery. There was even a legal category known as "present absentees," who were very much present as Arab citizens of Israel but who were legally accounted to be "absentees" because they had been absent from their village on a certain date—and therefore could be legally robbed of their land. The largest portion of this stolen land went to the kibbutzim—not only the kibbutzim run by the Mapai (right-wing social democrats) but even more went to the kibbutzim of the Mapam (who claimed to be left socialists), whose leaders regularly made clear that their hearts bled for the plight of the Israeli Arabs. However, their hearts also bled for their land, even more.

Along the border areas, Palestinian Arabs were pushed over the line into the Gaza Strip, or into Jordan, and then they were shot on sight as "infiltrators" if they tried to come back. It was in ways like this—which I sketch here only briefly —that Israel's rulers created the massive Arab refugee problem. Literally they surrounded the country with a circle of hatred—*hatred which they themselves had caused*—the hatred of the despoiled Palestinian Arabs looking over from the other side of the border and seeing their own lands being tilled by strangers whom the Zionists had brought from thousands of miles away to take their place.

This robbery is not transmuted into justice just because some of these strangers were Jewish refugees from Europe against whom another crime had been committed by someone else. The Zionist agencies welcomed these despairing refugees to their new life by putting them on the marches of the hate-encircled state so that they would have to defend themselves, their lives, and their stolen gifts, from the previous Arab owners. (Thus the "exiles" were not only "ingathered" but also very useful.)

Meanwhile in Israel, the 10 percent of the Palestinian Arabs left—who had not only not taken up arms but had not fled— were placed under military control like an occupied enemy people, and discriminated against in many ways. It is not without reason that they have been called the "niggers of Israel";

but as a matter of fact the American Negroes would not have taken lying down what the Israeli Arabs had to endure for two decades.

On the borders—for example, in the Gaza Strip—the dispossessed and robbed Arabs lived a wretched existence under the control of Egypt, but the Egyptians only used them for their own purposes as pawns, while keeping their help to a minimum. They were not admitted into Egypt proper. They were forced to fester there so that their misery and hatred might make them a bone in the throat of the Israelis; at the same time Israel was as little interested as Nasser in arriving at a deal for the settlement of the Arab refugee problem.

Every now and then some of the refugees would "infiltrate" —that is, slip across into Israel to visit his own land or till his own soil or try to take back his own belongings—and would be shot to death by those same Jewish policemen and guards who so delighted the heart of the Jewish tourist mentioned earlier. As a result the Israelis complained bitterly about the "infiltrators" who were so evil as to do this. The terrible situation escalated. Infiltrators began to commit acts of sabotage on the property that had been stolen from them, or struck out more blindly at the robbers. The Israelis began to resort to organized military reprisals to terrorize them into acquiescence. In 1953 there was a massacre organized by Israeli armed forces in the Arab village of Kibya. In 1955— a year that more or less marked a turning-point for the worse —there was a big attack by an organized Israeli military force on Gaza; more and more Israeli leaders oriented toward "preventive" war, since military force was their only answer to the problem created by their own crimes. This was the traditional and classic answer of the militarist and expansionist mentality; it is the same answer as was recommended by General MacArthur on how to treat Koreans and Chinese and other such "gooks"—you show them who's master—that's what they can understand, etc. The answer of the Israeli militarists was, similarly: kill and terrorize the "gooks" and "teach them a lesson" so that they won't do it again.

There were negotiations over the plight of the Arab refugees but neither side was interested in a real settlement—not the Israeli side and not the Egyptian and Arab side. For Nasser, the Arab refugees leading their wretched existence were useful tools to harass the Israelis. As for Israel, at the same time that they argued that they could not restore the land to the Arabs they had robbed, they were industriously bringing in whole Jewish populations, from Yemen and Morocco, for example (not to speak of the whole Jewish population of the U.S. which Ben-Gurion was so vainly anxious to move to Israel). There was plenty of room in Israel for such hundreds of thousands of Jews, but in the negotiations over the Arab refugee problem there was not a *dunam* of land that could be spared. The decisive thing to remember is that, from the Zionist viewpoint, for every single despoiled Arab who would be readmitted to Israel there was a Jew who could therefore not be "ingathered."

The problem was not *how* Israel and the Arab states could have made peace; the problem was that neither side wanted to make peace, except of course on capitulatory terms. They did not then, and they do not now.

For Nasser, the Israel issue was a pawn in the inter-Arab struggle for power. It was also a useful distraction from the internal failures of his bureaucratic-military regime, which lacked any progressive domestic program. In both Egypt and Jordan, the pressure of the refugees within the country was relieved only by pointing them outward, against Israel. As for Israel, it must be remembered that Zionism still did not rule the "Land of Israel" as the Zionist program demanded; the "Land of Israel" still included territories outside of the state of Israel. Israeli expansionism was implicit in this, and also in the fact that, if room was going to be made for the millions of "exiles" who were to be ingathered, more land was needed. In 1955 Israeli leaders (some eagerly convinced of the necessity of "preventive" war, some dragging their feet) were looking for some pretext to launch a war against Egypt and the Arab alliance. As it happened, British and French imperialism brought them to launch that aggression themselves. In 1956, openly and in the sight of the whole world, side by side with the two leading European imperialisms (of which it was once again a junior partner), Israel invaded Egypt as its partners struck at the Suez Canal.

The point is not that Nasser is or was a dove of peace, himself, as has been made clear. One of the reasons why Nasser was not in a position to give warlike substance to his blowhard threats was that he was too preoccupied with internal difficulties and too weak. But if Nasser was no dove, it is still true that Israel exposed itself to the whole world as an open aggressor in alliance with European imperialism. Every dirty expansionist plan it had been accused of turned out to be true.

Even after the British and French enterprise failed, Israel fought to retain the land it had grabbed in Egypt and gave it up only after immense international pressure.

This pattern must be remembered in the light also of the way in which the recent Third War was initiated: i.e. with Nasser taking the situation to the brink, talking loudly about destroying Israel, while the Israelis went straight to the business at hand by precipitating the shooting war.

There is one other story to be told for this period—the story of a pogrom. This pogrom was directed against an Arab village in Israel named Kfar Kassem. On the day that Israel attacked Egypt in 1956, the Israeli government declared a new curfew for its Arab citizens (who, remember, were under military control anyway, even without a war). The new decree advanced the curfew from 11 p.m. to 5 p.m. Israeli officers showed up in Kfar Kassem, as well as other places, to make known the change on that day. They were told that the men had already gone out to the fields; the officers' reply was, roughly speaking, "Don't bother us with details." In the evening, when the men of the village returned from working in the fields after the new curfew hour, they were shot down in cold blood by the Israeli soldiers—for violating a curfew that had never been told them. The government admitted that 46 men were thus killed; the number wounded was not made public. The government admission applied only to Kfar Kassem but it was reliably reported that the same thing happened that day at other Arab villages. Even this much was admitted by the government only after a week had passed and the reports could no longer be hushed up. All of Israel was appalled. Some underlings were made the scapegoats.

It was clear, then, that the Zionist program of making Israel a "state like any other state" had come true: it had its own Jewish policemen, it had its own soldiers, it had its own militarists, and now it had its own pogroms.

In 1967 the road that started in Deir Yassin and goes through Kfar Kassem has now reached the bank of the Jordan, where Arab refugees are once again being pushed out and around by the Israelis, as they have been for the last 20 years. It would be useful to go through the whole chapter subsequent to 1956, leading up to the Third War, but, aside from time considerations, we would only find that it is more of the same thing: the tragedy of one reactionary chauvinism versus another reactionary chauvinism.

There is an image that haunts me, about this whole tragic

embroilment in the Middle East. Buck deer in the mating season will fight each other, and now and again it has happened that they will entangle their antlers and be unable to disengage. Unable to break loose, unable to win, locked in a static hopeless combat until they die and rot and their bleached bones are found by some hunter in the forest, their skeletons are grisly evidence of a tragedy which destroyed them both, ensnarled.

It may be that, in the Middle East entanglement, the Arabs, or some of the Arabs, can survive this conflict. But it is doubtful whether, in the long run, the Jews of Israel can. What the Zionists have made out of Israel is a new ghetto—a state ghetto with state boundaries. That's not a new life for the Jews; that is more of the old life of which the Jews have had more than their share. This generation of Zionist hawks ruling Israel is a curse. No matter how many more great military victories they win, the sea of Arab peoples ringing them cannot be eliminated from the picture, and hatred grows. It may be another decade or two before the Arab states become modernized enough to wage war effectively; and then it will take more than euphoria over military heroes to point a way for Israel.

There are some in Israel who know and say what has been said here—more who know and fewer who say—and it is to be hoped that the next generation will be more willing to listen to their kind, to the kind of Jews who represent what is best in the history of Jewish humanism and social idealism rather than those who worship the Moloch of a "state like any other state."

Perfidy and Aggression

By N. T. Fedorenko*

The attention of the whole world has been focussed in these past days on the Middle East, where Israel has committed open and perfidious aggression against the Arab states.

The United Nations Organization, whose mission it is to maintain international peace and security, naturally could not

* N. T. Fedorenko, Soviet Permanent Delegate to the U.N., played a leading part in the United Nations' discussions before, during and after the crisis of June, 1967. His article appeared in the Soviet weekly *New Times*, June 28, 1967.

pass by the Israeli aggression. First the Security Council was urgently called into session, to discuss, in particular, the Soviet demand for cessation of hostilities by Israel and withdrawal of Israeli troops from U.A.R., Jordanian and Syrian territory occupied as a result of the aggression. Then, on the initiative of the Soviet Union, a special emergency session of the General Assembly was convened on June 17.

The Security Council debates showed up the broad imperialist conspiracy against the Arab states and peoples of the Middle East. It was proved that the Israeli aggression was not an accidental thing, not the result of any mistake or misunderstanding. No, it was a carefully plotted imperialist provocation, the timing of which was planned on all sides. This aggression was to secure political changes in the Middle East in the interest of imperialism, notably American imperialism, to alter the "balance of strength" in the area. Its purpose was to undermine the Arab national-liberation movement, to weaken the progressive regimes in the U.A.R., Syria and other Arab countries. Israel acted as the instrument of more powerful imperialist states, and above all the U.S.

The Israeli army was built up and trained with the help of the imperialist Western Powers. Tel Aviv was given every protection and encouragement, particularly in Washington, to prepare it for aggression against the Arab states.

The peoples of the U.A.R. and other Arab countries have scored historic victories in these past years in their struggle to attain national independence and freedom. Important social restructuring and reform in the interests of the working masses has been carried out in these countries. The imperialists could not stomach the fact that in this struggle the Arab peoples lean on the friendship and support of the Soviet Union and other socialist states.

Writing in *U.S. News and World Report,* General Max Johnson, formerly planning officer for the U.S. Joint Chiefs of Staff, openly voiced the sentiment of the American military chiefs. "The growing hostility of Middle Eastern nations towards the United States and friendliness towards the Soviet Union," he wrote, "has been a strategic loss of great proportions." And he linked the events in Vietnam with the position in the Middle East, pointing out that this area was a "strategic crossroads" between Europe, Asia and Africa.

And indeed, remote though Southeast Asia and the Gulf of Tonkin are geographically from the Middle East and the Eastern Mediterranean, few will question that the American aggression in Vietnam was bound to have the most pernicious effect on the general political situation in the world; and it was by no means the last factor in Israel's aggression against the Arab states.

The colonialists also refused to accept that Arab riches should belong to the Arabs themselves and that it is the Arab countries' lawful right to determine their own path of development. The imperialist forces got busy and the Israeli aggression was unleashed just when more and more of the Arab countries had begun taking measures to consolidate national independence.

The Israeli aggression is pointed against the national freedom and state independence of the millions of Arabs—from Kuwait, Damascus and Baghdad to Cairo, Algiers and Casablanca. There is not a shadow of doubt that behind Tel Aviv stand the imperialist forces which want to hamstring the free national development of the Arab states. It is these forces that lavishly supplied Tel Aviv with the needful means and gave it economic, moral and political assistance and support.

It should be added that behind the Israeli extremists it is easy to discover not only the Pentagon generals but the incorrigible militarists in West Germany. That Bonn has directly abetted the Israeli extremists is not to be concealed by any smokescreens of "neutrality." Bonn not only engaged in incitement, it not only sacrificed diplomatic relations with a number of Arab states for the sake of close partnership with Israel; it also supplied arms and equipment for the Israeli army. At the height of the Middle East crisis, West Germany demonstratively dispatched a large consignment of gas-masks to Israel. Thus there grew up on the soil of fevered militarism, on the common basis of adventurism, of hatred for all things progressive, of hostility to the Arab peoples' struggle to consolidate independence and achieve social progress, an alliance of Tel Aviv extremist circles not only with Washington but with Bonn.

On the eve of the Israeli attack an atmosphere of hysteria was artificially created in the country and tension whipped up to prepare the ground for aggression. The Arab states were showered with accusations. The events that followed showed that the U.A.R., Syria and the other Arab states had no aggressive intentions, that they had not been preparing to strike, and that it was Israel that had been girding feverishly for its brigand attack on the Arab countries. It was not the peoples, not the Arab countries that had an interest in kindling military conflict, but the forces of imperialism, the oil monopolies, of whom Israel is the confederate.

It is not surprising that when the question of Israel's aggression against the Arab states came before the Security Council, the aggressor had open defenders and abettors there, who sought to obstruct the work of the Council and enable Israel to ignore the Council's decisions, gain time for more conquests, and carry out its criminal plans.

That is why the Security Council had to hold a practically continuous series of emergency meetings and pass three separate resolutions on what was in effect one and the same question, reiterating its demand that Israel cease hostilities forthwith.

Thanks to the support given them by the United States—a permanent member of the Security Council—and by certain other members of the Council, who prevented the passage of a decision condemning the aggressor and demanding the immediate withdrawal of his troops to the positions held before the hostilities, the Tel Aviv rulers were able insolently to ignore the Security Council decisions and continue and extend their aggression, overrunning more and more Arab territory.

Even after the Security Council had ordered an immediate ceasefire and termination of hostilities, Israel treacherously—contrary to two Security Council resolutions (of June 6 and 7)—invaded the Syrian Arab Republic, occupied part of its territory, and bombed Cairo and the Damascus area.

The Tel Aviv rulers deliberately deceived the Security Council, assuring it that Israel was complying with its decisions while in reality they continued the aggression. It came to light during the debates that the bombing attacks on Cairo and Damascus and the invasion of Syria had taken place at the very time when Israel's representative in the Security Council had been making his hypocritical speeches and misleading Council members so as to distract attention from the criminal acts of the Israeli military. The Israeli authorities also did everything they could to prevent the U.N. observers on the spot from discharging their functions and keeping the Security Council informed of what was happening.

This perfidy of Tel Aviv was indignantly condemned by the socialist and Afro-Asian members of the Security Council. The Soviet delegation called the Council's attention to the dangerous war psychosis that has come to reign in the Israeli capital. Threats and ultimatums of a rare insolence and cynicism have been issuing from there. Plans of expansion, plans of seizing new territories, plans of recarving the map of the Middle East have been intensively prepared.

The overweening aggressors have taken over the notorious nazi theories of geopolitics, of Lebensraum, of establishing a "new order" and "vital frontiers" in the Middle East. The peoples are familiar with these ultimatums, these insensate theories, this talk of a "new order" and of recarving the political map. It was the nazi conquistadors that set out to recarve the map of Europe and the world, and attempted by armed force to impose what they called a "new order," until the fascist beast's spine was broken by the combined efforts of the Soviet Union and other peoples. How monstrous that these devices of the nazi brigands, condemned by the International Military Tribunal in 1946, have now been revived by a government claiming to represent a people which suffered so bitterly at the nazi butchers' hands!

Incoming reports show that the Arab population of Gaza, Jerusalem and other areas is being forcibly driven out. In the territories seized by Israeli troops occupation authorities are being set up, military governors of towns and regions are being appointed. Judging by all the indications, the system is being employed which the nazi invaders used in the countries they occupied in World War II.

Israel's Prime Minister Eshkol declared on June 12: "Have no illusions, Israel will not agree to revert to the situation which existed until a week ago. . . . We are entitled to determine what are the true and vital interests of our country and how they shall be secured. The position that existed until now shall never again return." General Moshe Dayan has proclaimed the same ambitions, declaring the other day that "if they [the Arab countries] don't want to talk to us, to sit down with us, then we shall stay where we are." "I don't think," he went on, "that we should in any way give back the Gaza strip to Egypt or the western part of Jordan to King Hussein."

Do these statements not show up the aggressor's true face and his expansionist plans, carefully laid long beforehand and executed when he thought the moment opportune?

Nor are the Israeli aggressors original in their methods of carrying out their expansionist policies. Like the nazis, they try to deceive the peoples by shifting the blame to the victim of aggression. They also emulate their American masters, who are waging barbarous war on the Vietnamese people and trying to dictate terms from positions of strength.

The facts go to show that, in the Middle East and in Southeast Asia and in Latin America alike, the same criminal hand is at work and the same imperialist methods are being employed. Like the soil of Vietnam, Arab soil has been drenched with napalm, and on it, too, infamous crimes against civilian populations have been and are still being perpetrated. It is all part of a single imperialist plot against freedom-loving peoples defending their sovereignty and freedom against colonial oppressors, upholding the great cause of national liberation.

In the Security Council the representative of Jordan, in a wrathful indictment of Tel Aviv, pointed to the similarity of Israel's policy and methods to the policy and methods of the nazis. "Both," he said, "have the concept of expansion, both have the concept of race, both have the concept of force, of acquiring lands by invasion and the use of force, and both have fifth columns."

Already in the first hours of Israel's aggression against the Arab states the Soviet Union branded the Israeli invaders and firmly demanded condemnation of their perfidious and criminal acts, immediate cessation of hostilities and the withdrawal of Israeli troops behind the armistice lines.

In a resolution tabled on June 8, the Soviet Union called on the Security Council to emphatically condemn Israel's aggressive acts and its violation of the Security Council resolutions, the U.N. Charter and the principles of the United Nations, and to demand that Israel immediately cease hostilities against neighbouring Arab states and withdraw all its troops from their territory to behind the armistice lines.

However, the United States, Britain and some other Western Powers, set their face against condemnation of the aggressor and the demand for the immediate withdrawal of his troops from the occupied territories. The Security Council proved unable to pass the decision that the emergency dictated. Yet under the U.N. Charter, as the organ primarily responsible for the maintenance of international peace and security, it should have done so.

Some Western representatives even tried to make out that the question of the withdrawal of Israel's troops from the occupied territories should be linked with some sort of other conditions, with a general settlement in the Middle East, and so on and so forth. The Soviet delegation firmly rejected all such attempts.

The Washington diplomats hastened to introduce their own resolution, which, so far from condemning Israel's aggression and demanding the withdrawal of its troops, actually attempted to put the Arab states at a disadvantage vis-à-vis the aggressor and hedge about the withdrawal of Israeli troops with various demands which in the final count would limit the Arab states' sovereign rights. Essentially, the American resolution only encouraged the Israeli extremists' expansionist ambitions. Accordingly, the Arab countries and the Soviet Union decidedly rejected it.

The Soviet delegation asked the U.S. and other Western delegations outright: Did they agree to the immediate and unconditional withdrawal of Israel's troops from the territories it had seized to behind the armistice lines? Were they willing to recognize that continued occupation of Arab territory by the Israeli armed forces was unlawful, criminal and contrary to the U.N. Charter and the elementary principles of modern international law? But the Security Council never did get a clear answer to these questions.

The representatives of India and Mali emphasized in their Security Council speeches the need to order withdrawal of both sides' armed forces behind the armistice lines and only then discuss other problems, relating to so-called deeper causes of the tension in the Middle East. The stand taken in the Council by India, in particular, was based on the well-known principle of international law that an aggressor must not be allowed to profit by his aggression.

Because of the Western Powers' attitude, however, the Security Council at the initial stage was only able to order the cessation of hostilities. But that was only a preliminary measure, essential to protect the victims of aggression from Israel's brigand forces. It was altogether insufficient. For it was the Security Council's duty under the U.N. Charter to put an end to the aggression and restore the lawful rights of the attacked Arab states—the U.A.R., Syria and Jordan.

The Soviet Union accordingly continued to insist that the Security Council should vote on the Soviet resolution. Yet even in the concluding phase of the Council's work the attitude of the Western members, notably the U.S. and Britain, who openly support Israel's aggressive policy, made it impossible for the Council to pass the necessary decision.

The Soviet resolution's demand for the immediate withdrawal of Israeli troops from the occupied Arab territories received the votes of the socialist (U.S.S.R. and Bulgaria) and Afro-Asian (India, Mali, Ethiopia and Nigeria) member countries of the Council. The Western states, while not venturing to vote openly against this lawful and just demand, resorted to the "hidden veto" by abstaining. Thus, the Soviet resolution did not go through.

Heavy responsibility for this rests on the states which failed in their duty as members of the Security Council. The result was to produce a situation that called for emergency action by the United Nations and all freedom-loving countries to stop the continuing aggression in the Middle East.

It was clear that further discussion of the matter in the Security Council could not at present yield the proper results. It thus became necessary to seek other ways of exerting a sobering influence on the aggressor.

In the circumstances the Soviet government felt that the U.N. General Assembly should discuss the situation, in accordance with Article 11 of the U.N. Charter, and take decisions designed to liquidate the consequences of the aggression and effect the immediate withdrawal of Israeli troops behind the armistice lines.

The Soviet government asked for a special emergency session of the U.N. General Assembly to be convened immediately for this purpose. A majority of U.N. member states responded at once with support for the Soviet government's proposal. It is significant, however, that the United States and Israel opposed this Soviet initiative.

The special emergency session of the General Assembly opened in New York on June 17. In view of the great importance of the question before it, the Soviet delegation is led by Premier Kosygin. Many other leading statesmen of U.N. member nations are also attending. The session has only begun. But one can already say that except for a narrow group of accomplices of the aggressor, the members of the U.N. uphold the rights of the Arab peoples.

Even now the Israeli aggressors remain on the soil they have seized from neighbouring Arab peoples. What are they counting on? Is Tel Aviv perhaps waiting for a special invitation? Does it think that the peoples of the world, the United Nations Organization, will accept its seizure and occupation of foreign territory? Does it imagine that the Arab countries, the Soviet Union, the socialist states and other freedom-loving peoples will allow it to profit by its insolent and perfidious aggression, to dictate terms from positions of strength, the positions of an invader seeking to wrest away by force lands that belong to Arab countries?

Anyone who imagines any such thing is profoundly mistaken. The Tel Aviv government should have no illusions: Israel will have to pay in full for its brigand actions. And the United Nations Organization must pass its authoritative judgment, must do its duty under the Charter.

New York
June 17

Holy War

By I. F. Stone*

Stripped of propaganda and sentiment, the Palestine problem is, simply, the struggle of two different peoples for the same strip of land. For the Jews, the establishment of Israel was a Return, with all the mystical significance the capital R implies. For the Arabs it was another invasion. This has led to three wars between them in twenty years. Each has been a victory for the Jews. With each victory the size of Israel has grown. So has the number of Arab homeless.

Now to find a solution which will satisfy both peoples is like trying to square a circle. In the language of mathematics, the aspirations of the Jews and the Arabs are incommensurable. Their conflicting ambitions cannot be fitted into the confines of any ethical system which transcends the tribalistic. This is what frustrates the benevolent outsider, anxious to satisfy both peoples. For two years Jean-Paul Sartre has been trying to draw Israelis and Arabs into a confrontation in a special number of his review, *Les Temps Modernes.* The third war between them broke out while it was on the press.

This long-awaited special issue on *Le conflit israélo-arabe* is the first confrontation in print of Arab and Israeli intellectuals. But it turns out to be 991 pages not so much of dialogue as of dual monologue. The two sets of contributors sit not just in separate rooms, like employers and strikers in a bitter labor dispute, but in separate universes where the simplest fact often turns out to have diametrically opposite meanings. Physics has begun to uncover a new conundrum in the worlds of matter and anti-matter, occupying the same space and time but locked off from each other by their obverse natures, for-

---

* I. F. Stone, a Washington correspondent for twenty-five years, is publisher and editor of *I. F Stone's Weekly.* This essay first appeared in the *New York Review of Books* August 3, 1967, and is reprinted by permission of the author.

ever twin yet forever sundered. The Israeli-Arab quarrel is the closest analogue in the realm of international politics.

The conditions exacted for the joint appearance of Israelis and Arabs in the same issue of *Les Temps Modernes* excluded not only collaboration but normal editorial mediation or midwifery. Claude Lanzmann, who edited this special issue, explains in his Introduction that the choice of authors and of subjects had to be left "in full sovereignty" (*en toute souveraineté*) to each of the two parties. The Arabs threatened to withdraw if an article was included by A. Razak Abdel-Kader, an Algerian who is an advocate of Israeli-Arab reconciliation. When the Israelis objected that *Les Temps Modernes* at least allow Abdel-Kader to express himself as an individual, the Arabs insisted on an absolute veto: there would be no issue if Abdel-Kader were in it.

In his Preface Jean-Paul Sartre lays bare the conflicting emotions which led him to embark on so difficult a task as to attempt the role—in some degree—of peacemaker between Arab and Israeli. They awaken the memories of his finest hours. One was that of the Resistance. "For all those who went through this experience," M. Sartre writes, "it is unbearable to imagine that another Jewish community, wherever it may be, whatever it may be, should endure this Calvary anew and furnish martyrs to a new massacre." The other was Sartre's aid to the Arabs in their struggle for Algerian independence. These memories bind him to both peoples, and give him the respect of both, as the welcome he received in both Egypt and Israel last year attests. His aim in presenting their views is, he says wistfully, merely to *inform*. His hope is that information in itself will prove pacifying "because it tends more or less slowly to replace passion by knowledge." But the roots of this struggle lie deeper than reason. It is not at all certain that information will replace passion with knowledge.

The experiences from which M. Sartre draws his emotional ties are irrelevant to this new struggle. Both sides draw from them conclusions which must horrify the man of rationalist tradition and universalist ideals. The bulk of the Jews and the Israelis draw from the Hitler period the conviction that, in this world, when threatened one must be prepared to kill or be killed. The Arabs draw from the Algerian conflict the conviction that, even in dealing with so rational and civilized a people as the French, liberation was made possible only by resorting to the gun and the knife. Both Israeli and Arabs in other words feel that only force can assure justice. In this they agree, and this sets them on a collision course. For the Jews believe justice requires the recognition of Israel as a fact; for the Arabs, to recognize the fact is to acquiesce in the wrong done them by the conquest of Palestine. If God as some now say is dead, He no doubt died of trying to find an equitable solution to the Arab-Jewish problem.

The argument between them begins with the Bible. "I give this country to your posterity," God said to Abraham (Gen. XV:18) "from the river of Egypt up to the great river, Euphrates." Among the Jews, whether religious or secular mystics, this is the origin of their right to the Promised Land. The opening article in the Arab section of *Les Temps Modernes* retorts that the "posterity" referred to in Genesis includes the descendants of Ishmael since he was the son of Abraham by his concubine Ketirah, and the ancestor of all the Arabs, Christian or Muslim.

All this may seem anachronistic nonsense, but this is an anachronistic quarrel. The Bible is still the best guide to it. Nowhere else can one find a parallel for its ethnocentric fury. Nowhere that I know of is there a word of pity in the Bible for the Canaanites whom the Hebrews slaughtered in taking possession. Of all the nonsense which marks the Jewish-Arab quarrel none is more nonsensical than the talk from both sides about the Holy Land as a symbol of peace. No bit of territory on earth has been soaked in the blood of more battles. Nowhere has religion been so zestful an excuse for fratricidal strife. The Hebrew *shalom* and the Arabic *salaam* are equally shams, relics of a common past as Bedouins. To this day inter-tribal war is the favorite sport of the Bedouins; to announce "peace" in the very first word is a necessity if any chance encounter is not to precipitate bloodshed.

In biblical perspective the Jews have been going in and out of Palestine for 3,000 years. They came down from the Euphrates under Abraham; returned from Egypt under Moses and Joshua; came back again from the Babylonian captivity and were dispersed again after Jerusalem fell to the Romans in 70 A.D. This is the third return. The Arabs feel they have a superior claim because they stayed put. This appearance side by side in *Les Temps Modernes* provides less than the full and undiluted flavor of an ancient sibling rivalry. Both sides have put their better foot forward. The Arab section includes no sample of the bloodcurdling broadcasts in which the Arab radios indulge; the Israeli, no contribution from the right-wing Zionists who dream of a greater Israel from the Nile to the Euphrates (as promised in Genesis) with complete indifference to the fate of the Arab inhabitants. On neither side is there a frank exposition of the *Realpolitik* which led Arab nationalists like Nasser to see war on Israel as the one way to achieve Arab unity, and leads Jewish nationalists like Ben Gurion and Dayan to see Arab disunity and backwardness as essential elements for Israeli security and growth. No voice on the Arab side preaches a Holy War in which all Israel would be massacred, while no voice on the Israeli side expresses the cheerfully cynical view one may hear in private that Israel has no realistic alternative but to hand the Arabs a bloody nose every five or ten years until they accept the loss of Palestine as irreversible.

The picture, however, is not wholly symmetrical. There is first of all the asymmetry of the victorious and the defeated. The victor is ready to talk with the defeated if the latter will acquiesce in defeat. The defeated, naturally, is less inclined to this kind of objectivity. The editor, Claude Lanzmann, speaks of an "asymmetry between the two collections of articles which derives at one and the same time from a radical difference in their way of looking at the conflict and from the difference in the nature of the political regimes in the countries involved." Even if not expressly authorized by their governments or organizations to participate, M. Lanzmann explains, all the Arabs except the North Africans wrote only after consultation and defend a common position while the Israelis "as is normal in a Western style democracy" speak either for themselves or for one of their numerous parties. But this diversity may be exaggerated. On the fundamental issue which divides the two sides, no Arab contributor is prepared to advocate recognition of the state of Israel, while only one Israeli contributor is prepared to advocate its transformation into something other than a basically Jewish state.

The depth of this nationalistic difference may be measured by what happened to Israel's Communist party. Elsewhere national centrifugal tendencies have made their appearance in the once monolithic world of communism. In Israel the same nationalist tendencies split the Communist party into two, one Jewish the other Arab. The days when Arab Communists faithfully followed Moscow's line straight into the jails of Egypt, Iraq, Syria, and Jordan by supporting the 1947 partition plan have long passed away. Today Arab and Jewish

Communists no longer find common ground.[1] It would be hard to find an Arab who would agree with Moshe Sneh, head of the Jewish Communist party (Maki) in Israel, when he told *L'Express* (June 19-25), "our war is just and legitimate. What united the 13 Arab States against us, irrespective of their regime, was not anti-imperialism but pan-Arabism and anti-Jewish chauvinism." He added boldly that Moscow in supporting the Arabs had "turned its back on the politics of the international left and on the spirit of Tashkent." But even Sneh's bitter rival, Meir Vilner, the Jewish leader of, and one of the few Jews left in, the Arab Communist party (Rakka) expresses himself in *Les Temps Modernes* in terms with which no Arab contributor to it agrees. M. Vilner is for the return of all the refugees who wish to, for full equality to Arabs in Israel and for a neutralist policy, but he defends the existence of Israel as a legitimate fact and denies that "one can in any way compare the people (of Israel) to Algerian colons or the Crusaders." The comparisons rejected by the leader of the Arab Communist party in Israel are the favorite comparisons of the Arabs outside Israel. The diversity of viewpoint on the Israeli side thus ends with the basic agreement on its right to exist, and to exist as a Jewish state. This is precisely where the Arab disagreement begins.

The gulf between Arab and Jewish views becomes even clearer when one reads two supplementary pieces contributed by two French Jews, Maxime Rodinson, a distinguished sociologist and Orientalist, and Robert Misrahi, a well-known writer of the Left. The former takes the Arab and the latter the Zionist side. But while M. Misrahi's article appears with the Israelis, M. Rodinson's contribution—by far the most brilliant in the whole volume—appears alone. He refused, for reasons of principle, to appear in the Arab ensemble. It is not hard to see why. For while M. Rodinson gives strong support to every basic Arab historical contention, he is too much the humanist (and in the last analysis no doubt the Jew) to welcome an apocalyptic solution at the expense of Israel's existence. There is still a gulf between M. Rodinson's pro-Arab position and the most moderate view any Arab statesman has yet dared express, that of Tunisia's President Bourguiba. Bourguiba's famous speech in Jericho, March 3, 1965, is re-

---

[1] The relative strength of the two since the split may be seen from the fact that the Jewish branch was able to elect only one deputy while the Arab branch, which draws the largest vote among the Arab minority, elected three, two Arabs and one Jew.

printed in an appendix by *Les Temps Modernes,* along with an interview he gave *le Nouvel Observateur* (April 15) a month later. But Bourguiba's speech, though it created a sensation by its relative moderation, merely suggested that the Arabs proceed to regain Palestine as they did Tunisia by a series of more or less peaceful compromises. When *le Nouvel Observateur* asked him whether this did not imply the progressive disappearance of the State of Israel, he would not go beyond the cryptic reply, "That is not certain."

The Arab section of the symposium is nevertheless far from being uniform. A Moroccan, Abdallah Laroui, a professor of literature in Rabat, not only ends by saying that the possibilities of peaceful settlement must be kept open because a war would settle nothing, but even goes so far as to express the hope that the time may come when a settlement is possible without making a new exile, i.e., of the Israelis, pay for the end of another exile, i.e. of the Arabs from Palestine. He even suggests that under certain conditions, a Jewish community "with or without political authority"—a most daring remark—may prove compatible with Arab progress and development.

When we examine these conditions, we come to the heart of the fears expressed by the Arabs in this symposium. The Palestinian Arabs, from the first beginnings of Zionism, foresaw the danger of being swamped and dislodged by Jewish immigration. Neighboring Arab States feared that this immigration would stimulate a continuous territorial expansion at their expense and create a Jewish state powerful enough to dominate the area. The relative size and population of Israel when compared to its Arab neighbors are deceptive and may make these fears seem foolish, but historically the Middle East has often been conquered and dominated by relatively small bands of determined intruders. Even now, as the recent fighting showed, tiny Israel could without difficulty have occupied Damascus, Amman, and Cairo, and—were it not for the big powers and the UN—dictated terms to its Arab neighbors.

It was the attempt of the British to allay Arab apprehension by setting limits on Jewish immigration that precipitated the struggle between the British and the Jews. The 1917 Balfour Declaration, when it promised a "Jewish National Home" in Palestine, also said—in a passage Zionists have always preferred to forget—"that nothing shall be done which may prejudice the civil and religious rights of the existing non-Jewish communities in Palestine." British White Papers in 1922, in 1930, and again in 1939 tried to fulfill this companion pledge by steps which would have kept the Jews a permanent minority. It is this persistent and—as events have shown—justifiable Arab fear which is reflected in M. Laroui's article. In calling the Palestine problem "A Problem of the Occident" his basic point is that if the Occident wipes out anti-Semitism, or keeps it within harmless proportions, making refuge in Israel unnecessary for the bulk of Jewry, and Israel divorces its politics from the Zionist dream of gathering in all the Jews from Exile, this will end the danger of an inexorable expansion in search of *"lebensraum"* at the expense of the Palestinian Arabs, and finally make peace possible between the two peoples. Since immigration into Israel has dwindled in recent years, this Arab fear seems at the moment less a matter of reality than of Zionist theory and of a past experience which leads them to take it seriously.

The suggestion that Israel abandon its supra-nationalist dream finds its only echo on the other side of this collection of essays in Israel's No. 1 maverick and champion of Arab rights, Uri Avnery. Avnery was born in Germany in 1923 and went to Palestine at the age of ten, the year Hitler took power. He began his political career on the far nationalist right, as a member of the Irgun terrorist group in the struggle against the British, but has since swung over to the far left of Israeli opinion, to the point where he is considered anti-nationalist. In the wake of the first Suez war, he supported the Egyptian demand for evacuation of the Canal Zone and in 1959 he formed an Israeli committee to aid the Algerian rebels. At one time he organized a movement which asserted that the Israelis were no longer Jews but "Canaanites" and therefore one with the Arabs, forcibly converted remnants of the same indigenous stock. When this far-out conception attracted few Jews and even fewer Canaanites, he formed a "Semitic Action" movement which has now become "the Movement of New Forces." This polled 1.2 percent of the vote in the 1965 elections and by virtue of proportional representation put Avnery into Parliament. Avnery has been more successful as a publisher. He has made his weekly *Haolam Hazeh* ("This World") the largest in Israel by combining non-conformist politics with what the rather puritanical Israelis call pornography, though that weekly's girlie pictures would seem as old-fashioned as the *Police Gazette* in America.

Avnery writes in *Les Temps Modernes* that he would turn
Israel into a secular, pluralist, and multi-national state. He
would abolish the Law of Return which gives every Jew the
right to enter Israel and automatically become a citizen.
Avnery says this pan-Judaism of Zionism feeds the anti-Zion-
ism of pan-Arabism by keeping alive "the myth of an Israel
submerged by millions of immigrants who, finding no place to
settle, would oblige the government to expand the country
by force of arms."

Yet Avnery, who asks Israel to give up its Zionist essence,
turns out to be a Jewish nationalist, too. After sketching out
a plan for an Arab Palestinian state west of the Jordan,
Avnery writes, "The Arabic reader will justly ask at this
point, 'And the return of Israel to the limits of the UN Plan
of 1947?' " Since Israel in the 1947-48 fighting seized about
23 percent more territory than was allotted to it in the 1947
partition plan, this implies a modification of frontiers in
favor of the Arab state which was supposed to be linked
with it in an economically united Palestine. But to this
natural Arab question Avnery replies,[2] "Frankly we see no
possibility of this kind. The Arab armies are already 15
kilometers from Israel's most populous city (Tel Aviv) and
at Nathanya are even closer to the sea." The Arabs may feel
that Avnery is as unwilling to give up the fruits of conquest
as any non-"Canaanite." Avnery is as reluctant as any conven-
tional Zionist to see his fellow Canaanite too close to Tel Aviv.

It is easy to understand why neither side trusts the other. In
any case M. Sartre's symposium is a confrontation largely of
moderates and Leftists, and on neither side do these elements
command majority support. Another complexity is that while
in settled societies the Left tends to be less nationalistic than
the Right, in colonial societies the revolutionary left is often
more nationalistic than the native conservative and propertied
classes.

The overwhelming majority opinion on both sides, even as expressed in a symposium as skewed leftward as this one, shows
little tendency to compromise. The Arabs argue that Israel
is a colonialist implantation in the Middle East, supported
from the beginning by imperialist powers; that it is an enemy
of Arab union and progress; that the sufferings of the Jews

---

[2] Avnery was writing, of course, before the new outbreak of warfare had
again changed these borders to Israel's advantage.

in the West were the consequence of an anti-Semitism the Arabs have never shared; and that there is no reason why the Arabs of Palestine should be displaced from their homes in recompense for wrongs committed by Hitler Germany. M. Laroui alone is sympathetic enough to say that if the Jewish National Home had been established in Uganda, the Arabs who felt compassion for the sufferings of the Jews of Europe would have shown themselves as uncomprehending of the rights of the natives as the West has been in Palestine. At the other end of the Arab spectrum a fellow Moroccan, a journalist, Tahar Benziane, ends up in classic anti-Semitism, blaming the Jews themselves, their separatism and their sense of superiority, for the prejudice against them. Benziane sees the only solution not just in the liquidation of Israel but in the disappearance of world Jewry through assimilation. His would indeed be a Final Solution. This bitter and hateful opinion, widespread in the Arab world, explains why Nazism found so ready an echo before the war in the Middle East and Nazi criminals so welcome a refuge in Egypt. It also disposes of the semantic nonsense that Arabs being Semite cannot be anti-Semitic!

The Zionist argument is that the Jewish immigration was a return to the Jewish homeland. Robert Misrahi even goes so far as to argue that the Jews had an older claim to Palestine than the Arabs since the Jews had lived there in the ancient kingdom of the Hebrews long before the Hegira of Mohammed! Misrahi argues the familiar Zionist thesis that their struggle against Britain proves them to be anti-imperialist, that their colonies are socialist, that their enemies are the feudal elements in the Arab world, and that the Arab refugees are the moral responsibility of the Arab leaders since it was on their urging that the Arabs ran away.

There is a good deal of simplistic sophistry in the Zionist case. The whole earth would have to be reshuffled if claims 2,000 years old to *irredenta* were suddenly to be allowed. Zionism from its begining tried to gain its aims by offering to serve as outpost in the Arab world for one of the great empires. Herzl sought to win first the Sultan and then the Kaiser by such arguments. Considerations of imperial strategy finally won the Balfour Declaration from Britain. The fact that the Jewish community in Palestine afterward fought the British is no more evidence of its not being a colonial implantation than similar wars of British colonists against the mother country, from the American Revolution to Rhodesia. In the

case of Palestine, as of other such struggles, the Mother
Country was assailed because it showed more concern for
the native majority than was palatable to the colonist minority.
The argument that the refugees ran away "voluntarily" or
because their leaders urged them to do so until after the fighting was over not only rests on a myth but is irrelevant. Have
refugees no right to return? Have German Jews no right
to recover their properties because they too fled?

The myth that the Arab refugees fled because the Arab radios
urged them to do so was analyzed by Erskine B. Childers in the
London *Spectator* May 12, 1961. An examination of British
and US radio monitoring records turned up no such appeals;
on the contrary there were appeals and "even orders to the
civilians of Palestine, *to stay put.*" The most balanced and
humane discussion of the question may be found in Christopher Sykes's book *Crossroads to Israel: 1917-48* (at pages
350-57). "It can be said with a high degree of certainty,"
Mr. Sykes wrote, "that most of the time in the first half of
1948 the mass exodus was the natural, thoughtless, pitiful
movement of ignorant people who had been badly led and
who in the day of trial found themselves forsaken by their
leaders. . . . But if the exodus was by and large an accident of
war in the first stage, in the later stages it was consciously
and mercilessly helped on by Jewish threats and aggression
toward Arab populations . . . It is to be noted, however, that
where the Arabs had leaders who refused to be stampeded
into panic flight, the people came to no harm." Jewish
terrorism, not only by the Irgun, in such savage massacres as
Deir Yassin, but in milder form by the Haganah, itself "encouraged" Arabs to leave areas the Jews wished to take over
for strategic or demographic reasons. They tried to make as
much of Israel as free of Arabs as possible.

The effort to equate the expulsion of the Arabs from
Palestine with the new Jewish immigration out of the Arab
countries is not so simple nor so equitable as it is made to
appear in Zionist propaganda. The Palestinian Arabs feel
about this "swap" as German Jews would if denied restitution
on the grounds that they had been "swapped" for German
refugees from the Sudetenland. In a sanely conceived settlement, some allowance should equitably be made for Jewish
properties left behind in Arab countries. What is objectionable
in the simplified version of this question is the idea that Palestinian Arabs whom Israel didn't want should have no objection

to being "exchanged" for Arabic Jews it did want. One up-rooting cannot morally be equated with the other.

A certain moral imbecility marks all ethnocentric move-ments. The Others are always either less than human, and thus their interests may be ignored, or more than human, and therefore so dangerous that it is right to destroy them. The latter is the underlying pan-Arab attitude toward the Jews; the former is Zionism's basic attitude toward the Arabs. M. Avnery notes that Herzl in his book *The Jewish State,* which launched the modern Zionist movement, dealt with working hours, housing for workers, and even the national flag but had not one word to say about the Arabs! For the Zionists the Arab was the Invisible Man. Psychologically he was not there. Achad Ha-Am, the Russian Jew who became a great Hebrew philosopher, tried to draw attention as early as 1891 to the fact that Palestine was not an empty territory and that this posed problems. But as little attention was paid to him as was later accorded his successors in "spiritual Zionism," men like Buber and Judas Magnes who tried to preach *Ichud,* "unity," i.e. with the Arabs. Of all the formulas with which Zionism comforted itself none was more false and more enduring than Israel Zangwill's phrase about "a land without people for a people without a land." Buber related that Max Nordau, hearing for the first time that there was an Arab population in Palestine, ran to Herzl crying, "I didn't know that—but then we are committing an injustice." R. J. Zwi Werblowsky, Dean of the faculty of letters at the Hebrew University, in the first article of this anthology's Israeli section, writes with admirable objectivity, "There can be no doubt that if Nordau's reaction had been more general, it would seriously have paralyzed the *élan* of the Zionist movement." It took refuge, he writes, in "a moral myopia."

This moral myopia makes it possible for Zionists to dwell on the 1900 years of Exile in which the Jews have longed for Palestine but dismiss as nugatory the nineteen years in which Arab refugees have also longed for it. "Homelessness" is the major theme of Zionism but this pathetic passion is denied to Arab refugees. Even Meir Yaari, the head of Mapam, the leader of the "Marxist" Zionists of Hashomer Hatzair, who long preached bi-nationalism, says Israel can only accept a minority of the Arab refugees because the essential reason for the creation of Israel was to "welcome the mass of immigrant Jews returning to their historic father-land!" If there is not room enough for both, the Jews must

have precedence. This is what leads Gabran Majdalany, a
Baath Socialist, to write that Israel is "a racist state founded
from its start on discrimination between Jew and non-Jew."
He compares the Zionists to the Muslim Brotherhood who
"dream of a Muslim Israel in which the non-Muslims will be
the gentiles, second-class citizens sometimes tolerated but
more often repressed." It is painful to hear his bitter re-
proach—

> Some people admit the inevitably racist character of Israel
> but justify it by the continual persecutions to which the Jews
> have been subjected during the history of Europe and by the
> massacres of the Second World War. We consider that, far
> from serving as justification, these facts constitute an aggra-
> vating circumstance; for those who have known the effects of
> racism and of discrimination in their own flesh and human
> dignity, are less excusably racist than those who can only
> imagine the negative effects of prejudice.

When Israel's Defense Minister, Moshe Dayan, was on
Face the Nation June 11, after Israel's latest victories, this
colloquy occurred.

> SYDNEY GRUSON: (*The New York Times*): Is there any pos-
> sible way that Israel could absorb the huge number of Arabs
> whose territory it has gained control of now?
> GEN. DAYAN: Economically we can; but I think that is not in
> accord with our aims in the future. It would turn Israel into
> either a binational or poly-Arab-Jewish state instead of the
> Jewish state, and we want to have a Jewish state. We can ab-
> sorb them, but then it won't be the same country.
> MR. GRUSON: And it is necessary in your opinion to maintain
> this as a Jewish state and purely a Jewish state?
> GEN. DAYAN: Absolutely—absolutely. We want a Jewish state
> like the French have a French state.

This must deeply disturb the thoughtful Jewish reader.
Ferdinand and Isabella in expelling the Jews and Moors from
Spain were in the same way saying they wanted a Spain as
"Spanish," (i.e. Christian) as France was French. It is not
hard to recall more recent parallels.

It is a pity the editors of *Les Temps Modernes* didn't widen
their symposium to include a Jewish as distinct from an Israeli
point of view. For Israel is creating a kind of moral schizophrenia in world Jewry. In the outside world the welfare of
Jewry depends on the maintenance of secular, non-racial,
pluralistic societies. In Israel, Jewry finds itself defending a

society in which mixed marriages cannot be legalized, in which non-Jews have a lesser status than Jews, and in which the ideal is racial and exclusionist. Jews must fight elsewhere for their very security and existence—against principles and practices they find themselves defending in Israel. Those from the outside world, even in their moments of greatest enthusiasm amid Israel's accomplishments, feel twinges of claustrophobia, not just geographical but spiritual. Those caught up in Prophetic fervor soon begin to feel that the light they hoped to see out of Zion is only that of another narrow nationalism.

Such moments lead to a reexamination of Zionist ideology. That longing for Zion on which it is predicated may be exaggerated. Its reality is indisputable but its strength can easily be overestimated. Not until after World War II was it ever strong enough to attract more than a trickle of Jews to the Holy Land. By the tragic dialectic of history, Israel would not have been born without Hitler. It took the murder of six million in his human ovens to awaken sufficient nationalist zeal in Jewry and sufficient humanitarian compassion in the West to bring a Jewish state to birth in Palestine. Even then humanitarian compassion was not strong enough to open the gates of the West to Jewish immigration in contrition. The capitalist West and the Communist East preferred to displace Arabs than to welcome the Jewish "displaced persons" in Europe's postwar refugee camps.

It must also be recognized, despite Zionist ideology that the periods of greatest Jewish creative accomplishment have been associated with pluralistic civilizations in their time of expansion and tolerance: in the Hellenistic period, in the Arab civilization of North Africa and Spain, and in Western Europe and America. Universal values can only be the fruit of a universal vision; the greatness of the Prophets lay in their overcoming of ethnocentricity. A Lilliputian nationalism cannot distill truths for all mankind. Here lies the roots of a growing divergence between Jew and Israeli; the former with a sense of mission as a Witness in the human wilderness, the latter concerned only with his own tribe's welfare.

But Jewry can no more turn its back on Israel than Israel on Jewry. The ideal solution would allow the Jews to make their contributions as citizens in the diverse societies and nations which are their homes while Israel finds acceptance as a Jewish State in a renascent Arab civilization. This would end Arab fears of a huge inflow to Israel. The Jews have as much reason to be apprehensive about that prospect as the Arabs.

It can only come as the result of a sharp recrudescence in persecution elsewhere in the world. Zionism grows on Jewish catastrophe. Even now it casts longing eyes on Russian Jewry. But would it not be better, more humanizing, and more just, were the Soviet Union to wipe out anti-Semitism and to accord its Jews the same rights of cultural autonomy and expression it gives all its other nationalities? The Russian Jews have fought for Russia, bled for the Revolution, made no small contribution to Russian literature and thought; why should they be cast out? This would be a spiritual catastrophe for Russia as well as Jewry even though it would supply another flow of desperate refugees to an Israel already short of Jews if it is to expand as the Zionist militants hope to expand it.

Israel has deprived anti-Semitism of its mystique. For the visitor to Israel, anti-Semitism no longer seems a mysterious anomaly but only another variant of minority-majority friction. *Es is schwer zu sein a Yid* ("It's hard to be a Jew") was the title of Sholom Aleichem's most famous story. Now we see that it's hard to be a goy in Tel Aviv, especially an Arab goy. Mohammad Watad, a Muslim Israeli, one of the five Arabic contributors to the Israeli side of this symposium, begins his essay with words which startlingly resemble the hostile dialogue Jews encounter elsewhere. "I am often asked," he writes, "about my 'double' life which is at one and the same time that of an Arab and that of an Israeli citizen." Another Arab contributor from Israel, Ibrahim Shabath, a Christian who teaches Hebrew in Arabic schools and is editor-in-chief of *Al Mirsad*, the Mapam paper in Arabic, deplores the fact that nineteen years after the creation of Israel "the Arabs are still considered strangers by the Jews." He relates a recent conversation with Ben Gurion. "You must know," Ben Gurion told him, "that Israel is the country of the Jews and only of the Jews. Every Arab who lives here has the same rights as any minority citizen in any country of the world, but he must admit the fact that he lives in a Jewish country." The implications must chill Jews in the outside world.

The Arab citizen of Israel, Shabath complains, "is the victim today of the same prejudices and the same generalizations as the Jewish people elsewhere." The bitterest account of what they undergo may be found in an anonymous report sent to the United Nations in 1964 by a group of Arabs who tried unsuccessfully to found an independent socialist Arab movement and publication. Military authorities despite a Supreme Court order refused to permit this, and the courts declined to overrule the military. Their petition is reprinted in the Israeli section of this symposium. Though the military rule complained of was abolished last year, and police regulations substituted, it is too soon—especially because of the new outbreak of warfare—to determine what the effect will be on Arab civil liberties. Israelis admit with pleasure that neither in the Christian villages of Central Galilee nor in the Muslim villages of the so-called "Triangle" was there the slightest evidence of any Fifth Column activity. Those Israelis who have fought for an end of all discrimination against the Arabs argue that they have demonstrated their loyalty and deserve fully to be trusted.

It is to Israel's credit that the Arab minority is given place in its section to voice these complaints while no similar place is opened for ethnic minority opinion in the Arabic section. Indeed except for Lebanon and to some degree Tunisia there is no place in the Arab world where the dissident of any kind enjoys freedom of the press. There is no frank discussion of this in the Arab section. One of the most vigorous and acute expositions of the Arab point of view, for example, is an article by an Egyptian writer, Lotfallah Soliman, who has played a distinguished role in bringing modern ideas to the young intellectuals of his country since World War II. His autobiographical sketch says cryptically if discreetly "He lives presently in Paris." I stumbled on a more candid explanation. In preparing for this review, I read an earlier article in *Les Temps Modernes* (Aug.-Sept. 1960) by Adel Montasser on *La répression anti-démocratique en Egypte*. Appended to it was a list of intellectuals imprisoned by Nasser. Among them was Lotfallah Soliman. Obviously it's hard to be a free Egyptian intellectual in Nasser's Egypt. Many of those then imprisoned have since been freed, but it is significant that a writer as trenchant and devoted as Soliman has to work in exile.

It is true that the full roster of Arab minority complaints in Israel had to be presented anonymously for fear of the the authorities. But in the Arab section of this book no place was allowed even anonymously for the Jewish and the various Christian minorities to voice their compaints. As a result the Arab contributors were able to write as if their countries, unlike Europe, were models of tolerance. They hark back to the great days of Arabic Spain where (except for certain interludes not mentioned) Christian and Jew enjoyed full equality, religious, cultural, and political, with the Muslim: Spain did not become synonymous with intolerance, Inquisition, and obscurantism until the Christian Reconquest. But today no Arab country except, precariously, Lebanon, dimly resembles Moorish Spain. As a result the Jews from the Arabic countries tend to hate the Arab far more than Jews from Europe who have never lived under his rule, which often recalls medieval Christiandom. A glimpse of these realities may be found in the most moving article in this whole symposium. This is by Attalah Mansour, a young Christian Arabic Israeli novelist of peasant origin who has published two novels, one in Arabic and the other in Hebrew, and worked as a journalist on Avnery's paper *Haolam Hazeh* and on the staff of *Haaretz,* Israel's best and most objective daily paper. M. Mansour knows doubly what it is to be a "Jew." He is as an Arab a "Jew" to the Israelis and as a Christian a "Jew" to the Muslims. He tells a touching story of an accidental encounter in (of all places) the Paris Metro with a young man who turned out like him to be Greek-rite Christian though from Egypt. They exchanged stories of their troubles, like two Jews in the Diaspora. "We in Egypt," the younger stranger told him, "have the same feelings as you. There is no law discriminating between us and the Muslims. But the governmental administration, at least on the everyday level, prefers Mahmoud to Boulos and Achmed to Samaan"—i.e. the man with the Muslim name to the man with the Christian. "Omar Sherif the well known movie actor," the Egyptian Christian added, "is Christian in origin. But he had to change his Christian name for a Muslim to please the public." In Israel, similarly, Ibrahim often becomes Abraham to pass as a Jew and to avoid widespread housing discrimination.

If in this account I have given more space to the Arab than the Israeli side it is because as a Jew, closely bound emotionally with the birth of Israel,[3] I feel honor bound to report the

[3] I first arrived in Palestine on Balfour Day Nov. 2, 1945, the day the Haganah blew up bridges and watch towers to begin its struggle against the British and immigration restrictions. The following spring I was the first newspaperman to travel with illegal Jewish immigrants from the Polish-Czech

Arab side, especially since the US press is so overwhelmingly pro-Zionist. For me, the Arab-Jewish struggle is a tragedy. The essence of tragedy is a struggle of right against right. Its catharsis is the cleansing pity of seeing how good men do evil despite themselves out of unavoidable circumstance and irresistible compulsion. When evil men do evil, their deeds belong to the realm of pathology. But when good men do evil, we confront the essence of human tragedy. In a tragic struggle, the victors become the guilty and must make amends to the defeated. For me the Arab problem is also the No. 1 Jewish problem. How we act toward the Arabs will determine what kind of people we become: either oppressors and racists in our turn like those from whom we have suffered, or a nobler race able to transcend the tribal xenophobias that afflict mankind.[4]

Israel's swift and extraordinary victories have suddenly transmuted this ideal from the realm of impractical sentiment to urgent necessity. The new frontiers of military conquest have gathered in most of the Arab refugees. Zionism's dream, the "ingathering of the exiles," has been achieved, though in an ironic form; it is the Arab exiles who are back. They cannot be gotten rid of as easily as in 1948. Something in the order of 100,000 have again been "encouraged" to leave, but the impact on public opinion abroad and in Israel has forced the State to declare that it will allow them to return. While the UN proves impotent to settle the conflict and the Arab powers are unwilling to negotiate from a situation of weakness, Israel can to some degree determine its future by the way in which it treats its new Arab subjects or citizens. The wrangles of the powers will go on for months but these people must be fed, clothed, and housed. How they are treated

---

border through the British blockade. In 1947 I celebrated Passover in the British detention camps in Cyprus and in 1948 I covered the Arab-Jewish war. See my *Underground to Palestine* (1946) and *This Is Israel* (1948). I was back in 1949, 1950, 1951, 1956, and 1964.

[4] In September, Black Star will publish a vigorous little book *The Aryanization of the Jewish State* by Michael Selzer, a young Pakistani Jew who lived in Israel. It may help Jewry and Israel to understand that the way to a fraternal life with the Arabs inside and outside Israel must begin with the eradication of the prejudices that greet the Oriental and Arabic-speaking Jews in Israel who now make up over half the population of the country. The bias against the Arab extends to a bias against the Jews from the Arab countries. In this, as in so many other respects, Israel presents in miniature all the problems of the outside world. Were the rest of the planet to disappear, Israel could regenerate from itself—as from a new Ark—all the bigotries, follies, and feuds of a vanished mankind (as well as some of its most splendid accomplishments).

will change the world's picture of Israel and of Jewry, soften or intensify Arab anger, build a bridge to peace or make new war certain. To establish an Arab state on the West Bank and to link it with Israel, perhaps also with Jordan, in a Confederation would turn these Arab neighbors, if fraternally treated, from enemies into a buffer, and give Israel the protection of strategic frontiers. But it would be better to give the West Bank back to Jordan than to try to create a puppet state—a kind of Arab Bantustan—consigning the Arabs to second-class status under Israel's control. This would only foster Arab resentment. To avoid giving the Arabs first-class citizenship by putting them in the reservation of a second-class state is too transparently clever.

What is required in the treatment of the Arab refugees Israel has gathered in is the conquest both of Jewish exclusivism and the resentful hostility of the Arabs. Even the malarial marshes of the Emek and the sandy wastes of the Negev could not have looked more bleakly forbidding to earlier generations of Zionist pioneers than these steep and arid mountains of prejudice. But I for one have a glimmer of hope. Every year I have gone to Palestine and later Israel I have found situations which seemed impossible. Yet Zionist zeal and intelligence overcame them. Perhaps this extraordinarily dynamic, progressive, and devoted community can even if need be transcend its essential self.

I was encouraged to find in this volume that the most objective view of the Arab question on the Israeli side was written by Yehudah Harkabi, a Haifa-born professional soldier, a brigadier general, but a general who holds a diploma in philosophy and Arabic studies from the Hebrew University and from Harvard. He has written a book on *Nuclear War and Nuclear Peace*. His article "Hawks or Doves" is extraordinary in its ability to rise above prejudice and sentiment. He does not shut his eyes at all to the Arab case. He feels peace can come only if we have the strength to confront its full human reality. "Marx affirms," he concludes, "that knowledge of the truth frees man from the determinism of history." It is only, General Harkabi says, when Israel is prepared "to accept the truth in its entirety that it will find the new strength necessary to maintain and consolidate its existence." The path to safety and the path to greatness lies in reconciliation. The other route, now that the West Bank and Gaza are under Israeli jurisdiction, leads to two new perils. The Arab populations now in the conquered territories make guerrilla war possible within Israel's own boundaries. And externally, if enmity deepens and tension rises between Israel and the Arab states, both sides will by one means or another obtain nuclear weapons for the next round.

This will change the whole situation. No longer will Israeli and Arab be able to play the game of war in anachronistic fashion as an extension of politics by other means. Neither will they be able to depend on a mutual balance of terror like the great powers with their "second strike" capacity. In this pygmy struggle the first strike will determine the outcome and leave nothing behind. Nor will the great Powers be able to stand aside and let their satellites play out their little war, as in 1948, 1956, and 1967. I have not dwelt here on the responsibility of the great Powers, because if they did not exist the essential differences in the Arab-Israeli quarrel would still remain, and because both sides use the great Power question as an excuse to ignore their own responsibilities. The problem for the new generation of Arabs is the social reconstruction of their decayed societies; the problem will not go away if Israel disappears. Indeed their task is made more difficult by the failure to recognize Israel since that means a continued emphasis on militarization, diversion of resources, and domination by military men. For Israel, the problem is reconciliation with the Arabs; the problem will not go away even if Moscow and Washington lie down together like the lion and the lamb or blow each other to bits. But the great Powers for their part cannot continue the cynical game of arming both sides in a struggle for influence when the nuclear stage is reached. It is significant that the one place where the Israeli and Arab contributors to this symposium tend to common conclusions is in the essays discussing the common nuclear danger. To denuclearize the Middle East, to defuse it, will require some kind of neutralization. Otherwise the Arab-Israeli conflict may some day set off a wider Final Solution. That irascible Old Testament God of Vengeance is fully capable, if provoked, of turning the whole planet into a crematorium.

I. F. Stone Reconsiders Zionism

By Marie Syrkin*

In a lengthy review of *"Le conflit israelo-arabe,"* the special issue of Jean-Paul Sartre's *Les Temps Modernes* devoted to the Arab-Israel conflict, I. F. Stone re-examines the Zionist case, (the *New York Review of Books,* August 3, 1967). Mr. Stone explains that "as a Jew, closely bound emotionally with the birth of Israel" he felt "honor bound to report the Arab side, especially since the U.S. press is so overwhelmingly pro-Zionist." Whatever the reasons for his posture, his conclusions and arguments must stand on their own. It is unfortunate that his declared stance as the man of "rationalist and universalist ideals" offers a protective shade to the weighted scale in which he judges Arab and Jewish claims. Familiar misstatements dismissed as the usual anti-Israel line when coming from Arab propagandists, the American Council for Judaism or Mr. Fedorenko, are admittedly more distressing when repeated by a respected writer of intellectual independence. Mr. Stone concludes: "If God as some now say is dead, He no doubt died of trying to find an equitable solution to the Arab-Jewish problem." I am more inclined to attribute the demise to despair at the wilful casuistry of some of the high-minded disputants.

In reviewing the Arab and Israeli contributions to *Les Temps Modernes,* Mr. Stone complains that both sides "have put their better foot forward." The Arabs fail to include their "blood-curdling broadcasts" demanding the extermination of Israel; the Israeli section offers no contribution from "right-wing Zionists" with expansionist dreams, also "no voice on the Arab side preaches a Holy War in which all Israel would be massacred, while no voice on the Israeli side expresses the cheerful cynical view one may hear in private that Israel has no realistic alternative but to hand the Arabs a bloody nose every five or ten years until they accept the loss of Palestine as irreversible."

This plea for honesty disguises a dishonest equation. The cries for the extermination of Israel, as every reader of the daily

* Marie Syrkin, formerly a Professor of English Literature, is now a member of the Jewish Agency Executive in New York. Her answer to I. F. Stone was published in *Midstream,* October, 1967. © The Theodor Herzl Foundation, Inc.

press knows, emanate, beginning with Nasser, from the Presidents, Prime Ministers and Foreign Ministers of the Arab states; the expansionist visions of "the right-wing Zionists" are limited to a small group of extremists who at no time since the creation of Israel have controlled its government or have made its policy. On what basis does Mr. Stone equate the openly declared official policy of all the Arab states with the views of minority groups in Israel whose programs have been consistently repudiated by the Israeli people and government? And by what yardstick are the Arab will for a "Holy War in which all Israel would be massacred" and the Israeli will to oppose this ambition given a common measure? Mr. Stone describes the Israeli determination as "cheerfully cynical." Neither the adverb nor the adjective seems appropriate. I, too, have heard in many not so private conversations in Israel the view that as long as Arabs were bent on the destruction of the country, Israelis would be obliged to demonstrate, at whatever sacrifice, that it cannot be done; but to detect cheer or cynicism in this resolution is, to say the least, far-fetched.

The burden of Mr. Stone's analysis is the dispossessed Arab, and no matter where his argument strays he returns to this central question. Of the Arab refugees, Mr. Stone writes: "The argument that the refugees ran away 'voluntarily' or because their leaders urged them to do so until after the fighting was over not only rests on a myth but is irrelevant. Have refugees no right to return? Have German Jews no right to recover their properties because they too fled?" And he continues: "Jewish terrorism, not only by the Irgun, in such savage massacres as Deir Yassin, but in milder form by the Haganah itself, 'encouraged' Arabs to leave areas the Jews wished to take over."

First as to the "myth." It is hard to understand why Mr. Stone finds it necessary to quote a notoriously pro-Arab advocate like Erskine Childers or any other commentator to make his point. Mr. Stone was in Israel in 1948 and gave an enthusiastic account of the Israel struggle. In *This Is Israel,* published in 1948, Mr. Stone wrote: "Ill-armed, outnumbered, however desperate their circumstances, the Jews stood fast. The Arabs very early began to run away. First the wealthiest families went; it was estimated that 20,000 of them left the country in the first two months of internal hostilities. By the end of January, the exodus was already so alarming that the Palestine Arab Higher Committee in alarm asked neighboring Arab countries to refuse visas to these refugees and to seal the borders against them. *While the Arab guerrillas were moving in, the Arab civilian population was moving out."* (Emphasis added—M.S.)

Mr. Stone goes on to describe the "phenomenon" of the "sudden flight" of Arabs from Tiberias and Haifa. Not one word in Mr. Stone's first-hand, on-the-spot report suggests the "milder" terrorism of the Haganah which he now discovered in retrospect. On the contrary, his own account fully supports the "myth." Admittedly, Mr. Stone is entitled to change his mind about the rights of the Zionist case in the course of twenty years—there have been changes of heart in regard to Israel from Soviet Russia to De Gaulle—but he should not revise history. Either what he himself saw in 1948 or what he reads now about 1948 is accurate. Which is the myth and who is being mythopoic?

I can bear witness to the correctness of Mr. Stone's 1948 reporting. In June 1948, when I arrived in Israel the overwhelming sentiment of the Israelis was still bewilderment at the "phenomenon" of the mass flight of the Arabs. As I pieced together the diverse explanations, a fairly consistent picture emerged. The first waves of departure—in January by the well-to-do Arabs, in March by thousands of Arab villagers from the Sharon coastal plain after the picking of the citrus crop—were clearly in response to the directives of their leaders in anticipation of Arab bombardment. The Jewish farmers were so troubled by what the departure boded that they begged the Arabs to stay. This phase of the exodus was obviously disciplined and well-organized.

The process gathered momentum as the fighting increased and the Jews, instead of being driven into the sea, were proving victorious. When the Arabs of Tiberias suddenly fled in long convoys (the British provided transport) the astonished Jewish Community Council of Tiberias issued the following statement: "We did not dispossess them; they themselves chose this course. But the day will come when the Arabs will return to their homes and property in this town. In the meantime let no citizen touch their property." Such was the initial reaction in April, 1948.

The circumstances surrounding the flight of 70,000 Arabs from Haifa after the Haganah victory on April 22 has fortunately been fully reported by the British authorities who are surely free of the suspicion of pro-Jewish bias. On April

26 the Haifa British Chief of Police, A. J. Bridmead, reported: "The situation in Haifa remains unchanged. Every effort is being made by the Jews to persuade the Arab populace to stay and carry on with their normal lives, to get their shops and businesses open and to be assured that their lives and interests will be safe." In a supplementary report issued the same day, Bridmead repeated: "An appeal has been made to the Arabs by the Jews to reopen their shops and businesses in order to relieve the difficulties of feeding the Arab population. Evacuation was still going on yesterday and several trips were made by Z craft to Acre. Roads too were crowded. *Arab leaders* (my emphasis) reiterated their determination to evacuate the entire Arab population, and they have been given the loan of 10 three-ton military trucks as from this morning to assist the evacuation." On April 28 Bridmead was again reporting: "The Jews are still making every effort to persuade the Arab population to remain and settle back into their normal lives in the town."

A British eye-witness account published in the London *Economist* (October 2, 1948) offers an explanation for the stampede: "So far as I know, most of the British civilian residents whose advice was asked by Arab friends told the latter that they would be wise to stay. Various factors influenced their decision to seek safety in flight. There is but little doubt that by far the most potent of these factors was the announcement made over the air by the Arab Higher Executive urging all Arabs in Haifa to quit. The reason given was that upon the final withdrawal of the British the combined armies of the Arab States would invade Palestine and drive the Jews into the sea."

All this is familiar, readily available information and I am bringing Mr. Stone no news. I am concerned with his readers. It is obvious from the dates that the Arab exodus began months before "such savage massacres as Deir Yassin," which took place on April 9. (Note Mr. Stone's plural though the outrage perpetrated by the Irgun was a unique occurrence deplored and repudiated by the Jewish community of Palestine.) It is also obvious from Bridmead's report that "Arab leaders" with whom he was negotiating insisted on the evacuation of Haifa. None of this precludes the irrational panic and mass psychosis to which the Arabs fell prey; the exodus assumed proportions not anticipated by its instigators. However, the Jews can hardly be held responsible for the too complete success of the Arab scheme to clear the decks for an Arab invasion. The Arabs of Nazareth, who did not join the exodus, and other villages in Galilee that followed the example of Nazareth, were well able to withstand the Haganah "encouragement" that Mr. Stone suspects. The most straightforward explanation of Arab flight is still that provided by the Jordanian daily, *A—Difaa,* which voiced the sentiments of the refugees themselves: "The Arab governments told us, 'Get out so that we can get in.' So we got out, but they did not get in." (September 6, 1954.)

The Arabs fled; they were not driven out. Equally true is that the Jews of Palestine, at first baffled and alarmed by something they could not understand, subsequently shed no tears for defectors who had cast their lot with the Arab invaders. The Arab onslaught transformed the situation physically and psychologically.

So much for the "myth." How about Mr. Stone's argument that it is in any case "irrelevant"? When Mr. Stone asks, "Have German Jews no right to recover their properties because they too fled?" his implied comparison of the Palestinian Arabs with the Nazi victims and consequently of the Israelis and the Nazis is disquietingly reminiscent of the crudest Arab propaganda and of the diatribes of the representatives of the Soviet Union at the General Assembly. It is shocking to hear this line from Mr. Stone. What choice except the gas chamber remained for German Jews who did not manage to escape? Mr. Stone can hardly pretend that the Arabs ran from systematic extermination. This "too" thrown in so casually to associate the fate of German Jewry with that of the Palestinian Arabs in the reader's mind is a sample of Mr. Stone's fair play. If Mr. Stone is convinced of the unqualified right of all refugees to return, why does he not raise his voice for the return of millions of German refugees to East Prussia, Pomerania and Silesia? In the context of war and its aftermaths, such a demand would be as absurd as in the case of the Arab refugees. However, reparation for abandoned Arab property is another matter and subject to negotiation as the Israeli government has repeatedly stated.

The Arab states have made no secret of the objective of an Arab "return"—the liquidation of Israel. Nasser put it simply and candidly: "If the Arabs return to Israel, Israel will cease to exist." (*Zürcher Woche,* September 1, 1961.) The numerous official Arab pronouncements on "the refugees' right to annihilate Israel" are not the statements of extremist groups but official Arab policy enunciated by Arab statesmen. Consequently when Mr. Stone asks, "Have refugees no right to return?" and conjures up the image of despoiled and persecuted German Jews, he should consider Shukairy's Palestine Liberation Organization, an army of 300,000 refugees concentrated in the Gaza strip. That a would-be invading army fails of its purpose does not make it innocent or innocuous.

A good example of the complexities of the situation is provided by the new refugee problems resulting from the Israeli victory of June, 1967. Some 150,000 Arabs fled from the West Bank of Jordan to the East Bank. They fled for a variety of reasons chief among them the conviction that Israeli soldiers would massacre them; they had been promised that the victorious Arabs would slaughter every Israeli "man, woman and child." Hussein's broadcast to his people gave full instructions as to how to treat a conquered enemy: "Kill the Jews wherever you find them. Kill them with your hands, with your nails and teeth." It is hardly surprising that Arabs so commanded expected no better from the soldiers of Israel. As in 1948, Arab atrocity propaganda back-fired. But unlike 1948 the Israelis were neither bewildered nor alarmed. If Arabs preferred the East Bank of the Jordan to life on the West Bank under Israeli occupation, Israelis could readily make peace with this predilection. They remembered how savagely Jordan had shelled Jerusalem despite all urging by Israel that Hussein not join the Arab attack. They knew that had Israel been defeated there would have been no Jewish equivalent of the East Bank and no Jewish refugees. Nevertheless, after the cessation of hostilities, Israel agreed to repatriate all *bona fide* residents of the West Bank who had fled. Yet after this decision, in the course of the negotiations, the Jordanian Finance Minister, Abdul Wahab Majali, publicly urged the refugees to return "to help your brothers continue their political action and remain a thorn in the flesh of the aggressor until the crisis had been solved." It is hardly surprising that after this pronouncement some members of the Israeli Cabinet, meeting on August 13, several days after the Jordanian Finance Minister's counsel, raised the question of the advisability of the return of these "thorns." Though the Cabinet re-affirmed its previous decision despite this blatant provocation, no government can be expected to welcome a returning Fifth Column, even the Israeli.

No doubt just as Mr. Stone, despite his own testimony of 1948, now finds it possible to write of "the expulsion of the Arabs from Palestine" so the contemporary reports of correspondents who watched the trek of Arabs across the Allenby Bridge from the West Bank to the East Bank will weigh little with the scribes of the future or, for that matter, of the present. Already the whole anti-Semitic, anti-Israel cabal from fascist to Communist, from Black Power to White Power, is in full swing, as Soviet cartoons à la Streicher and accounts of Israeli "massacres" of Arabs in the publications of S.N.C.C. and of the white supremacist National States Rights party indicate. The notion that T.V., radio and instant reporting have made the distortion of events taking place under our eyes more troublesome than in the past appears to be increasingly naive. The Arab who on the Israeli side of the Allenby Bridge testifies in the presence of the Red Cross and neutral observers that he is leaving voluntarily, and signs a document to that effect, may tell an opposite tale to the Jordanians on the other side of the bridge. That the Jordanian government urges refugees to return and even ventures to recommend insurrection merely confirms the statement of the UNRWA chief representative in West Jordan who stated on July 4 that not one of the 20 refugee camps in West Jordan was affected by the hostilities during the war, nor one resident killed. (Reported by Martha Gellhorn in *The Guardian*.)

In a sense Mr. Stone is right when he declares that the discussion as to whether Arab refugees fled voluntarily or were driven out is "irrelevant." It is irrelevant because his objection to the resettlement of Arab refugees or to any reasonable accommodation with reality is based on his rejection of the right of Israel to exist as a Jewish State. He believes that General Dayan's statement, "We want a Jewish state like the French have a French state" must "deeply disturb the thoughtful Jewish reader." He is equally shocked by a reported conversation with Ben Gurion in which the latter said: "You must know that Israel is the country of the Jews and only of the Jews. Every Arab who lives here has the same rights as any minority citizen in any country of the world, but he must admit the fact that he lives in a Jewish country." Mr. Stone observes, "The implications must chill Jews in the outside world."

Presumably he accepts the existence of France, or Soviet Russia, or China, or the United States without frost-bite.

While we judge the democratic character of these states by the rights enjoyed by their ethnic or religious minorities, each of these states has a dominant majority culture. Why is a Jewish state, while giving full political rights to all its citizens and prepared to respect their cultural and religious differences, more disturbing than any other democratic national state? Israeli Arabs speak Arabic and are Moslems or Christians; the Jewish majority speaks Hebrew and is Jewish, and the Arabs would be the first to protest linguistic or religious "integration." Their minority rights are precious just as are the rights of minorities in the United States or, hopefully, in Soviet Russia. But Mr. Stone, thoroughly congealed, is only able to compare a Jewish state with Spain of the Inquisition and, in an indecent innuendo, with "more recent parallels."

If Mr. Stone were advocating the abolition of all national states and raising the vision of the Federation of the World and the Parliament of Man his ideological horror of a "Jewish country" would be comprehensible. But he is not unfurling a belated internationalist banner under whose folds the tribes will merge. On the contrary, he is sympathetic to national claims, and particularly sensitive to the claims of Arab nationalism. It is only Jewish nationalism that by definition becomes "narrow," "tribal," "exclusive," or "racist." For Israel to call itself a Jewish State is "supra-nationalist," unlike the other countries of the earth whose national character leaves thoughtful Jews and non-Jews unchilled. In the vocabulary of Jewish leftists as of Jewish bourgeois assimilationists (*vide* the Council of Judaism's espousal of Mr. Stone), Jewish nationalism is always "chauvinism"; it is never "emergent," "renascent," "progressive," "revolutionary." No matter how many national "liberation movements" may burgeon with radical and liberal approval in Asia or Africa, Jewish nationalism is a suspect growth to be eradicated as energetically by the hammer and sickle as by the fascist axe. A totalitarian Egypt, where former Nazi henchmen not only receive refuge but are influential in the government, is acclaimed in preference to socially advanced Israel. The Left has long abandoned its old-fashioned Utopian enchantment with internationalism and has developed a sturdy regard for the national identity of all the tribes of the globe—yellow, black, red—with the one exception already noted. I am certain that the same Russian Communists who proscribe the study of Hebrew in the Soviet Union as reactionary will, without batting an eyelash, endorse

S.N.C.C.'s suggestion that Swahili be taught in American public schools.

Mr. Stone finds nothing reprehensible in love of country if Arabs do the loving. Writing in *Ramparts* (July, 1967) he writes: "The refugees lost their farms, their villages, their offices, their cities, their country." In the mounting crescendo of this listing, the climactic "their country" is worth noting. And in the *New York Review of Books* he comments on the longing of the Arab refugees for Palestine. " 'Homelessness' is the major theme of Zionism but this pathetic passion is denied to Arab refugees." The homelessness in question here is, of course, national homelessness.

Mr. Stone stresses not only the Arab refugee who—whatever the explanation—left his home and his home town but the Palestinian who lost his country. And he charges the Zionists with a "moral imbecility" which enabled them to ignore the existence of a native Palestinian population when they began the return to the ancient homeland. Through the Jewish return to Palestine a Palestinian people was ruthlessly dispossessed. Here Mr. Stone echoes the theme song of Arab belligerence.

Though it seems late in the day to re-argue the ABC's of the Zionist case, the current barrage from both the extreme Right and Left makes a few reminders mandatory, particularly as many well-intentioned people are troubled by such charges. Did Jewish aggressors set up their homeland in total disregard of a native people with prior claims?

Now for the ABC's: To make his point Mr. Stone comes up with all kinds of nuggets from his mining of *Les Temps Modernes*. Herzl never mentioned the Arabs in *The Jewish State* (1896); Nordau wept when he learned of the existence of Arabs. Mr. Stone fails to mention the fact that by the time Herzl wrote *Old-New Land*, he was well aware of the Arabs and dreamed of happy co-existence. But whatever were the deficiencies of early Zionist fantasies, the Balfour Declaration issued in 1917 took full cognizance of the 600,000 local Arabs. The underlying assumption of the Declaration was that while over 97% of the huge territories liberated by the Allies from the Turks would be devoted to the setting up of independent Arab states, the "small notch" of Palestine would be reserved for the creation of a Jewish state. This "small notch" (Lord Balfour's term) was in 1922 further reduced by two-thirds through the amputation of the East Bank of Palestine for the establishment of Transjordan, later Jordan.

By the time the Mandate was in effect, five independent Arab states were established on the territory freed from Turkish rule. Saudi Arabia, Iraq, Syria, Lebanon and Transjordan were allotted an area covering, 1,200,000 square miles. The ten thousand square miles left to Western Palestine constituted less than 1% of the total area and was less than a third of the area originally promised by the Balfour Declaration. The Partition Resolution of 1947, accepted by the Jews and fought by the Arabs, further lopped away at the continually diminishing "notch." A glance at the map of the region shows the ratio between the huge Arab lands and the tiny state of Israel.

But the Arabs and their supporters reject this comparison as irrelevant. That the Arabs received much and the Jews little has nothing to do with the case. Arab nationalism cannot be sated by less than 100% gratification; 90% plus won't do. What about the Palestinian Arabs? Why should they surrender their Palestinian identity to become Syrians or Jordanians as the Jews irrationally suggest? True, all Arabs are brothers when the Pan-Arab dream beckons but it is criminal imperialist aggression to suggest that the Arabs, particularly the Palestinians, relinquish one jot of their national claim because of Jewish need, Hitler's victims and the rest. Such is the Arab argument.

If a genuine Palestinian nationalism had been violated then it would be Quixotic folly to ask the Arabs of Palestine to abandon their rights in favor of the unfortunate Jews. But did such a violation take place? At the end of World War I the inhabitants of the land treasured for centuries by Jews as Zion did not view themselves as a distinct Palestinian nation. *Palestine did not exist as a political or national entity as far as the Arabs were concerned.* For them it was merely a geographical locality, the south of Syria. Whereas no one doubts the fierce authenticity of Arab nationalism, *Palestinian* Arab nationalism is an artificial creation with no roots before the British Mandate. As recently as May 31, 1956, Ahmed Shukairy, the extremist chief of the Palestine Liberation Organization, declared before the Security Council: "It is common knowledge that Palestine is nothing but southern Syria."

Nor were the Zionist pioneers who came to an abandoned wasteland forty or fifty years ago afflicted by "moral imbecility." They may have been simple-minded in believing that the swamps they drained, the stony soil they irrigated—incidentally, swamps and deserts *purchased* at fancy prices by the Jewish National Fund—would make them welcome neighbors, but there was nothing wrong with their ethics. They were socialist idealists who believed that to reclaim a marsh through their own toil and devotion and to establish agricultural settlements on soil on which no one had been able to live for generations was a gain for all and a loss to none. They took literally the business about to each according to his need from each according to his capacity. The result of their personal sacrifices was the green country-side which now enables Arabs to point to the flourishing land of which they were "despoiled."

Simple-minded though the pioneers may have been in believing that their physical reclamation of desolate wastes would win them affection or gratitude, they were right in their estimate of the economic and demographic results of their labor. Far from dispossessing Arabs Zionist colonization resulted in their numerical increase.

According to the 1922 census taken by the British Government only 186,000 Arabs lived in the area which later became Israel. The increase in the Arab population of Palestine took place not only because of a very high rate of natural increase due to improved health conditions and standards of living but also because Palestine became a country of Arab *immigration* from adjacent Arab countries. Arabs were attracted, mainly from Syria and Egypt, to the Jewish areas of Mandated Palestine by the swift industrial and agricultural growth which the Jews had started and were constantly enlarging and diversifying. This is confirmed by the testimony in an UNRWA bulletin of 1962:

> A considerable movement of people is known to have occurred, particularly during the Second World War years when new opportunities of employment opened up in the towns and on military works in Palestine. These wartime prospects and, generally, the higher rate of industrialization in Palestine than in neighboring countries attracted many immigrants from those countries, and many of them entered Palestine without their presence being officially recorded.
> (UNRWA Reviews, Information Paper No. 6, Beirut, September, 1962.)

In the whole of Palestine the Arab population doubled between 1920 and 1940, growing from 600,000 to well over a million. In Jordan, closed to Jewish immigration, the population remained static. Paradoxically, in the period between the issuance of the Balfour Declaration and the establishment of Israel, Palestine changed from a country of Arab emigration to one of Arab immigration—a phenomenon observable in none of the adjacent Arab countries.

Perhaps the most telling demonstration of what had actually taken place has ironically been provided by Israel's June victory. When publicity focused on the Arab refugees, the overwhelming bulk were discovered dwelling on the West Bank, the part of Palestine annexed in 1948 by Jordan, and in Gaza, the Palestinian city, occupied by Egypt. The refugees, maintained by UNRWA in camps whose standard of living was higher than that of many an Arab village, had never left Palestine.

Will Mr. Stone, who deplores "Lilliputian nationalism," make a holy cause of a fixation on a particular village or street? No matter how dear a home or a home town to the residents, people are shifted despite their wishes for so trivial a cause as the construction of a new dam or highway. Israel, a country of immigrants gathered from remote corners of the world, understandably perceives no gross injustice in the resettlement of Arabs on territory formerly Palestine—or on adjacent territory—a resettlement requiring no adjustment in landscape, language, climate, religion or social mores. The opposition of the Arab states to any of the numerous proposals for the productive resettlement of the Palestinian Arabs is predicated on the simple proposition that Israel must be destroyed. Economically, territorially, above all, humanly, the deliberately created Arab refugee problem lends itself to just solution once the Arab premise of the liquidation of Israel swiftly through a hostile influx or slowly through an uncontrolled demographic change is abandoned. The pseudo-humanitarian premise that Arab nationalism in full panoply down to its most tenuous ramifications merits tender regard, whatever the cost to the one small Jewish state, only bolsters Arab appetite and intransigeance.

In addition to dwelling on the "expulsion" of the Arabs, Mr. Stone finds much wrong with Israel. He complains that Israel is creating a kind of "moral schizophrenia in world Jewry." Outside Israel, Jewish welfare depends on the existence of "secular, non-racial, pluralistic societies"; yet Jews defend a society in Israel in which "the ideal is racial and

exclusionist." Israel is a theocratic state, with second-class
Arab citizens and with ingrained prejudice against oriental
Jews. Mr. Stone makes these charges categorically without
offering a shred of evidence of their truth. Blanket denuncia-
tions, if false, can only be answered with a blanket denial.
The one specific point Mr. Stone makes ("In Israel Jewry
finds itself defending a society in which mixed marriages cannot be legalized") is patently untrue. Both in Israel and outside of Israel the requirements of rigid orthodoxy instead of
being defended, are constantly under attack. If Mr. Stone
read the Hebrew press he would appreciate the vigor of its
self-criticism in this and other respects. Israel has many im-
perfections but to pretend that any of its inadequacies are its
"ideal" rather than the result of human failure or of the economic and political pressures to which the small beleaguered
land has been subject since its establishment is again to judge
Israel by an invidious criterion applied to no other people.
No country in the world has so bold a social vision or has
tried so bravely to integrate the excluded of the earth who
came to it—were they survivors of the gas chambers or despoiled Oriental Jews. Born in great travail to find an answer
for Jewish need and to achieve Jewish national independence,
it is not called upon to answer non-existent needs or desires
which have ample scope for their satisfaction elsewhere.

Mr. Stone perceives a growing divergence between Jew and
Israeli: "the former with a sense of mission as a Witness in
the human wilderness, the latter concerned only with his own
tribe's welfare." The reverse, of course, is true. It is the
Israelis whose concerns are global, whose emissaries pene-
trated Hitler's Europe, who brought Eichmann to justice,
whose instructors teach new and advanced social techniques
to emergent countries in Africa, whose kibbutzim serve as
laboratories to Africans and Indians and Burmese and Europeans, whose social dynamism and accomplishments inspire
all poor and undeveloped countries. The world sympathy for
Israel last June was not a tribute to tribal egoism but to
courage and vision on an unprecedented scale.

Mr. Stone makes another nasty charge. Since Zionism
"grows on Jewish catastrophe," it now "casts longing eyes on
Russian Jewry." Mr. Stone wants to know if it would not be
better if the Soviet Union wiped out anti-Semitism and gave
equal rights to its Jewish citizens. Better than what? Better
than another large-scale Jewish catastrophe which Israel ap-

parently desires? This is a disgraceful accusation. Israel is in the foreground of Jewish agitation for unrestricted cultural rights for Russian Jews. Among the rights sought is the right of emigration for those Russian Jews who have families in Israel or elsewhere. Were there to be free emigration from Russia, Israel would be delighted if Russian Jews came. But that is a very different matter from desiring another "catastrophe" which would supply "another flow of desperate refugees to an Israel already short of Jews if it is to expand as the Zionist militants hope to expand it." Here we get a double dig; not only is Israel lusting for Jewish tragedy but it is expansionist. Let me tell Mr. Stone a secret: not only Zionist "militants" want Jewish immigration; all Israel does. The call for *"Aliyah"* (Immigration) has gone out not to "expand" but further to develop the country. Ben-Gurion's great dream is to "expand" into the Negev, the desert that constitutes two-thirds of Israel. This creative vision—to regenerate sand and stone as the Emek was reclaimed—is Israel's "hope." Mr. Stone who so eloquently expounds universal values and universal visions should be warier of lending his authority to vicious anti-Israel smears.

Finally Mr. Stone suggests: "The ideal solution would allow the Jews to make their contributions as citizens in the diverse societies and nations which are their homes while Israel finds acceptance as a Jewish State in a renascent Arab civilization. This would end Arab fears of a huge inflow to Israel." At first reading, most Zionists would enthusiastically embrace such a solution; that's what they have been wanting all along—a renascent Jewish state to be accepted by a renascent Arab civilization. Stone might be quoting Herzl. But a second reading is less reassuring. To calm Arab fears of a "huge inflow," Jewish immigration to Israel would presumably be restricted (though Mr. Stone appreciates that the prospect of an inundation is slight). If, despite his cautious phrasing, I read Mr. Stone correctly, the one group that the "exclusionist" Jewish state could rightly exclude would be Jews. Such is the *reductio ad absurdum* of Mr. Stone's universalism.

Given a will to peace on the part of the Arabs all the problems of the Arab-Israeli conflict can be settled reasonably and to the advantage of Jew and Arab. This includes the definition of boundaries and the integration of refugees into a productive life, but the elementary recognition of Israel's right to exist is the precondition of any settlement. And the emergence of Israel as a Jewish country with the same rights for self-defense and normal development as other democratic countries should scar no psyche able to envision "renascent" civilizations all over the globe.

A word of warning should be added. The Zionist visionaries who came with the Bible and socialist tracts to build a "just society" in the desert have lost many illusions. They have learned the stern lessons of recent history. I have watched this transformation. In 1936, on my first visit to Palestine I attended a seder in Ein Harod, a kibbutz in the Emek. In addition to the traditional questions—why is this night different?—the children asked *Kashes* of their own. One of the questions was, "Why do the Arabs live on the hills and we in the valley?". The answer, understandable only to those aware of the exposed position of the kibbutzim was, "Because we want peace and friendship."

The children who heard this answer grew up to fight for hills in three wars since 1948. Last July, three weeks after the end of the 1967 battles, I was in Galilee in a kibbutz shelled for months from the Syrian ridges. I saw the destroyed cottages and the underground shelters where the children routinely slept. The next morning I visited the Golan heights, the fortified Syrian hills bristling with Russian armor from which Syrian soldiers equally routinely attacked the kibbutz. The ridge was scaled by Israeli soldiers on the last day of the fighting and the bunkers dismantled in one of the toughest fights of the war. Perhaps the most illuminating circumstance of this battle was that the kibbutzim, not the Israeli military, insisted on the capture of the ridge: "Our children must sleep in bed not in shelters." Anyone standing among the masses of Russian armor on the ridge and seeing the guns pointed at the settlements would probably find it difficult to continue prating about Israeli expansionism. Until the Arabs make peace, Israel needs viable borders; as long as Israel is under attack by Arabs who outnumber her twenty to one, it will perforce be militant. If instead of indulging in strictly one-sided pieties, the self-declared humanists and universalists would unequivocally grant the rights of the farmer in valley rather than of the gunner on the hill, peace might come sooner. Otherwise the enemies of Israel may be caught in the vise of a self-fulfilling prophecy to the detriment of all.

THE ARAB-ISRAELI WAR

The Consequences of Defeat

By Bernard Lewis*

Since the end of the third Arab-Israeli war the vocabulary of Middle Eastern politics has been enriched with a new formula —"the removal of the consequences of aggression." The phrase presents some obvious difficulties of definition concerning the origin of the aggression, the nature of its consequences and the manner of their removal. All these are subject to a wide diversity of interpretations. However, the meaning of the Arab states in putting forward this formula as a demand is quite clear; it is that Israel is the aggressor, that the occupation of Arab lands and the departure of their Arab inhabitants are the consequences of aggression, and that these consequences should be reversed.

It is possible that in certain circumstances the conquerors might be willing to give up their conquests; it is even conceivable that the refugees might return—though this would make them unique among the countless millions in Europe, Asia and Africa who have fled or been driven from their homes in our brutal century. But far more has happened than the occupation of lands and the movement of peoples, important as these may be. In the world of reality, events cannot be unmade, and their effects persist, even when their results vanish. Sometimes these events are of such dimensions as to involve radical reassessments: governments reassess policies at the periphery of their interests and people at the center of crisis reassess their governments. It seems likely that the war and crisis in the Middle East in the summer of 1967 formed such a turning point. The four chief parties concerned —the Arabs, Israel, the Soviet Union and the West—must have been pondering the significance of these events and the lessons to be learnt from them.

The Russians were involved in the crisis from the start— indeed, without descending to the conspiratorial conception of history or returning to the polemics of the cold war, we

* Bernard Lewis is Professor of the History of the Near and Middle East at the University of London. Reprinted by special permission from *Foreign Affairs*, January, 1968. Copyright by the Council on Foreign Relations, Inc., New York.

can say with reasonable assurance that they had no small part in creating it. One contribution, which they shared with other powers, was the dispatch of large quantities of modern, sophisticated weapons to the area; another, more distinctively their own, was their unswerving support for the Arab states in any and every encounter, irrespective of circumstances. A good example of this is the recurrent problem of clashes on the Syrian-Israeli border. Most observers—and governments—were content to treat each incident on its merits and to blame one side or the other as seemed appropriate. But the Soviet Government invariably supported the Syrians, even when they were palpably in the wrong, and on several occasions even used its veto in the Security Council to save the Syrians from a mildly critical resolution. On November 3, 1966, the veto was applied against an inoffensive resolution sponsored, among others, by two African states—a remarkable indication of how far the Soviet Government was prepared to go in support of its Arab protégés.

This kind of action would in itself have led Arab governments to form a high—and, as it turned out, exaggerated—assessment of Soviet willingness to stand by them in a crisis. There is, in addition, some evidence of Soviet help at a more intimate level than the politics of the United Nations. Syrian gunnery on the border, it is said, showed a degree of professional efficiency out of accord with the previous and subsequent performances of the Syrian army; Syrian diplomacy, on both border issues and questions of oil transit payments, was conducted with a professional finesse that suggested greater reserves of skill and experience than are normally available to short-lived governments in Damascus.

In his television address on Friday, June 9, President Nasser explained how the crisis had begun. On May 15, he said, it had become clear from Israeli statements that they intended to attack Syria. This was confirmed by information from Syrian sources and also by reports from the Egyptian intelligence services. Moreover, "our friends in the Soviet Union informed the parliamentary delegation which visited Moscow early last month that there was a premeditated intention to attack Syria. It was our duty not to stay with our arms crossed. It was a duty of Arab solidarity, and also a guarantee for our national security." It was for this reason, said the President, that he had sent his forces to the frontier. This had led successively to the withdrawal of UNEF, the Egyptian occupation of Sharm el-Sheikh, and the declaration of a blockade of the Gulf of Aqaba, since "the passage of the enemy flag in front of our troops was intolerable, and inflicted the deepest wound on the feelings of the Arab nation."

President Nasser of course acted, as always, by his own choice, but we may believe him when he says that the original impetus came from Syrian and Russian warnings. Both Syrian and, what is more important, Russian spokesmen have throughout taken the same line. But were these warnings based on a genuine danger—or even on a genuine belief that such a danger existed? The evidence adduced, apart from vague references to information received, consisted of two points: an alleged concentration of large Israeli forces on the Syrian frontier, and menacing speeches by Mr. Eshkol. Neither piece of evidence amounts to much. The speeches were no more than routine warnings of reprisals in what had become a standardized pattern, intended to discourage Syrian and soothe Israeli hotheads—an exercise which should have been familiar to Arab leaders. The troop concentration, as is clear from the reports of the U.N. truce observers, never took place. The Syrians may have misread the situation and panicked; the Russians will not have done so, and the conclusion is inescapable that the Soviet Government, for reasons of its own, either planned or connived at the launching of what became a new and dangerous crisis in Israel-Arab relations.

The suggestion has been made that the Soviet purpose was to provide a distraction in the Middle East and thus relieve the pressure on Viet Nam. This would assume, first, that they intended, from the start, to create a major international crisis, involving the powers and especially the United States, and, second, that they counted on the willingness of the United States to become involved. Both assumptions seem unlikely. A more probable explanation is that they aimed at something much more limited and local, a scare rather than a crisis, and that its purpose was to save the tottering Syrian régime from collapse. The Soviets had invested a good deal of time, effort and money in the left-wing Baathist government and had achieved a closer relationship with it than with any other government not under communist control. In May 1967, that government, and with it the Soviet position in Syria, was in grave danger. It was already more than a year old—a dangerous age in Damascus. Based on an uneasy alliance between members of Muslim religious minority groups, it was unpopular with the Sunnis,[1] and further weakened by the split between Alawis and Druzes. Worst of all, some of its supporters had gratuitously antagonized the powerful Islamic establishment. Like other "revolutionary" and "progressive" régimes in the Arab world, the Baathists had confined their radicalism to politics and economics and had usually refrained from attacking Islamic beliefs, traditions or institutions. They had therefore encountered nothing more than the grumbles of a population accustomed to acquiesce in the vagaries of authoritarian government. There are, however, limits to acquiescence, and at the beginning of May the publication in an army-sponsored magazine of an article denouncing religion and belief in God evoked a menacing wave of popular resentment against a régime which now seemed to be threatening the most cherished values of a Muslim people. The government beat a hasty retreat, attributing the article to the C.I.A., but the damage was already done. The Baathists and their Russian backers may well have decided that a little diversion, based on the unfailing theme of Palestine, might be useful. As the crisis developed, and seemed to be tending toward a diplomatic victory for the revolutionary Arab states, and therefore for Russia, wider and more tempting prospects appeared—the collapse of Western influence, the consolidation of Russian influence in the revolutionary Arab states, and its extension to the remaining Arab states in the Middle East and North Africa.

In backing them so far, the Russians were clearly assuming that the Arabs would win—if necessary in a war, but probably without one. The West would be hypnotized into accepting Arab demands; Israel, abandoned by her Western friends, perhaps even under their pressure, would be forced to give way. The dispatch of a Russian fleet to the eastern Mediterranean, of a strength obviously insufficient to confront the U.S. Sixth Fleet, can only have been intended to overawe Israel, with American acquiescence. The world would learn that the friends of the Soviets prosper, while the friends of the West do not.

For a while the world seemed to be learning just that. The West faltered and fumbled; Israel, unsure of Western attitudes, hesitated; President Nasser, triumphant, threw caution to the winds. After nationalizing the Suez Canal in 1956, he

---

[1] At one time the Baathist government was known as the *'Adas* (lentil) régime—an acronym of 'Alawis, Druzes and Isma'ilis.

had astutely sat back, declared himself satisfied and left the next move to his opponents. After closing the Straits of Tiran, he declared explicitly that this was a preliminary to the final confrontation with Israel, for which he was now ready. The other revolutionary Arab states were with him; even his Arab enemies felt obliged to make the necessary accommodations. That the Russian encouraged him to go so far is unlikely; they certainly did not prevent him.

The six-day war and its sequel showed that the Russians had failed badly in their military and political intelligence and assessments—not perhaps of the West, but of Israel and the Arabs. No doubt they were misled about the one by their own anti-Semitic stereotypes, about the other by the wishful thinking of their Arab informants. The correction of error is difficult in a dictatorship. By Monday evening, June 6, informed opinion—by Tuesday almost everyone in the free world— knew how the battle was going. It was not until Tuesday night (Wednesday morning in the Middle East) that the Soviet delegate to the U.N. agreed to an unconditional cease-fire. The extra time he had striven to gain for the Arabs served only to consolidate their defeat.

From Wednesday morning the signs multiplied that the Russians were engaged in a reappraisal—probably agonizing. They were surprised, disconcerted and very angry. Their public fury was directed against Israel; in addition, they were probably not unmoved by the swift collapse of Arab arms and by President Nasser's attempt, through the false charge of American and British participation, to drag them into war.

The Russians had reason to be angry. Soviet prestige—the reputation of Soviet arms and guidance, the value of Soviet friendship, the credibility of Soviet warnings—had received a damaging blow, with far-reaching repercussions. The Russians had suffered this blow because, through the extent of their commitment to the Arabs, they had in effect entrusted the safety of Soviet prestige to the keeping of Arab governments over which they had no real control. They had taken great chances, which turned out badly; they had done so for very dubious gains. The Arab leaders were very unwise to assume that the Soviets would accept, for their sake, risks which they had not accepted for Berlin or Viet Nam. This miscalculation was disastrous for the Arabs; it was also most unfortunate for the Soviet Union.

The root of the trouble was that the Arab governments, even that of Syria, were not satellites, and were therefore ultimately uncontrollable. The Soviet Government, in dealing with the Middle East, found themselves in a position of responsibility without power—a reversal of their normal experience. It is not surprising that they were disturbed.

In this predicament, the Soviet leadership had, basically, a choice between two policies: either to consolidate its hold on the revolutionary Arab governments and transform them into satellites, or to attempt some measure of disengagement. This in turn is linked with the larger, global choice before them, between détente and coexistence, on the one hand, and active hostility toward the United States on the other. Both choices are affected by changing and conflicting pressures within the collective leadership which succeeded Khrushchev.

One of these pressures is that of the so-called Stalinists—more precisely, the exponents of repression and chauvinism. These circles are strongly affected by old-fashioned anti-Semitism, which can become a powerful factor in determining attitudes both toward a Jewish state and toward its enemies. The point is sometimes made that Jewish or pro-Jewish sentiments can lead to unbalanced and unrealistic policies. This is of course true. It is equally true, though less obvious, that anti-Jewish sentiments can have the same effect. The hysterical violence and traditional anti-Semitic symbolism of Soviet attacks on Israel show that the offenses of the Israelis, in Soviet eyes, were greatly aggravated by the fact that they were Jews. These Soviet reactions also suggest that one of the motives of a pro-Arab policy may have been a desire to hurt the Jews, and that this emotional impulse may have warped the judgment of policy-makers and led them to a degree of indulgence to Arab wishes which was ultimately harmful to Soviet and even Arab interests. This phenomenon is not unknown in other countries; in the Soviet Union it was not countered or corrected by any pressure, emotional or otherwise, in the opposite direction.

II

Anti-Jewish prejudice may have pushed the policy of supporting Arab nationalism to ill-judged extremes; it was not of course the sole or even the main motive for this policy, which rested on a fairly realistic assessment of the condition of the Arab world and the importance of the Middle Eastern bridge-head for Soviet activities in Asia and Africa.

This importance was enhanced, rather than reduced, by the Arab defeat, and for the moment there was much to tempt the Russians into a closer involvement. The régimes they had supported were in danger of overthrow, with further damaging effects to Soviet prestige. China seemed ready to usurp Russia's place as the patron of Arab nationalism, and was gaining the support of Arab communists. The blow to Western influence, on the other hand, was far heavier than to Russian influence, and affected even those countries that were under conservative régimes. For a while the Russians seem to have toyed with the idea of establishing communist régimes in the Arab lands—and then to have abandoned it as too dangerous.

It is not difficult to see why. To transform the Arab countries into satellites would be an expensive, difficult and hazardous operation, and would never be safe unless the régimes were sustained, as in Eastern Europe, by the threat or presence of Soviet force. Even in Eastern Europe, this policy has become precarious; it would be still more so in countries that have no land frontier with the Soviet Union. Moreover, such an intervention in the Arab lands would endanger the new, hard-won and greatly valued understanding with Turkey and Iran—both of them, despite their recent rethinking, still members of Western-oriented alliances. In addition, it soon became clear that the Chinese menace was not yet a serious factor, and that the collapse of Western influence was by no means as complete as had at first appeared. The Syrian episode had shown that Islam was still the strongest loyalty of the people, and that outraged Islamic feelings could still shake or destroy a government which really tried to enforce its "progressive" and "revolutionary" principles. An attempt to create "popular democracies" could arouse very powerful forces indeed.

Finally, and most important of all, the danger of a direct confrontation with the United States remained. It was this danger that had induced the Soviet Government, at the height of the crisis, to draw back from armed intervention to save the Arabs. An adventurous policy in the Middle East could easily lead to a new danger of confrontation—and to another withdrawal, with even more damaging effects on Soviet prestige. In avoiding an entanglement with the Arabs and a collision with the United States, the Soviet leadership would be faithful to tradition. During the centuries of expansion, by which the principality of Muscovy grew into the great Russian Empire, the greater Soviet Union and the still greater Soviet bloc, two principles were almost always respected: to advance by land into adjoining regions to which troops and settlers could easily be moved, and to avoid a clash with a superior or even an equal power.

The dilemma of the Soviet Government was acute. A closer involvement in the Middle East was too dangerous—yet disengagement seemed politically impossible. The collective leadership could not make the sudden changes of policy that were possible for Stalin or Khrushchev; the internal pressures were too strong, and the status of the Soviet Union as a superpower was heavily committed. The Russian demand to Egypt, at the time of President Podgorny's visit, for a purge of bourgeois elements in the Egyptian Government and army, could be interpreted either way—as a prelude to Bolshevization or to abandonment. As an emergency measure, an airlift of arms was organized, to save the Nasserist and Baathist régimes from collapse. But while Soviet prestige clearly required that these régimes survive the war and its immediate aftermath, it did not necessarily require their indefinite continuance, and at one point there were some indications that the Soviets might regard them as expendable. Later they seem to have decided to hold on to President Nasser, and to support him against his possible successors on the left or the right. To do this, they needed to undertake some further reequipment of the Egyptian armed forces, and to extend—and more especially to publicize—their own military and political activities in Egypt. Whether these represent a holding operation or a new adventure is an open question. It is still too early to assess the future development of Soviet policy in the Middle East, nor indeed is it certain that this policy has yet been decided. Much will obviously depend on the attitudes of the Western powers and, above all, of the United States.

There are, however, some signs of its probable direction. The Soviets will certainly continue to give vociferous support to the Arab case against Israel, especially at the United Nations. They will try to salvage their battered prestige and hope that, as on previous occasions, they will find someone in the West to help them in this task. But in all probability they will take care not to get into a position again where their prestige can be endangered by governments and armies which they do not control. The most likely development is a policy based on relations with individual Arab states rather than on

Arabism, and aimed at the kind of relationship that they have sought to establish with Turkey, Iran and Pakistan. The question is how far they will be allowed to extricate themselves if they desire to do so.

Like the Soviet Union, the Western powers have been able to draw certain inferences from what has happened. For a while it seemed that the West, and particularly the United States, had been outmanœuvred. The ring was closing around Israel: even pro-Western Arab rulers, whatever their real feelings, were lining up behind President Nasser. Communist Russia could support Arab nationalist demands to the full; the United States and Britain, captives of their own freedom and their own standards, could not, and were thus forced to appear as enemies of the Arabs. Their only choice was of what kind: as enemies to be respected and conciliated, or to be despised and ignored. For the United States, a far more terrible choice was being prepared—whether to abandon Israel to destruction, or to be trapped in a land war in Southwest as well as Southeast Asia.

Fortunately for the United States, no such choice was needed. Through no particular wisdom or merit of their own, the Western powers emerged from a dangerous situation with what turned out to be only minor injuries. Like the Russians, they had learned that their control over their friends was very limited. They were fortunate in that the state which was generally regarded as their protégé did not need to be rescued. The danger remained.

For a while, it seemed that despite their failure against Israel, the Russians had won a considerable political success against the United States and Britain, which found themselves being ignominiously evicted from most Arab countries. But even this was deceptive. The two most powerful Arab weapons against the West—the oil boycott and, for Britain, the sterling balances—both proved ineffective. The stoppage of oil exports did greater and swifter damage to the sellers than to the buyers. Arabian money transferred from London to Switzerland, at low or no interest rates, found its way back to London, to earn high interest for its new custodians. Even the closing of the Suez Canal did less harm than was feared, and for the United States even brought some marginal advantage —some additional exports and the slowing down of Russian supplies to North Viet Nam. The inconvenience to Britain was more serious, but much of this was of a transitional nature, until new arrangements could become fully effective.

The heaviest sufferers were India, some other Asian and East African states, and above all the Egyptians themselves.

As the flames and the dust subsided, there were signs that the damage to Anglo-American diplomacy was less severe than had at first appeared. Some Arab leaders were beginning to wonder whether they were wise to identify themselves entirely with one camp in the global conflict, and whether indeed they had chosen the right one. Before very long, several Arab states began to make overtures to the West, and even President Nasser flew a kite, no doubt expecting, on the basis of past experience, that Western governments would respond with eager gratitude to the opportunity once again to feed his people and sustain his régime. This time, however, he had overestimated the American capacity to absorb calumny, abuse and injury, and the response from Washington was disappointing. In London he fared somewhat better, though the extent of British complaisance, and its value to Egypt, are still not clear.

That President Nasser should have found it necessary to seek London's good offices—for pressure in Jerusalem or intercession in Washington—is a measure of the failure of another kind of Western policy, that of General de Gaulle. Previous French policy toward Israel had been based on the assumptions that nothing could be achieved with the Arab states, and that one small ally in the Middle East was better than none at all. In a calculation unconnected with the Middle East, both assumptions were now abandoned. By supporting the Russian and Arab line against Israel, the General incurred some immediate losses—in the political and commercial good will of Israel, and in the confidence of Europe, at a time when the credibility of his friendship was rather important to him. In compensation, he gained warm words from Moscow and the Arab capitals. Whether he will gain any more from them is dubious. They for their part have already learnt that his support made no real difference to them; they are unlikely to pay for more than they receive.

III

In the West as in Russia the question that arises is a basic and simple one—how much trouble is the Middle East worth? On both sides there seems to be a growing appreciation of the advantages of disengagement—as far as is feasible—from an area of high risks, great costs, dubious returns and, above all, of diminishing importance, as it is being bypassed by strategic, economic and technological developments and over-shadowed by the urgent problems of East Asia. These must, increasingly, dominate political and strategic thinking in Washington and Moscow.

For the powers of the Communist and Western blocs the possibility exists, however remotely, of extricating themselves from the Middle Eastern quicksands. No such possibility is open to the countries of the Middle East, which must make the best they can of conditions in their area—including, for as long as may be necessary, the policies of the great and not-so-great powers. The lessons of the war will thus appear to these countries in a somewhat different form.

What Israel learnt is what victors always learn from victory —that is, that they were right all along. On two points in particular the crisis and war confirmed Israeli beliefs: that their survival depended, ultimately, on their willingness and ability to fight for it, and that they could not trust the United Nations, where their enemies had a built-in position of advantage. The Soviet veto in the Security Council is always available to the Arabs, even on the most trivial matters; the combination of the Communist bloc and the quaintly named "nonaligned" states in the General Assembly is sufficient to prevent any solution acceptable to Israel, if not to enforce one acceptable to the Arabs. "If the Arabs table a resolution tomorrow that the earth is flat," said an Israeli minister, "they can count on at least 40 votes."

Reliance on their own military and political strength in the Middle East and mistrust of "United Nations auspices" are two basic Israeli conclusions from recent events. A third is that, of all the powers of the outside world, the only one that really matters to Israel is the United States. Even in the euphoria of victory, Israelis know that American good will is fundamental to them. Basically, there are three things that Israel wants from Washington: first, to deter the Russians, as in June 1967, from direct military intervention against them; second, to refrain from imposing, alone or with others, a solution which Israel judges contrary to her interests; third, to ensure that Israel's armaments do not fall dangerously be-low the level of the Arab states. In other words, they wish to be sure that the Americans will neither undermine their position nor allow Russia to do so. Given this assurance, they feel confident that they can cope with their Arab neighbors.

The ultimately more serious problem of their Arab subjects, with its implications for the whole future of their state, society and ethos, remains unresolved, and there is little sign of agreement, inside Israel, on how to tackle it.

A victory, said the Duke of Wellington, is the greatest tragedy in the world, except a defeat. The Arabs suffered this greater tragedy, and the problems confronting them—problems of understanding and of action—have a terrible urgency quite different from the milder dilemmas of the Americans, the Russians, even of the Israelis.

The first and obvious question was—what went wrong? Why had they suffered a double defeat—a military defeat in the field, at the hands of a nation inferior in numbers, weapons, territory and resources, and a political defeat at the United Nations, despite every appearance of overwhelming political superiority? At the moment of crisis and war, it was the Arab states which found themselves isolated from world opinion, and even some of those governments which supported them were clearly acting against their own public opinion at home.[2] Even the full mobilization of the Soviet regular and auxiliary forces in the General Assembly failed to secure the necessary majority for the resolutions that the Arabs wanted. It was a political defeat hardly less striking than the military defeat which had preceded it.

War and defeat are the classical motors of social and political change. Sometimes they lead to major transformations, as in Germany and Russia after the First World War; sometimes to a mood of sullen resentment and withdrawal, as in the South after the American Civil War, and in Spain after 1898. Defeat is especially cogent when inflicted by the carriers of another civilization with a different and challenging religion or ideology. The defeat in Palestine in 1948 was the first such shock suffered directly by the Eastern Arabs. The earlier defeats of Islam at the hands of West and East European imperialism had been sustained by the Turks and Persians, who, as the dominant peoples of Islam, had shielded the Arabs from the realities of politics and war. The vague encounters of the Anglo-French period added little of value to their experience; on the contrary, by providing easy vic-

---

[2] The line-up of communist, fascist, personal, revolutionary and traditional dictatorships on the Arab side raises difficult problems for those who believe that economics and ideology, not politics, are the determining factors in international as in other affairs.

tories over embarrassed and halfhearted opponents they fostered a dangerous illusion of strength.

The shock of defeat in 1948, in place of the expected victory parade, was all the greater in that it was inflicted, not by the mighty imperial powers, but by the despised and familiar Jews. The *nakba* (disaster), as the Arabs called it, gave rise to an extensive literature, much of it concerned with the political and military blunders of Arab leaders, but some of it, as for example the well-known works by Mr. Musa Alami and Professor Constantine Zurayk, attempting to penetrate to the deeper social and cultural causes of the Arab failure.

Politically, the defeat was seen as a failure of the régimes— the parliamentary and constitutional monarchies and republics —which had conducted the war. The lesson learnt was the need for a more radical and more violent approach. The traditional and authoritarian régimes, as in Jordan and Saudi Arabia, managed to survive, but the liberal-style régimes in Syria, Egypt and Iraq were swept away. They were succeeded by military governments, with programs of revolutionary change, later designated socialism, and of Arab nationalism. In international relations, their anti-Western attitudes gradually became pro-Soviet, when the Soviet Union finally emerged as the most serious and dangerous antagonist of the West and of Western civilization.

The second defeat, in 1956, brought no comparable soul-searching or upheaval. This was because the military defeat was compensated by a great political victory, and because the significance of the struggle was blurred by myths. Three beliefs, in particular, shaped Arab thinking on these events: first, that Egypt was defeated by France and Britain, not just by Israel; second, that a cause of defeat was Arab disunity, which left Egypt alone to face the tripartite attack; third, that Egypt was saved from the consequences of defeat by the intervention of Russia, her new friend since the previous year.

The third of these is an obvious myth—a successful combined effort of delusion and self-delusion. The record of October and November 1956 makes it quite clear that the Soviet Government did not speak out until the American President and other spokesmen had explained, not once but several times, that the United States did not support Britain, France or Israel, and disapproved of their action. Then and only then did the Soviets take up the Egyptian cause and utter dire threats against the aggressors. And even after that, they were powerless to secure the Israeli withdrawal from Sinai, which was brought about by the American Government alone. Yet the myth of the Soviet rescue became an article of faith, and was reaffirmed by King Hussein in Moscow as late as October 3, 1967.

The military myths were more excusable, and were, in part at least, solidly based on fact. Egypt had indeed fought alone; Israel had not. The Egyptian interpretation of events was further encouraged by a flow of revelations and confessions.[3] The study of these revelations may well have contributed to President Nasser's—perhaps also to Moscow's—misjudgment of the relative military and political strengths of Israel and Egypt.

The myth of 1956—Egypt, alone, embattled and ultimately victorious against three enemies—stood for more than ten years. The events of 1967 should finally have dispelled it. This time the defeat was political as well as military. Three Arab states on Israel's borders, with help from others, were overwhelmed by Israel alone. There have been attempts to refurbish the old myths and create new ones; they have had only limited success.

There is still little willingness to face the facts—far less than in 1948-49, when discussion was still free and often realistic. The relatively minor defeat of that time was called *nakba*, disaster. The far greater defeat of 1967 is firmly labelled *naksa*, setback. This word is used even in press translations or summaries of foreign comments, and serves to render such terms as defeat and disaster, which are tabu. The universal adoption of this word is a striking example of the nationalization of language and its use to control thought and conceal reality.

Discussion so far has been mainly on the tactical level, and has concentrated on such things as military and political errors and unwise propaganda. In some Arab countries, as for example, in North Africa and South Arabia, rulers and leaders have been quick to draw inferences from the new balance of power within the Arab world, and to realign their policies accordingly. There are as yet few outward signs of any desire to examine the deeper causes of the Arab predicament: the basic weaknesses of Arab society in an age of disruption and transi-

---

[3] Notably by General Dayan's "Diary of the Sinai Campaign" (Hebrew, 1965; English translation 1966) and by the publication in *The Times* of London, April 29-May 6, 1967, of Mr. Anthony Nutting's account of the Suez crisis, later brought out in book form, "No End of a Lesson: the Story of Suez."

tion; the inadequacy of Arab political structures and ideas;[4] the widening sociological and therefore technological gap.

What are the prospects of peace in the Middle East? In the outside world, the realists, like other people, are divided into two groups: the pro-Arab realists, who say that it is unrealistic to expect the Arabs to recognize Israel, and the pro-Israel realists, who say that it is unrealistic to expect Israel to relinquish her gains without substantial guarantees. Stated in this form, the two views are mutually exclusive—and both could well be right. There is, however, a faint hope that the Arabs may in the last resort prove less implacable than the pro-Arabs in their hostility to Israel. One Arab leader, President Bourguiba, was prepared, however reluctantly, to accept the fact of Israel's existence even before the war. Other leaders in the East may be coming to the conclusion that some form of recognition is the least disagreeable of the alternatives that face them. The problem remains whether, in a context of unstable régimes, contested succession and external incitement, they will have the courage and ability to act on such beliefs.

In the past, it has sometimes been argued that the Arab-Israeli conflict prevents great-power agreement, sometimes that the great-power conflict prevents the Arabs and Israelis from coming to terms. Certainly outside intervention has more than once increased tensions, provoked crises and prevented solutions. The effect of the United Nations on problems in the Middle East and elsewhere has often been like that of modern medicine on major diseases—enough to prevent the patient from dying of natural causes, but not enough to make him well. Chronic invalidism is not a happy state.

It may well be that the best hope for the Middle East lies in its diminishing importance, which may in time lead to the great powers losing interest in the area. This would not be the first time. The decline of European interest in the Middle East in the fifteenth and sixteenth centuries, and its effects, are well known. An earlier example may be found in the fourth century A.D., when the last of a long series of wars between Rome and Persia came to an end. While the struggle between the two great powers of the ancient world continued, both were active in Arabia—politically, militarily, commercially. During the long peace from 384 to 502 A.D., both lost in-

---

[4] It is striking that, of the three Arab armies engaged, the Jordanian, with every disadvantage of numbers, terrain and armament, acquitted itself best. Simple, old-fashioned tribal and monarchical loyalties were more effective in maintaining morale than the revolutionary nationalism of Egypt and Syria.

terest. During the centuries of neglect, the trade routes were diverted, the caravan cities abandoned and much of Arabia reverted to nomadism.

It would not be easy for the great powers to lose interest and might well be painful for the Middle East, where the final fulfillment of the long-standing demand for the end of imperialism could have disconcerting political and economic effects. Without foreign stimulation, there would be grave danger of deterioration and regression; without foreign irritants, there might also be some hope of peace.

Is Peace in the Middle East Possible?

By Walter Laqueur*

Beyond the artillery duels at Suez, beyond the Security Council meetings and the Arab summits, the search is going on for solutions to the Middle East conflict. A scheme for an autonomous Arab state on the west bank of the Jordan has been proposed; there are blue-prints for an Israeli-Jordan confederation, even for a binational state. A corridor giving Jordan access to the Mediterranean has been suggested, as has the internationalization of the Sinai Desert. There are even pretenders to the throne of the Kingdom of Jerusalem—one in Nathania, one in London and, for all one knows, others elsewhere. The settlement of the Gaza Strip refugees on the west bank is envisaged by some, a new canal from Eilat to Ashdod by others, to make Suez unnecessary.

Such suggestions are only natural; war is usually followed by a peace settlement of sorts, a compromise between extreme demands and positions. Unfortunately, there is at this moment little hope that the Arab-Israeli war will end in such a fashion. Most of the schemes that have been advanced, however well-meaning and ingenious, are irrelevant. The more ambitious they are, the more quickly they collapse at the first collision with harsh facts. Had the recent war been over the possession of certain territories, over the refugee question, over the Jordan waters—or over all these bones of contention together—

* Walter Laqueur is Director of the Institute of Contemporary History and the Wiener Library in London, Professor at the University of Reading and Professor in the History of Ideas and Politics at Brandeis University. His article appeared first in *The New York Times Sunday Magazine,* August 27, 1967. © 1967 by The New York Times Company. Reprinted by permission.

solutions could be found. It would take a few months, at most a few years, for passions to cool down, and then, after much haggling, a sensible compromise could be worked out. The extremists on both sides would shout, "No, never!" But in the course of time most people would be reconciled to the new state of affairs. After a generation, with a little luck, the *modus vivendi* reached would no longer be questioned.

If there were such a chance, Israel would be well-advised to seize it with both hands: "Agree with thine adversary quickly, while thou art in the way with him." No sacrifice—not even Jerusalem—would be too heavy to insure a lasting peace between Israel and its Arab neighbors. (Jerusalem is the crown of the state, it is now claimed; Israel cannot exist without it. But Israel did exist without the Wailing Wall for 19 years; the state would not collapse without it.) However, the struggle is not about Jerusalem, about the borders of Israel, the refugees or the Jordan waters. To reduce it to a simple formula, it is a conflict between Arab pride and dignity and Jewish survival. Such a conflict cannot be solved by territorial concessions or Jordan water projects, of which there are by now a half-dozen. Technically, the refugee problem *could* be solved—an international loan of several billion dollars would make their absorption possible, some on the west bank, others in underpopulated regions of Iraq and Syria. But all these schemes presuppose Arab willingness to negotiate with Israel, to accept the existence of the Jewish state. And for this they are not yet ready.

Their case is well-known; Palestine was an Arab country up to the end of the First World War, when Britain imposed the Jewish community on the Arabs, who were thus asked to atone for the sins of the Christian peoples of Europe. Following Zionist invasion and aggression, the Jewish refugee problem was solved by creating an Arab refugee problem. The establishment of a Jewish state was thus a crying injustice; moved by collective guilt feelings about the Jews, the European peoples ignored the fact that morally, and in every other respect, right was on the side of the Arabs.

The case is familiar, and so are the counterarguments: that Palestine was a Turkish province inhabited by a few hundred thousand Arabs at the time of the Balfour Declaration; that Jerusalem had a Jewish minority well before 1917; that Zionism has built up a flourishing country from what was largely desert; that a Jewish state came into being because the Arabs rejected a binational state; that Israel expanded beyond the borders of the United Nations resolution of 1947 as a result of invasion by Arab armies; that the loss of a war is a misfortune, but not a moral argument; that nations have never come into being in accordance with the moral law, but as the result of migration, settlement, invasion and other forms of peaceful, or not so peaceful, conquest. All this is familiar; no useful purpose will be served by pursuing this discussion.

It was the historical misfortune of the Jewish state that it appeared as a latecomer among the nations, and that it came into conflict with a people who had grave, if different, problems of their own. The Arabs are a proud people, with a long and distinguished history. They kept the flame of civilization burning while most of Europe was shrouded in darkness. But this golden age was followed by centuries of sad decline until, in the 19th century, it was suddenly realized that the West, which they had despised and ignored, had forged ahead in every respect, while the Arab world had stagnated. Attempts were made to copy the institutions of the West; their failure generated resentment and hatred.

This kind of response was not peculiar to the Arabs: there have been similar reactions in other parts of the world. There are interesting parallels between the Cultural Revolution in China and the present irrational eruptions in the Arab world; the Middle Kingdom, like the Arab world, had for centuries ignored the "Western barbarians" until it woke up to the painful realization of its own backwardness. Wounded national pride made it imperative to catch up with the technological achievements of the West—which, it soon turned out, was not so easy as had at first been thought. There was also a profound urge to seek revenge for all the humiliations suffered during the colonial age. In the case of the Arabs, the creation of Israel, and the Arab failure to destroy the Jewish state, was a further blow to national pride.

Nasser saw it as his main task to restore Arab self-respect and dignity. He did his best to modernize his country; given Egypt's desperate poverty, this was an uphill struggle in which no quick results could be expected. Meanwhile, national pride was to be restored by defiance of the West and by intense propaganda which conjured up a dream world of Arab power and glory.

At first there was much goodwill toward Nasserism. In their willingness to come to terms with this movement, the Western powers, especially America, leaned over backward, ignoring attacks and insults. Like progressive parents, they showed infinite patience toward the misdeeds of their young. The results were calamitous.

In the meantime, a new generation had grown up in the Arab world, spoon-fed on the new slogans: Arab might was invincible, the confrontation with Israel inevitable. Why wait? Why not remove at once that Western outpost, the "imperialist poisoned dagger," as they called it? This was the attitude of the new generation of revolutionary and progressive Arab nationalists. But the progressive veneer was not very deep; there was as much hatred for the Jewish worker as for the Jewish capitalist. In Lebanon, traditionally the least fanatical Arab country, a popular singer aroused applause on the eve of the last war with a new song about Israel: "Kill them, crush them, suck their blood." The Syrian Government was (and is) almost Maoist in its inspiration: it constantly emphasizes the class struggle, the proletarian nations, the vanguard of the working class. But when it really got excited, its broadcasts assumed a different tone: "By God, if it is decreed that we have to wade through seven seas of blood and that the whole nation has to sink in blood to get revenge for its honor and dignity, then we will wade through the seas of blood and we will risk everything. . . ." No more atheism, class struggle or dialectical materialism; instead, God, blood, nation, revenge, honor, dignity.

Then came the five-day war and the totally unexpected defeat. Placards in the streets of Cairo and Damascus still displayed quaking little Jews cowering under the bayonets of steady-eyed, confident Arab soldiers. It was totally inexplicable, and utterly unacceptable. The self-image of the Arabs was that of a proud people distinguished above all by courage and the military virtues; the Jews were cowards who would not dare to fight. The war had been seen as a walkover. Surely Israel could not have defeated the Arab armies single-handed. Surely it was the element of surprise, the treacherous sudden attack for which the Arabs had been unprepared.

A generation educated in the belief that Arab armies are invincible could not possibly accept defeat, nor would it consider for a single moment that both its self-appraisal, and its image of Israel, may have been mistaken. Instead there was a call to renew the fighting immediately. If Nasser was a spent force, salvation would come from Boumediene and the Syrian leaders. Boumediene is a political featherweight, whose army was worsted even by the Moroccans—numerically inferior and not one of the world's greatest fighting forces. Nasser, even in defeat, is a giant in comparison with the men who rule in Damascus.

But these are the imperatives of a desperate situation: new heroes are needed to wreak revenge. There are some sensible voices, calling for self-criticism and a more realistic policy, but they are half-muted; they come from faraway countries like Tunisia and Morocco. Those nearer Israel do not dare to speak up: the director of Cairo Radio was no doubt right when he said that the Arabs would kill any leader contemplating peace with Israel. The Arab Governments had armed thousands of Palestinian volunteers (not to mention their own peoples); they had promised the liberation of Palestine; for more than a decade they had proclaimed that Israel was a cancer in the body politic of the Arab world and that it would be eradicated. They cannot now retreat. They fear that in their rage and frustration the masses would turn against them. The masses cannot be told that it is, for the time being, hopeless to continue the war.

It is not a reassuring picture—the Arabs, "lost in stormy visions, keep with phantoms an unprofitable strife." Nor does it leave much room for optimism. But any scheme to settle the Middle East crisis which ignores these psychological currents is doomed from the outset.

There are, in theory at any rate, three possibilities for a peaceful settlement. According to one school of thought, a solution could be imposed if only someone powerful enough would take the initiative. There would be resistance from both sides, especially from the Arabs. But provided there was courageous leadership, the fires of passion would die down after the inevitable period of shouting ("We shall never surrender").

Israel could be made to give up much, though not all, of its territorial conquests, if presented with a real, foolproof, big-power guarantee of its frontiers, and an Arab recognition of its existence. Israel would undertake to accept back all those refugees who wanted to return, the assumption being that not many would. Jordan would receive a corridor to the Mediterranean, or some other arrangement could be made. Israel would be given the right of free passage through the Suez Canal—in the very near future if not immediately. United Nations forces would be stationed permanently along the borders, and some of the most critical spots could be demilitarized (Sharm el Sheik, Sinai, the Syrian hills overlooking Galilee).

A special status would be worked out for Jerusalem, safe-guarding Israel sovereignty, Arab rights, free access to every-one—perhaps as an Israeli-United Nations codominion. The transfer of a permanent U.N. commission to Jerusalem might be envisaged. There would be substantial international loans for the Jordan waters project, and for other Arab-Israeli de-velopment schemes to make cooperation attractive.

Not all Arab countries would be willing to collaborate im-mediately, but once negotiations started between Israel and one Arab government, the conviction would grow in all Arab capitals that recognition of Israel could not be indefinitely postponed. It might take years, success might be only partial, but in the end a new *modus vivendi* would emerge; in due time it would be tolerated, if not enthusiastically accepted, by both Arabs and Jews.

I wish I could feel more optimistic about these visions; there are a great many variants, but they are all based on too many assumptions that are, at present, unreal. They all imply American-Soviet cooperation, but the Soviet Union does not see the slightest reason to impose any solution on the Arabs that would be unacceptable to them. Nor should the extent to which Moscow and Washington can impose solutions be over-rated. For the Arab capitals there is always China in the event of a Soviet "betrayal."

It is unlikely that any Israeli Government (except perhaps one headed by Dayan, an unlikely contingency at present) would be able to convince the public that some of its recent gains should be given up. Israelis would no doubt argue that a new great-power guarantee would be no more reliable and effective than any previous one. What if agreement were reached about the freedom of passage through the Suez Canal and the Straits of Tiran, and then Nasser, after a few years, again imposed a blockade? Since there are no foolproof guar-antees, would it not be more prudent from the Israeli point of view to hold on to what they have? If one or several Arab leaders decided to enter into negotiations with Israel, would there be any certainty that they would not be doing so merely to gain time, until they were ready for the next round of fight-ing? Should Israel pay for a recognition which might well be meaningless? Assuming even a sincere wish on the part of some Arab leaders to reach agreement with Israel, what guar-antee is there that it would be honored by their successors? In the present state of turbulence in the Arab world, no ruler is secure. Those most likely to talk with Israel are the ones most exposed, their countries most vulnerable to a Syrian-style coup. In the present mood, demagogues preaching war are infinitely more in line with the general sentiment in the Arab world than responsible leaders aiming at constructive solutions. Why talk to Israel, if the defeat of the "Zionist gangster state" is just a matter of one more attempt? (It used to be the "gangster dwarf state," but the dwarf has grown.) Surely the far greater resources of the Arab states will prevail; next time the Arab armies will not wait for the enemy to attack—the element of surprise will give them victory.

Israeli diplomats have argued for a long time that there is only one obstacle to lasting peace in the Middle East—the absence of courageous Arab leadership. It is, I fear, an oversimplification. Arabs have been accustomed for two decades to an "I-am-more-anti-Israel-than-thou" competition among the Arab leaders. It is quite unrealistic to expect that any one of them now will tell his people that it was a mistake and that it is all over.

The second school of thought maintains that it is up to Israel to make not only the first step but also most of the concessions. For, even if the Israelis have won one campaign, they have not won the war. Israel is still a small enclave surrounded by 80 million enemies. Time works for the Arabs; in the long run, Israel cannot defeat them. It will survive only if it ceases to be a Western outpost and integrates itself into the Afro-Asian world to which it really belongs; it must join the third world if it is to survive.

Within a big Arab federation, Israel would play an important role. True, the Arabs may demand the cessation of immigration—but then, not many immigrants will come anyway. Half of Israel is now Middle Eastern in origin, and there have been Israeli voices advocating integration in recent years. The only realistic policy in the long run is therefore to recognize that revolutionary Arab nationalism is the wave of the future, the present victory merely a brief episode interrupting an irreversible historic movement—the rise to political consciousness of the Arab masses, as personified by Nasser and the Syrian leaders. Consequently, Israel should extend the hand of friendship to the Arab leaders, give up all its gains and perhaps go even further and try to win Arab friendship by accepting Nasser's leadership.

There may be a grain of truth in this series of arguments.

Nasser-style or Syrian-style radical Arab nationalism may well
prevail in more Arab countries in the coming years; the long-
term survival of Israel is not yet assured. Gestures play an in-
ordinate role in the Middle Eastern politics (a few declarations
by de Gaulle made the Arabs forget that he, not America,
equipped the Israeli Army). It is possible that some Israeli
gestures of goodwill toward the Arabs, some unilateral acts or
concessions, would have a beneficial effect, and it is a matter
of regret that they have not been made.

Yet basically, this school of thought is mistaken in most of
its assumptions. Whether a big population is a blessing or a
curse in the modern world is by no means certain; what matters, militarily as well as technologically, is quality, not quantity. If the Arab-Israeli conflict were to go nuclear, the Arab
countries, above all Egypt, would be as much exposed as
Israel. Whether time works for the Arabs is not certain either;
for the last 20 years it has not. As a result of their refusal to
live in peace with Israel, the Arab countries have had to spend
a good share of their gross national product on armaments and
various kinds of anti-Israel warfare. As a result, the real
growth of their economies has been very small—in the region
of 2.5 per cent per annum. (Israel's rate of growth has been
almost three times as high.)

The present outlook for the Arab world—especially Egypt,
Syria and Jordan—is grave: it faces economic ruin. And yet
today the Arabs feel obliged to devote an even higher per-
centage of their income to rearming. Talk about the wave of
the future is meaningless unless supported by Soviet or Chinese
(or Japanese or Western) rates of growth. But even if the
future of the Arabs were much brighter, even if time were
working for them, how could Israel become a member of the
Arab world?

Geographically and historically, Israel is, of course, far
closer to the Mediterranean world—Italy, Greece, Turkey—
than to the Afro-Asian bloc. The third world is passing through
a profound crisis—politically, socially, economically—a crisis
nowhere more palpably felt than in the Arab countries. There
has been little if any advance toward political stability and
economic progress. In recent years the Arab countries have
fallen further back in comparison with both the Western and
the Eastern bloc, and this has produced a profound malaise
bordering occasionally on collective hysteria. Israel has by no
means solved its own problems, but it has tackled moderniza-
tion fairly successfully; it is a far from perfect country, but it

is reasonably democratic, reasonably effective. It could try to cut its ties with the Jews in the West; it could attempt to copy Egypt or Syria, with demonstrations in the streets of Jerusalem and Tel Aviv crying, "Down with American imperialism! Long live Frantz Fanon and the third world!" Such behavior might warm the hearts of some observers in the West, but it would carry little conviction in the Arab world.

A reasonable man may try to gain the confidence and friendship of the unreasonable by behaving like them, but it is not the surest way to success. The political psychology of backwardness is an organic growth; hate and resentment are the products of certain mechanisms that do not exist in Israel. Israel was never a colony and does not suffer from a colonial hangover; it has been successful where most Arab countries have failed. Israel could pretend to be part of the "wretched of the earth," but I fear no one would believe it. Countries like Egypt and Syria are at present in (to put it cautiously) a disturbed frame of mind. One must sympathize with them in their plight and hope for a change in the not-too-distant future. But agreement cannot be reached by voluntary adaptation to political psychosis. The present delusions in the Arab world may not last; there is hope of change in the long term, hope of a sobering-up process and more rational response to the challenges facing the Arab world. Then, and only then, will there be a chance for a real meeting of minds.

There is a third, less spectacular way to work for peace in the Middle East—by trying to defuse some of the most explosive issues. The administration of conquered territories presents Israel with enormous economic problems (unemployment on the west bank is now 20 per cent). In the long haul, there will be grave security problems, too, and the full implications of absorbing a million Arabs into Israel have not yet been entirely grasped in Israel. When they are, there may be greater readiness to negotiate. But, on the whole, what is negotiable as far as Israel is concerned will probably shrink as time passes. *Rien ne dure que le provisoire.* If the Arabs are unwilling to enter into direct negotiations, if they make preparations for a new war, the conviction will grow in Israel that it may as well hold onto its new territories, which give it undoubted military advantages.

The Arab states, above all Egypt and Jordan, and to a lesser degree Syria, are at present under far greater pressure. Jordan has lost half its agricultural output, Egypt half its foreign currency earnings. This means economic disaster, for Russia cannot indefinitely support Egypt's economy. And who is going to save poor Jordan? Yet Nasser, or whoever may succeed him, can in no circumstances enter into direct negotiations with Israel; so long as Nasser refuses, King Hussein has to refuse, too.

After the present round of inconclusive talks among Arab leaders, they will probably agree that while recognition of Israel and a peace settlement are out of the question, there should be talks through some intermediary in an attempt to solve certain particular issues: Egypt wants to reopen the Suez Canal to regain some of its foreign currency earnings; Jordan wants to negotiate about the refugees and the west bank. Yet even the choice of a mediator presents difficulties. America and Russia cannot mediate for obvious reasons, and Israel has reservations about France. Will it be Mr. Fanfani then, or Mr. Maurer? Israel may agree to the reopening of the canal if there is free passage for Israeli ships. It is more than doubtful whether Nasser could accede to this demand, even if there should be a face-saving formula. Prospects for a partial agreement with Jordan are better, but even this is not likely to come soon.

Public opinion in the Arab world (outside Jordan) is not aware of the extent of the military defeat and does not see the necessity for any compromise with Israel. The leaders are aware of the defeat, but they cannot undo now the effects of many years of anti-Israel propaganda. Nor can they switch their policy suddenly. Israel contends that the reward of victory should be peace; the Arabs, that there cannot be peace and that there should be unconditional withdrawal. Between these two positions there is no meeting ground.

A total Israeli victory would have compelled the Arab countries to change their position, but in Arab eyes what has happened is only a temporary setback. The Soviet Union is said to have replaced about half of the Arab aircraft and a quarter of the tanks; in a year, all the losses may be made good. But much more than that—and years of retraining—will be needed for a successful offensive against Israel. The Crusaders, it is said, were defeated by the Arabs after many decades; but are such historical parallels really of much help in recent times? Algeria and Syria press for the immediate renewal of a Chinese-style people's war. But the equation is not convincing: Dayan is not Marshal Ky, the Palestine Liberation Army is not the Vietcong, and Syria is not China. Israel would not be defeated; at most it would again be provoked into full-scale military action.

My own feeling is that the present confusion in the Arab world will persist for a long time, that attempts may be made in both directions—halfhearted negotiations and perhaps a little guerrilla war. At present, and for years to come, the Arab leaders can make neither war nor peace. No decisive action should be expected; and as the economic and political difficulties of the various regimes grow more severe, there will be more internal crises, greater instability. This long-drawn-out crisis may in the end have a sobering effect: the Arabs may realize that "dull and endless strife" is unprofitable, that the unsuccessful attempt to defeat Israel, which is sapping their strength and energy, is gradually making the Middle East a backwater of history, and preventing the general development of the Arab world. The Israeli victory will still be painful, but it would no longer receive priority in Arab eyes, and gradually energies would be directed into different channels to prevent even greater disasters to the Arab cause than the loss of Palestine. This is a possibility; unfortunately, it is no certainty; in any case, it will be a long haul back.

There is a sharp conflict of interest between America and Russia in the Middle East: the Soviet Union has now gained access to Middle East bases and warm-water ports, admittedly at an enormous price, and its political influence in Egypt and Syria seems unassailable. The United States aim, on the other hand, is not to allow the eastern Mediterranean to become a Soviet *mare nostrum*. But there is also a sphere of common interest: neither power wants another war which could have more dangerous consequences than even the one in Vietnam. The one way to prevent a war is to limit the arms race, to isolate the conflict as much as possible.

Montesquieu once said: "Happy the nations whose annals of history are boring to read." The boring years in the Middle East were always the happy ones. It cannot be too often stressed that the intrinsic importance of the Middle East is usually overrated in both East and West. If the West showed that it could get along indefinitely without Arab oil and even without the Suez Canal, that Egypt and Syria are simply not that important, it would be the greatest possible contribution not only to Middle Eastern mental hygiene but also to improved relations between the West and the Arab world. So long as the Nassers, Boumedienes and Attassis feel that the whole world's attention is focused on them, they will fret and strut on the Middle Eastern stage, adopting dramatic poses, uttering dire threats.

There is no cure for the Middle East sickness, but there is one sure way to alleviate it: to reduce the problems to their real size, not to take so terribly seriously the pocket Napoleons and Mao Tse-tungs, their trips, speeches, declarations, threats and promises. They flourish with publicity and wither when ignored. Half the battle for the future of the Middle East will be won on the day when news about this part of the world will be relegated from Page 1 to Page 16 in *The New York Times* and other leading newspapers.

A Selective Bibliography

ZIONISM

Alex Bein: *Theodore Herzl*, Philadelphia, 1940.

Adolf Boehm: *Die zionistische Bewegung*. 2 vols. Berlin and Jerusalem, 1935/37.

Israel Cohen: *The Zionist Movement*. New York, 1946.

Benjamin Halpern: *The Idea of a Jewish State*. Cambridge, Mass., 1961.

Arthur Herzberg (ed.): *The Zionist Idea. A historical analysis and reader*. New York, 1960.

Leonard Stein: *The Balfour Declaration*. London, 1961.

Chaim Weizmann: *Trial and Error*. New York, 1949.

ARABISM AND THE ARAB WORLD

George Antonius: *The Arab Awakening*. Philadelphia, 1939; London, 1946.

Erskine B. Childers: *The Road to Suez: A study of Western-Arab relations*. London, 1962.

Charles D. Cremeans: *The Arabs and the World*. New York, 1963.

Sami Hadawi: *Bitter Harvest, Palestine 1914-1967*. New York, 1967.

Sylvia Haim (ed.): *Arab Nationalism*. An anthology. Berkeley, 1962.

Kemal H. Karpat (ed.): *Political and Social Thought in the Contemporary Middle East*. New York, 1968.

Tom Little: *Modern Egypt*. New York, 1967.

Gamal Abdel Nasser: *The Philosophy of the Revolution*. Cairo, 1964.

Mohammed Neguib: *Egypt's Destiny*. London, 1955.

H. Z. Nuseibeh: *The Ideas of Arab Nationalism*. Princeton, 1956.

Maxime Rodinson: *Israel and the Arabs*. London, 1968.

Fayez Sayegh: *Arab Unity: Hope and Fulfilment.* New York, 1958.
Keith Wheelock: *Nasser's New Egypt.* New York, 1960.

PALESTINE

Esco Foundation for Palestine: *Palestine: A study of Jewish, Arab and British policies.* 2 vols. New Haven, 1947.
Paul L. Hanna: *British Policy in Palestine.* New York, 1942.
J. C. Hurewitz: *The Struggle for Palestine.* New York, 1950.
John Marlowe: *The Seat of Pilate. An Account of the Palestine Mandate.* London, 1959.
Royal Commission on Palestine: *Palestine Royal Commission Report.* London, 1937.
Sir Ronald Storrs: *Memoirs. (Orientations)* New York, 1937.
A Survey of Palestine. (3 Vols.) Government Printing Office. Jerusalem, 1945/6.
Christopher Sykes: *Crossroads to Israel. Palestine from Balfour to Bevin.* London, 1965.

ISRAEL

David Ben Gurion: *Rebirth and Destiny of Israel.* New York, 1954.
——— *Years of Challenge.* London, 1963.
Marver H. Bernstein: *The Politics of Israel: The First Decade of Statehood.* Princeton, 1957.
Abba Eban: *Voice of Israel.* New York, 1957.
Walter Eytan: *The First Ten Years. A Diplomatic History of Israel.* New York, 1958.
Leonard Fine: *Politics in Israel.* Boston, 1967.
Don Peretz: *Israel and the Palestine Arabs.* Washington, 1958.
Terence Prittie: *Israel, Miracle in the Desert.* New York, 1967.
Nadav Safran: *The United States and Israel.* Cambridge, Mass., 1963.

THE THREE WARS

E. L. M. Burns: *Between Arab and Israeli.* New York, 1962.
Winston S. Churchill and Randolph S. Churchill: *The Six Day War.* London, 1967.
Rony E. Gabbay: *A Political Study of the Arab-Jewish Conflict: the Refugee Problem.* Paris, 1959.
Robert Henriques: *One Hundred Hours to Suez. An Account of Israel's Campaign in the Sinai Peninsula.* London, 1957.
David Kimche and Dan Bawly: *The Sandstorm: The Arab-Israeli War of 1967.* London, 1968.
Jon and David Kimche: *Both Sides of the Hill.* New York, 1960.
Walter Laqueur: *The Road to Jerusalem. The Origins of the Arab-Israeli Conflict.* New York, 1968.

Netanel Lorch: *The Edge of the Sword. Israel's War of Independence 1947–49.* New York, 1961.

Terence Robertson: *Crisis. The Inside Story of the Suez Conspiracy.* London, 1965.

Hugh Thomas: *Suez Affair.* New York, 1966.

Constantine Zurayk: *The Meaning of the Disaster.* Beirut, 1956.

OTHER BOOKS

Lukasz Hirszowicz: *The Third Reich and the Arab East.* London, 1966.

Charles Issawi: *Egypt in Revolution. An Economic Analysis.* New York, 1963.

Malcolm Kerr: *The Arab Cold War 1958–1964.* London, 1965.

Walter Laqueur (ed.): *The Middle East in Transition.* New York, 1958.

Bernard Lewis: *The Middle East and the West.* New York, 1964.

Patrick Seale: *The Struggle for Syria.* New York, 1965.